Older Bereaved Spouses

Older Bereaved Spouses

Research with Practical Applications

Edited by
DALE A. LUND
Gerontology Center
University of Utah
Salt Lake City, Utah

● HEMISPHERE PUBLISHING CORPORATION
A member of the Taylor & Francis Group

New York   Washington   Philadelphia   London

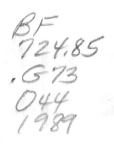

OLDER BEREAVED SPOUSES: Research with Practical Applications

1 2 3 4 5 6 7 8 9 0   B R B R   9 8 7 6 5 4 3 2 1

This book was set in Times Roman by Hemisphere Publishing Corporation. The editors were Mark A. Meschter and Chris Milord; the designer was Sharon Martin DePass; the production supervisor was Peggy M. Rote; and the typesetters were Linda Andros and Sharon L. Kohne. Braum-Brumfield, Inc. was printer and binder. Cover design by Renée E. Winfield.

Library of Congress Cataloging-in-Publication Data

Older bereaved spouses.

    (Series in death education, aging, and health care,
ISSN 0275-3510)
    Includes index.
    1. Bereavement in old age.   2. Widows—Psychology.
3. Widowers—Psychology.   I. Lund, Dale A.   II. Series.
[DNLM: 1. Bereavement.   2. Single Person—in old age.
3. Single Person—psychology.   BF 575.G7 044]
BF724.85.G73044   1989   155.9'37   88-32901
ISBN 0-89116-803-6 (case)
ISBN 1-56032-240-3 (paper)
ISSN 0275-3510

Contents

Contributors

Doug Abbott *University of Nebraska, Lincoln, Nebraska 68583.*

Elizabeth A. Berman *Miami Beach, Florida 33154.*

Edgar W. Butler *Department of Sociology, University of California, Riverside, California 92521.*

Michael S. Caserta *Gerontology Center, College of Nursing, University of Utah, Salt Lake City, Utah 84112.*

M. Cherie Clark *Stein Gerontological Institute, Miami Jewish Home and Hospital for the Aged, Miami, Florida 33137.*

Heidi Cover *Geriatric Research, Educational and Clinical Center, Veterans Administration Medical Center, Palo Alto, California 94304.*

Margaret F. Dimond *College of Nursing, University of Washington, Seattle, Washington 98195.*

Alicia Duran *Counseling Center, University of Utah, Salt Lake City, Utah 84112.*

Martin V. Faletti[†] *Stein Gerontological Institute, Miami Jewish Home and Hospital for the Aged, Miami, Florida 33137.*

Judy Farnsworth *College of Nursing, University of Utah, Salt Lake City, Utah 84112.*

Dolores Gallagher *Geriatric Research, Educational and Clinical Center, Veterans Administration Medical Center, Palo Alto, California 94304.*

Kathleen A. Gass *Rutgers University, College of Nursing, Newark, New Jersey 07102.*

Jeanne M. Gibbs[†] *Stein Gerontological Institute, Miami Jewish Home and Hospital for the Aged, Miami, Florida 33137.*

Michael Gilewski *Veterans Administration Outpatient Clinic, Los Angeles, California 90013.*

Patricia Hanley-Dunn *Veterans Administration Medical Center, Palo Alto, California 94304.*

Merry S. Juretich *College of Nursing, University of Utah, Salt Lake City, Utah 84112.*

Gay C. Kitson *Department of Anthropology and School of Medicine, Case Western Reserve University, Cleveland, Ohio 44106.*

Steven Lovett *Veterans Administration Medical Center, Palo Alto, California 94304.*

Dale A. Lund *Gerontology Center, College of Nursing, University of Utah, Salt Lake City, Utah 84112.*

[†]Deceased.

Roberta Mou   *Catholic Community Services, Tucson, Arizona 85717.*

James Peterson   *Ethel Percy Andrus Gerontology Center, University of Southern California, Los Angeles, California 90089-0191.*

Marjorie A. Pett   *College of Nursing, University of Utah, Salt Lake City, Utah 84112.*

Rachel A. Pruchno   *Philadelphia Geriatric Center, Philadelphia, Pennsylvania.*

David A. Redburn   *Lander College, Greenwood, South Carolina 29646.*

Mary Joan Roach   *Case Western Reserve University School of Medicine, Division of Medicine, Cleveland Metropolitan General Hospital, Cleveland, Ohio 44109.*

Tonya L. Schuster   *Ethel Percy Andrus Gerontology Center, University of Southern California, Los Angeles, California 90089-0191.*

Susan K. Shaffer   *Gerontology Center, College of Nursing, University of Utah, Salt Lake City, Utah 84112.*

Larry W. Thompson   *Geriatric Research, Educational and Clinical Center, Veterans Administration Medical Center, Palo Alto, California 94304.*

Charles W. Turner   *Department of Psychology, University of Utah, Salt Lake City, Utah 84112.*

Jan Van Pelt   *Gerontology Center, College of Nursing, University of Utah, Salt Lake City, Utah 84112.*

Sally Van Zandt   *Department of Human Development and the Family, University of Nebraska, Lincoln, Nebraska 68583-0811.*

Preface

This is the most satisfying part of the entire book to write because I want to dedicate this book to Martin Faletti and Jeanne Gibbs who worked together on the bereavement study at the Stein Gerontological Institute within the Miami Jewish Home and Hospital for the Aged. Both Marty and Jeanne died at relatively young ages and before their study was completed. Although they were able to write several papers based on the study, they did not have the opportunity to learn all that they wanted and to disseminate it to others. It was possible, however, to include a chapter from their study because of the dedicated work of Cherie Clark and some editorial input from me.

I know that Marty would have been pleased to have his work included, because he was always committed to sharing his research findings with others. I miss his presence at the annual meetings of the Gerontological Society of America, particularly his enthusiastic presentations. The lunches and evening socials with him also were memorable. It was over 5 years ago that Marty, with encouragement from Hannelore Wass, tried to get a similar group publication together. Because of conflicting schedules and competing priorities at the time, Marty was unable to get the help he needed from me, Ed Butler, Margaret Dimond, Dolores Gallagher, and Larry Thompson. All of us finally collaborated, along with others, and the book became a reality. I feel that one small piece of Marty and Jeanne's unfinished business has now been completed.

Most of us who study or deal with professional issues related to death and dying know how important it is to express our feelings and emotions when we lose people who are important to us. Although others were closer than I was to Marty and Jeanne, I highly respected their work, found them to be caring and personable, and thoroughly enjoyed their company. I know that I join with Cherie Clark, Elliot Stern, Joyce Levitt, others at the Miami Jewish Home and Hospital for the Aged who worked with Marty and Jeanne, and their families and many friends in formally acknowledging our sadness, that we miss them, that they will not be forgotten, and that we are pleased to have been part of their lives and to have had them part of ours. I hope that their deaths will help many of us to keep our daily activities in their proper perspective and as a consequence to be thoughtful and selective in how we use our time.

Dale A. Lund

Acknowledgments

Many people have contributed to the book and their efforts should be recognized. First and most importantly were the many bereaved, nonbereaved, and divorced persons who agreed to participate in the nine studies conducted by the authors. Without their willingness to share very personal and sensitive feelings, in many cases several times, our understanding of bereavement would be severely limited. Also, I am indebted to the 30 other authors for their willingness to include in this book findings from their research. It would have been relatively easy for them to have sent their manuscripts to professional journals for publication, so I appreciate both the confidence that they had in me and the patience they showed.

Three colleagues deserve special recognition for their direct and indirect contributions to the book. I thank Margaret Dimond for giving me the opportunity of working with her on the longitudinal study and for stimulating my interest in bereavement research. Hannelore Wass, perhaps more than anyone else, was the major force behind this project. She recognized the need for a book on older bereaved spouses, encouraged my efforts, and facilitated the slow but continual process. I appreciated her unwavering support and advice and her willingness to include the book in Hemisphere's Series in Death Education, Aging, and Health Care. Michael Caserta, a close friend, colleague, and skilled researcher was instrumental in the process by coauthoring four of the chapters and assisting with the review of every other chapter. He has been a key person in my own social support network, particularly throughout this project.

This book would never have been possible without the support of the National Institute on Aging, which provided funding for six of the nine studies. Their staff, particularly Ronald Abeles and Marcia Ory, were valuable sources of information and excellent facilitators during the course of our studies.

Several research assistants and typists at the University of Utah Gerontology Center contributed to the book. Chris Kay, Rebecca Hill, and Susan Shaffer were most helpful in their careful proofreading and compiling of the lengthy reference lists in my chapters. Their willingness to assist with these tedious but important tasks and to do them cheerfully and efficiently is most appreciated. Mary Beth Aiken, Birgit Robinson, and Jenna Kae Whiting were excellent typists of my chapters and displayed considerable patience with me as I continually made changes in the changes that I had already made.

Finally, I want to thank my wife, Patty, and my two children, Matthew and Angie, for their willingness to give me some quiet time to work on the book. They are a fun family, and it was difficult for me to miss out on a few activities with them. I hope that they will understand these inconveniences, which I promise will not occur too often in the future.

Dale A. Lund

Introduction

PURPOSE

Two of the underlying reasons for compiling this book are that very little research has been done on spousal bereavement in later life and that when such research is published, it is frequently spread among a wide array of professional journals. It is certainly possible to locate most of these sources but only after considerable time and effort has been expended. This book, therefore, is intended to help fill this information gap by bringing together, in a single volume, some of the most recent findings from investigators who are currently doing research on this topic. All of the chapters present new findings which have not been published previously.

Besides adding information about older spouses to the growing amount of bereavement literature, this book has three specific purposes. The first is to present recent research findings on older bereaved spouses that add to our knowledge about the degree of impact that bereavement has on well-being, the factors believed to influence adjustments, and the larger issue of coping with loss in later life. The second is to present research-generated information that will be of practical value to a variety of professionals, service providers who interact with older bereaved spouses, students, members of bereaved persons' social support networks, and bereaved spouses who are interested in learning more about the commonalities and uniquenesses of their experiences. Much of the book's content will be of particular interest to educators, researchers, and students in the behavioral, social, and health sciences; practitioners, clinicians, and counselors such as gerontologists, nurses, physicians, social workers, psychiatrists, and family therapists; administrators and staff of community service agencies and organizations such as state units on aging, area agencies on aging, long-term care facilities, home health care agencies, and hospices; clergy; and, finally, public officials who make decisions regarding policy, planning, and funding for social and health services. The third purpose is to stimulate interest in others to conduct more research on bereavement in later life and to develop appropriate and innovative interventions based on research findings. The final chapter in this book provides an integrated and organized summary of the many specific findings so that the information will be more useful to those who might plan interventions or conduct research.

DISTINGUISHING FEATURES

The book also has three important distinguishing features of which the reader should be aware. First, the studies and chapters reflect a multidisciplinary approach that recognizes that no single discipline has a monopoly on knowing how to study bereavement, what questions should be asked, and what the answers are. This approach assumes that many disciplines have unique contributions to make and that a more comprehensive understanding will result from divergent perspectives. Thirty-one authors representing seven disciplines (anthropology, health education, human development, nursing, psychology, social work, and sociology) contributed to the book.

The second distinguishing feature is that all of the chapters present new findings from recent studies, most of which used longitudinal designs. Six of the nine studies described in the book were longitudinal, with data collected from bereaved spouses as early as 14 days after the death (Chapter 4) and as late as 58 years (Chapter 5). Also, six of the studies were supported by grants from the National Institute on Aging.

The large number and heterogeneity of the research participants is the third feature. Collectively, 2,727 people participated in the nine studies, including 2,113 who were bereaved or widowed, 317 who were nonbereaved controls, and 297 who were divorced. Much of the heterogeneity among the participants resulted from the geographic diversity of the study locations. Respondents lived in six different states, including states in the western, midwestern (e.g., a rural sample in Nebraska), north central, and southeastern regions of the United States. Because the focus of the book was on older adults, most of the bereaved and nonbereaved were between the ages of 50 and 93, with a mean of about 72 years. The divorced respondents ranged in age from 18 to 69, with a mean of about 50 years. Because many of the earlier studies of bereavement and widowhood did not include men in their samples, it is noteworthy that among the studies in this book, men constituted 31% of the bereaved, 41% of the nonbereaved, and 16% of the divorced. Although most of the respondents were Caucasians, some studies included blacks and Hispanics. Religious diversity also was present, with some representation of Catholics, Protestants, Mormons, Jews, and nonaffiliated persons.

ORGANIZATION

The 16 chapters were organized into four parts. Part I, "Impact and Course of Bereavement," consists of four chapters that present findings from four prospective longitudinal studies. Each of these chapters addresses questions dealing with the degree of impact that bereavement in later life has on the mental and physical health of the surviving spouses, the periods of time when difficulty and distress are the greatest, and the proportions of people who experience major coping difficulties. Chapter 1, by Lund, Caserta, and Dimond, presents data on the subjective well-being of bereaved and nonbereaved spouses at six time periods, from 4 weeks to 2 years after the death. Chapter 2, by Thompson, Gallagher, Cover, Gilewski, and Peterson, focuses on measures of psychopathology obtained four times, from 6 weeks to 30 months after the death. In chapter 3, Van Zandt, Mou, and Abbott report on the impact and course of bereavement by focusing on several indicators of mental and physical health of rural elders. Their study followed the same respondents from 6 weeks to $3^1/2$ years post–death event, with four data collection periods. Chapter 4, by Faletti, Gibbs, Clark, Pruchno, and Berman, also examines mental and physical health outcomes, with an emphasis on depression. Their study had up to five data collection periods, ranging from 14 days to 18 months after the death. All four chapters include findings for both men and women and report on comparisons of bereaved and nonbereaved respondents.

Part II, "Factors Influencing Bereavement Adjustments," includes seven chapters. Chapter 5, by Schuster and Butler, and chapter 6, by Duran, Turner, and Lund, have as a primary focus the role of social support in alleviating the stress and threats to mental health functioning which can accompany the bereavement process. Chapter 6 is somewhat unique in its analyses where early depression is used as an explanation of subsequent stress. The findings presented in Chapter 5 are from a longitudinal study initiated in 1963, with follow-up assessments in 1977 and 1984. Chapter 6 reports on data from the same longitudinal study presented in chapter 1. Chapters 7 and 8 are based on data from a cross-sectional study by Gass. The bereaved respondents were all in their first year of bereavement. Gass's chapters appear together because both focus on the influence that appraisal of the bereavement situation has on health and psychosocial functioning. They also follow the two chapters on social support because Gass included related measures that deal with the amount and strength of resources. Chapter 9, by Gallagher, Lovett, Hanley-Dunn, and Thompson, and chapter 10, by Caserta, Van Pelt, and Lund, both examine coping strategies. Chapter 9 presents findings from the same longitudinal study described in Chapter 2, and Chapter 10 reviews data obtained from the longitudinal study described in Chapters 1 and 6. Chapter 9 deals primarily with the influence of specific types and frequencies of coping strategies on physical and mental health outcomes. While Chapter 10 discusses the advice that older bereaved spouses offer to others who are in similar situations, it is quite likely that the advice reflects some of their own coping strategies. The various types of advice were then correlated with a variety of outcome measures. Chapter 11, by Lund, Caserta, Dimond, and Shaffer, is based on the baseline data and an additional survey from respondents in a self-help group intervention study. This chapter explores the relationships between competencies in performing tasks of daily living and several physical and mental health outcomes.

Because it is important to understand the broader context of spousal bereavement that places it in the category of major losses, Part III consists of three chapters that compare bereavement or widowhood with divorce. Both situations are usually recognized as highly stressful losses that can initiate major life transitions. Chapter 12, by Farnsworth, Lund, and Pett, makes use of data from some of the bereaved respondents described in Chapters 1, 6, and 10 and from an additional study of recently divorced persons. The bereaved and divorced were matched with respect to age, gender, and time since loss, and then compared on several indicators of loss-related feelings and behaviors and life satisfaction and depression. Chapters 13 and 14, by Kitson and Roach, present data from a comparative study of widowhood and divorce conducted in Ohio. Female respondents provided data approximately 3 months after their loss. These two chapters not only compare widows and divorcées in terms of their social and psychological adjustments but they examine the correlates of these adjustments in both loss situations.

Part IV, "Interventions and Implications for Research," consists of only two chapters, but they focus on extremely important aspects of bereavement. Chapter 15, by Lund, Redburn, Juretich, and Caserta, is basically a description of a controlled intervention study where older bereaved adults were asked to participate in small self-help groups as part of a research project. The focus of the chapter is on the identification and suggested resolution of practical problems that were experienced during the study of 26 such groups. Chapter 16 consists of 15 conclusions that I believe summarize some of the major highlights of the findings presented in the previous chapters, with the addition of my own interpretation from other relevant studies. These conclusions cover issues about the impact, course, and predictors of bereavement adjustments among older spouses. Equally important are the 14 implications for future interventions and research. Personally, I hope that this final chapter will be helpful to those who are looking for some brief and clear conclusions regarding what is presently known about older bereaved spouses and where we might best turn our attention for future interventions and research.

I

Impact and Course of Bereavement

The first four chapters form much of the core foundation for the book, because they provide information regarding the impact spousal death in later life has on the surviving spouse and what the course of bereavement is like. These descriptive accounts of bereavement over time are particularly needed when we know so little about the course or process of adjustment of older spouses. Some of the fundamental questions that these chapters address are: To what extent does the death affect the mental and physical health of the bereaved? Are there particular times when coping difficulties are greatest? How long does the adjustment process last? After these questions are considered, Part II examines more closely the factors that help to explain why some people experience greater difficulty than others (or, conversely, why some do not have as much difficulty).

Each of the first four chapters provide information from separate prospective longitudinal studies in different parts of the United States. The study in Chapter 1 was conducted in Salt Lake City; Chapter 2, in Los Angeles; Chapter 3, in rural Nebraska; and Chapter 4, in Miami. The research designs in the four studies were particularly appropriate for generating information about the process of adjustment, because they had multiple assessment periods covering up to the first $3\frac{1}{2}$ years of bereavement. They also were prospective in that the male and female participants provided information as they moved through the process rather than recalling what they had done or how they had felt years earlier. This feature is important because it adds greater accuracy, reliability, and richness to the data on grief and bereavement.

The findings from these four studies have considerably more impact as a group than they would if they were presented separately, for each study has limitations regarding the representativeness of its sample and, to some extent, the generalizability of its findings. Although these limitations cannot be dismissed, it is important to note that the findings of the four studies are remarkably similar even though there was considerable variation among the research participants. These commonalities in the impact and course of bereavement are highlighted in the final chapter of the book.

1

Impact of Spousal Bereavement on the Subjective Well-Being of Older Adults

Dale A. Lund, Michael S. Caserta, and Margaret F. Dimond

In order to assess the degree of impact that bereavement has on older adults, 108 bereaved spouses and 85 matched nonbereaved controls who completed six questionnaires over 2 years were compared on three indicators of subjective well-being. The bereaved were moderately more depressed in the first few months of bereavement, but their levels of depression declined gradually over time and became similar to those of the nonbereaved. Bereaved respondents also had slightly lower life satisfaction, but only in the 1st month of grief. Both samples had equally high perceived health scores. The discussion focuses on why bereavement did not have more negative impact than expected and on suggestions for measuring more transitory dimensions of subjective well-being.

Two decades ago, Holmes and Rahe[1] acknowledged the death of one's spouse as the most severe negative life event that can be encountered in adult life. The impact of such an occurrence is multidimensional, because it influences a person physically, emotionally, socially, and economically.[2] Numerous aspects of one's daily life are altered and adjustments must be made. New tasks need to be accomplished,[3] new identities are formed,[4-6] social attachments[7] and connectedness[8] are altered, new perspectives are learned,[9] and social relationships and interactions are changed.[10-11] Also, although not all of the research findings are consistent, there is evidence that suggests a linkage between the stress of bereavement and higher rates of morbidity and mortality.[12]

In order to limit the scope of bereavement-related outcomes in this study and

Revision of a paper presented at the Annual Meeting of the Gerontological Society of America, New Orleans, LA, November 1985. The bereavement study was funded by a grant from the National Institute on Aging (R01 AG02193). Staff support was also provided by the Gerontology Center at the University of Utah.

3

yet allow for multidimensional assessments, it was necessary to select a conceptual focus that was consistent with both of these goals. Since there are diverse outcomes, the conceptual framework should help to organize them in a meaningful way. Additionally, the focus should be capable of adding to theoretical and methodological developments in gerontology, facilitate comparisons of findings from other studies of outcomes associated with stressful situations, and accept, with limitations, the validity of self-reported measures. These objectives can be achieved by studying bereavement's impact on subjective well-being.

Subjective well-being is generally regarded as a multidimensional construct that encompasses both stable and transitory dimensions as well as global and specific indicators.[13-18] Although there is considerable dispute concerning the operationalization and conceptualization of subjective well-being, there is some agreement that it includes a general state of perceived psychological well-being and a variety of happiness and satisfaction dimensions. While more theoretical clarity is needed, subjective well-being is particularly appropriate for the study of bereavement.

Since the major purpose of this study was to assess the degree and duration of impact that the death of a spouse in later life has on the survivor's well-being, we selected indicators that were consistent with the literature on bereavement and subjective well-being. The three indicators utilized in this investigation—depression, life satisfaction, and perceived health—cover the continuum from specific to global and from transitory to stable dimensions.

A major component of subjective well-being given much attention in the bereavement literature is constituted by depressive symptoms.[19-21] Of the three indicators, depression would be considered more transitory and domain-specific, because it encompasses aspects of one's daily concerns such as sleeping, eating, fatigue, irritability, and decision making. It has been seen to appear early in the bereavement process,[22] and in some cases, persists for relatively long periods of time.[23-26] In their review of the research findings on this topic, Osterweis et al.[12] suggest that 10–20% of bereaved persons were still exhibiting depressive symptoms one year after the death of the spouse. Carey's[24] figure approached 25% and Bornstein et al.[27] found 17% were depressed. Van Rooijen[25] found significant differences at 18 months between widowed and nonwidowed women across all age categories. Our research estimated that 18% of the sample of bereaved elders were still experiencing major coping difficulties after 2 years.[28]

It must also be noted, however, that while the prevalence of depressive symptoms is often elevated among bereaved populations, the levels may not approach what experts would define as a clinical affective disorder.[29] Still, there is concern for those individuals who show no evidence of improvement after a period of time.

Another widely accepted component of subjective well-being is life satisfaction. This is considered theoretically to be a more global and stable dimension[15] that exhibits little change over time.[30,31] Most of the items in the scale require respondents to reflect on their entire life and their plans for the future. While there is generally considerable stability in life satisfaction, little empirical evidence exists about the impact of a significant loss such as conjugal bereavement. A previous study by the authors did find life satisfaction of a group of bereaved elders to change over a 2-year period.[32] On the other hand, since the group was not compared to a similar nonbereaved group, the previous analyses were unable to assess the degree of impact that bereavement had on life satisfaction. Since life satisfaction has been conceptually associated with morale[33] as well as empirically correlated with health,[30,34] it would be helpful to investigate how an event such as the death of a spouse may impact it by using a nonbereaved sample for comparison.

The final dimension of subjective well-being in this investigation is how someone perceived his or her own health. Since self-ratings of physical health are frequently based on both stable and transitory properties, health is conceptually located in the middle of the well-being continuum between depression and life satisfaction. The health item had a time frame of several weeks, which also helps to substantiate that it should be considered between the more immediate situation addressed by the depression items and the broader life review frame of the life satisfaction items. Lawton et al.[17] specifically recommend that self-rated health be included as a measure of subjective well-being. While some epidemiological evidence exists pointing to increased morbidity and mortality as a possible outcome of conjugal bereavement,[29,35] researchers also have found that perceived health is predictive of these outcomes.[36] Perceived health has been reported to be a useful and valid indicator of general physical health, for high correlations have been observed between how respondents assessed their own health and more objective measures.[37,38] Furthermore, and more important for the topic of bereavement, perceived health measured over time has been considered useful as an indicator of general distress.[12]

While research examining the impact of bereavement on a variety of outcomes has been on the increase, there has been little effort to integrate such outcomes into a subjective well-being conceptualization. In addition to its conceptual framework, the present study was also somewhat unusual in that it focused on an elderly sample, included males, had an early assessment following the death, was longitudinal, and included a nonbereaved control group for comparison purposes. The primary contribution of this study to the existing bereavement literature is that it assesses the amount of impact that conjugal bereavement has on the subjective well-being of older adults over a 2-year period.

METHODS

The data utilized in this investigation were part of a longitudinal descriptive study of bereavement among the elderly that was completed in 1983 in the Salt Lake City metropolitan area (the University of Utah study). Other findings from this study have been published,[28,32,39-41] but none of the articles have systematically compared the bereaved and nonbereaved samples to determine the relative impact that the death of a spouse has on subjective well-being. However, articles have provided descriptions of bereavement over time, explored various predictors of bereavement adjustments, and reported on methodological issues related to the study. Chapters 6, 10, and 12 in this book also report on data from this study.

Sampling

Recently bereaved spouses aged 50 and over were identified through the use of local newspaper obituaries in order to complete the first interview or questionnaire as early as 3 weeks following the spouse's death. Official mortality data obtained later from the State Department of Health Statistics revealed that this procedure missed only 9% of the actual deaths for those in the same age category.

No significant gender, age, or socioeconomic differences were found between those who had a published obituary and those who did not.

All potential bereaved participants were randomly assigned to either a home interview group (N = 104) or a mailed questionnaire group (N = 88) in order to test for an interview effect. No major interviewer effect was observed,[39] so the two samples have been combined into one sample for further statistical analyses. A total of 192 bereaved people participated in the study.

Due to the early assessment and the longitudinal design, 61% of the potential bereaved respondents refused to participate. The most common reasons for refusal were extreme busyness, extreme upset, poor health, and advice from adult children not to participate. A 1-year follow-up telephone interview with a random sample of those who had refused to be in the study (N = 111), indicated that their self-reported health was slightly lower than those who had participated. They did not differ, however, in age, gender, socioeconomic status, perceived coping, perceived stress, and rate of remarriage. This does not entail that the participants were experiencing the bereavement process in the same way but they were similar with respect to several important considerations.

Nonbrereaved older adults were identified through the use of public voter registry data and were selected on the basis of sex, age, and socioeconomic area of residence. In order to reduce the number of matching procedures, a matched nonbereaved person was selected only for each of the 104 bereaved respondents in the interview group. The refusal rate for this sample was 50 percent and the major reasons for refusal were busyness and lack of interest. The first two questionnaires for each of the nonbereaved participants were delivered by a research assistant according to the same procedures as those used for the mailed questionnaire group of bereaved participants. In both samples, the respondents completed them without the assistance of an interviewer and returned them by mail.

Procedure

All of the 192 bereaved persons were asked to complete questionnaires at six times during the first 2 years of bereavement: 3 to 4 weeks (T_1), 2 months (T_2), 6 months, (T_3), 1 year (T_4), 18 months (T_5), and 2 years (T_6) after the death. With the exception of the demographic variables, all six questionnaires were essentially the same. The survey instruments took approximately 1½ to 2 hours to complete. The 104 nonbereaved controls completed similar questionnaires at the same six times. Since their questionnaires did not include the items pertaining to specific aspects of bereavement (e.g., cause of death, coping, etc.), they required only 45 minutes to complete the questionnaires.

Attrition data for the bereaved and nonbereaved samples were quite similar, but the nonbereaved had a higher proportion who completed questionnaires at all six times. Twenty-eight (14.6%) of the bereaved discontinued or dropped out of the study because they were too busy, too ill, lacked interest in the project, or had moved away. Additionally, 4 males and 4 females (4.7%) died during the 2nd year of the study. Eight (7.7%) of the nonbereaved stopped participating, primarily because they were too busy or lacked interest. Two nonbereaved males and 2 nonbereaved females (3.8%) died during the 2nd year of the study. Regarding the continuity of their participation, 108 (56.3%) of the bereaved completed questionnaires at all six times, compared with 85 (81.7%) of the nonbereaved. Much of the lower rate of completion among the bereaved group can be attributed to the design of the study, which allowed bereaved persons to enter at (T_2) rather than (T_1) if they were reluctant to answer questions as early as 3 weeks following the death. Fourteen bereaved persons (13.5%) elected to begin at (T_2).

Samples Utilized for Statistical Analyses

Because of theoretical and methodological considerations, only the respondents who completed all six questionnaires were utilized in the statistical analyses. In order to address the important theoretical issue of changes in subjective well-being over the course of 2 years, it is more consistent to compare the scores of the same set of people rather than the scores of the unique set of people who happen to complete a given questionnaire. The statistical comparisons also are more accurate, since the variation in sample size from one time period to another is reduced. Therefore, the samples consisted of 108 bereaved and 85 nonbereaved older adults.

Since it was critical to assess biases resulting from the elimination of respondents, statistical tests were done to identify any significant differences between those who completed questionnaires at all six times and those who missed one or more. They were compared on sociodemographic characteristics (age, gender, and SES) and the three measures of subjective well-being discussed above. There were no significant differences between the bereaved who were eliminated from further analyses and those who were included. The same was also true for the nonbereaved participants who did not complete all six questionnaires.

Instruments

Two well accepted and standardized scales were used to assess the two ends of the subjective well-being continuum. Depression was measured by the Self-Rating Depression Scale[42] and life satisfaction by the LSI-A.[43] Both scales have been widely used with aging populations and have documented sociometric properties.[44-46] Perceived health was measured by a single seven-point Likert-type item. The questionnaire item read, "How would you describe your health during the past several weeks according to the scale below?" Respondents then selected a printed number from 1 (poor) to 7 (excellent). Although single-item measures are recommended with caution, they have been found to be useful and predictive in health and social science research.[37,47-49]

The three measures of subjective well-being were obtained for all six of the data-gathering times. Since each of these measures has its own unique conceptual features, the measures were treated separately in the statistical analyses. This permits more specificity in assessing the multidimensional effects of bereavement than if they were combined into one global measure of well-being.[35]

Respondent Characteristics

Both the bereaved and nonbereaved samples have been described in other publications,[32,41] but it is essential to this article to indicate some of their most relevant descriptive features. It also is important to note that the demographic characteristics of the 108 bereaved and 85 nonbereaved respondents were very similar. Therefore, any differences between the samples in their levels of subjective well-being are less likely to be due to the demographic variables than to the deaths of the spouses.

The bereaved sample was 78.9% female and 96.3% Caucasian. The mean age of the bereaved group at the beginning of the study was 67.6 years (SD = 8.2) and 80.7% had finished high school. Similarly, the nonbereaved group was also primarily white (98.8%) and female (77.4%). The mean age was 66.3 years (SD = 7.8) and 80.5% had completed high school. Respondents in both samples were equally representative of the upper, middle, and low socioeconomic districts within the larger metropolitan area. Approximately 72% of the bereaved and non-bereaved were Mormons. While the degree of Mormonism is of concern regarding the generalizability of the findings, we have found that very few differences exist between the bereavement experiences of the Mormons and non-Mormons. They did not differ on any of the measures of subjective well-being utilized in this investigation.

RESULTS

In order to determine the initial impact of bereavement on subjective well-being, as well as to assess the effect over time, analyses of variance with repeated measures were conducted on depression, life satisfaction, and health between bereaved and nonbereaved samples. The analysis revealed the bereavement had a significant initial effect upon depression, $F(1, 155)$ = 9.37, p < .01. The mean depression score (see Fig. 1) for the bereaved at T_1 was 39.4, which was significantly higher than for the nonbereaved group (M = 33.3). Tests for the effect of time produced similar results. Even though time as a main effect did not yield statistical significance, the results pertaining to the interaction of time and bereavement status indicate that once the two groups were treated separately, they were found to change at different rates. $F(5, 151)$ = 2.70, p < .05. This relationship is clarified when the mean depression scores for each group at each time period are observed. While the mean scores for the nonbereaved group did not change substantially between each time period, the mean depression scores for the bereaved showed a steady decrease through the first 1½ years (at T_5 M = 36.5) and then a slight increase (at T_6 M = 37.7). These findings indicate that the degree of depression associated with bereavement gradually subsides but does not drop to the level of the nonbereaved at any time during the first 2 years. It must also be noted, however, that even though the bereaved sample means are elevated, they do not reach clinical levels according to the suggested cutoff scores of 40[42] and 48.[46] This is also consistent with the findings of Gallagher et al.[29] On the other hand, using 48 as the cutoff score, a higher proportion of the bereaved respondents had scores in the clinical range, although the percentages in general were fairly low. Among the bereaved, 10% (at T_5) to 17% (at T_3) had scores in that range during the 2 years of the study; the equivalent percentages for the nonbereaved were from 5% (at T_1) to 12% (at T_4). The most notable difference in the proportions of those depressed occurred at T_1 (16% and 5% respectively). This was the only time when the proportions differed significantly according to chi-square tests (χ^2 = 4.93, df = 1, p < .05).

Borderline significance was found regarding the initial effect of bereavement on life satisfaction, $F(1, 143)$ = 3.63, p < .06. In this case, the nonbereaved (M = 15.5) had a higher mean life satisfaction score than the bereaved group (M = 13.5) (See Fig. 2). While some changes in life satisfaction were observed over time, $F(5, 139)$ = 2.83, p < .05, these changes were statistically independent of bereavement status. The interaction effect of bereavement and time was not

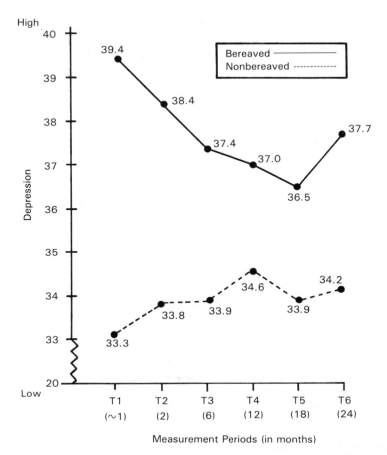

FIG. 1   **Depression scores of bereaved and nonbereaved respondents over 2 years.**

significant. As indicated by the mean scores at each time, the bereaved respondents showed a slight general increase in life satisfaction whereas the nonbereaved showed a slight decrease over time. Finally, at T_6, the differences between the two groups were minimal (mean for bereaved = 14.4; mean for nonbereaved = 14.8). There appears to be a small effect on life satisfaction due to bereavement in that the nonbereaved scores are consistently slightly higher than the bereaved. On the other hand, the initial difference at T_1, which is the greatest, seems to be due more to something unaccounted for inflating the scores of the nonbereaved than to the deaths of the spouses suppressing the scores of the bereaved group. These findings support the notion that life satisfaction is a relatively stable dimension of subjective well-being.

Finally, no initial effect due to bereavement was found pertaining to perceived health. The mean perceived health scores at T_1 showed little difference between bereaved ($M = 5.0$) and nonbereaved ($M = 5.2$). Changes over time, however, were observed for both groups, $F(5, 180) = 3.31$, $p < .01$, although

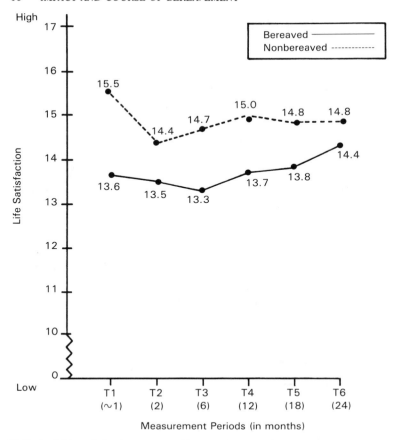

FIG. 2   Life satisfaction scores of bereaved and nonbereaved respondents over 2 years.

the changes in mean scores (see Fig. 3) were not very large between the times of measurement. More importantly, because the interaction between bereavement status and time was not significant, both groups changed at roughly the same rate. This indicates that bereavement had neither an immediate nor protracted effect on perceived health.

DISCUSSION

The most obvious impact of spousal bereavement on the subjective well-being of the older adults in this study was on the depression dimension. This was particularly noticeable at the earliest time period (3 to 4 weeks following the death). Over the 2 years of the study, there was a marked decrease in depression, but the levels for the bereaved still exceeded those of the nonbereaved. However, since the proportion of bereaved with depression scores of clinical significance ranged from 10% to 17%, it is important to acknowledge that the majority of them were not clinically depressed. These findings are consistent with other recent longitudinal studies,[26,32,50] which report that depression was greatest in the first several weeks, that there was a gradual decline over time, and that for many depression was not a severe outcome.

Our conceptualization of depression as a transitory and domain-specific dimension of subjective well-being was supported by the findings in that it was the most sensitive of the three indicators to the effects of spousal death. Since depression is likely to be considered the most domain-specific of the three indicators, it is reasonable and consistent with the findings to suggest that spousal bereavement has greater impact on characteristics at this level than on those which are more global, such as life satisfaction.

At the other end of the well-being continuum, life satisfaction was only slightly impacted by the death of a spouse. This was not surprising, since it is generally conceptualized as relatively stable, and the LSI-A requires a respondent to review or reassess much of his or her entire life. Even though the death of a spouse is traumatic and stressful, our findings suggest that it is unlikely that bereaved older adults will immediately make major changes in how they view their lives. In fact, 2 years later, the mean life satisfaction scores for the bereaved were nearly identical to the nonbereaved. Alternatively, it might be emphasized that

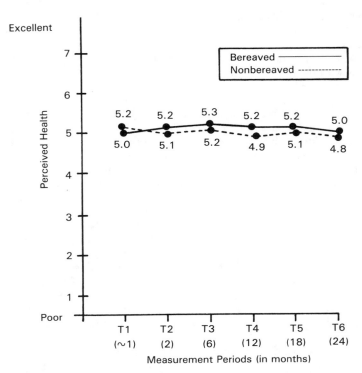

FIG. 3 Perceived health scores of bereaved and nonbereaved respondents over 2 years.

since life satisfaction is such a stable trait, spousal bereavement must be a powerful event to impact it at all. Perhaps with younger samples and studies over longer periods of time, the cumulative effects of spousal bereavement might have a greater impact on life satisfaction. In either case, our conclusion is that life satisfaction is relatively unaffected by the death of one's spouse in later life.

Our results concerning self-reported health were somewhat unexpected, since Thompson et al.,[35] found that their bereaved respondents rated their health more poorly than a nonbereaved comparison group on a similar one to seven single-item measure. Their bereaved sample mean scores were very similar to those of the bereaved respondents in our study; however both groups were found to have relatively good health. The reason Thompson et al. observed a negative impact of spousal bereavement on perceived health might be due to the unusually high health scores of their comparison group, who were recruited from senior centers, residential facilities, and a university emeriti center. Our nonbereaved were identified through voter registry files. It is possible that the different findings were the result of different sampling procedures. Their findings also were limited to 2 months after the death; as they analyze additional data periods, the observed negative effect might dissipate. Although Zisook and Shuchter[26] did not use a measure of perceived health in their study, they concluded that there were no substantial changes in medical functioning, in terms of physician visits, illnesses, and worrying about health, over 5 data periods covering the first 4 years of widowhood. More replication studies are needed to resolve some of these matters, but it should be noted that our findings revealed no substantial effects of bereavement on perceived health.

Regarding perceived health as a measure of subjective well-being, our findings are consistent with the argument that it is more stable and global that transitory, at least among relatively healthy samples of bereaved and nonbereaved older adults. If changes are occurring, it is not sensitive enough to detect them. Also, if perceived health is adversely affected by the death of a spouse, it may take much longer than 2 years for the impact to be realized.

A general conclusion of this study is that the death of a spouse in later life does impact the surviving spouse's subjective well-being but not to the extent that many would expect, particularly since the situation is often regarded as the most stressful of all life events. Also, the negative impact was only apparent with respect to the transitory dimension of well-being. These conclusions, however, should be viewed with caution. First, subjective well-being was assessed by only three specific indicators. Even though they cover various levels of assessment, other more sensitive measures should be considered. Horley's[15] suggestion to include a finer "elemental" level of measurement to assess day-to-day concerns is recommended, because it would be better able to identify everyday types of changes. These measures would be particularly useful for studies of various bereavement interventions, because important changes that result from them might otherwise go undetected. Also, it may be unreasonable, for example, to expect self-help groups to impact such global dimensions as life satisfaction and perceived health.

A second reason for caution concerning these findings is that the selected measures were self-reports and also were utilized in quantitative analyses. It is possible that observational and clinical techniques might result in somewhat different conclusions. The study from which the present data were drawn also included a large amount of qualitative information obtained from tape recorded interviews. The bereaved respondents in the interview sample were given the opportunity to respond to a series of less structured and more open-ended questions. These qualitative data are presently being content analyzed. There are, however, already a few indications from the transcripts that some of the bereaved respondents might have had greater difficulty than their quantitative scale scores would imply. It would be premature at this point to claim this, but it is possible that the quantitative and qualitative data could lead to slightly different conclusions. Since there are strengths and limitations of both quantitative and qualitative approaches, we suggest that our present conclusions be identified with the self-report and quantitative procedures that were utilized.

Clearly, more longitudinal research with appropriate control groups is needed to clarify the effects that spousal bereavement has on subjective well-being and other important outcomes. We recommend that investigators use multidimensional assessments, particularly those at the elemental and domain-specific levels. Given our conclusions, it also would be appropriate to ask research questions related to why spousal bereavement does not result in more negative outcomes than some recent publications have reported.

REFERENCES

1. Holmes, R. H., & Rahe, R. H. (1967). The social readjustment rating scale. *Journal of Psychosomatic Research, 11,* 213–218.
2. Shuchter, S. R., & Zisook, S. (1986). Treatment of spousal bereavement: A multidimensional approach. *Psychiatric Annals, 16,* 295–305.
3. Worden, J. W. (1982). *Grief counseling and grief therapy: A handbook for the mental health practitioner.* New York: Springer.
4. Lopata, H. Z. (1975). On widowhood: Grief work and identity reconstruction. *Journal of Geriatric Psychiatry, 8,* 41–55.
5. Parkes, C. M., & Weiss, R. S. (1983). *Recovery from bereavement.* New York: Basic Books.
6. Saunders, J. M. (1981). The process of bereavement resolution: Uncoupled identity. *Western Journal of Nursing Research, 3,* 319–332.
7. Bowlby, J. (1980). *Attachment and loss, Vol. 3. Loss, sadness and depression.* New York: Basic Books.
8. Lofland, L. H. (1982). Loss and human connection: An exploration into the nature of the social bond. In W. Ickes & E. S. Knowles (Eds.), *Personality, roles and social behavior.* New York: Springer-Verlag.
9. Silverman, P. (1985). *Widow-to-widow.* New York: Springer.
10. Lopata, H. Z. (1979). *Women as widows.* Cambridge MA: Schenkman.
11. Raphael, B. (1983). *The anatomy of bereavement.* New York: Basic Books.
12. Osterweis, M., Solomon, F., & Green, M. (1984). *Bereavement: Reactions, consequences and care.* Washington, DC: National Academy Press.
13. Carp, F. M., & Carp, A. (1983). Structural stability of well-being factors across age and gender, and development of scales of well-being unbiased for age and gender. *Journal of Gerontology, 38,* 572–581.
14. George, L. K. (1981). Subjective well-being: Conceptual and methodological issues. In C. Eisdorfer (Ed.), *Annual review of gerontology and geriatrics (Vol. 2).* New York: Springer.
15. Horley, J. (1984). Life satisfaction, happiness, and morale: Two problems with the use of subjective well-being indicators. *The Gerontologist, 24,* 124–127.
16. Lawton, M. P. (1983). The varieties of well-being. *Experimental Aging Research, 9,* 65–72.
17. Lawton, M. P., Kleban, M. H., & diCarlo, E. (1984). Psychological well-being in the aged: Factorial and conceptual dimensions. *Research on Aging, 6,* 67–97.
18. Liang, J. (1984). Dimensions of the Life Satisfaction Index A: A structural formulation. *Journal of Gerontology, 39,* 613–622.

19. Glick, I., Weiss R. S., & Parkes, C. M. (1974). *The first year of bereavement.* New York: John Wiley & Sons.
20. Sanders, C. M. (1980). A comparison of adult bereavement in the death of a spouse, child, and parent. *Omega, 10,* 303–322.
21. Sanders, C. M. (1980). Comparison of younger and older spouses in bereavement outcomes. *Omega, 11,* 217–232.
22. Gallagher, D. E., Breckenridge, J. N., Thompson, L. W., & Peterson, J. A. (1983). Effects of bereavement on indicators of mental health in elderly widows and widowers. *Journal of Gerontology, 38,* 565–571.
23. Barrett, C. J., & Schneweis, K. M. (1980). An empirical search for stages of widowhood. *Omega, 11,* 97–104.
24. Carey, R. G. (1979). Weathering widowhood: Problems and adjustments of the widowed during the first year. *Omega, 10,* 163–174.
25. van Rooijen, L. (1979). Widows' bereavement: Stress and depression after 1½ years. In I. G. Sarason & C. D. Spielberger (Eds.), *Stress and anxiety.* Cambridge, MA: Winthrop.
26. Zisook, S., & Shuchter, S. R. (1986). The first four years of widowhood. *Psychiatric Annals, 16,* 282–294.
27. Bornstein, P., Clayton, P., Halikas, J., Maurice, W., & Robins, E. (1973). The depression of widowhood after thirteen months. *British Journal of Psychiatry, 122,* 561–566.
28. Lund, D. A., Dimond, M. F., Caserta, M. S., Johnson, R. J., Poulton, J. L., & Connelly, J. R. (1985). Identifying elderly with coping difficulties after two years of bereavement. *Omega, 16,* 213–224.
29. Gallagher, D. E., Breckenridge, J. N., & Thompson, L. W. (1982). Similarities and differences between normal grief and depression in older adults. *Essence, 5,* 127–139.
30. Baur, P. A., & Okun, M. A. (1983). Stability of life satisfaction in late life. *The Gerontologist, 23,* 261–265.
31. Gubrium, J. F., & Lynott, R. J. (1983). Rethinking life satisfaction. *Human Organization. 42,*30–38.
32. Lund D. A., Caserta, M. S., & Dimond, M. F. (1986). Gender differences through two years of bereavement among the elderly. *The Gerontologist, 26,* 314–320.
33. Lawton, M. P. (1977). Morale: What are we measuring? In C. N. Nydegger (Ed.), *Measuring morale: A guide to effective assessment.* Washington, DC: Gerontological Society.
34. Tate, L. A. (1982). Life satisfaction and death anxiety in aged women. *International Journal of Aging and Human Development, 15,* 299–305.
35. Thompson L. W., Breckenridge, J. N., Gallagher, D. E., & Peterson, J. A. (1984). Effects of bereavement on self-perceptions of physical health in elderly widows and widowers. *Journal of Gerontology, 39,* 309–314.
36. Mossey, J. M., & Shapiro, E. (1982). Self-rated health: A predictor of mortality among the elderly. *American Journal of Public Health, 72,* 800–808.
37. LaRue, A., Bank, L., Jarvik, L., & Hetland, M. (1979). Health in old age: How do physicians' ratings and self-ratings compare? *Journal of Gerontology, 34,* 687–691.
38. Linn, B. S., & Linn, M. W. (1980). Objective and self-assessed health in the old and very old. *Social Science and Medicine, 14A,* 311–315.
39. Caserta, M. S., Lund, D. A., & Dimond, M. F. (1985). Assessing interviewer effects in a longitudinal study of bereaved elderly adults. *Journal of Gerontology, 40,* 637–640.
40. Lund, D. A., Dimond, M. F., & Caserta, M. S. (1984). *Effects of religion and religious activity on bereavement among the elderly: A comparison of Mormons and non-Mormons.* Salt Lake City: Intermountain West Long Term Care Gerontology Center.
41. Lund, D. A., Caserta, M. S., Dimond, M. F., & Gray, R. M. (1987). Impact of bereavement on the self-conceptions of older surviving spouses. *Symbolic Interaction, 9,* 235–244.
42. Zung, W. (1965). A self-rating depression scale. *Archives of General Psychiatry, 12,* 63–70.
43. Neugarten, B., Havinghurst, R., & Tobin, S. (1961). The measurement of life satisfaction. *Journal of Gerontology, 16,* 123–143.
44. Jegede, R. O. (1976). Psychometric properties of the self-rating depression scale (SDS). *Journal of Psychology, 93,* 27–30.
45. Kane, R. A., & Kane, R. L. (1981). *Assessing the elderly: A practical guide to measurement.* Lexington, MA: D.C. Health.
46. Kitchell, M. A., Barnes, R. F., Veith, R. C., Okimoto, J. T., & Raskind, M. A. (1982). Screening

for depression in hospitalized geriatric medical patients. *Journal of the American Geriatrics Society, 30,* 174–177.

47. Maddox, G. L., & Douglas, E. B. (1973). Self-assessment of health: A longitudinal study of elderly subjects. *Journal of Health and Social Behavior, 14,* 87–93.

48. Palmore, E., & Weiner, M. B. (1972). Health and social factors related to life satisfaction. *Journal of Health and Social Behavior, 13,* 68–130.

49. Tissue, T. (1972). Another look at self-rated health among the elderly. *Journal of Gerontology, 27,* 91–94.

50. Faletti, M. V., & Berman, E. A. (1984, November). *The role of person and death event characteristics in longitudinal outcomes in spousal bereavement.* Paper presented at the annual meeting of the Gerontological Society of America, San Antonio.

2

Effects of Bereavement on Symptoms of Psychopathology in Older Men and Women

Larry W. Thompson, Dolores Gallagher, Heidi Cover, Michael Gilewski, and James Peterson

In this chapter we investigate the extent of psychological distress in nine domains of psychopathology as measured by the Brief Symptom Inventory. Bereaved men and women aged 55 and above were evaluated at three points in time over a 30-month period and were compared to nonbereaved counterparts at the same points in time. In general, the bereaved were initially more distressed than the controls, but over time their distress levels were considerably reduced. Women were generally more symptomatic than men—regardless of bereavement status. These effects remained even when the contribution of various covariates were statistically removed. Taken together, these data indicate that the distress associated with the early stages of bereavement mitigates over time, so that after 2½ years the bereaved strongly resemble their nonbereaved counterparts in measures of a variety of aspects of psychological distress.

Recent evidence has shown that many elderly individuals experience considerable distress during the bereavement process,[1-3] but that their distress is likely to subside with time.[2] Most of the reports dealing with the impact of spousal loss in the elderly have focused on the depression and anxiety that commonly result.[4] A question addressed in the present study pertains to whether other symptoms of psychopathology show similar trends during the course of adapting to spousal bereavement. Earlier work has also raised questions concerning sex differences during bereavement. Some researchers have reported significant differences between older males and females in measures of psychological distress,[5] whereas others have tended to minimize these differences.[2,6] The present study examines whether older men and women manifest different symptoms in response to spousal

This research was supported in part by a grant from the National Institute on Aging (RO1 AG01959) to Larry W. Thompson.

loss as reflected in the various subscales of the Brief Symptom Inventory developed by Derogatis.[7]

METHOD

Sample Selection

The procedure for sample selection is described in detail in an earlier paper by Gallagher et al.[1] Chapter 9 also reports on findings from this study. Briefly, it can be stated that this was a volunteer sample comprising of 211 bereaved (113 women and 98 men) aged 55 to 80 (mean for men = 69.76; women = 66.43) who were contacted through death certificate records. A sociodemographically similar comparison sample of 163 persons (78 women and 85 men) aged 55 to 80 (mean for men = 70.97; women = 68.22) was obtained through senior centers and the like. The participants in the latter group were either married at the time of entry into the study or, if single, had not lost a spouse through death or divorce in the past 5 years.

Times of Measurement

The initial interview occurred from 6 to 9 weeks after the death of the spouse; the mean time was approximately 8 weeks. Subjects were interviewed at three points in time following the initial interview: 6 months, 1 year, and 2½-years. However, the 6-month data was not included in the results reported here, as there were problems with missing data for that time point.

Measures

Both interview and self-report measures were included at each evaluation point, which are described in greater detail in an earlier paper.[1] The interview was highly structured to minimize the influence of interviewer interpretations. It included questions covering demographic data, religious practices, general coping strategies, recent and earlier stresses, nature of the support network, health status, and self perceptions of physical and mental health. Self-report scales included measures of grief, indices of psychological distress and general level of functioning, and an index of morale and general well-being. Of particular interest is the Brief Symptom Inventory (BSI).[7]

The BSI is a self-report scale that measures psychopathology along nine primary symptom dimensions: somatization, obsessive compulsive features, interpersonal sensitivity, depression, anxiety, hostility, phobic anxiety, paranoid ideation, and psychotic features. The scale is an abbreviated version of the SCL-90 and contains 53 items. Each item is rated on a 5-point distress scale (0–4) ranging from "not at all" to "extremely." It has high test-retest reliability and high internal consistency.[8] Also, norms are available for older groups.[9] The BSI was administered at each time of measurement to both bereaved and control respondents.

RESULTS

The means and standard deviations for the nine symptom subscales are included in Table 1 for the three different times of measurement (2 months, 12 months, and 30 months postloss). Distributions for all variables tended to be

TABLE 1   Means and Standard Deviations for Nine Subscales of the Brief Symptom Inventory for Control and Bereaved Men and Women over Time[a]

	Bereaved				Control			
	Males		Females		Males		Females	
	M	SD	M	SD	M	SD	M	SD
Somatization								
T_1	.459	(.572)	.568	(.680)	.354	(.528)	.478	(.509)
T_3	.294	(.431)	.386	(.501)	.387	(.493)	.423	(.526)
T_4	.337	(.570)	.429	(.642)	.438	(.651)	.360	(.388)
Obsessive-compulsive								
T_1	.812	(.668)	1.08	(.823)	.645	(.619)	.858	(.708)
T_3	.722	(.602)	.833	(.725)	.694	(.645)	.766	(.746)
T_4	.635	(.712)	.867	(.747)	.772	(.787)	.778	(.611)
Interpersonal sensitivity								
T_1	.317	(.478)	.468	(.654)	.411	(.620)	.490	(.480)
T_3	.290	(.450)	.350	(.512)	.413	(.540)	.396	(.594)
T_4	.316	(.535)	.419	(.599)	.355	(.479)	.370	(.471)
Depression								
T_1	.890	(.739)	1.01	(.782)	.278	(.518)	.342	(.498)
T_3	.584	(.539)	.677	(.706)	.282	(.462)	.363	(.598)
T_4	.528	(.639)	.628	(.706)	.353	(.552)	.349	(.536)
Anxiety								
T_1	.499	(.569)	.783	(.774)	.279	(.461)	.554	(.414)
T_3	.384	(.513)	.560	(.592)	.254	(.353)	.416	(.507)
T_4	.331	(.507)	.518	(.712)	.315	(.508)	.436	(.475)
Hostility								
T_1	.256	(.337)	.298	(.466)	.377	(.521)	.317	(.378)
T_3	.190	(.279)	.226	(.331)	.335	(.388)	.243	(.373)
T_4	.196	(.550)	.269	(.519)	.410	(.516)	.348	(.475)
Phobic anxiety								
T_1	.191	(.342)	.383	(.621)	.144	(.333)	.344	(.600)
T_3	.143	(.270)	.245	(.491)	.113	(.229)	.285	(.522)
T_4	.082	(.277)	.231	(.509)	.140	(.307)	.303	(.584)
Paranoid ideation								
T_1	.358	(.455)	.407	(.583)	.438	(.532)	.380	(.421)
T_3	.298	(.423)	.286	(.400)	.487	(.585)	.357	(.492)
T_4	.371	(.593)	.400	(.568)	.453	(.565)	.369	(.516)
Psychoticism								
T_1	.478	(.462)	.539	(.592)	.256	(.392)	.275	(.394)
T_3	.362	(.357)	.335	(.422)	.212	(.278)	.262	(.432)
T_4	.314	(.434)	.404	(.576)	.281	(.387)	.234	(.437)

[a]Scale ranges from 0 (not at all) to 4 (extremely) for each item; subscale scores are obtained by summing scores for all items included in a given subscale and dividing the sum by the number of items.

skewed positively at all three times of measurement such that means were near the low-distress end of the distribution. Because the subscales are highly intercorrelated, these data were analyzed separately and as a full scale using a multivariate analysis of variance (MANOVA) approach. The MANOVA yielded a highly significant *group effect* ($F = 9.52$, $p < .001$), with the bereaved respondents manifesting more symptomatic distress than the controls. Females also had significantly more symptoms than males overall ($F = 3.02$, $p < .001$). In general, the symptoms measured by these scales decreased gradually across time ($F = 3.19$, $p <$

TABLE 2   F-Ratios for Between-Subjects Analysis of the Brief Symptom Inventory

	Group	Sex	Group X sex
Somatization	.136	1.86	.986
Obsessive-compulsive	.619	3.08†	.72
Interpersonal sensitivity	1.28	2.15	1.04
Depression	28.92**	1.55	.027
Anxiety	3.34†	9.85*	.081
Hostility	7.13*	.004	2.02
Phobic anxiety	.34	10.92**	.018
Paranoid ideation	1.22	.001	1.46
Psychoticism	8.44*	.684	.119

$**p < .001$. Two-tailed test.
$*p < .05$. Two-tailed test.
$^\dagger p < .10$.

.001), and this change was much more significant in the bereaved than in the control participants ($F = 6.31$, $p < .001$). There was a suggestion of a sex by time interaction, with females showing greater declines in symptoms than males, but no evidence of a third order interaction in these data. Repetition of the analyses using several covariates (e.g., background variables, coping strength, cumulative stress, and social support predictor components) did not change this picture appreciably.

A summary of the univariate analyses for the nine subscales is included in Tables 2–4. Inspection of these tables indicates that the bereaved were significantly higher on depression ($F = 28.92$, $p < .001$) and psychoticism ($F = 8.44$, $p < .05$) and significantly lower on hostility ($F = 7.13$, $p < .05$) than the controls. There also was a borderline effect of the bereaved having higher levels of anxiety ($F = 3.34$, $p < .10$). There were no group differences on the remaining subscales.

Bereaved women were higher than bereaved men on anxiety ($F = 9.85$, $p < .05$) and phobic anxiety ($F = 10.92$, $p < .001$) and nearly so on obsessive-compulsive features ($F = 3.08$, $p < .10$) (see Table 2). There were no gender differences on the six remaining subscales. There was no evidence of an overall

TABLE 3   F-Ratios for Analysis of Effect over Time of the Brief Symptom Inventory

	Linear	Quadratic
Somatization	.011	1.66
Obsessive-compulsive	1.43	.618
Interpersonal sensitivity	.003	.564
Depression	13.52**	.366
Anxiety	4.93*	1.81
Hostility	.125	11.12**
Phobic anxiety	3.89*	1.13
Paranoid ideation	1.83	3.31
Psychoticism	4.42*	4.30

$**p < .001$.
$*p < .05$.

TABLE 4   F-Ratios for Linear Analysis of the Brief Symptom Inventory

	Group × time	Sex × time	Group × sex × time
Somatization	.160	8.21*	.525
Obsessive-compulsive	2.73	3.38†	.503
Interpersonal sensitivity	3.76†	3.78†	.433
Depression	31.14**	1.66	.667
Anxiety	2.50	2.88†	.289
Hostility	.187	.165	.003
Phobic anxiety	1.02	1.37	.262
Paranoid ideation	.181	2.04	.012
Psychoticism	3.79†	.836	.809

**$p < .001$.
*$p < .05$.
$^\dagger p < .10$.

group by sex interaction. Again, the introduction of the four predictor components did not change this pattern of results.

Table 3 shows the effects across time for the nine subscales. There was a linear decrease in depression ($F = 13.52, p < .001$), anxiety ($F = 4.93, p < .05$), phobic anxiety ($F = 3.89, p < .05$), and psychoticism ($F = 4.42, p < .05$). The overall change across time for hostility was best explained by a quadratic (curvilinear) function ($F = 11.12, p < .001$), with no strong evidence for a linear relationship. Table 4 shows the interaction effects of group and sex by time.

There was a significant sex by time interaction on the somatization subscale ($F = 8.21, p < .05$), and it was still apparent when the predictor components were introduced. The means for the somatization subscale in Table 1 suggest that the women were slightly higher than the men at T_1, they showed a greater decrease from T_1 to T_3 than did the men, while the change from T_3 to T_4 was similar for both sexes. The obsessive-compulsive scale also showed a significant sex by time effect that was more evident in the quadratic component ($F = 4.44, p < .05$) than in the linear ($F = 3.38, p < .10$). This effect was removed when the coping strength components were introduced as predictors. The means in Table 1 indicate that the women were again higher than the men on obsessive-compulsive symptoms at T_1 and showed a greater decline from T_1 to T_3 than did the men. Also, the women showed a slight increase from T_3 to T_4, whereas the men remained essentially the same.

There was a marginal group by time and sex by time effect on the interpersonal sensitivity scale. Both the bereaved and the females were slightly higher at T_1 and showed a greater decline from T_1 to T_3 than their counterparts. The group by time effect was highly significant on the depression scale ($F = 31.14, p < .001$), and this remained unchanged with the introduction of the predictor components. Table 1 shows that the bereaved were substantially higher than the controls at T_1 and they showed a strong linear decline across the three times of measurement. The controls, on the other hand, showed no change across the 2^1/$_2$-year measurement period. There was a slight suggestion of a sex by time effect on the anxiety scale. Again the females were higher than the males and showed a greater linear decline than the males.

The means for the hostility scale (see Table 1) indicate that there was no linear tend across time. There was, however, a decrease in hostility from T_1 to T_3 and then an increase from T_3 to T_4. There was no sex by time or group by time interaction. There was a slight suggestion of a group by sex interaction, with the bereaved men showing less hostility than the other three groups at all three times of measurement and the control men showing more. This same trend was evident in the women, but was less pronounced.

Finally, Table 4 indicates that there was a marginally significant group by time effect on the psychoticism scale. The bereaved were endorsing more of the psychotic symptoms than the controls at T_1, but these symptoms declined from T_1 to T_3 for the bereaved while they remained essentially the same across time for the controls.

DISCUSSION

Overall these data suggest that older adults undergoing spousal bereavement have greater depression and anxiety and are more likely to manifest "psychot-iclike" symptoms than normal controls during the first few months following the death of the spouse. It should be noted that mean scores, in general, were in the mildly distressed range on all of the subscales; however, the bereaved responded to these items in a manner that suggests somewhat greater psychological distress than is typical for this age range on most subscales.[9] However, by the end of the 1st year, many of these symptoms decreased substantially or were not evident at all, and, by the end of the 2nd year, there was virtually no difference between be-reaved and nonbereaved groups on most of these symptom dimensions. This agrees with the recent work of Lund et al.[2] and suggests that a strong degree of resiliency characterizes the elder bereaved. It is interesting to note that symptoms of hostility were significantly less in the bereaved at 2 months following the death of the spouse, particularly in the men, and that this reduction in symptoms re-mained fairly stable over the 2-year period of measurement. Given the increased hardships that many of the bereaved participants had to undergo, one might have expected to see an increase in hostility, but this clearly was not the case.

It is also noteworthy that while the various predictor components associated with background variables by and large had significant effects on the dependent measures, their introduction into the covariance analyses had only minimal impact on the effects of group and sex and their interactions with time. Since there were sociodemographic differences between the bereaved and the controls and between the males and the females, it is noteworthy that the adjustments made to account for these differences did not modify the effects of bereavement or sex in the manifestation of symptoms. This suggests that the differences among these groups cannot be accounted for by differences in age or socioeconomic conditions. This point is noted because of recent work emphasizing the role that socioeconomic factors may play in the development of psychological distress.[10,11] While such factors clearly do impact symptom manifestation, they cannot account for the differences between the bereaved and nonbereaved who participated in this study.

It is also clear that the level of coping strength, the amount of cumulative stress, and the extent and quality of the social support network all did have effects on BSI symptom manifestation, but again these did not account for the effects of bereavement and sex when the adjustments were made in the covariance analyses. A similar interpretation can be made for the effects of sex. Examination of the F

ratios for the effects of covariates on the dependent measures shows that the level of cumulative stress had the highest effect on all of the nine scales. The higher the stress, the higher the score on the symptom scale. Coping strength had the second highest effect on eight of the nine scales. Individuals who reported using a variety of coping strategies had lower scores on the symptom scales. Social support had a greater impact on the obsessive-compulsive scale than did coping strength, but it also contributed significantly to the other scales. In particular, those who reported have more extensive social support systems experienced less distress as reflected in self-report of symptoms on the BSI. Although it is clear that these three domains do in fact impact significantly on the level of distress, as we originally predicted, they do not explain all the effects observed in the bereavement group. Thus, there is an effect of bereavement on the level of pathological symptoms experienced that is separate from these three domains.

Results of these analyses may be summarized in the following conclusions: (1) The initial psychological distress associated with early bereavement diminished over time for most elders in our sample. (2) Women endured more distress (irrespective of bereavement status) on this multidimensional measure than did the men. (3) These results remained unchanged even after several additional analyses were done to statistically control for the contribution of such covariates as sociodemographic status, coping strength, social support, and the impact of subsequent stressors. Thus, these findings may be considered fairly robust, at least for the generally well-educated volunteer sample assessed in this study. Further research is needed to elucidate the characteristics of elder bereaved persons whose symptoms do *not* remit with time so that appropriate interventions can be initiated.[12] It is also important to evaluate the impact of spousal bereavement on the everyday functioning of elders to increase knowledge about the relationship between functional status and the kind of data reflecting symptomatic distress obtained from the paper and pencil measure used in this and other studies of the mental health of elders.

REFERENCES

1. Gallagher, D. E., Breckenridge, J. N., Thompson, L. W., & Peterson, J. A. (1983). Effects of bereavement on indicators of mental health in elderly widows and widowers. *Journal of Gerontology, 38,* 565–571.
2. Lund, D. A., Caserta, M. S., & Dimond, D. F. (1986). Gender differences through two years of bereavement among the elderly. *The Gerontologist, 26,* 314–320.
3. Gallagher, D. E., & Thompson, L. W. (in press). Bereavement and adjustment disorders. In E. Busse & D. Blazer (Eds.), *Handbook of geriatric psychiatry* (2nd ed). Washington, DC: American Psychiatric Association.
4. Breckenridge, J. N., Gallagher, D. E., Thompson, L. W., & Peterson, J. A. (1986). Characteristic depressive symptoms of elder bereaved. *Journal of Gerontology, 41,* 163–168.
5. Heyman, D., & Gianturco, D. (1973). Long term adaptation by the elderly to bereavement. *Journal of Gerontology, 28,* 359–362.
6. Clayton, P. (1982). Bereavement. In E. Paykel (Ed.), *Handbook of affective disorders.* New York: Guilford Press.
7. Derogatis, L. (1977) *Brief symptom inventory: Administration scoring and procedures manual.* Baltimore, MD: Clinical Psychometric Research.
8. Derogatis, L., & Melisaratos, N. (1983). The Brief Symptom Inventory: An introductory report. *Psychological Medicine, 13,* 595–605.
9. Hale, W. D., Cochran, C. D., Hedgepeth, B. E. (1984). Norms for the elderly on the Brief Symptom Inventory. *Journal of Consulting and Clinical Psychology, 52,* 321–322.

10. Hirschfeld, R. M. A., & Cross, C. K. (1982). Epidemiology of affective disorders: Psychosocial risk factors. *Archives of General Psychiatry, 39,* 35–46.
11. Vernon, S. W., & Roberts, R. E. (1982). Use of the SADS-RDC in a tri-ethnic community survey. *Archives of General Psychiatry, 39,* 47–52.
12. Silverman, P., & Cooperband, A. (1975). Mutual help and the elderly widow. *Journal of Geriatric Psychiatry, 8,* 9–27.

3

Mental and Physical Health of Rural Bereaved and Nonbereaved Elders: A Longitudinal Study

Sally Van Zandt, Roberta Mou, and Doug Abbott

The mental health of elderly widows and widowers who reside in rural areas was explored over a 3½-year time span beginning shortly after the death of the spouse. Data from structured interviews and four self-report measures of mental and physical health status revealed no differences between widows and widowers. Differences did appear on measures of grief and perceived mental health between the widows and a matched group of control subjects. Although the physical health status of both groups decreased, the widowed persons reported a larger number of health problems.

INTRODUCTION

Becoming widowed is a difficult life transition for most, and for some it is a devastating personal crisis. The death of a spouse is not only an emotional loss but also a social loss, and it often entails major changes in life-style and role performance.[1-3]

The death of a spouse has long been recognized as a major life stressor, requiring more readjustment than any other life event.[4,5] Stressful life events, like widowhood, have been found to be associated with increased emotional and physical illness.[6-8] Bereavement can exacerbate existing mental and physical health problems, and it appears to have a role in precipitating new illnesses.[9] Adding further to the concern about widowhood are the demographic projections which reveal that because the proportion of the elderly in the population is increasing, more elderly persons will experience widowhood each year.[10]

Mental Health and Bereavement

The clinical literature contains numerous examples of mental health problems associated with bereavement;[4] however, the findings are inconsistent. Several earlier studies reported high levels of distress, but recent research has shown more moderate impact on mental health. For example, Parkes[11] states that bereavement can cause serious mental illness. The findings of Maddison[12] indicated a marked deterioration in mental health of widows compared to a nonwidowed sample. Neither study included persons over the age of 65, however. Research studies conducted by Clayton, Halikas, and Maurice[13] addressed the issue of depression associated with widowhood among the elderly. The researchers concluded that a predictor of depression at 1 year was the presence of the clinical syndrome of depression at 1 month. Additional research by Berardo[14] found greater psychological distress in the widowed elderly

Recent research by Breckenridge, Gallagher, Thompson, and Peterson[15] suggested, however, that older persons may "experience less severe distress than middle aged people" (p. 167), and Lund, Dimond, Caserta, Poulton, and Connelly[16] reported that only 18% of their sample were still experiencing major coping difficulties after 2 years of adjustment.

Heyman and Gianturco[17] revealed that the impact of bereavement on elderly persons' mental health was comparable for both men and women. Clayton[18] and Parkes and Brown[11] found that individuals in early stages of bereavement experience considerable psychological distress. These differences were independent of gender. Two other recent studies also reported that men and women had more similarities than differences in how they had coped with the death of their spouses.[19,20]

Physical Health and Bereavement

Bereavement has been associated with deterioration not only in the mental health but also in the physical health of the survivors.[8] Parkes[21] examined the medical histories and physicians' records of 44 widows and concluded that the number of physician consultations more than doubled during the first 6 months of bereavement. When the sample was further broken down into widows under and over age 65, the younger widows reported psychological complaints whereas the older widows reported increasing physical symptoms.

Heyman and Gianturco[17] and Clayton[18] investigated the physical health status of elderly widowed persons and observed no significant bereaved-control differences in health ratings, reported number of physician visits, physical symptoms, or incidence of hospitalization during a 1-year interval. Yet, despite the consensus among researchers regarding the stressful nature of bereavement,[6] the data on physical health deterioration in adults over the age of 60 are limited and provide conflicting results.[22]

Mortality and Bereavement

As an extension of physical illness experienced by the widowed, bereavement has also been shown to be associated with an increase in mortality rates.[23] Researchers Young, Benjamin, and Wallis[24] compared the mortality rate of widowers with that of married men of the same age and concluded that widowhood appeared to bring a 40% increase in mortality rates during the first 6 months of bereavement. However, further analysis revealed that for the period from 6 months to 5 years following bereavement, the mortality of widowers differed little from that of married men.

Rees and Lutkins[25] found a difference in mortality between bereaved and matched control samples of 7 : 1, with bereaved men having the highest mortality rates, especially in the first 6 months. Helsing, Szklo, and Comstock[26] found a higher risk of mortality for widows than widowers, a higher risk for young widows than older ones, a lower risk for widowed males who remarried than those who remained single, but no differences among widowed females whether or not they remarried.

Thus, it is difficult to predict exactly what effects bereavement can be expected to have on the physical and psychological status of elderly men and women. It is even more difficult to anticipate the impact of bereavement on older adults who live in rural areas, because there is no body of literature on this population. The authors speculate that the rural elderly would also experience a deterioration in mental and physical health following the death of their spouses. It is unclear, however, that they would differ in any substantial way as a result of having fewer formal resources available to them and as result of differences in their informal support networks.

A major problem in working with the bereaved elderly in rural areas is the dearth of research studies concerning this population. Many of the rural elderly live far from community services, and the question arises, "From where does their help come?" Longitudinal studies in this area are warranted in order to investigate the elderly's emotional responses to bereavement and to trace their changes over time. Therefore, the general purpose of this study was to investigate the bereavement adjustments of older adults who live in rural areas.

METHODOLOGY

Sampling

The participants of the research project belonged to either a bereaved or nonbereaved sample. The samples involved in the study resided on farms and ranches or in rural towns with populations of less than 15,000. In order to obtain participants for the bereaved sample, names were selected from obituary columns of local newspapers in southeastern Nebraska. The criteria used were age (over age 55), location (rural), and length of widowhood (less than a month from the death of the spouse). Letters were sent to all surviving spouses over age 55 to explain the study and enlist their cooperation. A stamped return postcard was enclosed to indicate willingness to participate. Mailings were sent to 633 persons. Of the 115 persons who responded (18%), only 25 women and 12 men met the age criteria. Because so few older men are surviving spouses, follow-up phone calls were made to the most recent widowers. Within a month, another 13 men agreed to participate. When asked about the return postcard, most stated they didn't think they had anything to offer but would be glad to participate in the study if we would come to their homes. Subjects agreeing to participate were contacted by telephone and personal interviews were arranged.

In choosing participants for the nonbereaved comparison sample, names were solicited chiefly from widowed persons being interviewed. These individuals were over age 55, and either were married or had not lost their spouse through death or divorce in the preceding 5-year period. Because these individuals had already been contacted by their friends, the researchers telephoned them and arranged personal interviews.

The samples were composed of 50 bereaved and 50 nonbereaved, with an equal distribution of men and women. The ages of the samples ranged from 55 to 92, with a mean age of 71.4 for bereaved men, 68.8 for bereaved women, 70.9 for nonbereaved men, and 70.5 for nonbereaved women. Forty-one percent of the sample had received 9–12 years of formal education. The men reported less formal education (20% with less than eighth grade) than their female counterparts (7%), and the majority of individuals who received advanced degrees were women (10%). The majority of the participants were unemployed or retired (65%), whereas 18% were employed full-time, 11% were employed part-time, and 6% were volunteers. The income levels of the participants were as follows: 12% had incomes of $3,000 to $4,999; 24%, $5,000 to $9,999; 35%, $10,000 to $19,999; 18%, $20,000 to $29,999. Four percent had less that $3,000 and 4% had incomes over $30,000. The participants were generally active members of religious groups including 72% of the bereaved men, 92% of the bereaved women, 100% of the nonbereaved men, and 96% of the nonbereaved women. The religious denominations of those in the sample were Lutheran (32%), Methodist (21%), Presbyterian (9%), Catholic (8%), Baptist (7%) and other (13%). Ten percent had no religious affiliation.

Procedure

Collection methods utilized in obtaining the data for this research included both structured interviews and self-report measures. Interviews by the senior researchers and trained graduate students were conducted in the homes of the participants, with the exception of two participants who chose to be interviewed at the university. Interviews proceeded according to the following schedule. The newly widowed persons were interviewed within 6 weeks to 4 months after the spouse's death T_1, 8 months later T_2, and approximately 1 year after the second interview T_3. The final interview was conducted 3½ years after the death of the spouse T_4. The interviews of the nonbereaved persons proceeded according to the same schedule. The interviews ranged in time from 45 minutes to 4 hours. Interviews for the nonbereaved were shorter than for the bereaved.

Over the 3½ years, 15 individuals were dropped from the study. Among the bereaved participants, 3 women remarried and 6 men remarried. Among the nonbereaved women, 3 became widowed and 1 of the 3 remarried. One bereaved man and 2 nonbereaved men died, leaving a total of 85 persons participating at T_4.

Instruments

A structured interview for widowed persons developed by Gallagher, Thompson, and Peterson at the Ethel Percy Andrus Gerontology Center, University of Southern California, was utilized.[20] (Their study is described further in chapters 2 and 9.) For the purpose of this research project, only those sections of the structured interview pertinent to the mental and physical health status of the participants were used. Comparable interviews with appropriate modifications in wording were conducted with the comparison nonbereaved sample.

Questions were asked concerning the participants' self-rating of their perceived mental health at the present time. The participants' ratings were made on a seven-point Likert-type scale, with higher scores denoting a more negative self-appraisal. Physical health was measured by the participants' self-ratings of their perceived physical health, the number of physical health problems experienced, and the number of visits to a physician.

The helpfulness of various support systems was measured by using a seven-point Likert-type scale, with higher scores denoting a more negative appraisal. Family, friends, religious participation, work, group activities, keeping busy, seeking information, learning from past experiences, sense of purpose, and crying or talking about the death were the support systems measured.

In addition to the structured interviews, the participants were instructed to complete a packet of self-reporting measures, which they returned by mail following each interview. For the purpose of this research project, only those parts of the inventory pertaining to the mental and physical health status of the participants were utilized; these included the Beck Depression Inventory, the Texas Inventory of Grief, and the Severity Index subscale of the Brief Symptom Inventory.

The Beck Depression Inventory (BDI) is a multiple-choice symptom scale developed to assess the severity of depression.[27] Psychometric properties of the BDI are reviewed in Beck[27] and adequate reliability in samples of the elderly population has recently been reported by Gallagher, Thompson, and Peterson.[4] According to Beck,[27] scores from 0 to 9 are normal, scores from 10 to 16 show mild depression, scores from 17 to 23 show moderate depression, and scores 24 and above show severe depression.

The Texas Inventory of Grief (TIG) is a Likert-type self report measure of past disruption and present grief following a death. The inventory consists of five subscales; however, only the subscale present grief was used for this research study. Reliabilities from .70 to .90 have been reported for the subscales present grief and past grief by Faschingbauer.[28] For comparison purposes, the nonbereaved were asked to recall a significant loss they had experienced during their adult years and to complete the inventory for that loss. Scores can range from 0 to 65, with higher scores indicating a higher level of grief.

RESULTS AND DISCUSSION

The purpose of this paper was to examine longitudinally the effects of bereavement among rural elderly in relation to their mental and physical health status. The findings regarding mental health are presented first.

Mental Health Status

BEREAVED VERSUS NONBEREAVED

It was expected that widowed persons would experience significantly more mental health problems over time than nonwidowed persons. Using a 2-group (bereaved, nonbereaved) by 4-time (T_1, T_2, T_3, and T_4) repeated measures analysis of variance, the results indicated a significant group by time interaction effect [$F = (3, 77) = 5.56$, $p < .002$]. The univariate comparison indicated a significant linear pattern [$F = (1, 77) = 14.89$, $p < .001$]. According to the data in Table 1, the mental health of the bereaved improved, while the perception of the nonbereaved of their mental health became more negative over time. At T_1, the bereaved scores were more negative than the nonbereaved scores, but by T_4 the bereaved self-reports had improved to the point where they were actually more positive than those of the nonbereaved.

On the BDI, there was also a significant group by time interaction effect [$F = (3, 58) = 6.25$, $p < .001$]. The univariate comparison in Table 1 indicates a

TABLE 1   Mean Scores on Measures of Mental and Physical Health of Elderly Bereaved and Nonbereaved over 3½ Years[a]

	Time periods			
	T_1	T_2	T_3	T_4
Perceived mental health				
Bereaved	2.81	2.65	2.14	1.89
Nonbereaved	2.10	2.03	2.23	2.48
Beck Depression Inventory				
Bereaved	9.17	7.60	7.37	5.93
Nonbereaved	4.18	4.30	5.82	6.07
Texas Inventory of Grief				
Bereaved	42.81	39.15	35.96	35.65
Nonbereaved	29.86	27.14	26.00	26.79
Perceived physical health[b]				
Bereaved	2.62	2.46	2.65	2.11
Nonbereaved	2.30	2.08	2.35	2.60
Number of physical problems				
Bereaved	3.56	2.62	2.73	2.81
Nonbereaved	2.10	1.30	1.98	1.90
Number of physician visits				
Bereaved	1.19	1.27	2.95	3.43
Nonbereaved	.88	2.20	3.50	3.13

[a]High scores denote poor mental health, high depression and high grief.
[b]1 = better health and fewer problems; 7 = poor health and more problems.

significant pattern interaction $[F = (1, 58) = 17.64, p < .001]$ in that the bereaved had decreasing levels of depression while nonbereaved had increasing levels of depression over time. Although the bereaved began the study with depression scores slightly above normal, at the end both groups were nearly the same and were well within the normal range.

On the TIG, there was a group effect; the bereaved experienced higher levels of grief than the nonbereaved $[F = (1, 54) = 25.12, p < .001]$. The results also indicated a significant effect by time $[F = (3, 54) = 3.98, p < .013]$. The time effect seemed to indicate a linear pattern $[F = (1, 54) = 11.01, p < .002]$. No interaction effect was observed between group and time. Both bereaved and nonbereaved levels of grief decreased similarly over time (see Table 1).

Data from Gallagher, Breckenridge, Thompson, and Peterson[20] revealed their widows had higher levels on measures of grief and lower perceived mental health than their nonwidows. Findings from the present study are in agreement with observations by Clayton[18] and Parkes and Brown[11] that individuals in the early stages of bereavement experience psychological distress; over time however, the bereaved experienced psychological distress similar to that experienced by their nonbereaved counterparts.

BEREAVED MEN VERSUS BEREAVED WOMEN

It was also posited that widowed men and women would experience similar levels of mental health problems over time. Using repeated measures analysis of variance, bereaved men and bereaved women reported no group differences on perceived mental health, the TIG, and the BDI. These findings are consistent with those recently reported by Gallagher et al.[20] and Lund, Caserta, and Dimond,[19] suggesting that the impact of spousal loss on the mental health of elders is comparable for both men and women.

The results of the comparison between the bereaved men and women on these mental health variables did indicate a time effect. Both bereaved men and bereaved women reported gradual improvement in mental health [$F = (3, 37) = 5.07 p < .005$] showing a linear pattern [$F = (1, 37) = 11.77, p < .002$]. They also showed decreasing levels of grief and depression over time [$F = (3, 30) = 4.41, p < .012$], the decreases again possessing linear patterns [$F = (1, 30) = 13.04, p < .001$ for depression, and $F = (3, 26) = 7.13, p < .001$ and $F = (1, 26) = 19.10, p < .001$ for grief]. Schaie and Willis[29] offer one plausible explanation why the perceived mental health of some widowed persons improved over time. They argue that individuals experience grief in two stages. In the first stage of acute grief, the widow or widower attempts to adjust to the loss of the spouse. During the second stage, the bereaved individual gradually reconstructs an identity as a partnerless person with greater feelings of competence and independence. Thus, the perceived mental and physical health of both men and women improves over the years.

Physical Health Status

BEREAVED VERSUS NONBEREAVED

Repeated measures analysis of variance was also used to compare the physical health of the bereaved and nonbereaved groups. There were no significant group or time differences, but the univariate comparison indicated a significant linear interaction [$F = (1, 77) = 6.21, p < .015$]. Although some fluctuation was evident, the bereaved generally perceived their physical health as slightly improving over time and the nonbereaved sample perceived their physical health to slightly decrease. The mean scores, which indicate generally positive ratings for both groups, are presented in Table 1.

The bereaved, however, reported experiencing significantly more health problems than the nonbereaved [$F = (1, 77) = 8.77, p < .004$]. There was also a time effect [$F = (3, 77) = 4.15, p < .009$] showing a quadratic effect by time [$F = (1, 77) = 10.44, p < .002$]. At T_2, the number of health problems reported by both the bereaved and nonbereaved was less than at times T_1, T_3, and T_4. No group by time interaction was observed, however, indicating the changes over time were similar for both the bereaved and nonbereaved. Their mean scores are presented in Table 1.

There were no differences between the bereaved and the nonbereaved on incidence of hospitalization. There were also no group differences on physician visits, but there was a time effect [$F = (3, 77) = 9.20, p < .001$] showing a linear pattern [$F = (1, 77) = 24.82, p < .001$]. The number of visits to physicians increased over time for both the bereaved and nonbereaved, as indicated by their mean scores in Table 1.

BEREAVED MEN VERSUS BEREAVED WOMEN

There were no group differences between the bereaved men and women on their perceived physical health, the number of reported health problems, or the incidence of hospitalization. Again, no differences were found between the bereaved on number of physician visits, though there was a time effect [$F = (3,$

37) $= 6.45, p < .001$] showing a linear pattern [$F = (1, 37) = 9.31, p < .004$]. Both bereaved men and bereaved women reported an increasing number of physician visits over time.

One major finding from this study is that there were no significant differences between the bereaved men and the bereaved women on any of the measures of physical health over the 3½ years. This finding is consistent with the findings of Breckenridge, Gallagher, and Peterson for 2 months after the death and with the findings of Lund et al.[19] for 2 years after the death. It is not consistent with the findings of Gerber, Rusalem, Hannon, Battin, and Arkin[30] or Parkes and Brown.[11]

A second finding was in the mortality rate of the two groups. One of the bereaved men died 2 years after the death of his wife and two of the nonbereaved men died during the time of the study. None of the women died during the 3½ years of the study, although the wives of two nonbereaved men became widowed. This finding is considerably different from the findings of Parks, Murray, and Fitzgerald;[23] Young, Benjamin, and Wallis[24] and Rees and Luthkins.[25] Given these small numbers, however, one must be cautioned against drawing inferences. Further investigations on large samples are needed to adequately explore this relationship.

Although the bereaved did report a greater number of health problems over time than the nonbereaved, the number of physician visits increased over time for both samples. This finding is consistent with what one would expect from persons aged 55–92. It was interesting that the bereaved persons' perceptions of their health improved over time whereas the perceptions of the nonbereaved persons declined, even though both groups showed increases in the number of physician visits. This could be due in part to the bereaved persons' expecting their health to deteriorate more than it actually did; therefore, compared to what they anticipated, it seemed to them their physical health was quite good.

Support Systems

Interviews with the bereaved persons revealed the importance of various support systems in facilitating the process of bereavement from the acute grief of stage 1 to the independence of stage 2. At T_1, family and church were the most helpful supports. By T_4, family and friends were the most helpful. Group activities and seeking information were the least helpful.

The support system information suggests the importance of warm, caring, one-to-one relationships for both widowed men and women. Men may try to lose themselves in their work in the beginning, often because their wives were their best friends. As time continues, however, they can rebuild relationships with others and build new friendships. Women may say to themselves, "I've been through rough times before and I can do it again," but by T_4 they, too, are willing to share themselves with friends and loved ones in order to move forward into the future. Lund, Dimond, and Juretich[31] also found that many of the older adults in their study had a similar willingness to share.

SUMMARY

The results of this research indicated that bereaved persons had slightly more mental health problems than the comparison nonbereaved persons during the first several months, but the differences disappeared over time. Although the bereaved perceived their physical health as improving over time, the number of physician visits actually increased. It should be noted that the majority of research studies previously conducted have found significant differences between the bereaved and nonbereaved. Therefore the results of this study should be viewed tentatively. Another reason to evaluate the results of this study with caution was the small, voluntary, nonrandom nature of the sample which consisted of older adults residing within rural areas.

Additional research using larger random sample containing persons from various geographic regions and with different ethnic or racial backgrounds is warranted. These additional efforts will permit an examination and evaluation of sample differences in the adaptations of elders to conjugal bereavement. It is further suggested that in addition to documentation, future research will facilitate programs in assessment, intervention, and prevention, enabling the survivors of spousal loss to better cope with the challenges of widowhood.

CONCLUSIONS AND IMPLICATIONS FOR COUNSELORS AND EDUCATORS

Overall, the data suggest that there were fewer differences than expected between the mental and physical health of newly widowed older persons and the health of counterparts who were not widowed or had been widowed more than 5 years. There also were no gender differences among the widowed. Both men and women experienced similar symptoms in response to spousal death. Mental health problems associated with bereavement and grief were less notable than expected. Physical health problems also did not appear to be as bad as the widowed individuals had expected.

Although the researchers do not wish to minimize the problems associated with the loss of a mate at any time in life, the elderly in this study may have suffered less than expected for two reasons. First, all of the older persons interviewed (both bereaved and nonbereaved) had suffered a previous loss and had survived. Each one had utilized various coping mechanisms and support systems that had worked and that could be counted on to work in the case of bereavement. Second, widowhood may not be as difficult if it is almost an expected life event.[32] When friends are dying, there is a feeling of living "on borrowed time"; death can occur at any moment.

As noted, the intensity of grief among the widowed persons did decrease over the 3 1/2 years of this study, which may indicate either that the support systems utilized were adequate or that grief was experienced in two stages.[29] The result is that perceived mental health improved over the years and that physical health seemed more related to age than to widowhood.

The rural Nebraska elderly are typically independent and self-sufficient, with strong family ties and few community support systems. Older men need either assistance in building friendships or some structure in which they can be together so friendships can develop. Older women need a confidant who will encourage them in the process of becoming more independent.

Counselors and educators can provide opportunities for older persons (both bereaved and nonbereaved) to discuss bereavement with each other. Seminars and discussions on bereavement led by qualified professionals are popular and can provide such opportunities. Balkwell[33] suggested that counselors and educators should encourage family members to identify whether or not a confidant exists for the bereaved older person. If desired, they can help friends and family members learn listening skills so that the confidant role can be filled.

Scheidt[34] suggested placing mental health paraprofessionals in available local sites or providing gerontological training for those people already working there. The independent rural elderly who typically refuse state and local social service assistance can be encouraged to maintain that independence with minimal training and professional assistance. Those who have managed their grief with positive outcomes could also serve to help others in similar situations, particularly in rural areas where trained professionals are rare. These older persons are valuable resources for others.

REFERENCES

1. Balkwell, C. (1981). Transition to widowhood; A review of the literature. *Family Relations, 30,* 117–127.
2. Kalish, R. (1987) Older people and grief. *Generations, 11(3),* 33–38.
3. Parkes, C. M., & Weiss, B. (1983). *Recovery from bereavement.* New York: Basic Books.
4. Gallagher, D. E., Thompson, L. W., & Peterson, J. A. (1982). Psychosocial factors affecting adaption to bereavement in the elderly. *International Journal on Aging and Human Development, 14(2),* 79–95.
5. Sanders, C. M. (1981). Comparison of younger and older spouses in bereavement outcome. *Omega, 11(3),* 217–232.
6. Holmes, T. H., & Rahe, R. (1967). The social readjustment rating scale. *Journal of Psychosomatic Research, 11,* 213–218.
7 Fenwick, R., & Barresi, P. M. (1981). Health consequences of marital-status change among the elderly: A comparison of cross-sectional and longitudinal analysis. *Journal of Health and Social Behavior, 22(2),* 106–116.
8. Strobe, M. S., & Strobe, W. (1983). Who suffers more? Sex differences in health risks of the widowed. *Psychological Bulletin, 93(2),* 279–301.
9. Osterweis, M. (1985Z). Bereavement and the elderly. *Aging, 348,* 8–14.
10. American Association of Retired Persons (AARP) and U.S. Department of Health and Human Services, Administration on Aging (1985). *A profile of older americans.* Washington, DC: American Association of Retired Persons.
11. Parkes, C. M., & Brown, R. J. (1972). Health after bereavement: A controlled study of young Boston widows and widowers. *Psychosomatic Medicine, 34,* 449–461.
12. Maddison, D. (1968). The relevance of conjugal bereavement for preventive psychiatry. *British Journal of Psychology, 41*223–233.
13. Clayton, P., Halikas, J., & Maurice, W. (1972). The depression of widowhood. *British Journal of Psychiatry, 120,* 71–78.
14. Berardo, F. M. (1970). Survivorship and social isolation: The case of the aged widower. *Family Coordinator, 19(1),* 11–25.
15. Breckenridge, J. N., Gallagher, D. E., Thompson, L. W., & Peterson, J. A. (1986). Identifying elderly with coping difficulties after two years of bereavement. *Omega, 16,* 213–224.
17. Heyman, D. K., & Gianturco, D. T. (1973). Long-term adaptation by the elderly to bereavement. *Journal of Gerontology, 28(3),* 359–362.
18. Clayton, P. J. (1974). Mortality and morbidity in the first year of bereavement. *Archives of General Psychiatry, 30(6),* 747–750.
19. Lund, D., Caserta, M., & Dimond, M. (1986). Gender differences through two years of bereavement among the elderly. *The Gerontologist, 26,* 314–320.
20. Gallagher, D. E., Breckenridge, J. N., Thompson, L. W., & Peterson, J. A. (1983). Effects of bereavement on indicators of mental health in elderly widows and widowers. *Journal of Gerontology, 38(5),* 565–571.
21. Parkes, C. M. (1964). Effects of bereavement on physical and mental health: A study of the medical records of widows. *British Medical Journal, 2,* 274–279.
22. Thompson, L. W., Breckenridge, J. N., Gallagher, D. E., & Peterson, J. A. (1984). Effects of

bereavement on self-perceptions of physical health in elderly widows and widowers. *Journal of Gerontology, 39(3),* 309–314.
23. Parkes, C. M., Murray, B. B., & Fitzgerald, R. G. (1969). Broken heart: A statistical study of increased mortality among widows. *British Medical Journal, 1,* 740–743.
24. Young, M., Benjamin, B., & Wallis, C. (1963). The mortality of widowers. *Lancet, 2(7305),* 454–456.
25. Rees, W., & Lutkins, S. (1967). Mortality of bereavement. *British Medical Journal, 4,* 13–16.
26. Helsing, K. J., Szklo, M., & Comstock, G. W. (1981). Factors associated with mortality after widowhood. *American Journal of Public Health, 71(8),* 802–809.
27. Beck, A. (1967). *Depression: Clinical, experimental and theoretical aspects.* New York: Harper & Row.
28. Faschingbauer, T. R. (1981). *Texas revised inventory of grief manual.* Houston: Honeycomb Publishing.
29. Schaie, K. W., & Willis, S. L. (1986). *Adult development and aging.* Boston: Little, Brown.
30. Gerber, E., Rusalem, R., Hannon, N., Battin, D., & Arkin, A. (1975). Anticipatory grief and aged widows and widowers. *Journal of Gerontology, 30,* 225–229.
31. Lund, D., Dimond, M., & Juretich, M. (1985). Bereavement support groups for the elderly: Characteristics of potential participants. *Death Studies, 9,* 309–321.
32. Thompson. L. W., & Gallagher, D. E. (1985). Depression and its treatment in the elderly. *Aging, 348,* 14–18.
33. Balkwell, C. (1985). An attitudinal correlate of the timing of a major life event: The case of morale in widowhood. *Family Relations, 34,* 577–581.
34. Scheidt, R. J. (1984). A taxonomy of well-being for smalltown elderly: A case for rural diversity. *The Gerontologist, 24,* 84–89.

4

Longitudinal Course
of Bereavement in Older Adults

Martin V. Faletti, Jeanne M. Gibbs, M. Cherie Clark,
Rachel A. Pruchno, and Elizabeth A. Berman

Data were obtained from interviews with 251 bereaved spouses aged 55–93 concerning their physical and psychosocial adjustments over the 18 months following the death. Half of the participants were first interviewed as early as 14–28 days postdeath and the others entered the study 6–8 weeks postdeath. Most of the analyses were performed on the 181 spouses who had complete data sets at T_2, T_3, and T_4. The findings revealed that depression and other psychosocial indicators were relatively low throughout the 18 months, with the highest levels at 2 months. Findings from ANOVA tests are presented regarding the effects of gender, occupational status, perceived health, religious affiliation, characteristics of the death situation, and the spousal relationship.

   This chapter represents a revision, compilation, and summary of several conference papers describing data collected as part of a project funded by a National Institute on Aging research grant (AG02061) and designed to examine bereavement in older adults. Several of these papers were originally written by the principal investigator of this project, the late Dr. Martin Faletti. The late Dr. Jeanne Gibbs was project director and authored one of the papers. Other collaborators on the papers summarized here were Dr. Rachel Pruchno and Elizabeth A. Berman.[1,6] The information presented here reflects the results of earlier analyses of the data and are not meant to provide a comprehensive summary of the entire study. Other analyses of these data are being completed by other investigators noted for their expertise in bereavement and aging. The preliminary results reported here do provide some insight into a few important factors affecting the course and consequences of the bereavement process. Moreover, these findings add to the literature base regarding the development of an integrative model of bereavement that includes the roles of supportive networks and the characteristics of the survivor and death event as factors influencing the intensity and duration of bereavement consequences in elderly surviving spouses.

OVERVIEW OF RESEARCH GOALS AND METHODOLOGY

The overall goal of this 3-year longitudinal study was to identify the relative roles of survivor characteristics, death event characteristics, supportive networks, and interventions in mediating the intensity and duration of negative consequences associated with bereavement in a sample of older surviving spouses. The study examined changes in physical and psychosocial functioning over an 18-month period following the death event and also examined the structure of and changes in supportive networks impacting on the bereaved survivor during this period. The analyses and results reported in this chapter focus on a subset of the questions dealt with in the study as a whole. These questions reflect some of the specific concerns of the Miami Jewish Home and Hospital for the Aged, which provides acute and long-term community services to older people experiencing mental and physical health problems.

Beyond the theoretical issue of whether critical parameters surrounding the relationship and aspects of the death event are significant predictors of the course of bereavement, this study sought to discover (1) the extent to which survivor, relationship, and death event characteristics might provide some estimate of risk for significant psychological dysfunction during the course of the first 18 months of bereavement and (2) in what time frame such dysfunction might be most manifest. In addition, as a result of early analyses, a number of methodological issues were addressed regarding the various assessment measures used in the study.

Sample Development

High refusal rates in previous studies suggested there would be significant obstacles for participant recruitment. In order to lessen the problems of recruitment and to conduct the study in as sensitive a way as possible, a community contact network was developed in which community liaisons served both as mediators between the potential participants and the interviewers and as referral sources.

Three formal groups were identified that traditionally provide caregiving services to the newly bereaved: (1) people in the medical community, (2) the funeral directors, and (3) the clergy and others in their community. Agency representatives from each of these groups were approached about the project and asked for their cooperation in functioning in the contact-mediation role. In some instances, the community contacts worked in conjunction with each other (e.g., a funeral director contacted the cleric who officiated at the funeral). The contact was accomplished through sending an explanatory letter and brochure to agencies, organizations, and persons in these three caregiving groups. In many cases, these efforts were followed up with presentations and personal visits by the project director and staff. The utilization of a contact was coupled with an individually directed letter and brochure sent to the surviving spouse.

Daily newspaper obituaries were used for the purpose of identifying those who died at age 55 or over and had surviving spouses in Dade County, Florida, and of identifying community contacts who could be utilized to mediate the initial contact. Sampling was accomplished by random selections from the obituary entries prior to exploration of the contact and potential solicitation of the respondent. However, participants were also initially acquired by self-presentation or as referrals from contact sources. Community contacts with knowledge of potential respondents also helped provide information not available from obituaries. In order to ensure some representation of anticipated death, approximately 37% of the study participants were identified through local hospice organizations.

Sample Description

A total of 251 bereaved elderly spouses (aged 55 years and older) were studied; 171 (68.1%) were female and 80 (31.9%) were male. The mean age of the participants was 72.5 years and the age range was 55–92 years. Health and psychosocial data were collected on half of these participants 14–28 days postdeath and then again 6–8 weeks postdeath. The remaining half of the sample was interviewed for the first time 6–8 weeks postdeath. These two entry points were utilized to compare patterns of early versus later effects. With the exception of early versus nonearly entry into the study, all participants were treated identically. Study participants were measured at the early or nonearly entry points, followed by measurements at 7 months, 13 months, and 18 months postdeath. In addition, since the effect of anticipatory grieving on the course of bereavement was of interest, an attempt was made to recruit participants for whom the death event was sudden and participants who expected the death of the spouse. The resulting sample was composed of 62% who expected the death of the spouse and 38% who did not.

Table 1 provides a descriptive comparison of the full study sample ($N = 251$) and the participants who completed all of the outcome assessments at T_2, T_3, and T_4 ($n = 181$). This comparison is important, because most of the analyses concerning changes over time utilized only those with more complete data sets. Otherwise the comparisons at various time periods would not be of the same set of people. As the figures indicate, those with more complete data (the subsample) were similar to the full sample in terms of their gender, age, years of education, occupational status and rankings, income, and religious affiliation. This is to be expected, because those with complete data composed 72% of the full sample. The largest occupational categories in the subsample were clerical (29%), administrative (19%), housewife (15%), and business managers (15%). Their income levels revealed that about 65% made above $20,000 per year and 35% made below that figure. Sixty-five percent were retired. Because some of the sample were identified through services provided by the Miami Jewish Home and Hospital for the Aged, there was a substantial number of Jewish participants in the subsample (58%). The next largest groups by religious affiliation were Protestants (21%) and Catholics (17%).

Measures and Interview Procedures

The interview protocols comprised measures of (1) psychosocial outcome using the Beck Depression Inventory (BDI)[7] and the Hopkins Symptom Check Lists (HSCL);[8] (2) social network characteristics using a modified version of the Kahn and Antonucci[9] circle diagram for social network assessment with specific questions related to functional supportive and affective roles of social agents placed in the network; (3) life events using a checklist; (4) last illness characteristics using a checklist; and (5) one aspect of the mutuality of closeness of the

TABLE 1   Demographic Characteristics: Total Study Sample and Those with Complete Data at T_2, T_3, and T_4

	Total sample $(N = 251)$[a]		Complete data sample $(N = 181)$[b]	
	%	(n)	%	(n)
Gender				
Male	31.9	80	34.8	63
Female	68.1	171	65.2	118
Age				
55–64	21.9	55	23.8	43
65–74	39.0	98	37.6	68
75–84	35.5	89	33.7	61
85+	3.6	9	4.9	9
Respondent occupation level[c]				
Higher executive	3.6	8	4.0	7
Business manager	14.2	32	15.3	27
Administrative	18.7	42	18.8	33
Clerical	29.7	67	29.0	51
Housewife	16.4	37	15.3	27
Skilled manual	8.0	18	8.0	14
Semiskilled	6.7	15	6.2	11
Unskilled	2.7	6	3.4	6
Income level				
$0–5,000	4.6	9	4.5	7
5,000–10,000	11.7	23	11.5	18
10,001–14,999	7.1	14	7.1	11
15,000–19,999	12.2	24	11.5	18
20,000–24,999	18.2	36	17.9	28
25,000–34,999	19.3	38	17.3	27
35,000–49,999	12.2	24	13.5	21
50,000+	14.7	29	16.7	26
Respondent occupational status				
Full-time employment	12.6	29	12.9	23
Part-time employment	9.1	21	10.1	18
Retired	63.9	147	65.2	116
Unemployed				
Work sought	7.0	16	5.6	10
Choice	7.4	17	6.2	11
Religious affiliation				
Protestant	21.6	49	20.9	37
Jewish	57.3	130	57.6	102
Catholic	17.2	39	16.9	30
Other	3.9	9	4.6	8

[a]Average years of schooling = 11.0.
[b]Average years of schooling = 11.9.
[c]See Holingshead, A. D., & Redlick, F. C. (1958). *Social class and mental illness*. New York: John Wiley & Sons.

relationship between the spouses using a shared task inventory. For the early entry group, the data base included the psychosocial measures at T_1 (14–28 days post-death) and T_2 (6–8 weeks postdeath). The first social network assessment and the last illness characteristics checklist were also used at the T_2 interview for this group. The late entry participants were administered psychosocial measures, the network assessment, and the last illness characteristics checklist at their initial interview (6–8 weeks postdeath). All participants then received psychosocial, social network, and life events measures at the three follow-up interviews at 5-month intervals. The last illness characteristics checklist was administered again, along with the shared task inventory, at the T_4 interview to examine the role of closeness of the spousal relationship and previous caretaking in the early course of bereavement.

The focus on expectation of death, characterization of the last illness, and care burden stemmed from an interest in the suggested hpenomenon of anticipatory grieving and its effect on the course of bereavement following the actual death. Self-report (yes-or-no format) questions were used to measure expectation of spouse's death, providing care at home, and help with care at home from persons outside the household. Differences in patterns of outcome for subgroups of the group who expected the death led to the inclusion of a supplemental instrument, the shared tasks inventory, to solicit specific information on care tasks performed. The item set attempted a rough index of care burden as reflected in the range of tasks performed. Eleven items composed the inventory, and scoring was by item count of yes responses; for analysis purposes, scores were placed into three groupings: 0, 1-4, and 5-11. The rationale was that groupings were more robust and would potentially smooth variance associated with items of potentially uneven salience in care burden.

RESULTS

Table 2 presents summary results for 181 cases in the complete data subsample on the BDI and on the HSCL subscales and gives the number of deaths among the study participants at each of the five data periods.

As seen in Table 2, the overall BDI means were not highly elevated and there was a trend toward reductions in mean BDI scores over time for the sample as a whole. Only 5% of the full sample were severely depressed. Scores 0–13 on the BDI are considered to reflect a mild depression; 14–24, mild to moderate depression; and 25 +, severe depression. The relative lack of severe depression seen in these samples is consistent with other reports of low overall rates of clinical depression in bereaved samples.[10] The remaining analyses focused on examining the extent to which this was a constant effect over all cases or whether other factors operated to produce different effects in different subgroups.

The mean scores on the HSCL subscales (depression, somatization, anxiety, and obsessive-compulsive) also illustrate relatively low levels of these potential mental health difficulties. Each of the mean scores were lower at T_5 than they were at T_1, with the exception of the somatization subscale, which remained at the same level. Only eight deaths occurred in the subsample (4.4%) during the 18-month study period, seven of them within the first 13 months.

Survivor Characteristics

Table 3 presents means, standard deviations, and a summary of effects for gender, occupational status, religious affiliation, and perceived health on the depression scale (BDI). The outcome assessments were limited to T_2, T_3, and T_4.

The three components of socioeconomic status and age were not dichotomized for ANOVAs. As was suggested in outcome means for the sample as a whole, depression as reflected in the BDI means was significantly higher at the 2-

TABLE 2 Summary Data for Selected Outcome Measures

		1 Month (T$_1$, n = 104)	2 Months (T$_2$, n = 181)	3 Months (T$_3$, n = 181)	13 Months (T$_4$, n = 181)	18 Months (T$_5$, n = 181)
Beck Depression Inventory						
Percent in	X(SD)	10.2(7.3)	10.3(7.8)	9.2(7.7)	9.0(8.2)	9.9(9.0)
	0–13	66.3	69.1	74.0	74.0	67.3
Score range	14 +	33.7	30.9	26.0	26.0	32.7
Hopkins Symptom Checklist						
Depression (range 11–44)	X(SD)	19.3(6.2)	19.1(6.1)	17.4(5.7)	17.1(5.9)	16.4(6.9)
Somatization (range 13–52)	X(SD)	17.8(5.9)	18.0(5.6)	17.4(5.6)	17.8(5.9)	17.7(7.2)
Anxiety (range 8–32)	X(SD)	12.8(5.5)	12.3(5.1)	11.3(5.1)	11.3(4.6)	10.9(5.7)
Obsessive-Compulsive (range 9–36)	X(SD)	14.7(5.5)	13.8(5.1)	13.2(5.1)	13.1(4.6)	13.4(5.7)
Number of deaths		—	1	3	3	1

TABLE 3 Results Summary: ANOVA Contrasts of BDI Scores on Selected Survivor Variables

| Variable | Level | (N) | 2 Months (T$_2$) | | 7 Months (T$_3$) | | 13 Months (T$_4$) | | ANOVA effects summary | | | | | |
| | | | | | | | | | Between | | Within | | Interaction | |
			X	(SD)	X	(SD)	X	(SD)	F	p	F	p	F	p
Gender	Male	(63)	9.19	(8.12)	8.74	(7.99)	8.31	(8.69)						
	Female	(118)	11.02	(7.63)	9.50	(7.69)	9.36	(8.08)	1.19	NS	3.88	.02	.68	NS
Occupational status	Working	(41)	6.60	(5.51)	5.21	(5.83)	5.04	(5.77)						
	Retired	(127)	11.16	(7.89)	10.37	(7.95)	9.77	(8.28)	10.95	.001	5.27	.005	1.55	NS
	Seeking work	(10)	17.00	(9.68)	12.00	(8.49)	15.80	(11.17)						
Perceived health	Better	(137)	9.06	(7.20)	8.10	(7.32)	7.59	(7.38)						
	Same	(33)	13.33	(8.08)	11.15	(6.87)	12.09	(9.09)	13.07	.001	1.67	NS	.49	NS
	Worse	(11)	18.00	(8.66)	17.63	(10.15)	17.27	(9.79)						
Religion	Non-Jewish	(79)	8.37	(6.78)	8.20	(6.89)	7.36	(7.19)						
	Jewish	(102)	11.94	(8.26)	10.04	(8.35)	10.26	(8.87)	6.89	.009	4.75	.009	1.79	NS

month interview than at later interviews. The main effect for interview time (repeated measure) was significant for three of the four analyses reported here. While mean levels for females were higher than for males, the differences were not statistically significant. Main effects were found for occupational status, religious affiliation, and perceived health; none of the three were associated with significant interaction effects.

The main effect for perceived health status regardless of the time of interview was predicted from other literature. Specifically, Jarvik and Perl[11] reported a strong correlation between physical illness and depression in the aged. In addition, studies of morale or life satisfaction emphasize the importance of health status as a correlate of a sense of well-being.[12] The strength of this relationship is further substantiated in its consistency across points 5 and 10 months.

The occupational status effect was unexpected, particularly as regards its strength. The pattern across levels of occupational status (i.e., working, not working by choice, retired, and not working but desiring work) can be viewed in several ways. In one respect, the data for not working but desiring to work could reflect some frustration in implementing desired objectives. However, the separation in means for each of three groups could be viewed as supportive of the notion that engagement in activity is associated with more adaptive outcomes. Working requires attention to be focused in directions other than the loss, while not working may provide more options for focusing attention on problems and dissatisfaction. However, it should be noted that the small size of the group not working but desiring to work dictates caution in drawing such inferences. Analyses of social networks data, which assessed what the respondent does for others, could provide an approach to examining social engagement and whether its effects support this view of activity and adaptation.

The presence of a significant main effect for religious affiliation and the large number of participants identifying themselves as Jewish is potentially problematic, since this factor encompasses both ethnic and religious components. While it must be taken into account in making interpretations, it is not now viewed as a confounding factor given the absence of a significant interaction effect between affiliation and time from the death. It is difficult to speculate as to whether cultural effects underlie generally higher levels of experienced depression or whether other factors disposing one toward more intense depression or more reporting of symptoms are simply more represented in this group.

Relationship Variables

The most striking feature of the results for the two shared task variables (Table 4) is the strong main effect for shared social and recreational tasks, with more sharing associated with lower mean levels of depression. While one might intuitively expect the opposite and posit that more sharing patterns would exacerbate the loss, these results do not support this view. Given that the items represent survivors' retrospective assessments of the sharing of tasks and activities, it is possible that the responses may reflect adaptation of recall as a result of the need to remember life with the spouse in a certain way, akin to social desirability. However, it is equally possible that they reflect the association between relationships which were, on the whole, close or mutual and less regret at things not done, a definite possibility given the results from the death situation variables.

Given the socialization of these older cohorts, there was some interest in the

TABLE 4 Results Summary: ANOVA Contrasts of BDI Scores on Selected Survivor Variables

| | | | 2 Months (T_2) | | 7 Months (T_3) | | 13 Months (T_4) | | ANOVA effects summary | | | | | |
| | | | | | | | | | Between | | Within | | Interaction | |
Variable	Level	(n)	X	(SD)	X	(SD)	X	(SD)	F	p	F	p	F	p
ADL shared tasks	Low	(73)	10.8	(10.8)	10.6	(7.6)	9.5	(7.8)						
	Moderate	(75)	9.7	(7.4)	8.5	(7.4)	9.1	(8.8)	.81	NS	7.67	.001	2.18	NS
	High	(33)	10.8	(9.1)	7.7	(8.5)	7.4	(8.0)						
Social/recreation	Low	(10)	13.0	(9.3)	13.8	(9.1)	12.9	(10.8)						
	Moderate	(24)	11.7	(7.8)	12.1	(7.7)	13.0	(9.2)	4.03	.01	.07	NS	1.65	NS
	High	(147)	9.9	(7.7)	8.4	(7.5)	8.0	(7.7)						

effect of activities of daily living (ADL) sharing, particularly whether a gender interaction with ADL sharing would associate with depression. Based on previous findings, the general prediction was that a more acute sense of loss would be experienced by males than by females, a suggestion which was not supported by results from a specific test of this interaction.

Death Situation

Preliminary examination of death situation data (Table 5) suggested a significant effect for death expectation, with sudden death cases evidencing more intense depression at early time periods, although the interaction with time was not significant.

Evidence of some planning (e.g., discussion of business and finances, life insurance, and wills) was not associated with depression in significant main or interaction effects. Two items indexed retrospective desire for change; specifically, they asked survivors if they would have done things differently during the last illness or made different death situation arrangements. Positive responses were considered as evidence of regret and were predicted to be associated with higher depression. Evidence for this was found in the significant main effect showing higher depression in the group responding positively on the retrospective desire for change items.

Where last illnesses or conditions suggested protracted caring, some impact of care burden as reflected in doing daily tasks was expected, especially as part of participation in a hospice program. In addition, sleep loss has previously been suggested as a correlate of depression, so the protocol included this item. Care burden as operationalized here was not significant as a main effect, and, contrary to expectation, the pattern of means suggests more caring is associated with lower levels of depression. Similarly, sleep loss had no main or interaction effects, even though means did suggest higher mean depression scores for the group reporting some sleep loss.

The effect for hospice participation, a significant interaction with time of interview, is interesting in that this factor appears to identify a group which, unlike most patterns noted, is relatively similar to the nonhospice group at the early point but remains elevated at later points. There was some information to indicate that part of this might be an effect of selection, since at least ten hospice subjects were involved in therapy and showed highly elevated BDI scores. It is, however, difficult to attribute this effect solely to 10 of 77 cases in this group.

Methodology Notes

A number of methodological issues were raised in the course of the study and as a result of preliminary findings. In an attempt to examine and improve the assessment measures used in the present study, a number of analyses were conducted using both the psychosocial outcome data as well as the social network data. A brief summary of the results of these analyses follows.

PSYCHOSOCIAL OUTCOME DATA

There was concern in the present study about using instruments originally developed to measure psychopathologies such as clinical depression (e.g., the BDI and the HSCL) with normal elderly populations. Using such instruments has become a common practice among researchers surveying normal elderly populations.

TABLE 5 Results Summary: ANOVA Contrasts of BDI Scores on Selected Survivor Variables

Variable	Level	(N)	2 Months (T_2) X	(SD)	7 Months (T_3) X	(SD)	13 Months (T_4) X	(SD)	Between F	Between p	Within F	Within p	Interaction F	Interaction p
Death expectancy	Expected	(128)	9.45	(7.09)	8.78	(7.19)	8.58	(7.80)	3.25	NS	7.94	.001	2.22	NS
	Sudden	(52)	12.80	(9.02)	10.26	(8.89)	10.11	(9.43)						
Preparation fiscal plan	No	(22)	11.10	(7.50)	10.6	(7.10)	10.0	(8.50)	.60	NS	1.71	NS	.14	NS
	Yes	(159)	10.2	(7.80)	9.0	(7.80)	8.8	(8.20)						
Retrospective desire for change	No	(113)	9.3	(7.60)	8.7	(7.80)	8.2	(7.70)	3.62	.05	6.05	.002	1.16	NS
	Yes	(68)	12.1	(7.80)	10.1	(7.70)	10.2	(9.00)						
Careload	None	(104)	10.4	(8.00)	9.6	(8.10)	8.7	(8.50)						
ADL home care	1–4 tasks	(39)	12.2	(7.60)	9.6	(7.30)	11.5	(8.70)	2.30	NS	4.27	.01	1.60	NS
	5–11 tasks	(38)	8.2	(7.00)	7.7	(7.30)	7.0	(6.40)						
Hospice	No	(104)	10.21	(8.43)	8.15	(8.08)	7.96	(8.83)	2.84	NS	4.10	.01	3.51	.03
	Yes	(77)	10.62	(7.00)	10.71	(7.15)	10.40	(7.31)						
Lost sleep	Yes	(78)	10.92	(7.59)	9.48	(7.72)	10.39	(8.53)	1.42	NS	4.88	.008	2.67	NS
	No	(103)	9.98	(8.00)	9.05	(7.86)	7.90	(7.98)						

TABLE 6   Hopkins Symptom Checklist Subscales and Items after Principal Component Analysis

Subscales and items[a]

Anxious behavior (alpha = .79)
  Sweating
  Feeling confused
  Having to do things very slowly in order to be sure you were doing them right
  Having to check and double-check what you do
  Trouble concentrating
Anxiety (alpha = .66)
  Nervous or shakiness inside
  Suddenly scared for no reason
  Feeling tense or keyed up
Depressive behavior (alpha = .69)
  Crying easily
  Constipation
  Difficulty in falling asleep or staying asleep
  A lump in your throat
Depression (alpha = .82)
  Feeling low in energy or slowed down
  Feeling lonely
  Feeling blue
  Worrying or stewing about things
  Your feelings being easily hurt
Withdrawn/disengagement (alpha = .69)
  Unable to get rid of bad thoughts or ideas
  Loss of sexual interest or pleasure
  Feeling no interest in things
  Wanting to be alone

[a]The item poor appetite did not load on any of the five subscales.

Such efforts often yield distributions with limited variance, which makes data interpretation difficult. An analysis was conducted to identify a set of items from an often-used self-report symptom inventory (the Hopkins Symptoms Checklist) that behave as traditional state measures in order to develop a test to assess the multidimensional components of stress in an elderly community-dwelling population.

Twenty-one variables that behaved statistically as state indicators were identified and subjected to a principal component analysis. Five factors were interpreted based on theoretical rationale: (1) anxious behavior, (2) anxiety, (3) depressive behavior, (4) depression, and (5) withdrawal/disengagement. Scale reliabilities (alpha coefficients) ranged from .66 to .82. See Table 6 for specific items within each of these subscales. The results suggested that the instrument is a useful research measure and service screening tool, particularly for service providers concerned with identifying a normal elderly population who is likely to be at risk for mental health problems.

SOCIAL NETWORK DATA

Earlier preliminary results indicating an interaction between increased levels of depressed affect and unexpected death occurring in those persons with fewer agents in their social network led to the development of methods to operationalize social or supportive network changes over time with respect to composition and function. The following sections summarize a number of these analyses performed on data collected using the modified version of the Kahn and Antonucci[9] social network circle diagram. Briefly, a circle diagram comprising four concentric circles was given to respondents. They were asked to place themselves in the center of the diagram and think about the people who were important in their life at that moment in time. They were then asked to place the names of these people into the three circles. The most important person or persons were to be placed in the first circle, the next most important in the second circle, and the next most important in the outer circle.

An analysis was conducted to determine whether the high proportion of networks incorporating family agents is a constant characteristic in the bereaved elderly (continuing long after the death event) or whether this reflects a more timebound phenomenon in which family members increase contact when death is imminent and then move to more distant roles as time passes. Specifically, the relationship between characteristics of social or supportive networks and affective and functional consequences over the 17-month period following the death of a spouse was examined. Results demonstrated the degree of change in role composition over time (i.e., 2 weeks and 8 weeks) for the agents. At 2 weeks postdeath, the inner circle contained a greater proportion of close family relatives and the second circle contained other relatives and friends. The third circle more likely contained friends. Two months after the death event, the inner circle still retained a similar number of close family members, while the number of other relatives declined slightly and the number of friends increased slightly. In the second circle, the average number of close family and friends was stable, while the number of other relatives declined. However, the proportional representation changed in this circle, not only for other relatives but also for friends. The third circle remained relatively unchanged.

Therefore, data indicated that, for the study participants, social or supportive networks reflected a dominance of close family in the inner circle, which also had the most agents. Other relatives were represented in the inner and middle circles and friends were more likely to be found in the outer circle. Thus, in this group, close family in the inner circle remained proportionally more stable over time. Other relatives appeared to increase over time, as did friends, but their respective proportional representation changed in different directions, with friends gaining (i.e., .36 : .32 vs. .11 : .16). The middle circle was similar in this respect. Thus, close family members do not necessarily stay with the older bereaved spouse; friends and more distant relatives and peers generally "take over" as time passes.

Drawing on Kahn and Antonucci's[9] theory of social convoys, a separate series of analyses was conducted to determine what best predicts agent placement in a convoy, that is, (1) role position or (2) giving and receiving various psychological and functional utilities with respect to the respondent. The total sample of bereaved elderly was broken down into those people residing in a long-term care facility and those living in the community. Social network data for these two samples were subjected to a series of discriminant analyses. Included in separate discriminant analyses for each of the two samples were (1) relationship variables and (2) psychological utility variables. In addition, a discriminant analysis using functional utilities was calculated for the community sample. In contrast to Kahn and Antonucci's[9] theory that location in the first circle (and to a lesser extent the second circle) is determined by the supportive quality of the relationship in terms of focal person utility variables and not role relationship variables, data from this analysis showed that membership in the first and second circles was best predicted for both the community and institutional samples by relationship variables. As for the best predictor of membership in the third circle, it was an even split between relationship and psychological utility variables for the institutionalized sample; for the community sample, the best predictor was the set of functional utility variables.

These results clearly support the efficacy of role relationship frequencies as variables which discriminate convoy circle membership among both instutionalized and community-dwelling bereaved elderly. The data further suggest that giving and receiving psychological utility and functional variables are not as useful for predicting circle membership. Interpretation of results in terms of the theory postulated by Kahn and Antonucci suggests the need to view convoys as multidimensional and to distinguish social convoys from support convoys. Social convoys are limited to people who are important to the focal person in terms of psychological closeness, while support convoys include people with whom the focal person is involved in giving and receiving relationships. Thus, prediction of agent placement in a convoy must be done by assessing role relationships (e.g., family, friend, or other relationship), psychological utilities (e.g., giving or receiving affect or affirmation), and functional utilities (e.g., giving or receiving direct aid). Finally, the data suggest that the role of convoys in predicting well-being of older persons may become clearer when the distinction is made between social and support convoys. It may be that while social convoys may be phenomenological representations of social worlds which mediate the stress of life, support convoys are likely to be useful in explaining why some older people are better able to continue to function in the face of life's stressors than others.

DISCUSSION

The results from preliminary approaches to assessment of survivor, relationship, and death situation factors and their effects on the course of bereavement in elderly widowed persons suggest a more complex dynamic than was originally expected. The pattern in early bereavement suggests that an intuitive view of survivor or death situation factors may be useful in at least discriminating cases likely to be appropriate for some intervention. The postdeath association between expecting the event, preparing for it, and being involved in providing care during the last illness does give some support to the notion that some grieving or relevant coping work may go on prior to the death and thus is not seen following it. Having time to dwell on problems or the experience of problems due to the lack of work, long-term group counseling, or other activities (as opposed to engagement in work or other activities), together with expressions of regret and the negative consequences of caring (e.g., sleep loss), is an intuitively satisfactory explanation for the exacerbation of depression following the death event.

The dominant trend toward early elevation and overall lessening of depression over time also square nicely with conventional wisdom, as does older age as a factor in discriminating less depressed cases. While the variance contributed by personality factors is unspecific, and while such factors doubtlessly contribute to the lack of clarity in the pattern of effects, these preliminary analyses suggest that the life situation and death situation play some role in outcomes. In general, the results of these analyses support the view that situational factors should be part of any model of bereavement and that they are potential discriminators of cases at risk for more negative consequences in bereavement, cases where interventions might be most useful.

REFERENCES

1. Faletti, M. V., & Berman, E. A. (1984). The role of person and death event characteristics in longitudinal outcomes in spousal bereavement. *Proceedings of the 37th Gerontological Society of America,* p. 83.
2. Faletti, M. V., & Pruchno, R. A. (1983). Social network change over time: Results from a sample of community aged. *Proceedings of the 36th Gerontological Society of America,* p. 288.
3. Gibbs, J. M., & Faletti, M. V. (1982). Supportive networks and coping in bereaved aged. *Proceedings of the 35th Gerontological Society of America,* p. 192.
4. Pruchno, R. A., & Faletti, M. V. (1983). The social world of our elderly: Structure vs. function. *Proceedings of the 36th Gerontological Society of America,* p. 288.
5. Pruchno, R. A., & Faletti, M. V. (1984). Convoys in later life: Social vs. support networks. Unpublished manuscript.
6. Pruchno, R. A., & Faletti, M. V. (1985). Measuring stress among community elderly: Sensitive indicators. *Proceedings of the 93rd Annual Meeting of the American Psychological Association,* p. 75.
7. Beck, A. T., Ward, C. H., Mendelsen, M., Mock, J., & Erbaugh, J. (1961). An inventory for measuring depression. *Archives of General Psychiatry, 4,* 561–571.
8. Derogatis, L. R., Lipman, R. S., Rickles, K., Uhlenhuth, E. H., & Covi, L. (1974). The Hopkins Symptom Checklist (HSCL): A self-report symptom inventory. *Behavioral Science, 19,* 1–15.
9. Kahn, R. L., & Antonucci, T. (1980). Convoys over the life course: Attachment roles and social status. In P. Baltes & O. Brim (Eds.), *Life span development and behavior* (Vol. 3) (pp. 253–286). New York: Academic Press.
10. Clayton, P. J., Halikas, J. A., & Maurice, W. L. (1972). The depression of widowhood. *British Journal of Psychiatry, 12,* 71–78.
11. Jarvik, L. F., & Perl, M. (1981). Overview of physiologic dysfunction and the production of psychiatric problems in the elderly. In A. Levenson & R. C. W. Hall (Eds.), *Psychiatric management of physical disease in the elderly* (pp. 1–15). New York: Raven Press.
12. Morgan, L. A. (1976). A re-examination of widowhood and morale. *Journal of Gerontology, 31,* 687–695.

Factors Influencing Bereavement Adjustments

The four chapters in Part I revealed that the death of a spouse in later life is a highly stressful experience and that the first few months are among the most difficult. Also, there is considerable variation in the way older bereaved spouses are impacted by the loss. Some of them were quite depressed, but a substantial number appeared to be managing the loss better than expected. Clearly, many of the bereaved were resilient, finding ways to cope and making some successful adjustments.

Chapters 5 through 11 examine many of the factors that might help explain why some bereaved spouses were more adversely affected and others were more resilient. These seven chapters report on five separate studies in California, Utah, and Ohio. Chapters 5 and 6 focus primarily on the relative importance of social networks and social support, with the assumption that they can buffer some of the negative effects of bereavement. Chapters 7 through 10 concentrate on the helpfulness of various coping strategies. Chapters 7 and 8 also examine how the spouses perceive or appraise their bereavement situations and how the appraisals might impact subsequent coping strategies and adjustments. Chapter 10 deals with the issues of coping by focusing on the advice that bereaved spouses offer to others in similar situations. It is likely that their suggestions reflect what was and was not helpful for them. Chapter 11 examines the influence of personal coping resources, such as the competencies and abilities used to manage the challenging tasks of daily life without one's spouse.

Other factors can possibly influence when, how, and what kinds of adjustments are made, but the seven chapters in Part II examine most of those which are expected to play important roles. The studies encompass personal, social, and community factors. Some of the research findings were expected, but many were not. Fortunately, the findings reveal some promising areas for future research and interventions; these are highlighted in chapter 16.

5

Bereavement, Social Networks, Social Support, and Mental Health

Tonya L. Schuster and Edgar W. Butler

This chapter explores the long-term impact of social networks and social support on mental health measures within the context of conjugal bereavement. This evaluation includes a comparison of the recall of support at the time of initial bereavement as well as current support. Social networks and affective and instrumental social support were measured by self-reports of respondents. A series of background dimensions were controlled in the analysis, including age, sex, income, length of widowhood, and activities of daily living (ADL). Overall, analytic results confirmed the importance of various social and demographic characteristics especially ADL, gender, and income, for mental health. Length of widowhood was significantly related only to future orientation.

Consistent with some previous research findings, these analyses showed the significant impact of social networks and social support on the mental health of the bereaved. However, previously conflicting findings also suggest that the necessity and impact of social networks and various types of support my be temporally specific. Thus, an examination of current mental health outcomes as impacted by the timing of social support, assessed at both the time of death (initial bereavement) and the time of interview, showed that early support was most helpful, with instrumental support being more predictive than affective.

Revision of a paper presented at the American Society on Aging, San Francisco, California, March 23, 1986. Appreciation is extended to the following granting agencies: NIMH (MH-08667), which funded the original 1963 baseline survey; NIE (G-74-0095) and NIA (AG00320), which funded the 1972, 1975, and 1977 follow-up surveys; and NIA (AG03857), which supported the follow-up survey reported in this chapter. Tonya L. Schuster expresses her gratitude to the Graduate Division, University of California, for graduate fellowship support. Linton Freeman, Hiroshi Fukurai, Ron Kessler, Dale Lund, Alexandra Maryansky, David Morgan, and Camille Wortman offered valuable suggestions at different stages in this research.

INTRODUCTION

Among the factors that have recently received attention in attempts to account for differential responses to death and bereavement are social networks and social support. While these concepts have at time been used interchangeably, there is an emerging literature clearly delineating their distinction. See Gallagher and Thompson[1] and Schuster[2] for reviews of this literature. Prior to the extensive use of the terms *social networks* and *social support,* literature on death and bereavement stressed the importance of family, kinship, and other persons in the bereavement process. The influence of such psychosocial factors on adaptation among the elderly has been extensively investigated. For recent examples of such research, see Cohen and Syme,[3] Dohrenwend and Dohrenwend,[4] Faletti,[5], and Antonucci.[6]

While all members of a social network are not necessarily supportive, the network may mediate the availability and provision of social support.[7] Bankoff[8] pointed out that two implicit assumptions in the support of literature are (1) that the more support a bereaved person receives, the better off that person is and (2) that the social support necessary for the bereaved person remains constant over time. However, conflicting research findings have prompted questions concerning the fluctuating influence of the type, source, and timing of social support. Moreover, emphasis has been placed on the importance of the social network at time of initial bereavement and on the potential aftereffects of the loss of other persons in the social network, which could even lead to social isolation.

Social networks, then, including family and kinship systems, may play an important role in variations found in bereavement responses. "Their structure and the manner in which they emphasize some relationships rather than others supply initial reference points for the concept of bereavement itself.[9]" Emphasis in our society is placed on members of the immediate nuclear family suffering the loss. This contrasts with societies where the family system is more extensive and individual members are less vulnerable when a death occurs. While the family typically is the major support of an individual during the time of crisis[10], it is problematic whether the nuclear family is equipped to handle this task.[11-13] Thus, the extent of support received from the total social network is of critical importance during bereavement.

Changes in social status or role occur when a wife becomes a widow. Friends and family may respond to this change in such a manner that it results in social deprivation for the widow. This deprivation is seen as the avoidance of the bereaved person and a general lessening of contact with others.[14,15] Specific ways in which a widow's relationships change depend on age, social class, and life style. In addition to losing a companion, widows tend to lose contact with married couples who were friends with them and their spouses.[15] "They are women in a male-dominated society without mates in a social network of couples.[16]" Widowhood may, then, have a long-term negative impact upon the friendship networks of older people. Widows eventually establish different kinds of networks than those formed during their marriages. They are likely to spend leisure time with women who like themselves, are widowed.[17] Hence, unless new contacts and friendships are made, survivors are likely to become more and more alone.[18]

There is consensus within the social network and social support literature that social support received from a social network during bereavement is crucial in the initial response to death as well as to the long-range adjustment of a bereaved person.[19,20] While some controversy exists concerning whether there are bereavement stages, there is no question that support received from a social network is important to long-term adjustment. In addition to social network and social support influences, a variety of background characteristics have been found in some cases to be related to mental health adjustment in bereavement, including age, gender, socioeconomic status and so on.[21]

Widows and widowers experience a significantly higher rate of mental disorders than those who are still married, especially among older people. Earlier research on the development of mental illness following bereavement also showed that an unusually large number of widows and widowers receive psychiatric care for the first time during bereavement.[21,22]

In the general population of older adults, married people have higher average well-being and life satisfaction than widows.[23] This difference in well-being may be mediated by time and the increasing proportion of peers who share the widowed status as one becomes older.[18,24] As length of widowhood increases, the level of a widow's morale also rises somewhat, until it approximates the morale of married women. This appears to be true in Britain and Denmark as well as in the U.S.[25] Loneliness can be mitigated by strong family ties, although peer relationships are also important.[18] Indeed, even one stable, intimate relationship with a friend is reported to be more closely associated with good mental health and higher morale that are high social interaction or stability in interaction and role.[26]

In summary, available research literature suggests, that social networks, social support, and a variety of background characteristics are related to bereavement adjustment.[27,28] The present study controls individual and demographic characteristics in order to ascertain the impact of social networks and social support at the time of spousal bereavement on subsequent long-term mental health. (For an extensive review of the relevant literature, see Schuster.[2]) Two hypotheses are addressed in this chapter: (1) that social networks and social support have a significant impact on the mental health of the bereaved; (2) that the timing of social support, in this case measured at the time of initial bereavement and the time of interview, differentially influence mental health outcomes.

METHODS

Sample

The data used here are part of a larger longitudinal study of a 1963 geographically and socioeconomically stratified random sample of 10.5% of the households in Riverside, California. In the original baseline research, one adult from each household was interviewed and asked to provide information on the entire family and on each member of the household. See Butler and Friedman[29] for a more elaborate description of the original research design and earlier follow-up surveys. The original sample included information on over 8,750 individuals. Subsequently, several specific follow-up research projects were carried out on various subsamples of this original sample. Each of these follow-up projects was concerned with a variety of measures of long-term adjustment. A 1984 follow-up of the elderly portion of the original 1963 sample is utilized in this chapter. The primary sample for this phase of the research includes all persons for whom data were collected in both 1963 and 1977, consisting of 723 potential respondents who were aged 57 years or older in 1984. One focus of the follow-up was on social networks and social support, especially as they related to bereavement among the elderly. For more information on this particular follow-up research, see Schuster.[2]

Although the original sample was a stratified random sample of Riverside, California, in 1963, the sampling for the special populations under consideration in the 1972, 1975, 1977, and 1984 follow-up studies preclude any claim to randomness or generalizability with regard to a general elderly population. The oldness of those in the sample resulted in a portion of the eligible respondents being medically unable to participate.

Instruments

This section explicates the primary concepts that are the focus of this research and presents the indicators used to measure each primary concept. The discussion is divided in terms of social and demographic variables, social networks, social support, and the mental health outcomes of anomia, anxiety, life satisfaction, future orientation, and perceived physical health.

SOCIAL AND DEMOGRAPHIC VARIABLES

Social and demographic variables of age, sex, and income (the previous year) were measured by standard interview questions. The number of years of widowhood was elicited by questions in the marriage history section of the interview schedule. The ability to carry out activities of a daily living (ADL) was determined by items derived from Kane and Kane.[30]

SOCIAL NETWORKS

In most bereavement literature, social network and social support have not been conceptually distinguished, either theoretically or methodologically. This confusion has resulted in inconsistent findings on the impact of interpersonal relationships for individuals adjusting to widowhood. Our research shows the utility of defining and measuring social networks and social support as separate but interrelated concepts.[2,31,32]

A social network approach examines the total social field within which an individual is embedded. Network analysts generally define a network as a set of nodes (persons) that are connected by a type of relation. Networks may be described in terms of their composition, structure, and content. In contrast to the "system-centered" network, which encompasses all possible interconnections linking individuals, emphasis here is on the "egocentric" or "personal" network, which incorporates ties to various people defined from the standpoint of the focal individual.

In this research, egocentric networks included persons in the network as defined or perceived by the respondent. Maintaining the distinction between social network and social support, the network measurement process involves eliciting from each respondent those persons who the respondent feels are close or important to him or her. As shown in Fig. 1, the perception of closeness was elaborated by having respondents place each network person in the inner, middle, or outer circle. This approach is based upon that suggested by Kahn[33] and Kahn and Antonucci,[34] especially as elaborated by Faletti[5] and Gibbs and Faletti.[35]

Additional questions regarding sex, relationship, distance away, marital status, age, circumstances of first meeting, length of time known, a series of measures of frequency of contact (in own home, their home, other places, by tele-

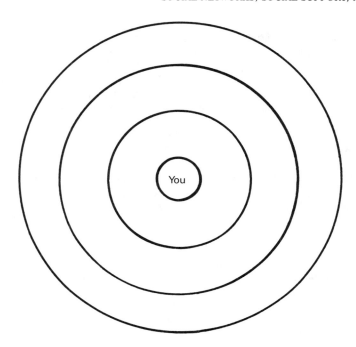

DIRECTIONS (abstract)

Please begin with the people you *feel closest* to: Is there any one person or persons that you feel so close to that it's hard to imagine life without them? Would you tell me their name(s)? (Is there any one else that you *feel* that close to?) (ENTER NAME AND NUMBER THEM IN *CIRCLE CLOSEST TO YOU* STARTING AT 12 O'CLOCK).

Now are there people to whom you may not *feel* quite so close, but who are still very important to you? Would you tell me their name? (Anyone else?) (ENTER NAME AND NUMBER THEM IN *MIDDLE CIRCLE* STARTING AT 12 O'CLOCK).

Are there people whom you haven't already mentioned who are close enough and important enough in your life that they should also be placed in your network? Would you tell me their name. (Anyone else?) (ENTER NAME AND NUMBER THEM IN *OUTER* CIRCLE STARTING AT 12 O'CLOCK).

FIG. 1 Diagram for Elicitation of Egocentric Networks. The circle took up a full page in the questionnaire. After the respondent completed his or her social network, one copy of the circle remained in the questionnaire, one copy was given to the respondent, and one copy was retained by the interviewer. The directions given here have been abstracted.

phone or letter), and other persons known in the network were systematically obtained on persons reported by the respondent to be in their network. While the network could contain an unlimited number of members, additional information was obtained for a maximum of 15 network members. This necessary constraint nevertheless allowed the study to be far more extensive than most studies on egocentric networks, which have typically examined a maximum of 6 network members. See Burt[36] and Fischer et al.[37] for examples of research utilizing a restricted number of possible network members. In this research, these first 15 members incorporated 83% of all network ties generated by these respondents. When appropriate in subsequent sections of the interview schedule, questions referred primarily to persons in the defined network, although anyone else who might have been involved was included as well.

While criticisms of actor-defined networks exist,[38] we explicitly reject such criticisms by accepting individuals' definition and perception of their social networks as being crucial to their behavior and well-being, especially in bereavement.[39] The major problem in this technique of measuring social networks is the extremely complex data reduction required to ascertain the various aspects of social networks beyond mere network size.[2]

Our approach allows a range of social network dimensions to be analyzed. In this chapter, two pieces of information about social networks are combined in the analysis: the number of persons in the network and the relative distribution in the inner, middle, and outer circles. This variable involves the construction of an index we call *network close*. Network close equals the sum of the people in the network weighted as follows: Persons in the inner circle were given a value of 3; those in the middle circle, a value of 2; and those in the outer circle a value of 1. Persons beyond the first 15 were almost always in the outer circle.

A second network characteristic, the frequency of contact with network members, is also included in the analyses. Frequency of contact was first summed within each network connection (across the five types of contact) and then summed across all network members. The resulting index indicates the total number of contacts per year with all network members. This index was then reduced to the number of contacts per day (as shown in Table 1, Results section). Individuals in the network residing with the respondent were coded at the maximum frequency of contact.

Measures of network size, closeness, and frequency of contact have often been utilized in previous research as measures of social support. In contrast, previous analyses of these data indicate that closeness and frequent contact with network members are necessary *but not sufficient* for the provision of social support from those members.[2,31]

SOCIAL SUPPORT

One of the assumptions of this research is that social networks and social support are conceptually and methodologically separate but interrelated concepts. Furthermore, they are interrelated in such a way that the provision of social support is a variable aspect of a network tie. Social support has been categorized in a variety of ways.[34,40-43] Two functional types of support are distinguished in this research: affective (emotional) and instrumental (task oriented). Affective support is concerned with persons confided in; talked to when upset, nervous, or depressed; and who call often. Instrumental support is concerned with more mundane activities, such as help with finances, chores, shopping, and errands and caring for the respondent when ill.

Support was also assessed at the time of initial bereavement. Support at time of death focuses on the respondent's recall of who helped most around the time of the death of the spouse. Support indices were constructed by first summing the number of persons providing each form of support and then summing occurrences of support across all network members. Each index, then, represents the total quantity of support received by the respondent, either currently or at the time of initial bereavement.

MENTAL HEALTH

Four dependent mental health scales were used to assess mental health (anomia, anxiety, life satisfaction, and future orientation); a fifth dependent variable was measured by perceived physical health (considered to be another aspect of mental health).

Anomia

Anomia, or self-to-others alienation, refers to a subjective state of an individual. During bereavement, individuals often experience feelings of alienation, powerlessness, and hopelessness and a desire to withdraw from others because life for them has become meaningless.[44] Anomia was measured by a scale developed by Srole,[45] which has been utilized extensively.[46-51] The scale consists of five agree-disagree statements, with a high score reflecting a low degree of anomia. The alpha for this scale was .68.

Anxiety

Chronic anxiety is defined as poor mental health and may lead to a clinical evaluation of mental illness and to physical illness[52] or even death. Items used to measure generalized anxiety were derived primarily from the work of Srole et al. reported in *Mental Health in the Metropolis*;[53] that work was subsequently made use of by others.[54] The scale consists of eight statements, with responses ranging from "never" to "often." A high score indicates low anxiety. The alpha for this scale was .65.

Life Satisfaction

Osterweis et al.[52] suggest that there is a convergence in explanatory models of the bereavement process, and they note that both in the psychodynamic perspective and in cognitive theories, importance is placed on meanings attributed to loss and what happens to a person's self-concept and life satisfaction as a result. Horowitz et al.[55] suggest that persons who have low life satisfaction have pathological responses in bereavement.[56,57] Similarly, persons having emotional problems carry negative views of life, themselves, their future, and experiences.[58] After several preliminary analyses, a series of life satisfaction items (LSI-B) were used in a summated scale.[59] The alpha was .69.

Future Orientation

A future orientation involves an investment in current life and hopefulness about the future. A favorable outcome of bereavement involves such a future orientation.[52,60-62] The future orientation scale was developed by the research staff and was first used on the middle-aged and elderly samples in this longitudinal research in 1977. They were created in an effort to delineate the extent to which individuals had a feeling that they would have an opportunity to carry out their plans for the future (e.g., they expected to be alive for some time in the future or they had not given up hope of a future). The scale consists of the following three agree-disagree items: (1) It is possible to plan ahead in life; (2) I think it is valuable to plan ahead the things I will be doing in the next few weeks or so; (3) I have made plans for things I'll be doing a month or year from now. A high score indicates a strong future orientation. The alpha for this scale was .65.

TABLE 1   Characteristics of Social Networks and Social Support

	M	SD	Range
Network size (unlimited)	9.13	7.81	0.00–38.00
Network size (limited to 15)	7.73	4.84	0.00–15.00
Total network closeness	19.82	11.69	3.00–45.00
Frequency of contact	5.55	4.11	0.07–21.23
Current affective support	5.04	4.36	0.00–20.00
Current instrumental support	3.50	3.37	0.00–14.00
Bereavement affective support	4.87	4.55	0.00–33.00
Bereavement instrumental support	6.19	4.24	0.00–21.00

Perceived Physical Health

Perceived physical health was measured by the standard ladder technique, where the top of the ladder represents perfect physical health and the bottom represents poor physical health. Respondents indicated at which rung of the ladder they belonged.

RESULTS

Because of the nature of the survey population, the sample is primarily elderly, with an average age of 75.35 years. Fifteen percent are under 64 years, 29% are from 65 to 74, and 56% are 75 years of age and over. Respondents are almost twice as likely to be female as male, which is understandable given the age and bereaved status of the sample. Recoding household income levels to the mid-point of ranges specified in the interview schedule yielded a mean income of $13,500 per year, with the majority of respondents having lower incomes. The range is $1,500 to $45,000.

The Activities of Daily Living Scale previously mentioned was constructed by summing items so that a higher score indicates a better overall level of physical functioning. Within the possible range, a mean level of 28 indicates that most of these respondents maintain a relatively high level of physical functioning. The number of years respondents have been widowed (years since initial bereavement) is quite variable in this sample, ranging from less than 1 year to 58 years, with a mean of 13 years. Very few respondents, then, have been bereaved for less than 1 or 2 years, and the great majority have been widowed for a relatively long time.

Characteristics of the constructed indices of social networks and social support are presented in Table 1. The networks of persons perceived to be close or important by respondents are quite diverse. When network size is unlimited, the networks range in size from 0 to 38, with an average size of 9; a mean of 8 network members results when network size is limited to 15. Previous analyses of persons in this sample showed that widows and widowers have significantly smaller networks than people who are married.[31]

The average total network closeness of about 20 indicates that a substantial proportion of network members of the bereaved were included in the close inner and middle circles of the network. Widow and widower networks are significantly more close in this sense than married networks.[31] Frequency of contact with network members is relatively high, although quite variable. The mean reflects an average of 5.55 contacts (of some type) per day across all network members.

TABLE 2   Characteristics of the Sample: Constructed Mental Health Scales

Mental health scale constructs	M	SD	Range
Anomia	14.41	4.74	5–24
Life satisfaction	29.49	6.58	11–45
Anxiety	21.94	3.73	13–31
Future orientation	10.73	3.14	3–15
Perceived physical health	3.33	0.92	1–5

Note. Higher score = better mental and physical health.

While virtually all respondents reported having some supportive ties in their network, the amount of social support received was relatively low. Previous analyses indicated that only about half of the perceived close ties were also perceived as providing either affective or instrumental support.[31] At the most recent data point, respondents on the average reported more affective support (mean of five occurrences across the network) than instrumental support (mean of four occurrences across the network). However, respondents on the average recalled more instrumental than affective support at the time of initial bereavement. Indeed, while the average amount of affective support reported currently and at time of bereavement was about the same, the level of instrumental support at the time of bereavement was much higher than the present level.

Table 2 reports the descriptive data on four mental health scales and the single item measure of perceived physical health. On the whole, these respondents have relatively good mental health, particularly life satisfaction, with the mean well above the midpoint of the actual possible range. Comparing their present physical health to perfect health on a five-rung ladder (the fifth rung representing perfect health), the great majority selected the third or fourth rung, with the others falling evenly above and below.

In order to test the research hypotheses, the next analytic stage required multivariate analyses to examine relative contributions of independent variables (controlling for the effects of background variables) with regard to mental health outcomes. Separate parallel multiple regression analyses for each of the five dependent measures of metal health were performed for this purpose (see Table 3). Each mental health measure was regressed on models of the following sets of independent variables. Background variables included those previously shown to influence mental health outcomes, and they were controlled in the analysis in order to assess clearly the impact of network and support variables. The network variables incorporated both network closeness and frequency of contact with network

TABLE 3   Results of Parallel Regression Analysis (R^2) of Mental Health Scales on Models of Background Characteristics, Social Networks, and Social Support

Model	Anomia	Life satisfaction	Anxiety	Future orientation	Perceived health
1. Background variables	15%	18%	13%	14%	13%
2. Model 1 + network	23	24	18	19	17
3. Model 1 + current support	25	25	19	21	18
4. Model 1 + bereavement support	27	33	20	24	19
5. Full model	27	33	20	24	19

members. Current support included affective and instrumental support. Support at time of bereavement also was characterized as affective and instrumental. The full model included all variables. The emphasis in the analyses was on increments to R_2 (or variance explained in dependent variables by the sets of independent variables in the various models).

Model 1 (Table 3) established a baseline by regressing each dependent mental health measure on the background variables alone. Model 1, by incorporating all background variables, confirmed the importance of these variables as "control" variables. Background variables of particular importance are gender, income, and ADL. Across all dependent variables, the explained variance accounted for by background variables was statistically significant, ranging from 13% for anxiety and perceived physical health to 18% for life satisfaction.

Across all dependent measures, sizable increases in explained variance were obtained with the addition of either network, current support, or support during bereavement (Models 2, 3, or 4); this is in contrast to Model 1, which contains only background variables. That is, controlling for the impact of background variables, all of these network and support dimensions exert a significant influence on current levels of mental health. Further, results across models confirm the differential but related influence of these variables.

Of particular significance here is that when the focus is on specific comparisons with the baseline model, both sets of support variables account for greater contributions to explained variance in mental health than do the network variables, with support at time of initial bereavement providing the greatest incremental gain in explained variance compared with Model 1. This result is even more striking, because in all cases the full model (Model 5), which incorporates all background, network, and support variables, does not account for any more of the variance than Model 4. Intercorrelations among network and support items did not exceed .43.

While this pattern of results was consistent across all five dependent variables, there were notable differences in the amount of incremental increases in explained variance across the measures. The smallest (although meaningful) increase occurred for the perceived physical health measure, with level of physical functioning (ADL) being the most pronounced predictive variable. The most prominent gain in explained variance was for life satisfaction with Model 3, which incorporated support at time of initial bereavement and accounted for 33% of the explained variance. That is, support at time of initial bereavement exerted a considerable influence on current life satisfaction (controlling for the impact of background characteristics including the number of years since bereavement).

DISCUSSION

Overall, the results confirmed the importance of various social and demographic characteristics to mental health in widowhood. For example, widowed females tend to have significantly lower life satisfaction and greater anxiety than widowed males. With other factors controlled, income was significantly positively related to eunomia (not being anomic) and to having a future-oriented outlook on life.

In contrast to some previous literature,[20] number of years widowed did not have a significant relationship to mental health outcomes for individuals in this sample, with the exception of a negative association with future orientation. The

ADL scale was significantly associated with all five outcomes. That is, when all other factors were held constant, a greater ability to carry out ADLs (or to function physically) was related to better mental health.

We began with the hypothesis that social networks and social support influence the mental health of the bereaved. The results revealed several important findings that confirmed the viability of that hypothesis. After the control of various social and demographic characteristics, social networks and social support incrementally contributed to explaining variation in all five dimensions of mental and physical health assessed, but in varying degrees. This suggests that long-term mental health adjustment is multidimensional. Contributions of the independent additions of social networks and of support measures in the analyses further confirmed that these separate, although related, concepts have a differential impact on the mental health of the bereaved. Specifically, the reported quantity of affective and instrumental social support, while related to network measures of closeness and frequency of contact, had a more important impact on mental health. Obviously this conclusion has significant research implications for those who measure "support" solely in terms of network size and/or frequency of contact, and it may partly account for inconsistencies among previous investigations. Further, the relatively greater influence of support measures for this bereaved sample is consistent with previous literature reviews[63,64] comparing research on general versus crisis populations.

Regarding the timing of support, our hypothesis was that there would be a differential impact of support currently and at the time of initial bereavement. These analyses relied on respondents' recall of support at time of death, and the limitations of recalled data, such as the influence of a person's current situation and deficiencies in recall capabilities, should be noted. Nevertheless, results suggest that support at the time of bereavement is more influential in explaining variation in current mental health than current support, even though the analyses statistically controlled for number of years widowed. In contrast to some literature, the analyses further suggest that affective support at the time of bereavement is no more important to current mental health than instrumental support at the time of bereavement. Overall, the impact of social support at the time of bereavement apparently continued for a long period of time for individuals in this sample. This finding implies that subsequent adjustment to the death of a spouse may depend substantially upon the support that the social network provides during this crucial life event.

This research shows that support received at time of death has a greater influence on current mental health than current support or current measures of network closeness and frequency of contact. The latter two measures have been used as measures of social integration, which has been consistently reported in the literature as being major problem in widowhood. Thus it must be considered extremely important that support during the actual crisis was paramount to current and long-term mental health outcomes.

Because this was an examination of the influence of social networks and social support on the long-term mental health of the bereaved, the impact of instrumental, as well as affective, support may appear to be questionable. There are at least two possible reasons for this finding. First, most research on the bereaved has focused on shorter-term adjustment, for example, up to 2 years. While at initial bereavement there may be a need for affective support, over the long term, instrumental support received at that time may be extremely important because of its usefulness in helping an individual work through problems associated with establishing a new lifestyle.[8,65] A small and close-knit social network providing strong affective support may be of crucial importance at one point but suffocating and inadequate when the person later begins to establish a new life.[66] In addition, current recollections may focus on the more currently salient instrumental support received than the affective support. Certainly the practical implications of this finding should be noted.

Because we examined long-term adjustment to bereavement, no evidence was presented concerning earlier stages of bereavement; in the analyses however, years widowed was only related to future orientation and not to the other mental health dimensions. It is possible, as Bankoff[8] suggests, that few supports at time of initial bereavement seem to make any difference but that many more seem to be effective over a longer period. The reasons for this phenomenon have not yet been investigated.

Finally, it is suggested that further research in this area consider in more detail the sources of support (e.g., family, friends, neighbors, etc.) and other characteristics of network members providing support. In addition, while the literature has focused primarily on support received from the social network, an argument could be made that reciprocal support (i.e., support provided by the bereaved to others) has implications for mental health and well-being.

REFERENCES

1. Gallagher, D. E., & Thompson, L. W. (1981–1982). Psychosocial factors affecting adaptation to bereavement in the elderly. *International Journal of Aging and Human Development, 14,* 79–95.
2. Schuster, T. L. (1987). *Social networks or social support: Clarification and consequences.* Unpublished doctoral dissertation, University of California, Riverside.
3. Cohen, S., & Syme, L. (Eds.). (1985). *Social support and health.* New York: Academic Press.
4. Dohrenwend, B. S., & Dohrenwend, B. P. (Eds.) (1984). *Stressful life events and their contexts.* New Brunswick, NJ: Rutgers University Press.
5. Falleti, M. V. (1986). *Supportive networks and coping in bereaved elderly.* Final progress report summary for NIA Grant No. AG-02061.
6. Antonucci, T. C. (1985). Social support: Theoretical advances, recent findings and pressing issues. In I. G. Sarason (Ed.). *Social support theory research and applications* (pp. 21–37). Boston: Martinus Nijoff.
7. Wellman, B., & Hall, A. (1986). Social networks and social support: Implications for later life. In V. W. Marshall (Ed.), *Later life* (pp. 191–231). Beverly Hills: Sage Publications.
8. Bankoff, E. A. (1983). Social support and adaptation to widowhood. *Journal of Marriage and the Family, 45,* 827–839.
9. Fulton, R. (Ed.) (1976). *Death and identity* (2nd ed., 246). Bowie, MD: Robert J. Brady.
10. Maddison, D., & Viola, A. (1968). The health of widows in the year following retirement. *Journal of Psychosomatic Research, 12,* 297–306.
11. Treas, J. (1977). Family support systems for the aged: Social and demographic considerations. *The Gerontologist, 17,* 486–491.
12. Heinemann, G. D. (1983). Family involvement and support for widowed persons. In T. Brubaker (Ed.). *Family relationships in later life* (pp. 127–148). Beverly Hills: Sage Publications.
13. Sussman, M. B. (1985). The family life of old people. In E. Shanas & R. H. Binstock (Eds.), *Handbook of aging and the social sciences* (2nd ed., pp. 415–449). New York: Van Nostrand Reinhold.
14. Spiegel, Y. (1977). *The grief process.* Nashville: Parthenon.
15. Glick, I. O., Weiss, R. S., & Parkes, C. M. (1974). *The first year of bereavement.* New York: John Wiley & Sons.
16. Gaine, L. (1974). *Widow.* New York: William Morrow.

17. Schuster, T. L., Morgan, D., & Butler, E. W. (1987, March). *Social networks and bereavement: How important are widow-to-widow contacts?* Paper presented at the American Society on Aging, Salt Lake City, Utah.
18. Blau, Z. S. (1973). *Old age in a changing society.* New York: Franklin Watts.
19. Dimond, M. F., Lund, D. A., & Caserta, M. S. (1987). The role of social support in the first two years of bereavement in an elderly sample. *The Gerontologist, 27,* 599–604.
20. Barrett, C. J., & Schneweis, K. M. (1980). An empirical search for stages of widowhood. *Omega, 11,* 97–105.
21. Parkes, C. M., & Brown, R. (1972). Health after bereavement: A controlled study of young Boston widows and widowers. *Psychosomatic Medicine, 34,* 449–461.
22. Stein, A., & Susser, M. (1951). Widowhood and mental illness. *Journal of Preventive Social Medicine, 23,* 106–110.
23. Larsen. R. (1978). Thirty years of research on the subjective well-being of older Americans. *Journal of Gerontology, 33,* 109–116.
24. Kutner, B., Fanshel, D., Togo, A. M., & Langner, T. S. (1956). *Five hundred over sixty.* New York: Russell Sage Foundation.
25. Shanas, E., Townsend, P., Wedderburn, D., Friis, Z. H., Milhof, P., & Stehouwer, J. (1986). *Old people in three industrial societies.* New York: Atherton Press.
26. Lowethal, J. F., & Haven, C. (1968). Interaction and adaptation: Intimacy as a critical variable. In B. L. Neugarten (Ed.), *Middle age and aging* (pp. 390-400). Chicago: University of Chicago Press.
27. Dimond, M. F. (1981). Bereavement and the elderly: A critical review with implications for nursing practice and research. *Journal of Advanced Nursing, 6,* 461–470.
28. Lopata, H. Z. (1973). *Widowhood in an American city.* Cambridge, MA: Schenkman.
29. Butler, E. W., & Friedman, S. (1984). Longitudinal studies of impaired competence in the community: A description of the Riverside Community Research Project (1963–1977). In S. A. Mednick & M. Harvey (Eds.), *Handbook of longitudinal research* (Vol. 2, 182–196). New York: Prageger.
30. Kane, R. A., & Kane, R. L. (Eds.). (1981). *Assessing the elderly: A practical guide to measurement.* Lexington, MA: Lexington Books.
31. Schuster, T. L., & Butler, E. W. (1987, April). *Social networks versus social support.* Paper presented at the Pacific Sociological Association, Eugene, Oregon.
32. Wellman, B., & Hall, A. (1986). Social networks and social support: Implications of later life. In V. W. Marshall (Ed.), *Later life* (pp. 191–213). Beverly Hills: Sage Publications.
33. Kahn, R. L. (1979). Aging and social support. In M. W. Riley (Ed.). *Aging from birth to death* (pp. 77–91). Boulder: Westview Press.
34. Kahn. R. L., & Antonucci, T. (1981). Convoys of social support: A life-course approach. In S. B. Kielser, J. N. Morgan, & V. K. Oppenheimer (Eds.). *Aging, social change* (pp. 383–405). New York: Academic Press.
35. Gibbs, J. M., & Faletti, M. V. (1982, November). *Supportive networks and coping in bereaved aged.* Paper presented at the 35th Gerontological Society of America, Boston, MA.
36. Burt, R. S. (1980). Models of network structure. *Annual Review of Sociology, 6,* 79–141.
37. Fischer, C., & Associates. (1977). *Networks and places: Social relations in the urban setting.* New York: The Free Press.
38. Kilworth, P. D., & Bernard, H. R. (1976). Informant accuracy in social network data. *Human Organization, 35,* 269–286.
39. Freeman, L. C., Romney, A. K., & Freeman, S. C. (1987). Cognitive structure and informant accuracy. *American Anthropologist, 89,* 310–325.
40. Mitchell, R. E., & Trickett, E. J. (1980). Task force report: Social networks as mediators of social support. *Community Mental Health Journal, 16,* 27–44.
41. Gottleib, B. H. (1985). Social networks and social support: An overview of research, practice, and policy implications. *Health Education Quarterly, 12,* 5–22.
42. Cobb, S. (1976). Social support as moderator of life stress. *Psychosomatic Medicine, 38,* 300–314.
43. House, J. S. (1981). *Work stress and social support.* Menlo Park, CA: Addison-Wesley.
44. Ramsey, R. W. (1979). Bereavement: A behavioral treatment of pathological grief. In P. O. Sioden, S. Bates, & W. S. Dorkens III (Eds.), *Trends in Behavior Therapy.* New York: Academic Press.

45. Srole, L. (1956). Social integration and certain corollaries: An exploratory study. *American Sociological Review, 21,* 709–716.
46. Pearlin. L. I. (1962). Alienation from work: A study of nursing personnel. *American Sociological Review, 27,* 314–326.
47. Bell, W. (1957). Anomie, social isolation, and the class structure. *Sociometry, 20,* 105–116.
48. Rose, A. M. (1962). Alienation and participation: A comparison of group leaders and the "mass." *American Sociological Review, 27,* 834–838.
49. Struening, E. L., & Richardson, A. H. (1965). A factor analytic exploration of the alienation, anomia, and authoritarianism domain. *American Sociological Review, 30,* 768–776.
50. Butler, E. W., Sabagh, G., & Van Arsdol, M. D., Jr. (1964). Demographic and social psychological factors in residential mobility. *Sociology and Social Research, 48,* 139–154.
51. Miller, C. R., & Butler, E. W. (1966). Anomia and eunomia: A methodological evaluation of Scrole's anomia scale. *American Sociological Review, 31,* 400–406.
52. Osterweis, M., Solomon, F., & Green, M. (1984). *Bereavement: Reactions, consequences, and care.* Washington, DC: National Academy of Sciences Press.
53. Srole, L., Langner, T. S., Michale, S. T., Opler, M. K., & Rennie, T. A. C. (Eds.). *Mental health in the metropolis: The Midtown Manhattan Study.* New York: McGraw-Hill.
54. Butler, E. W., Chapin. F. S., Jr., Hemmens, G. C., Kaiser, E. J., Stegman, M., & Weiss, S. F. (1969). *Moving behavior and residential choice: A national survey.* Washington, DC: National Academy of Sciences.
55. Horowitz, M., Wilner, N., Marmar, C., & Krupnick, J. (1980). Pathological grief and the activation of latent self-images. *American Journal of Psychiatry, 137,* 1157–1162.
56. Horowitz, M. (1979). *States of mind.* New York: Plenum.
57. Horowitz, M., Marmar, C., Krupnick, J., Wilner, N., Kaltreider, N., & Wallerstein, R. (1984). *Personality style and brief therapy.* New York: Basic Books.
58. Beck, A., Rush, J., Shaw, B., & Emergy, G. (1979). *Cognitive therapy of depression.* New York: Guilford Press.
59. Neugarten, B., Havighurst, R., & Tobin, S. (1961). The measure of life satisfaction. *Journal of Gerontology, 16,* 134–143.
60. Parkes, C. M., & Weiss, R. S. (1983). *Recovery from bereavement.* New York: Basic Books.
61. Vachon, M. L. S., Sheldon, A. R., Lances, W., Layall, W. A., & Freeman, S. J. J. (1982). Correlates of enduring distress patterns following bereavement: Social network, life situtation, and personality. *Psychological Medicine, 12,* 783–788.
62. Clayton, P. J., & Darvish, H. S. (1979). Course of Depressive Symptoms following the stress of bereavement. In J. E. Barrett (Ed.). *Stress and mental disorder.* New York: Raven Press.
63. House, J. S., & Kahn, R. L. (1985). Measures and concepts of social support. In S. Cohen & L. S. Syme (Eds.), *Social support and health* (pp. 83–108). San Diego: Academic Press.
64. Kessler, R. C., Price, R. H., & Wortman, C. B. (1985). Social factors in psychopathology: Stress, social support and coping processes. *Annual Review of Psychology, 36,* 531–572.
65. Walker, K. N., MacBride, A., & Vachon, M. L. S. (1977). Social support networks and the crisis of bereavement. *Social Science and Medicine, 11,* 35–41.
66. Hirsch, B. J. (1980). Natural support systems and coping with major life changes. *American Journal of Community Psychology, 8,* 159–172.

6

Social Support, Perceived Stress, and Depression following the Death of a Spouse in Later Life

Alicia Duran, Charles W. Turner, and Dale A. Lund

The present research examined the potential of social support to buffer the effects of stress and depression following the death of a spouse for 94 widows and widowers. The effects of social support on stress and depression were examined using a 2-year longitudinal panel design. Subjects completed questionnaires at different time periods after the death of the spouse: 3–4 weeks, 2 months, 6 months, 1 year and 2 years. The results of a structural regression analysis of the longitudinal data provided evidence that a stable social support system buffered the effects of stress 2 years after the loss of a spouse. The findings also suggest that changes in social support are related to changes in depression following the death of a spouse. However, the analysis did not provide evidence that social support was causally associated with depression.

Numerous researchers[1-4] have noted that social support can serve as a buffer against stressful life experiences. In discussing the moderating effects of social support on stressful events, Thoits[5] reasoned that "individuals with a strong social support system should be better able to cope with major life changes while those with little or no social support may be more vulnerable to life changes, particularly undesirable ones" (p. 145). Persisting, uncontrollable stress may eventually lead to clinically significant levels of depression.[6]

The importance of focusing on the stress of widowhood should be clear from the fact that the death of a spouse has been generally considered to be among the most stressful of all life events and that each year there are approximately 800,000 new widows and widowers in the United States.[7,8] The death of a loved one can be

Data were obtained from a study funded by the National Institute on Aging (R01 AG02193).

The authors are indebted to Mike Caserta for his assistance with the data analysis and to Len Haas, Juan Mejia, and Ernst Beier for their comments on an earlier draft of this manuscript.

especially stressful, since the survivor may be unable to do anything to control or prevent the loss. When death occurs unexpectedly, the individual also is unable to plan for the stressful event.

Social support has been identified as a key variable in the management of grief, especially in the loss of a spouse.[9-11] The present research used a longitudinal panel design to assess the long-term effects of social support on the perceived stress and depression of individuals following the death of a spouse.

SOCIAL SUPPORT AS A BUFFER TO STRESS

In general, stressful life events can impact existing social support by diminishing one's self-esteem and one's motivation to maintain social ties.[12] If one's social support does remain intact, stressful events may not be as devastating. Dimond[1] reasoned that the effects of social support depend upon the nature of the situation, the timing, and the availability of resources. Weiss[13] provided evidence that these three variables are instrumental in determining the extent to which social support can help buffer stressful events.

Cohen and Wills[14] differentiated between two types of effects of social support. First, social support can create a generalized beneficial effect in which an individual experiences stability of social relationships and an overall sense of well-being. In addition, social support can serve as a buffering mechanism against stressful events.

These researchers suggest that social support may intervene as a buffering mechanism at two different points: (1) between a stressful event and stress reaction and (2) between the experience of stress and the possible onset of a pathological outcome. In the first situation, social support may lessen a stress appraisal response by allowing the person at risk to perceive that others will provide resources needed to cope with the stressful event. In other words, an otherwise stressful situation may be relabeled to be minimally stressful due to anticipated support from others. In the second situation, social support may result in a solution or reduce the perceived importance of the problem.

Several studies provide evidence for a buffering effect by a person's social support system. The research identifies psychological mediators that counteract stressors and lead to greater feelings of self-esteem and personal efficacy.[15-17] During stressful situations, feelings of helplessness and loss of self-esteem frequently occur. Helplessness may result from one's feelings of inability to cope with situations which require effective responses. When the loss of self-esteem takes place, an individual may attribute the failure to cope to his or her own stable personality traits or general personal ability instead of to some external cause.[6]

The availability of a confidant or a supportive relationship with one or more individuals may provide self-esteem enhancement or informational support that counteracts the tendency to attribute failure to the self.[14] With this type of support, feelings of helplessness may decrease and self-esteem may increase.

SOCIAL SUPPORT FOR A SURVIVING SPOUSE

The loss of companionship and the expectations for the surviving spouse to assume a multitude of new roles and responsibilities can be overwhelming. Social networks may provide assistance with daily tasks such as household chores, car maintenance, or financial concerns. Interacting with others who have successfully adjusted to a similar loss can instill hope and provide coping skills or strategies for handling stressors resulting from the loss. The opportunity to engage in a social comparison process with other widows also offers the opportunity to verbalize negative emotions about the dead spouse and to establish that these emotions are in fact normal. Similarly, the opportunity to help others or reciprocate support enables an individual to feel good about him or herself.

Some researchers have provided evidence that a reciprocal relationship exists between social support and negative life events. One study showed that perceived levels of social support impacted negative events.[18] Individuals with high levels of perceived support actually reported fewer numbers of subsequent negative events over a period of time than did those with low levels.

SOCIAL SUPPORT, STRESS, AND DEPRESSION FOLLOWING THE DEATH OF A SPOUSE

In addition to the importance of social support, depression is another crucial factor affecting the outcome of the loss of a spouse. Individuals who experience greater levels of depression may have more difficulty adjusting to the loss. Social support, stress, and depression appear to have an interactive effect on the well-being of an individual. Social support has been shown to impact the course of depression and to offer protection against depression.[19]

Under the stress of adverse situations, social support may also prevent clinical depression or other emotional problems associated with aging from developing.[20-22] Miller and Ingham[23] found buffering effects for anxiety and depression through the use of a "diffuse support scale." A total of 1,060 individuals were involved in an interview procedure and were asked questions related to contacts with coworkers, relatives, neighbors, and membership in various clubs. The questions were designed to tap into the functional components of the social support system. In general, the researchers found significant interactions between the buffering effects of social support on the one hand and anxiety and depression on the other.

Several theorists propose that depressed individuals create hostility, withdrawal, and annoyance in others. These reactions can reinforce negative views that people have of themselves and their ability to relate to people in their support system.[3,24-26] By creating these negative feelings in others, willingness to help the depressed person greatly decreases, thus lowering the number of available support persons. With a loss of support, the cycle of depression may be perpetuated and prolonged.

Gore[27] conducted a study of 100 men who were unemployed when the factory they worked at closed down. Each man was asked about the supportiveness of his friends, wife, and relatives. Those males who were not immediately reemployed and who reported feeling unsupported had more symptoms of illness and higher serum cholesterol levels. In addition, lack of support was correlated with more depression regardless of whether the male was employed. This study provides evidence that social support can buffer both psychological and physical symptomatology.

BENEFITS OF LONGITUDINAL PANEL DESIGNS IN STUDYING DEPRESSION

Previous research suggests that social support, stress, and depression are intercorrelated. However, a causal relationship between these variables cannot be determined from a bivariate correlational analysis within a single measurement period.[28,29] Previous research has not determined whether depression is a contributing factor to social support or whether social support is a contributing factor to depression. One explanation for the relationship between these variables is that social support buffers the effects of a loss, thus lowering levels of depression and allowing bereaved individuals to recover more quickly. Therefore, changes in social support may contribute to subsequent changes in depression. An alternative explanation is that stable levels of depression may affect changes in social support. If depressed individuals continually alienate themselves from family and friends, their social support systems may decrease. Finally, changes in social support may be related to changes in depression, but researchers may not be able to determine the direction of causation.

Structural regression analyses of longitudinal panel designs permit researchers to examine the plausibility of hypothesized causal relationships between variables.[29] The present research used a longitudinal panel design to examine the relationship of social support to stress and depression following the death of a spouse.

METHODS

Sample and Procedure

The data utilized to assess the structural interrelationships among social support, stress, and depression were obtained from a longitudinal bereavement study by Dimond and Lund which has already been described in this book (Chapters 1 and 10). More detail on the methodology of the study can be found in other publications[30,31] and in Chapters 1, 10, 11, and 12.

A total of 192 bereaved spouses over the age of 50 (M = 67.7) completed questionnaires or interviews at six times over the first 2 years of bereavement. Seventy-four percent of the participants were females. The measurement times were 3–4 weeks (T_1), 2 months, 6 months (T_2), 1 year (T_3), 18 months, and 2 years (T_4) following the death. The data collected at 2 and 18 months were not utilized in the analyses in this report in order to minimize losses in sample size for statistical procedures that require complete data sets for each participant.

Instruments

This study incorporated several outcome measures to assess the stable and transitory characteristics of stress, depression, and social support. Each of the six questionnaires over the 2-year period included two standardized scales and a variety of single-item assessments. Specifically, the Zung Self-Rating Depression Scale[32] was utilized to assess the level of depression. The scale is composed of 20 items which relate to mood, affect, and physiological behaviors. The range of scores is from 20 (low) to 80 (high). According to the Self-Rating Depression Scale, a score below 40 is within the normal range of depression, 40–47 indicates minimal to mild depression, 48–55 indicates moderate to marked depression, and

56 or above indicates severe depression. The measure has good internal consistency, as suggested by Cronbach's alpha of .79.[33] Concurrent validity of .70 has also been established with the Minnesota Multiphasic Personality Inventory (MMPI). The Zung measure has been widely used with aging populations, which was a major consideration for its inclusion. In addition, each questionnaire obtained self-reported ratings for perceived stress, coping, health, and self-esteem measured by seven-point, single-item statements. Social support was measured by 3 items rated on scales from 1 (low) to 5 (high). The items were frequency of contact, the amount of mutual help, and mutual confiding. For more details on the scaling procedures, see Dimond, Lund, and Caserta.[11]

RESULTS

Depression scores obtained from the Zung Self-Rating Scale indicated 90% of the subjects did not have clinically significant levels of depression. Most of the analyses were based on 94 of the participants who had complete data sets at the four selected times. The means and standard deviations for the raw depression scores were as follows: (1) at 6 months, $M = 37.6$; $SD = 7.2$; (2) at 1 year, $M = 37.1$, $SD = 6$; and (3) at 2 years, $M = 38$, $SD = 6$. The means and standard deviations for stress were as follows: (1) at 6 months, $M = 5.3$, $SD = 1.1$; (2) at 1 year, $M = 5.3$, $SD = 1$, and (3) at 2 years, $M = 5$, $SD = 1.2$. For social support, the means and standard deviations were as follows: (1) at 6 months, $M = 12$, $SD = .8$; (2) at 1 year, $M = 12$, $SD = .52$. In general, the means for depression, stress, and social support remained relatively unchanged over the different times.

Cross-Sectional Analyses

Previous research suggests that social support, stress, and depression are interrelated. Researchers have proposed that stress leads to depression. Social support, however, can buffer the effects of stress and thereby lower depression.[14]

The present results are only partially consistent with prior research. Pearson product moment correlations were computed among the measures of stress, social support, and depression for each time of measurement. These results indicated that perceived stress and depression were positively correlated for each of the four times (Table 1). The magnitude of the relationship ranged from .34 to .43. Social support, however, was negatively correlated with depression only at the last mea-

TABLE 1   Cross-sectional Correlations for Stress, Social Support, and Depression

Time periods	Stress with depression	Social support with depression	Social support with stress
T_1	.43**	−.14	.08
T_2	.35**	−.16	−.05
T_3	.36**	−.11	.11
T_4	.34**	−.24*	−.07

Note. Cell entries are the Pearson product moment correlations between two measures at a single point in time. $N = 94$ for all correlated time periods.
*$p < .05$. **$p < .01$.

surement time, 2 years after the spouses death ($r = -.24$). Social support was not significantly correlated with stress during any of the measurement periods.

Structural Regression Analyses

Structural regression analysis was utilized to test the plausibility of each of three types of competing hypotheses about the causal relationships among depression, stress, and social support.[29] Specifically, the analysis was employed to test whether stable individual differences of one variable can predict changes in another variable. This analysis provides evidence as to whether a causal relationship exists between two variables over different periods of time. For example, the structural regression model was utilized to determine whether stable social support systems predict changes in depression over time, whether stable depression predicts changes in social support systems, or whether changes in social support are related to changes in depression.

The structural regression model examines potential causal relationships that could exist between two variables. That is, the causal relationships between the variables can exist in either direction (A determines B or B determines A). The structural regression model, however, can determine which causal relationship is the most plausible. In order to identify the most plausible causal relationship, the analysis is usually conducted between two variables over two or more points in time.

Essentially, each variable is divided into three components: (1) a stable or persisting value, (2) a transient or changing value, and (3) an error component or residual value. The stable or unchanging value can be estimated at time T_2 from observations made at time T_1. That is, the stable or enduring values from T_1 to T_2 make it possible to estimate the enduring components at T_2. These predictions are based on the autocorrelations (correlations between the same variable at different time periods) of the variable over time (see Table 2 for the autocorrelations of social support, stress, and depression). In contrast, the transient component of the T_2 measurement is the portion of the T_2 variable which cannot be predicted from the T_1 observations. A third component, described as the error or residual value, cannot be explained by either the transient or stable components of either variable.

If the stable components of one variable (A) can predict changes over time in another variable (B), then the stable components of the first variable (A) are identified as the most plausible cause of the relationship between the two variables. The plausibility of a causal relationship between A and B exists only if the stable components of B are not able to predict changing values in A.

TABLE 2   Autocorrelations for All Measures

Time periods	Stress	Social support	Depression
T_{1-2}	.70	.35	.74
T_{1-3}	.62	.29	.68
T_{1-4}	.71	.23	.61

Note. The numbers represent the correlation of a measure at one time with the same measure at a later time. For example, T_{1-2} represents the correlation between measures at T_1 and T_2.

TABLE 3   Correlations Between Stable and Transient Structural Regression Components

	Correlation of T_1 with:		
Structural components	T_2 (6 months)	T_3 (1 year)	T_4 (2 years)
Stable stress with transient social support	− .07	.03	− .003
Stable social support with transient stress	− .10	− .07	− .260*
Transient social support with transient stress	− .01	.14	.050
Stable social support with transient depression	.03	.06	− .060
Stable depression with transient social support	− .10	− .04	− .030
Transient social support with transient depression	− .12	− .04	− .250*
Stable depression with transient stress	.21*	.28*	.280*
Stable stress with transient depression	− .06	.03	− .020
Transient stress with transient depression	.13	.14	.030

*$p < .05$.

STRUCTURAL REGRESSION ANALYSIS OF SOCIAL SUPPORT, STRESS, AND DEPRESSION IN BEREAVED INDIVIDUALS

A structural regression analysis was performed to determine whether causal relationships existed over different time periods on each of these variables (social support, stress, and depression); the results are summarized in Table 3. For all three outcome measurement times (i.e., 6 months, 1 year, and 2 years), individuals who remained depressed experienced higher levels of stress over time. Results in Table 3 show that stable depression predicted residualized changes in stress. That is, those individuals who reported low (or high) levels of depression consistently over time also reported decreasing (or increasing) levels of stress over time.

Depression was significantly correlated with the perceived stressfulness of the loss only 3 weeks after the loss B (158) = .39, $p < .01$. A statistically significant relationship exists between the concurrent measures of depression and stress at 6 months B (128) = .212, $p < .02$, at 1 year B (131) = .28, $p < .001$, and at 2 years B (117) = .27, $p < .002$. These findings suggest that stable, continually depressed individuals did not show a reduction in their perceived level of stress.

A second finding suggests that stable or persisting social support was related to changes in stress. Although social support and stress were not significantly correlated immediately after the loss, individuals whose social support system persisted after 2 years were likely to experience less stress. That is, stable social support provided a statistically significant prediction of changes in perceived stress from 3 weeks to 2 years B (119) = − .26, $p < .005$. Stable social support, however, did not yield a significant prediction of change in perceived stress from 3 weeks to 6 months B(129) = − .10, $p > .1$ or to 1 year B (133) = − .07, $p > .1$.

One possible explanation for the relationship between social support and stress is that individuals recovering from the stress of bereavement may have been able to maintain more stable, persisting social support systems. In addition, stable social support systems might produce a reduction in the stress level of bereaved individuals.

DISCUSSION

One of the major conclusions from this study is that bereaved individuals who initially reported higher levels of depression also experienced higher levels of stress over a 2-year period. The effects of depression on the perceived stressfulness of the death of a spouse has both early and lasting effects after the loss. According to the results of the structural regression analyses, the impact of depression on stress can continue up to 2 years. The fact that stable depression was able to predict changes in stress warrants the search for effective interventions to help alleviate depression immediately or soon after the death.

While the existence of a correlation between two variables does not necessarily provide evidence of a causal relationship between them, causality does imply the existence of a correlation.[34] If two variables are causally related, they probably are correlated with each other. In contrast, if two variables are not correlated, they are not likely to be causally related. If the stable properties in variable A predict changes in variable B but the stable properties in variable B do not predict changes in A, the finding suggests that A is causally related to B.

A structural regression analysis provides indirect evidence about the existence of a causal relationship among variables. If a causal relationship exists between two variables, then the structural regression model provides evidence as to which variable causally affects the other. If a causal relationship exists between social support and stress, then the present findings support the view that social support causally affects stress.

Wills and Langner[35] proposed that a single stressful event may not place exceedingly difficult demands on a person. However, a multitude of accumulated problems may drain or overwhelm a person's coping abilities. Under these circumstances, the potential arises for depression or other serious disorders to occur. In the present study, those individuals who experienced lower levels of depression also consistently reported lower levels of stress. Determining what factors differentiate a person with high levels of depression from one with low levels of depression will be critical for understanding how the bereavement process can be facilitated. Levels of competence and social skills have been cited as factors impacting the buffering effect of social support and consequently affecting depression.[36,37] Some researchers have speculated that other factors affecting stress and depression include reduced financial income, poor health, the relationship to the deceased, and concurrent losses.[8] Researchers have estimated that 10 to 20% of the widowed will suffer depressive symptoms sometime during the bereavement process and that a small number are likely to become clinically depressed.[38]

A number of research studies have demonstrated that stable or persisting social support impacts the level of perceived stress. Mitchell et al.[12] proposed that longitudinal studies "need to consider: a) the type of stress: b) the type of support: c) the possible existence of nonlinear relationships: and d) the lag period involved" when examining stress-support relationships. Especially during the early stages of bereavement, support from family has been found to be helpful; later on, however, support from other widowed persons and neighbors was found to have a more positive impact.[39] In the present study, a relationship was not found between social support and stress measured immediately after the loss (i.e., at 6 months or 1 year).

An enduring social support system affected the stress level of a bereaved person only after 2 years. Researchers have provided evidence that bereavement is a long-term process extending beyond 1 year of time.[40,41] This evidence provides an explanation for the findings that social support is not related to stress until 2 years after bereavement. In essence, stable social support did predict changes in perceived stress from 3 weeks to 2 years. The fact that a structural regression analysis only provides indirect evidence about the existence of a causal relationship among variables makes it difficult to determine which changes were made as a result of which variable. If in fact an individual was experiencing low levels of stress, then the possibility of maintaining a stable social support system might increase. On the other hand, if a person's social support system remains relatively stable, then the level of stress might be reduced.

REFERENCES

1. Dimond, M. F. (1981). Bereavement and the elderly: A critical review with implications for nursing practice and research. *Journal of Advanced Nursing, 6,* 461–470.
2. Dohrenwend, B. S., & Dohrenwend, B. P. (1981). *Stressful life events and their contexts.* New York: Neal Watson.
3. Gottlieb, I. H., & Robinson, L. A. (1982). Responses to depressed individuals: Discrepancies between self-report and observer-rated behavior. *Journal of Abnormal Psychology, 91,* 231–240.
4 Turner, R. J. (1982). Social support as a contingency in psychological well-being. *Journal of Health and Social Behavior, 23,* 145–159.
5. Thoits, P. A. (1982). Conceptual, methodological, and theoretical problems in studying social support as a buffer against life stress. *Journal of Health and Social Behavior, 23,* 145–159.
6. Garber, J., & Seligman, M. E. P. (1980). *Human helplessness: Theory and applications.* New York: Academic Press.
7. Osterweis, M. (1985). Bereavement and the elderly. *Aging Magazine, 348.*
8. Osterweis, M., Solomon, F., & Green, M. (1984). *Bereavement reactions, consequences and care: A report of the Institute of Medicine.* Washington, DC: National Academy Press.
9. Lattanzi, M. E. (1982, November). Hospice bereavement services: Creating networks of support. *Family and Community Health, 5,* 54–63.
10. Rando, T. (1986). *Loss and anticipatory grief.* Lexington, MA: Lexington Books.
11. Dimond, M. F., Lund, D. A., & Caserta, M. S. (1987) The role of social support in the first two years of bereavement in an elderly sample. *The Gerontologist, 27,* 599–604.
12. Mitchell, R. E., & Moss, R. H. (1984). Deficiencies in social support among depressed patients: Antecedents or consequences of stress? *Journal of Health and Social Behavior, 25,* 438–452.
13. Weiss, R. S. (1976). Transition states and other stressful situations: Their nature and programs for their management. In G. Caplan & M. Killilea (Eds.), *Support Systems and Mutual Help* (pp. 213–232). New York: Grune & Stratton.
14. Cohen, S., & Wills, T. A. (1985). Stress, social support, and the buffering hypothesis. *Psychological Bulletin, 98,* 310–357.
15. Cohen, S., & Hoberman, H. (1983). Positive events and social support as buffers of life change stress. *Journal of Applied Social Psychology, 13,* 99–125.
16. Paykel, E. S., Emms, E. M., Fletcher, J., & Rassaby, E. S. (1980). Life events and social support in puerperal depression. *British Journal of Psychology, 136,* 339–346.
17. Pearlin, L. I., & Menaghan, E. G., Lieberman, M. A., & Mullan, J. T. (1981). The stress process. *Journal of Health and Social Behavior, 22,* 337–356.
18. McFarlane, A. H., Norman, G. R., Streiner, D. L., & Roy, R. G. (1983). The process of social stress: Stable, reciprocal, and mediating relationships. *Journal of Health and Social Behavior, 24,* 160–173.
19. Mueller, D. (1980). Social networks: A promising direction for research on the relationship of the social environment to psychiatric disorder. *Social Science and Medicine, 14A,* 147–161.
20. Blau, Z. (1973). *Old age in a changing society.* New York: Viewpoints.
21. Brown, G., Bhrolchain, M., & Harris, T. (1975). Social class and psychiatric disturbance among women in urban populations. *Sociology, 9,* 225–254.
22. Lowenthal, M., & Haven, C. (1968). Interaction and adaptation: Intimacy as a critical variable. *American Sociological Review, 33,* 20–30.
23. Miller, P. M., & Ingham, J. G. (1979). Reflections on the life events to illness link with some

preliminary findings. In I. G. Sarason & C. D. Spielberger (Eds.), *Stress and Anxiety* (pp. 313–336). New York: Hemisphere.

24. Coyne, J. C. (1976). Toward an interactional description of depression. *Psychiatry, 39*, 28–40.
25. Strack, S., & Coyne, J. C. (1983). Social conformation of dysphoria: Shared and private reactions to depression. *Journal of Personality and Social Psychology, 44*, 798–806.
26. Weakland, J. H., Fisch, R., Watzlawick, P., & Bodin, A. M. (1974). Brief therapy: Focused problem resolution. *Family Process, 19*, 13–18.
27. Gore, S. (1978). The effect of social support in moderating the health consequences of unemployment. *Journal of Health and Social Behavior, 19*, 157–165.
28. Kessler, R. C., & Greenberg, D. F. (1981). *Linear panel analysis: Models of quantitative change.* New York: Academic Press.
29. Rogosa, D. (1980). A critique of cross-lagged correlation. *Psychological Bulletin, 90*, 726–748.
30. Caserta, M. S., Lund, D. A., & Dimond, M. F. (1985). Assessing interviewer effects in a longitudinal study of bereaved elderly adults. *Journal of Gerontology, 40*, 637–640.
31. Lund, D. A., Caserta, M. S., & Dimond, M. F. (1986). Gender differences through two years of bereavement among the elderly. *The Gerontologist, 26*, 314–320.
32. Zung, W. (1965). A self-rating depression scale. *Archives of General Psychiatry, 12*, 63–70.
33. Jegede, R. O. (1976). Psychometric properties of the Self-rating Depression Scale (SDS). *Journal of Psychology, 93*, 27–30.
34. Mulaik, S. (1987). Toward a conception of causality applicable to experimentation and causal modeling. *Child Development, 58*, 18–32.
35. Wills, T. A., & Langner, T. S. (1980). Socioeconomic status and stress. In I. L. Kutash & L. B. Schlesinger (Eds.), *Handbook on stress and anxiety,* (pp. 159–173). San Francisco: Jossey-Bass.
36. Lewinsohn, P. M. (1974). A behavioral approach to depression. In R. Friedman & M. Katz (Eds.), *The psychology of depression: Contemporary theory and research* (pp. 157–176). New York: John Wiley & Sons.
37. Husaini, B. A., Neff, J. A., Newbrough, J. R., & Moore, M. C. (1982). The stress-buffering role of social support and personal confidence among the rural married. *Journal of Community Psychology, 10*, 409–426.
38. Clayton, P., & Darvish, H. (1979). Course of depressive symptoms following the stress of bereavement. In J. E. Barrett (Ed.), *Stress and mental disorder* (pp. 121–136). New York: Raven Press.
39. Bankoff, E. A. (1983). Social support and adaptation to widowhood. *Journal of Marriage and the Family, 45*, 827–839.
40. Carey, R. G. (1979). Weathering widowhood: Problems and adjustments of the widowed during the first year. *Omega, 10*, 163–174.
41. Parkes, C. M., & Weiss, R. S. (1983). *Recovery from bereavement.* New York: Basic Books.

7

Appraisal, Coping, and Resources: Markers Associated with the Health of Aged Widows and Widowers

Kathleen A. Gass

Conjugal bereavement is a major stressor associated with high morbidity rates in surviving spouses. This study focused on factors associated with the health dysfunction of widowed persons following bereavement and on similarities and differences between the genders on appraisal of bereavement, coping, resources, and health dysfunction. One hundred widows (M age = 71.3) and 59 widowers (M age = 71.1) were identified through church burial records from Catholic parishes and then interviewed. Questionnaires included Gilson, Bergner, Bobbitt, and Carter's Sickness Impact Profile; Folkman & Lazarus's Ways of Coping Checklist; Appraisal of Bereavement; and Assessment of Resources. Widows and widowers did not differ in physical and psychosocial dysfunction or in appraisal of bereavement; however, widows who appraised their bereavement as a loss with other anticipated threats had higher psychosocial dysfunction [$F (2, 92) = 6.84, p < .01$]. The more "wishful thinking," "mixed," "growth," "minimizes threat," "self-blame," "emotion-focused," and "overall problem-focused" coping used by widows, the higher their psychosocial dysfunction. Greater use of "minimizes threat" coping was related to higher physical dysfunction for widows. For widowers, only "self-blame" coping was related to higher psychosocial dysfunction. Resources which were related to less health dysfunction in women were social support, practicing death and mourning rituals, religious beliefs, control over bereavement, good prior mental health, and absence of other losses with bereavement. For widowers, control over bereavement, closeness to spouse, and absence of ambivalent feelings toward the deceased were related to less dysfunction. Men and women did not differ in the number of coping strategies they used or in the total amount of resources.

This research was supported by the Public Health Service National Research Fellowship (No. S F31 NU05527-03) and a grant from the School of Nursing, University of Wisconsin-Madison.

The author wishes to thank Dale A. Lund, Ph.D., for his careful review and helpful feedback on this chapter.

Conjugal bereavement is considered a major stressor associated with a higher morbidity and mortality rate in surviving spouses.[1-6] The effects of stress and poor self-care contribute to mortality.[7] The death of a spouse is often immediately followed by the grieving process and by role changes, and this increased stress may result in illness.[4] Conjugal bereavement is viewed as a time of transition that challenges the adaptive capacities of individuals.[7-10] Comparative data on health of older bereaved men and women and markers associated with health following bereavement are limited or provide conflicting results. Bereavement research has focused primarily on the morbidity and mortality of survivors following the death of a loved one. In investigations of conjugal bereavement, researchers have mixed the young widowed with the older widowed,[1,5] combined data on genders for analysis,[1,11] or mixed the widowed with other bereaved close relative,[6] thereby making comparisons between aged widows and widowers difficult. Some researchers have studied younger widowed persons (under the age of 60),[3,11-14] and, more recently, older widowed persons[15-18] who may be at greater risk for morbidity and mortality following conjugal loss because of limited coping resources.[19] Findings on the younger widowed may not be directly applicable to the aged widowed.

Some researchers have found men to be at greater risk for morbidity and mortality following bereavement at all ages than women.[6,20-23] Helsing and Szklo[24] found a higher mortality risk only for widowers 55 to 74 years of age. Others found no differences between the genders on health or coping following conjugal bereavement.[15,18,25,26]

Sampling and methodological differences likely contributed to differences in findings. For example, some researchers investigated select samples, such as bereaved patients on psychiatric units,[5] while others focused on older adults[16,25] or the younger bereaved.[3,11-13] Some studied persons who were widowed for over a year[1,11,13,25,27] while others focused on those recently widowed.[15,18] Age, sex, and length of bereavement may influence morbidity and mortality, which suggests there is a need to control and further investigate these variables when conducting bereavement research.

Identification of markers associated with health following bereavement can lead to a better understanding and better prediction of the health of widowed persons and provide knowledge which may help facilitate transition to widowhood and expedite the helping interventions of professionals who care for the bereaved. Key variables which can affect health following stressful experiences are appraisal of the stressful event, coping processes, and coping resources.[28,29] Little research has been done on the role of appraisal of bereavement and its influence on coping and health following conjugal loss.[16] Appraisal of a stressor has been found to influence the coping process and the health of nonbereaved individuals.[30-33]

It has been suggested that men and women have different adaptive outcomes regarding conjugal bereavement. Berardo[34] and Rees and Lutkins[6] reported that older men found it more difficult to adapt to the loss of a spouse than older women. However, Heyman and Gianturco[25] observed little or no gender differences in depression, happiness, and adjustment before and after conjugal bereavement. Johnson, Lund, and Dimond[9] found effective copers continued to cope effectively throughout 1 year following the death of a spouse, but the presence of persistent stress was negatively associated with coping ability and self-esteem a year later. The researchers concluded that adjustment to the stressfulness of conjugal loss must be confronted or the stress will impact on coping ability and self-esteem.

The death of a spouse is considered to be the most severe form of stress and requires considerable coping effort. Johnson, Lund, and Dimond[9] state that an explication of the dynamics of the bereavement process and the extent to which stress and coping are involved should be a primary issue in gerontological research. To date, limited research exists on the process of coping with bereavement or on the various coping strategies used by widows and widowers following bereavement and their importance to health.[35] Much research has utilized outcome measures which imply "coping," but this research has not directly made use of a coping theoretical framework or conceptualization. This is problematic, because researchers are not making use of an important and extensive body of literature which may assist them in better understanding and helping individuals to cope following bereavement.

Researchers have made gains in investigating the role of personal, social, and environmental resources and their impact on the health of bereaved individuals. Researchers have studied a single resource[3,21] or multiple resources[1,25] following bereavement, but they have seldom investigated gender differences in the use or availability of resources. The resources associated with health following bereavement which were investigated in the present study include helpful social supports;[2,36,37] the practice of rituals and beliefs which facilitate the grieving process;[37-39] the possession of religious beliefs which foster an acceptance or understanding of death;[1,25,40] knowledge of the grieving process through previous experience and through information on grieving or widowhood received from others;[10,41] opportunities for anticipatory grieving;[3,42] a prior history of good mental-emotional health;[10,43] absence of additional losses concurrent with bereavement;[19,36,37] a quality relationship with the spouse characterized by a healthy degree of closeness, minimal dependency, and lack of prolonged conflict or ambivalent feelings;[39,43,44] perception that the spouse's death was not preventable;[44] the ability to openly express grief;[37,45] belief in control over stressors;[8] and adequate finances.[14,46,47] The purposes of the present study were (1) to investigate appraisal of bereavement, coping patterns, and resources and their interrelationships and how they relate to the health of the aged widowed following conjugal bereavement and (2) to identify similarities and differences between the genders on appraisal of bereavement, coping, resources, and health status.

METHOD

Sample

One hundred widows and 59 widowers identified through church burial records from Catholic parishes in two midwestern cities were interviewed. Criteria for inclusion in the study were that (1) the spouse had died from 1 to 12 months prior to the interview (2) the potential participant was aged 54–85, and (3) the potential participant had not remarried or was not institutionalized. The participants were white and primarily Catholic ($N = 157$), aged 54–81 (mean age of widows = 71.3 years; mean age of widowers = 71.1 years), and bereaved for a time period ranging from 35 to 364 days ($M = 224$ days for widows; $M = 189$ days for widowers). Sixty-four percent of the widows and 65% of the widowers had completed high school or a higher level of education. Incomes ranged from $3,000 to over $11,000 a year, with 70% of the widows and 93% of the widowers reporting an income of over $7,000. Forty percent of the widows and 31% of the widowers had spouses who died a sudden death, while 60% of the widows and 69% of the widowers had spouses who died from a chronic illness. The mean number of days widows and widowers cared for their spouse before death was 487 and 596 days respectively.

Instruments

APPRAISAL OF BEREAVEMENT

One question was developed to assess the meaning of bereavement, and it was pilot tested with six widowed persons prior to its use in the study. Widowed persons were asked to choose which one of three statements reflected how they perceived their bereavement experience: "a harmful loss without other losses," a "harmful loss with other anticipated threats," or "a challenge." Widowed persons who defined their bereavement as "a loss without other losses" viewed the spouse's death as a great personal loss but felt there were no other bereavement-related losses, fears, or problems they could not manage. Widowed persons who had "other anticipated threats" defined their bereavement as a loss with many other losses, fears, and problems to anticipate and they worried that they would not be able to manage. Those who perceived widowhood as "a challenge" were determined to overcome or master their bereavement and they viewed widowhood as an opportunity for growth.

WAYS OF COPING CHECKLIST

Coping with bereavement was measured by the Ways of Coping Checklist developed by Folkman and Lazarus.[32] The checklist consists of 68 items that describe a range of behavioral and cognitive coping strategies that a person might use in a specific stressful situation. Examples of strategies include "Made a plan of action and followed it" and "Accepted sympathy and understanding from someone." The respondent answers either yes or no to each statement. Items are classified into overall problem-focused and overall emotion-focused coping categories or into seven different subcategories of coping: problem-focused, wishful thinking, mixed, (help-seeking/avoidance), growth, minimizes threat, seeks social support, and self-blame. Both the two-factor scales and seven-factor subscales were used in this study, because it was believed that the seven subscales would provide additional knowledge on the types of coping used by widowed persons. Scoring involved summing the number of ways of coping answered yes for each subscale. A coping strength score was obtained by summing the total number of coping strategies used by the respondent, including both desirable and less desirable coping methods. The summing of desirable and undesirable coping strategies is not Folkman and Lazarus's routine procedure for scoring the Ways of Coping Checklist. The decision to obtain a coping strength score was based on prior research findings which suggested that use of higher numbers of coping strategies was related to health in nonbereaved subjects.[48,49] Cronbach alphas in the present study for the two overall coping scales and the seven subscales were as follows: overall problem-focused (widows $\alpha = .69$; widowers, $\alpha = .56$), overall emotion-focused (widows α = .75; widowers, α = .74), problem-focused (widows, α = .62; widowers, α = .37), wishful thinking (widows, α = .66; widowers, α = .72), mixed (widows, α = .43; widowers, α = .58), growth (widows, α = .65; widowers, α = .49), minimizes threat (widows, α = .53; widowers, α = .47), seeks social support (widows, α = .48; widowers, α = .34), and self-blame (widows, α = .56; widowers, α = .56). Reliabilities were lower than those based on data from a community sample containing persons who coped with the stressful events of daily living,[32]which may reflect differences in the samples studied.[29]

ASSESSMENT OF RESOURCES

An assessment of resources (AR) instrument was developed for the study. It consisted of nine ordinal and seven dichotomous items drawn from the literature relative to psychological, social, and material factors which may influence bereavement outcome. The AR was scored based on the extent to which each resource was present. Dichotomous items logically required a yes or no response. These items received either a score of 0 (resource absent) or 3 (resource present). Ordinal items had four choices. Based on the respondent's answers, ordinal items were scored 3 (resource highly present), 2 (resource moderately present), 1 (resource minimally present), or 0 (resource absent). Resource strength was a sum of the scores on the 16 items. Content validity was established through a thorough review of the literature on factors influencing health following bereavement as well as through the assistance of widowed spouses who evaluated the questionnaire and confirmed the validity of the questions. Since 16 separate constructs were assessed, internal consistency reliability for the total instrument was not obtained.

SICKNESS IMPACT PROFILE

Health status was defined as physical and psychosocial dysfunction. The physical and psychosocial dimension subscales of the Sickness Impact Profile (SIP) were used. The SIP developed by Gilson et al.[50] is a 132-item, behaviorally based measure of sickness-related dysfunction and it provides a reliable and valid measure of health functioning. Separate reliability data do not exist for either of the dimension subscales. Test-retest coefficients (r = .97) and coefficients of internal stability (r = .94) for the overall instrument support a high level of reliability.[50] Examination of the relationship between SIP scores and other measures of dysfunction, including clinician assessments, self-assessments, and a related function assessment instrument, has provided evidence for the validity of the SIP as a measure of health dysfunction.[51] Items address activities involved in carrying on with one's life and reflect the person's perception of his or her performance of these activities. Examples of items include "I laugh or cry suddenly" and "I stay lying down most of the time." Subjects respond to only those items that describe them presently and are related to their health. Each item has an assigned scale value indicative of severity of dysfunction. The physical dimension score is calculated by adding the scale values for each item checked within categories for this dimension, dividing by the maximum possible dysfunction score for these categories, and then multiplying by 100. The psychosocial dimension score is obtained in a similar manner. For both dimensions, the larger the percentage score, the greater the impairment of health functioning.

Procedure

Pastors in Catholic parishes were contacted and their assistance was sought in obtaining names of widowed persons. The burial record book was used to obtain the date of death and the name and address of the surviving spouse. Those who met the sampling criteria were mailed a letter of explanation which invited them to participate in the study; they were also contacted by telephone to seek their participation and confirm they met sampling criteria. For those who agreed to participate, a home interview was scheduled. Interviews were conducted by a trained research specialist or by the researcher. Consent was obtained from the subject, and the Appraisal of Bereavement, Ways of Coping Checklist, AR, and SIP were administered in random order to control for possible order effects. Interviews ranged from 1 to 3 hours. One hour was needed for completion of the questionnaires; however, most participants had concerns or questions about the grieving process or widowhood which the interviewer addressed following the interview.

One hundred fifty-three women and 84 men were invited to participate in the study. Of these, 53 women and 25 men declined participation, yielding a refusal rate of 34% and 30% respectively. The reasons for refusal to participate included poor physical or mental health, difficulty talking about the death, advice of family members not to participate in the study, belief that bereavement was a private matter not to be discussed, shortness of time following bereavement, busyness, and involvement in important or additional stressful family situations. The reasons did not differ for the genders; however, men were less likely than women to state that it was too early following the death for a visit or to decline participation based on the advice of family members.

RESULTS

Similarities and Differences between the Genders on Demographic Variables and Health

There were no statistically significant differences between the genders on the demographic variables of age [$t(157) = .12$, $p = .90$], education [$t(157) = -.58$, $p = .57$, and length of time the subject cared for the spouse while ill before death [$t(157) = -.58$, $p = .56$]. There were differences in income level [$t(157) = 4.92$, $p < .001$], occupational status [$t(157) = -6.44$, $p < .001$], and time period of bereavement [$t(157) = 2.19$, $p < .05$]. Widowers had significantly higher incomes and occupational status than widows. Higher income was related to less psychosocial dysfunction ($r = -.36$, $p < .01$) and less physical dysfunction ($r = -.42$, $p < .001$) for widowers. There was a trend for higher income to be associated with less psychosocial dysfunction for widows, but it was not statistically significant ($r = -.18$, $p = .08$). Widowers were bereaved for a shorter time period than widows; however, the amount of time bereaved was not significantly correlated with any of the major research variables. Widows and widowers did not differ in type of death; that is, similar numbers of men and women had spouses who died from a chronic illness as opposed to suddenly [$\chi^2(1, N = 159) = 1.44$, $p = .23$].

Descriptive data analysis indicated that the sample as a whole was relatively healthy. The mean physical and psychosocial dysfunction scores for the widows were 7.51% ($SD = 9.44$) and 12.18% ($SD = 11.64$) respectively. For widowers,

TABLE 1 Means, Standard Deviations, and One-Way Analyses of Variance in the Three Appraisal Groups' Health Dysfunction Scores for Widows and Widowers

Subscale	Group 1 (without other losses)		Group 2 (other threats)		Group 3 (challenge)		F
	M	SD	M	SD	M	SD	
	Widows						
	(n = 30)		(n = 14)		(n = 51)		
Physical dysfunction	7.09	8.06	10.41	14.38	7.17	9.01	.68
Psychosocial dysfunction[a]	7.42	8.32	20.17	72.05	13.72	12.12	6.84**
	Widowers						
	(n = 22)		(n = 7)		(n = 30)		
Physical dysfunction[b]	7.40	8.43	15.29	9.52	6.14	8.34	3.31*
Psychosocial dysfunction[b]	11.66	9.34	22.95	9.22	12.84	10.30	3.68*

Note. df = 2.
[a]Scheffé post hoc comparisons show Group 2 differs from Group 1.
[b]Sheffé post hoc comparisons show Group 2 differs from Groups 1 and 3.
*p < .05. **p < .01.

the mean physical and psychosocial dysfunction scores were 7.69% (SD = 8.84) and 13.60% (SD = 10.28) respectively. Maximum possible scores were 100% physical and 100% psychosocial dysfunction. The mode on both SIP measures was 0% dysfunction. The SIP physical and SIP psychosocial dysfunction scores were correlated (r = .57 for widows; r = .70 for widowers) at the .001 level of significance. Results indicated no significant differences between the genders on physical [$t(157)$ = −.12, p = .90] and psychosocial [$t(157)$ = −.78, p = .44] health dysfunction.

Similarities and Differences between the Genders on Appraisal, Coping, and Health and the Relationship between Appraisal, Coping, and Health

In Table 1 the results of the one-way analyses of variance on the three appraisal groups' health dysfunction scores for widows and widowers are presented. The genders did not differ in how they appraised their bereavement [$\chi^2(2, N = 154) = .63 p = .73$]; however, widows who appraised their bereavement as "a harmful loss with other anticipated threats" had higher psychosocial dysfunction than widows who appraised their bereavement as "harmful loss without other losses." There were no significant differences among appraisal groups in physical dysfunction for widows. Widowers with "other anticipated threats" had significantly higher psychosocial and physical dysfunction than the other appraisal groups.

Only one significant difference was found between the genders on the Ways of Coping Checklist subscales. Widows used significantly more mixed (help-seeking/avoidance) coping than widowers [$t(157)$ = 2.63, p < .01]. Men (M = 29.80, SD = 7.51) and women (M = 30.31, SD = 7.89) did not differ in the numbers of coping strategies (coping strength) they used [$t(157)$ = .40, p = .69].

TABLE 2   Pearson Product Moment Correlation Coefficients of Ways of Coping with Dysfunction Measures for Widows and Widowers

Ways of coping	Physical dysfunction		Psychosocial dysfunction	
	Widows	Widowers	Widows	Widowers
Problem focused	− .05	− .07	.19	− .18
Wishful thinking	.06	.10	.31**	.25
Mixed	− .09	.11	.27**	.21
Growth	.04	− .16	.25*	− .08
Minimizes threat	.21*	.24	.20*	.12
Seeks social support	.07	− .01	.08	− .01
Self-blame	.07	.06	.41†	.28*
Overall emotion-focused	.10	− .16	.42†	− .11
Overall problem-focused	− .05	.18	.22*	.25

$*p < .05.$ $**p < .01.$ $^\dagger p < .001$, two-tailed.

Several ways of coping were related to health dysfunction. In Table 2, the Pearson correlations between ways of coping and the dysfunction measures for widows and widowers are presented.

For widows, the more wishful thinking, mixed, growth, minimizes threat, self-blame, overall emotion-focused, and overall problem-focused coping used, the higher the psychosocial dysfunction. Higher use of minimizes threat coping was related to higher physical dysfunction. For widowers, use of self-blame coping was related to higher psychosocial dysfunction. No ways of coping were significantly related to physical dysfunction for men. Use of more coping strategies (coping strength) was related to more psychosocial dysfunction ($r = .39$, $p < .001$) for widows but was not significantly related to their physical health dysfunction ($r = .04$, $p = .67$). Coping strength was not significantly related to widowers' psychosocial ($r = .16$, $p = .22$) or physical dysfunction ($r = .09$, $p = .56$).

Initially, two-way ANOVAS were done on gender by appraisal for ways of coping. There were no significant two-way interactions between sex and appraisal groups on any of the coping subscales; however, there were differences between appraisal groups on several ways of coping. To examine the differences, one-way analyses of variance using Scheffé post hoc comparisons were done. The means, standard deviations, and results of the one-way analyses of variance on the three appraisal groups' ways of coping scores for widows and widowers are presented in Tables 3 and 4 respectively.

There were significant differences in coping by widows who appraised their bereavement differently. Widows who appraised their bereavement as having "other anticipated threats" used more wishful thinking, mixed, self-blame, and overall problem-focused coping than widows who appraised their bereavement as a "loss without other losses." The "challenge" appraisal widows used less wishful thinking than widows who perceived "other anticipated threats" and they used more growth, problem-focused, and overall problem-focused coping than widows "without other losses." There were no differences found among the appraisal groups for widows regarding minimizes threat, seeks social support, and overall emotion-focused coping. There were no differences in coping among widowers who appraised their bereavement differently. For widows, appraisal groups differed significantly in coping strength. Widows "without other losses" used less coping strategies (lower coping strength) than the other two appraisal groups [F (2, 92) = 6.57, $p <$ .01]. For widowers, there were no statistically significant differences among appraisal groups in coping strength [$F(2, 56)$ = 1.13, p = .33].

Similarities and Differences between the Genders on Resources and the Relationship between Resources and Health

Differences between the genders were found for 2 of the 16 resources, namely, use of death and burial rituals and one aspect of the quality of the relationship. Significantly more widowers than widows followed all burial customs and rituals associated with the church. Widows followed most of the burial customs and rituals [$\chi^2(2, N$ = 159) = 11.88, $p <$ .01]. More widowers reported seldom having had disagreements or conflicts with their spouse than widows. Widows more often reported having had occasional disagreements [$\chi^2(2, N$ = 159) = 14.71, $p <$ .01]. Higher amounts of certain individual resources were associated with better health functioning. Table 5 presents the Pearson and biserial correlations for resources with dysfunction measures for widows and widowers.

The more the widows practiced death and mourning rituals, believed in their control over bereavement, and had no other losses with bereavement, the lower their physical dysfunction. More helpful social supports, stronger religious beliefs, more belief in control over bereavement, good prior mental-emotional health, and no other losses with bereavement were related to lower psychosocial dysfunction for widows. For widowers, higher control over bereavement and more closeness to spouse were related to less physical and psychosocial dysfunction. Absence of ambivalent feelings toward the deceased spouse was related to less psychosocial dysfunction for widowers. Men (M = 28.16, SD = 3.24) and women (M =

TABLE 3   Means, Standard Deviations, and One-Way Analyses of Variance in the Three Appraisal Groups' Ways of Coping Scores for Widows

Subscale	Group 1 (without other losses, n = 30)		Group 2 (other threats, n = 14)		Group 3 (challenge, n = 51)		F
	M	SD	M	SD	M	SD	
Problem focused[a]	5.00	2.03	6.64	1.95	6.37	2.37	4.39*
Wishful thinking[b]	10.10	2.87	13.29	2.20	11.04	3.23	5.42**
Mixed[c]	2.67	1.56	4.07	1.82	3.61	1.76	4.23*
Growth[d]	2.37	1.73	3.71	1.64	3.82	1.76	7.02**
Minimizes threat	3.43	1.25	3.29	.91	3.49	1.78	.10
Seeks social support	2.70	.60	2.36	.93	2.69	.55	1.69
Self-blame[e]	.40	.68	1.07	1.14	.57	.78	3.30*
Overall emotion-focused	17.50	4.05	20.93	4.43	20.16	5.58	3.42
Overall problem-focused[f]	9.03	3.12	12.86	2.77	11.26	3.39	7.84[†]

Note. Five widows appraised their bereavement as nonstressful and were not included in the analysis.
Note. df = 2.
[a]Groups 1 and 3 differ. [b]Group 2 differs from Groups 1 and 3. [c]Groups 1 and 2 differ. [d]Groups 1 and 3 differ. [e]Groups 1 and 2 differ. [f]Group 1 differs from Groups 2 and 3.
*$p <$ .05. **$p <$ .01. [†]$p <$ .001.

TABLE 4   Means, Standard Deviations, and One-Way Analyses of Variance in the Three Appraisal Groups' Ways of Coping Scores for Widowers

Subscale	Group 1 (without other losses, n = 22)		Group 2 (other threats, n = 7)		Group 3 (challenge, n = 30)		F
	M	SD	M	SD	M	SD	
Problem focused	5.73	2.23	5.43	1.72	5.47	1.81	.13
Wishful thinking	10.77	4.09	12.86	3.02	11.63	3.15	1.01
Mixed	2.41	1.65	4.00	1.83	2.33	2.02	2.37
Growth	3.14	1.83	4.14	1.46	3.37	1.61	.95
Minimizes threat	3.73	1.67	3.14	1.77	3.60	1.25	.42
Seeks social support	2.46	.67	2.71	.76	2.53	.73	.36
Self-blame	.68	.89	1.43	.79	.60	.89	2.55
Overall emotion-focused	18.64	5.88	22.00	2.83	19.40	5.13	1.09
Overall problem-focused	9.96	3.53	11.14	2.80	9.77	2.47	.63

Note. df = 2.

27.46, SD = 4.35) did not differ in the amount of their resources (resource strength) [$t(157)$ = -1.16, p = .25]; however, presence of higher amounts of resources was related to less psychosocial (r = $-.38$, p < .001) and physical (r = $-.22$, p < .05) dysfunction for widows. There were no statistically significant relationships between resource strength and psychosocial (r = $-.17$, p = .20) and physical (r = $-.12$, p = .36) dysfunction for widowers. For widows,

TABLE 5   Pearson Product Moment and Biserial Correlation Coefficients of Resources With Dysfunction Measures for Widows and Widowers

Resources	Physical dysfunction (r)		Psychosocial dysfunction (r)	
	Widows	Widowers	Widows	Widowers
Social support	$-.10$	.11	$-.35^{\dagger}$	$-.15$
Rituals practiced	$-.28**$	$-.06$	$-.08$	$-.22$
Religious beliefs	$-.11$	.12	$-.28**$	$-.00$
Lets out emotions	$-.05$	$-.07$	.01	$-.06$
Control over bereavement	$-.21*$	$-.30*$	$-.31**$	$-.36**$
Closeness to spouse	.03	.31*	.17	.28*
Dependency on spouse	.18	.10	.13	$-.11$
Disagreements/conflicts with spouse	.08	$-.19$	.18	$-.11$
Ambivalent feelings toward spouse	.04	$-.25$	.12	$-.40^{\dagger}$
		r_{bis}		
Information on grieving/widowhood	.01	.10	.04	.16
Previous experiences with losses	$-.30$	.02	$-.25$	$-.06$
Anticipatory grieving	$-.01$	.16	.04	.18
Good prior mental emotional health	$-.05$	$-.14$	$-.47**$	$-.15$
No other losses with bereavement	$-.35**$	$-.14$	$-.51^{\dagger}$	$-.17$
Death not preventable	.00	$-.15$	$-.19$	$-.11$
Adequacy of finances	$-.11$	$-.09$	.03	$-.00$

*p < .05. **p < .01. $^{\dagger}p$ < .001, two-tailed.

appraisal groups significantly differed in resource strength. Widows with other anticipated threats had lesser amounts of resources (lower resource strength) than the other two appraisal groups [$F(2, 92) = 7.62, p < .001$]. For widowers, there were no statistically significant differences among appraisal groups in resource strength.

Summary

Major findings can be summarized as follows. For widows, appraisal groups differed in their use of problem-focused, wishful thinking, mixed, growth, self-blame, and overall problem-focused coping but not in their use of minimizes threat, seeks social support, and overall emotion-focused coping. The more wishful thinking, mixed, growth, minimizes threat, self-blame, overall emotion-focused, and overall problem-focused coping used by widows, the higher their psychosocial dysfunction. The more minimizes threat coping used, the higher their physical dysfunction. More support, stronger religious beliefs, practicing rituals, control, good prior mental health, and no other losses were related to less health dysfunction in widows. Higher amounts of resources but not higher numbers of coping strategies were related to less dysfunction for widows. For widowers, appraisal groups did not differ in their use of ways of coping. More self-blame coping was related to higher psychosocial dysfunction. Higher control over bereavement, more closeness to the spouse, and absence of ambivalent feelings toward the spouse were related to less health dysfunction. Coping strength and resource strength were not significantly related to health dysfunction for widowers.

DISCUSSION

Findings from the present study indicated that widows and widowers did not differ in physical and psychosocial health dysfunction following bereavement. These findings are in agreement with Heyman and Gianturco,[25] Gallagher, Breckenridge, Thompson, and Peterson,[15] and Lund, Caserta, and Dimond[26] who found no differences in health following bereavement. They do not support Berardo's[20] findings, which suggested that widowers are at greater risk for morbidity following bereavement.

The findings suggest that appraisal of bereavement is a key marker associated with the health outcome of widows and widowers following bereavement. It may not be bereavement per se which affects the health of the widowed, but rather the meaning of the bereavement experience to the individual and the degree of threat perceived. The findings suggest that the "anticipatory threat" appraisal group was at greatest risk for health dysfunction following bereavement. Widowers in this group had higher psychosocial and physical dysfunction than widowers in the "without other losses" and "challenge" appraisal groups; "anticipatory threat" appraisal widows had poorer psychosocial health dysfunction than widows in the "without other losses" appraisal group. Differences among female appraisal groups on physical dysfunction were not statistically significant. One explanation for this lack of significant differences may be that serious impact on physical health may occur at a later time period following bereavement. The findings suggested that bereavement is a stressor which may impact more heavily on psychosocial health than on physical health, since the majority of statistically significant correlations were on the psychosocial health dysfunction measure.

The results for widows provide some support for the view that higher threat appraisal contributes to the use of less adequate ways of coping. Widows who perceived "other anticipated threats," the highest threat appraisal group, used more self-blame, wishful thinking, and mixed coping than widows "without other losses," the lowest threat appraisal group. The higher psychosocial dysfunction of widows who perceived "other anticipated threats" suggest that their higher use of self-blame, wishful thinking, and mixed coping may not be sufficient to reduce or eliminate the threats associated with bereavement. These ways of coping may be less desirable or less useful coping methods. The "challenge" appraisal group's higher use of growth, problem-focused, and overall problem-focused coping suggest that more adaptive, reality-oriented forms of coping are likely used when threats are comparatively mild. Appraisal groups for widows did not significantly differ in their use of minimizes threat, seeks social support, and overall emotion-focused coping, suggesting that widows used these ways of coping to a similar degree. There were no differences in coping for widowers who appraised their bereavement differently. This finding suggests that irrespective of the way men appraise bereavement, they tend to use similar ways of coping.

A limitation of the study was the type of measuring instrument used to assess appraisal. In response to a single question, individuals chose one type of appraisal from three options. Lazarus and Folkman[29] suggest that appraisal types may not be mutually exclusive. Thus, a multiple-item Likert scale which focuses on types of appraisal and the multifaceted dimensions of widowhood may warrant consideration for future research on appraisal of bereavement. According to Lazarus and Folkman, appraisal and coping are processes which can change over time. For this reason, a longitudinal design may be more useful in studying changes in appraisal and coping processes following bereavement.

Coping strength did not differ for the genders. There was only one gender difference regarding the ways of coping subscales, that is, women used more mixed coping than men. These findings suggest that men and women use similar ways of coping to manage their bereavement. For widows, coping is a reflection of the degree of threat appraisal; that is, the higher the threat appraisal, the higher the number of coping strategies used. Widows who perceived "other anticipated threats" used more coping strategies to deal with bereavement than the other two appraisal groups. Numbers of coping strategies utilized by widowers were not reflective of the degree of threat appraisal. Overall, more coping strategies were associated with more psychosocial dysfunction for women than men. Bereavement is a stressor which can be associated with many other stressful problems that also require coping, such as financial losses, taking over the daily living tasks of the deceased spouse, and loneliness. Each bereavement-related problem may require different types and amounts of coping, and the number of bereavement-related problems confronting a widowed person at one time may affect the amount of coping strategies used. Women may have been confronted with more bereavement-related problems than men, thereby needing to muster more coping, especially if the threat was high.

Men had a higher financial and occupational status than women. Other bereavement researchers have found widowers to have higher socioeconomic status than widows.[15] The higher incomes of widowers may have reduced the threat of bereavement for them and, in turn, reduced their need to employ more ways of coping. Atchley[46] found that widowers and widows who viewed their income as adequate were much less likely to encounter either social or psychological stress than were widowed persons with inadequate income. Economic provisions can affect the course of mourning and impact on an individual's life adjustment and health.[14,20,47] Adequate finances may help the individual purchase assistance with daily living tasks or may provide psychological comfort. Harvey and Bahr[52] concluded that most of the problems of widowhood, including lower morale and decrease in affiliation, are correlated more with income change than with change in marital status. Thompson, Breckenridge, Gallagher, and Peterson[18] found a greater likelihood of illness for women in lower income brackets. Findings from the present study are in agreement with prior research in that higher income was related to less psychosocial and less physical dysfunction for men and there was a trend for higher income to be associated with less psychosocial dysfunction for women.

A methodological problem likely influenced the findings. The low to moderate reliabilities on the coping subscales suggest that findings on ways of coping need to be viewed as tentative until additional support is provided through future research. It may be that coping is situation-specific, as suggest by Lazarus and Folkman,[29] and therefore utilizing scales developed from a factor analysis of coping responses to a different kind of stressor may not be appropriate for bereavement.

While widows and widowers did not differ in perceived availability or use of most individual resources (exceptions were use of burial customs and quality relationships with the spouse in terms of disagreements), the resources which were related to health functioning varied for the genders. More helpful social support, belief in control, religious beliefs, practicing rituals, absence of other losses with bereavement, and good prior mental-emotional health were associated with less dysfunction for widows. Higher control, more closeness to the spouse, and absence of ambivalent feelings toward the spouse were related to less dysfunction for widowers. Belief in control over bereavement was the only factor associated with both widows' and widowers' physical and psychosocial health; that is, the more perceived control over bereavement, the less physical and psychosocial dysfunction experienced by the individual. The findings suggest relationship factors, namely, more closeness to the spouse and absence of ambivalent feelings toward the spouse are more crucial to the health of widowers following bereavement.

Persons have been found to turn to God and religion during times of grief and bereavement.[25,35,37] Religion is seen as providing a source of meaning and sense of belonging to the bereaved, which in turn positively influences well-being.[40] Berardo[20] found sex differences on the religious variable in his investigation of 181 widows and 44 widowers. In contrast to widowers, widows were found to increase their church attendance following bereavement. Findings from the present study are in agreement with those of Berardo: Women more often attended church and practiced their religion to a higher degree than men following the death of the spouse. In addition, religious belief was a marker associated with the health functioning of widows but not widowers.

Resource strength did not differ for the genders; however, women who had more resources had less dysfunction than women who had fewer resources. There was some evidence that presence of resources decreased the degree of threat perceived for widows. The "other anticipated threat" appraisal group had a lower resource strength than the other two appraisal groups. For men, there was no statistically significant relationship between health dysfunction and resource strength. This finding may be due to there being few differences in individual resources among widowers who appraised their bereavement differently. The results suggest that the health of widows may be more keenly affected by the presence or absence of resources.

It is important to note that correlations between resources and the health dysfunction measures were weak to moderate. Also, most of the resources were not found to be significantly associated with either dysfunction measure. A comparatively healthy sample of widows and widowers, evidenced by the low mean and modal dysfunction scores, may account for the low correlations. Correlations between resources and the health dysfunction measures might have been greater with a less healthy sample. Nonsignificant findings may also be a reflection of the AR instrument, which consists of 16 items, with 1 item for each resource. A single item to measure a construct gives only an approximate or rough measurement. In addition, little variability in responses on a few resource items, such as previous experiences with losses through death, likely contributed to nonsignificant findings.

These results suggest that the health of widows and widowers is influenced by the appraisal of bereavement, the appraisal's relationship to coping, and the coping resources. Appraisal, coping, and resources may be useful markers to help identify widowed persons who are at risk for less healthy outcomes to bereavement.

Practical Implications

The findings have practical implications for professionals who help the bereaved cope with conjugal loss. Ways of coping employed by widows are reflections of threat appraisal. Professionals need to be aware that higher threat may be associated with less adaptive ways of coping, such as self-esteem or wishful thinking. Individuals working with the bereaved may need to develop strategies which facilitate a more positive reappraisal of bereavement and widowhood, especially for widowed persons who appraise their bereavement as being threatening. Research is needed to identify the appropriate times to introduce positive reappraisal. Bereavement counseling which addresses adaptive ways to cope with loss and the readjustment process may help widowed persons who are in need of assistance with coping. Professionals may also reduce threat appraisal by mobilizing resources. Focused intervention programs to help widowed persons identify and utilize appropriate coping strategies and resources need to be developed. Gender differences in resources associated with health functioning may need to be considered when developing interventions for the bereaved.

Although tentative, the findings suggest that certain factors may place widows at risk for morbidity following bereavement: appraisal of bereavement as having other anticipated threats; unhelpful social supports; limited belief in one's control over bereavement; perception of religious beliefs as being minimally helpful in understanding or accepting the death; limited use of death and mourning rituals; other losses at the time of bereavement; and a history of poor mental-emotional health. For widowers, such factors include appraisal of bereavement as having other anticipated threats; limited belief in control over bereavement; minimal closeness to spouse; and ambivalent feelings toward the spouse. These is a need to further investigate these and other risk factors in more detail. A clearer identification of risk factors would sensitize professionals to the widowed persons most prone to morbidity following bereavement.

REFERENCES

1. Bornstein, P. E., Clayton, P. J., Halikas, J. A., Maurice, W. L., & Robins, E. (1973). The depression of widowhood after thirteen months. *British Journal of Psychiatry, 122,* 561–566.
2. Clayton, P. J., Halikas, J. A., & Maurice, W. L. (1972). The depression of widowhood. *British Journal of Psychiatry, 120,* 71–78.
3. Glick, J. O., Weiss, R. S., & Parkes, C. M. (1974). *The first year of bereavement.* New York: John Wiley & Sons.
4. Kaprio, J., Koskenvuo, M., & Rita, H. (1987). Mortality after bereavement: A prospective study of 95,647 widowed persons. *American Journal of Public Health, 77,* 283–287.
5. Parkes, C. M. (1964). The effects of bereavement on physical and mental health: A study of the medical records of widows. *British Medical Journal, 2,* 274–279.
6. Rees, W. D., & Lutkins, S. G. (1967). Mortality of bereavement. *British Medical Journal, 4,* 13–16.
7. Brock, A. M. (1984). From wife to widow: A changing lifestyle. *Journal of Gerontological Nursing, 10,* 8–15.
8. Dimond, M. F. (1981). Bereavement and the elderly: A critical review with implications for nursing practice and research. *Journal of Advanced Nursing, 6,* 461–470.
9. Johnson, R. L., Lund, D. A., & Dimond, M. F. (1986). Stress, self-esteem and coping during bereavement among the elderly. *Social Psychology Quarterly, 49,* 273–279.
10. Silverman, P. (1979). *Widow-to-widow program: Final report to the National Institute of Mental Health.* (Administration on Aging, Microfiche No. CF 001 273). Rockville, MD: U.S. Department of Health, Education and Welfare.
11. Parkes, C. M., & Brown, R. J. (1972). Health after bereavement: A controlled study of young Boston widows and widowers. *Psychosomatic Medicine, 34,* 449–461.
12. Maddison, D. (1968). The relevance of conjugal bereavement for preventive psychiatry. *British Journal of Medical Psychology, 41,* 223–233.
13. Madison, D., & Viola, A. (1968). The health of widows in the year following bereavement. *Journal of Psychosomatic Research, 12,* 297–306.
14. Parkes, C. M. (1970). The first year of bereavement: A longitudinal study of the reaction of London widows to the death of their husbands. *Psychiatry, 33,* 444–467.
15. Gallagher, D. E., Breckenridge, J. N., Thompson, L. W., & Peterson, J. A. (1983). Effects of bereavement on indicators of mental health in elderly widows and widowers. *Journal of Gerontology, 38,* 565–571.
16. Gass, K. A. (1987). The health of conjugally bereaved older widows: The role of appraisal, coping and resources. *Research in Nursing and Health, 10,* 39–47.
17. Lund, D. A., Dimond, M. F., Caserta, M. S., Johnson, R. J., Poulton, J. L., & Connelly, J. R. (1985–1986). Identifying elderly with coping difficulties after two years of bereavement. *Omega, 16,* 213–224.
18. Thompson, L. W., Breckenridge, J. N., Gallagher, D. E., & Peterson, J. A. (1984). Effects of bereavement on self-perceptions of physical health in elderly widows and widowers. *Journal of Gerontology, 39,* 309–314.
19. Kastenbaum, R. (1969). Death and bereavement in later life. In A. Kutscher (Ed.), *Death and bereavement* (pp. 28–54). Springfield, IL: Charles C Thomas.
20. Berardo, F. M. (1967). Social adaptation to widowhood among a rural-urban aged population. (Administration on Aging, Microfiche No. CF001 335). Rockville, MD: U.S. Department of Health, Education, and Welfare.
21. Gerber, I., Rusalem, R., Hannon, N., Battin, D., & Arkin, A. (1975). Anticipatory grief and aged widows and widowers. *Journal of Gerontology, 30,* 225–229.
22. Kraus, A. S., & Lilienfeld, A. M. (1959). Some epidemiological aspects of the high mortality rate in the young widowed group. *Journal of Chronic Disease, 10,* 207–217.
23. Ward, A. (1976). Mortality of bereavement. *British Medical Journal, 1,* 700–702.

24. Helsing, K. J., & Szklo, M. (1981). Mortality after bereavement. *American Journal of Epidemiology, 114*, 41–52.
25. Heyman, D. K., & Gianturco, D. T. (1973). Long-term adaptation by the elderly to bereavement. *Journal of Gerontology, 28*, 259–362.
26. Lund, D. A., Caserta, M. S., & Dimond, M. F. (1986). Gender differences through two years of bereavement among the elderly. *The Gerontologist, 26*, 314–320.
27. Marris, P. (1958). *Widows and their families*. London: Routledge and Kegan Paul.
28. Lazarus, R. S. (1966). *Psychological stress and the coping process*. New York: McGraw-Hill.
29. Lazarus, R. S., & Folkman, S. (1984). *Stress, appraisal, and coping*, New York: Springer.
30. Aldwin, C., Folkman, S., Schaefer, C., Coyne, J. C., & Lazarus, R. S. (1980, September). *Ways of coping: A process measure*. Paper presented at the Annual Convention of the American Psychological Association, Montreal, Canada.
31. Coyne, J. C., Aldwin, C., & Lazarus, R. S. (1981). Depression and coping in stressful episodes. *Journal of Abnormal Psychology, 90*, 439–447.
32. Folkman, S., & Lazarus, R. S. (1980). An analysis of coping in a middle-aged community sample. *Journal of Health and Social Behavior, 21*, 219–239.
33. Folkman, S., Lazarus, R. S., Dunkel-Schetter, C., De Longis, A., & Gruen, R. J. (1986). Dynamics of a stressful encounter: Cognitive appraisal, coping, and encounter outcomes. *Journal of Personality and Social Psychology, 50*, 992–1003.
34. Berardo, F. M. (1970). Survivorship and social isolation: The case of the aged widower. *The Family Coordinator, 19*, 11–25.
35. Clark, P. G., Siviski, R. W., & Weiner, R. (1986). Coping strategies of widowers in the first year. *Family Relations, 35*, 425–530.
36. Maddison, D., & Walker, W. L. (1967). Factors affecting the outcome of conjugal bereavement. *British Journal of Psychiatry, 113*, 11057–1067.
37. Parkes, C. M. (1972). *Bereavement: Studies of grief in adult life*. New York: International Universities Press.
38. Bowlby, J. (1980). *Attachment and loss: Loss, sadness and depression*. New York: Basic Books.
39. Lopata, H. Z. (1975). On widowhood: Grief work and identity reconstruction. *Journal of Geriatric Psychiatry, 8*, 41–55.
40. Wuthrow, R., Christiano, K., & Kuzlowski, J. (1980). Religion and bereavement: A conceptual framework. *Journal of the Scientific Study of Religion, 19*, 408–422.
41. Clayton, P. J., Halikas, J. A., Maurice, W. L., & Robins, E. (1973). Anticipatory grief and widowhood. *British Journal of Psychiatry, 122*, 47–51.
42. Parkes, C. M. (1975). Determinants of outcome following bereavement. *Omega, 6*, 303–323.
43. Blank, R. H. (1969). Mourning. In A. H. Kutscher (Ed.), *Death and bereavement* (pp.204–206). Springfield, IL: Charles C. Thomas.
44. Bugen, L. A. (1977). Human grief: A model for prediction and intervention. *American Journal of Orthopsychiatry, 47*, 196–207.
45. Barry, M. (1973). The prolonged grief reaction. *Mayo Clinic Proceedings, 48*, 329–335.
46. Atchley, R. C. (1975). Dimensions of widowhood in later life. *The Gerontologist, 15*, 176–178.
47. Morgan, L. A. (1976). A re-examination of widowhood and morale. *Journal of Gerontology, 31*, 687–695.
48. Litman, G. K., Eiser, J. R., Rawson, N. S., & Oppenheim, A. N. (1979). Differences in relapse precipitants and coping behavior between alcohol relapsers and survivors. *Behavioral Research and Therapy, 17*, 89–94.
49. Jalowiec, A., & Powers, M. J. (1981). Stress and coping in hypertensive and emergency room patients. *Nursing Research, 30*, 10–15.
50. Gilson, B. S., Bergner, M., Bobbitt, R. A., & Carter, W. (1978). *The SIP: Final development and testing, 1975-1978*. Seattle, WA: University of Washington, Department of Health and Community Medicine.
51. Bergner, M., Bobbitt, R. A., Pollard, W. E., Martin, D. P., & Gilson, B. S. (1976). The sickness impact profile: Validation of a health status measure. *Medical Care, 14*, 57–67.
52. Harvey, C. D., & Bahr, H. M. (1974). Widowhood, morale and affiliation. *Journal of Marriage and the Family, 36*, 97–106.

8

Health of Older Widowers: Role of Appraisal, Coping, Resources, and Type of Spouse's Death

Kathleen A. Gass

The relationships between appraisal of bereavement, coping, resources, spouse's type of death, and health dysfunction were investigated in 59 older men (mean age = 71.1 years) who were widowed from 1 to 12 months prior to home interview. Widowers were compared on health status with 59 nonbereaved married controls (mean age = 71.1 years) who were matched by age and religion. Seven hypotheses derived from Lazarus's Stress-Coping Framework were tested. Data collection included the use of Folkman and Lazarus's Ways of Coping Checklist; Gilson, Bergner, Bobbitt, and Carter's Sickness Impact Profile; a subjective health rating using a Cantril ladder; and an assessment of the subjects' appraisal of bereavement, extent of resources, and spouse's type of death. Nonbereaved controls had significantly less physical ($t(116)$ = 2.02, $p < .05$) and psychosocial ($t(116)$ = 5.22, $p < .001$) dysfunction than widowers. There were no significant differences in subjective health ratings. Appraisal groups did not significantly differ in ways of coping; however, type of spouse's death was related to coping. Widowers whose spouse had died suddenly used more problem-focused, wishful thinking, self-blame, overall emotion-focused, and overall problem-focused coping as well as higher numbers of coping strategies than widowers whose spouse had died from a chronic illness. Control over bereavement, closeness to spouse, and absence of ambivalent feelings toward the deceased were related to less psychosocial or physical dysfunction. More closeness to spouse, absence of ambivalent feelings, and perception of having adequate finances were significantly related to higher health ratings. More coping strategies or resources were not significantly related to any of the health measures.

This research was supported by a Biomedical Science Research Grant and a grant from the School of Nursing, University of Wisconsin-Madison.

The author wishes to thank Dale A. Lund, Ph.D., for his careful review and helpful feedback on this paper.

There is increasing evidence that bereavement adversely affects the physical and psychological well-being of individuals. It is well documented that the death of a spouse can be extremely stressful[1] and the surviving spouse runs the risk of becoming ill or dying.[2-8]

Researchers who have studied mortality following bereavement have found widowed persons to have higher mortality rates than married nonbereaved persons,[5,9-12] with the greatest risk being shortly after bereavement.[5,13,14] In two investigations, the mortality rate of the bereaved did not exceed the rates of matched controls,[3,15] which may have been because of methodological differences (i.e., smaller samples were studied for shorter time periods).

Investigators studying morbidity following bereavement showed that widowed persons have more physical and mental illness than married nonbereaved control subjects. Gallagher, Breckenridge, Thompson, and Peterson[16] found bereaved spouses had significantly higher mean scores on the Beck Depression Inventory, the Severity Index from the Brief Symptom Inventory, and the Texas Inventory of Grief than did nonbereaved controls. Thompson, Breckenridge, Gallagher, and Peterson[17] investigated multiple indices of self-perceived physical health for 162 controls and for 113 older widows and 99 widowers 2 months after the death of the spouse. Although there were no differences in physician visits and hospitalizations, the widowed reported significantly more recently developed or worsened illnesses, greater use of new and prior medications, and poorer health ratings than the controls. Parkes and Brown,[7] comparing health indices for 68 bereaved widowed and matched controls, found that at 13 months the bereaved had more disturbances in sleep, changes of appetite and weight, depression, restlessness, strain, difficulty making decisions, and use of alcohol, tobacco, and tranquilizers. Bereaved and control groups did not differ significantly in self-reports of general health, but the bereaved were more likely to have been hospitalized during the preceding year. No significant differences were observed by Clayton[18] between bereaved and controls in health ratings or reported number of physical symptoms, physician visits, and hospitalizations during a 1-year period.

According to several studies, men are at greater risk for mortality and morbidity following the death of a spouse.[7,8,11,19-22] Jacobs and Ostfeld[5] concluded that the risk for morbidity was greater for men at all ages, particularly within 6 months following the bereavement. In comparing male and female widowed persons over 65 to married controls, Berardo[23] found a greater incidence of health problems in the widowed, with proportionately more poor health in widowers than in widows. Health problems increased with age of the bereaved. Parkes, Murray, and Fitzgerald[24] found a trend toward increased mortality risk among widowers as one went up the class scales. However, Lund, Caserta, and Dimond[25] and Gallagher et al.[16] found no significant differences between males and females in psychosocial morbidity. Conflicting findings and differential mortality and morbidity rates between widowers and widows indicate a need to investigate factors affecting the adaptation of men following bereavement.[26]

The type of death has been found to be associated with health outcomes following bereavement. Forewarning of death, which allows for potential anticipatory grieving, has been found to have a salutary effect on the adjustment of the widowed,[4,27] while sudden death of a loved one may contribute to more physical and mental distress in the bereaved and more intense grief reactions.[28-30] Anticipatory grief, it has been suggested, possesses adaptational value for the bereaved, in that the individual has the opportunity to begin to work through grief reactions, to prepare for necessary adjustments, and to make amends for wrongs done to the ill spouse by providing the spouse with special care and attention.[4,31] Lundin[29] studied 130 close relatives 8 years after bereavement and found that widowed persons whose spouses died suddenly had more pronounced grief reactions than when the death was expected.

The relatives of a person who died suddenly showed increased mourning, guilt feelings, numbness, and need to cry and missed the deceased person more. Lundin[32] found that sudden and unexpected loss resulted in a significantly higher morbidity rate during the first 2 years after bereavement than did expected loss. Sanders[31] interviewed 86 bereaved persons shortly after the death of a spouse or child and 18 months later. She found no statistically significant differences when the deceased died suddenly or died following a short- or long-term chronic illness; however, analysis of the data indicated some important trends. For example, the short-term chronic illness group had the most favorable adjustment to bereavement. The sudden death group had an internalized "anger-in" emotional response which produced prolonged physical stress. An "anger-out" response was characteristic of the long-term chronic illness group; this response did not sustain physical stress. High levels of social isolation were found in the long-term chronic illness group. Based on trends, Sanders concluded that there appears to be value in some preparation for loss as long as it is not over a protracted time period, which results in withdrawal of support.

Gerber, Rusalem, Hannon, Battin, and Arkin[22] found no significant differences in initial adjustment between individuals whose spouses died from acute illness and those whose spouses died from chronic illness; however, the bereaved who had protracted anticipatory grief had poorer medical adjustment 6 months after the loss (indicated by more physician office visits) and more occasions when they felt ill but did not contact a physician. Widowers did more poorly than widows in cases where the spouse cared for the loved one over an extended period of time. Clayton, Halikas, Maurice, and Robins[33] found that bereaved survivors (M age = 61) who experienced anticipatory grief were not significantly more depressed 1 year after the death than participants who had experienced the unexpected death of a spouse.

Much of the research on widowed persons to date has focused on morbidity and mortality outcomes associated with the death of a spouse. More recently, researchers have begun to focus on factors associated with adaptation to widowhood.[26] Because not all persons experience the same degree of morbidity or mortality following bereavement, variables which minimize these outcomes likely exist. Identification of factors which enable some individuals to be resilient in the face of stressors may expedite the task of translating research findings into prevention strategies. The type of stress appraisal, type of death, coping processes, and resources may be key factors which influence health outcomes.[34,35]

The purpose of this study was to examine (1) differences in health between bereaved widowers and married controls; (2) the appraisal of bereavement, coping patterns, resources, and health functioning of aged widowers within the context of Lazarus's Stress-Coping Framework; and (3) the influence of the type of death on the appraisal of bereavement, the coping, the resources, and the health of widowers.

THEORETICAL FRAMEWORK

According to Lazarus and Folkman,[35] appraisal, coping, and the presence of resources are interrelated and associated with health following stressful experiences. Whether bereavement is perceived as a threat depends on how it is appraised and whether coping strategies and resources are available to the surviving spouse.[34] Primary appraisal involves the meaning of the situation to the individual. According to this model, there are three types of stress appraisal: (1) harm or loss, which refers to the damage that has already occurred; (2) anticipated threat, which refers to the harm or loss that has not yet occurred; and (3) challenge, which refers to an opportunity for mastery or gain.[36] Stress appraisals call for the mobilization of coping efforts. Nonstress appraisals include irrelevant and benign-positive appraisals and do not require coping. When an event is evaluated as carrying no implications for the person's well-being, it is considered irrelevant. The person has no investment in the outcome, and thus there is nothing to be lost or gained. Benign-positive appraisal occurs if the outcome of the event is viewed as positive, that is, if the individual evaluates the event as preserving or enhancing well-being. Since the present study focused on the coping patterns of widowers, only participants who reported their bereavement to be stressful were interviewed.

Lazarus posited that appraisal influences the ways of coping employed to deal with a stressor. Stress reactions manifest themselves in health status and are reflections or consequences of coping processes. Secondary appraisal takes into account the coping options that are available to the person. Coping is defined as constantly changing cognitive and behavioral efforts in order to manage specific external or internal demands that are appraised as taxing or exceeding the resources of the person.

Psychological, social, and material resources affect appraisal and coping and, in turn, influence the degree of stress experienced. A person appraises an event as a threat or nonthreat by considering his or her available resources. Resources strengthen the individual's position with respect to the stressor. Some of the resources believed to be associated with health following bereavement include helpful social supports;[32,37] practicing rituals and beliefs which facilitate the grieving process;[38] possessing religious beliefs which foster an acceptance or understanding of death;[2,39] knowledge of the grieving process through previous experiences with loss and receiving information on grieving or widowhood from others;[33,40] opportunities for anticipatory grieving;[4,27] a prior history of good mental-emotional health;[40] absence of additional losses concurrent with bereavement;[37] a quality relationship with the spouse characterized by a healthy degree of closeness, minimal dependency, and lack of prolonged conflict or ambivalent feelings;[41] perception of the spouse's death as unpreventable;[42] the ability to openly express grief;[43] belief in control over stressors;[44] and adequate financial status.[45] Johnson, Lund, and Dimond[46] have also found self-esteem to be a resource which reduced early bereavement stress.

Situational factors also can positively or negatively influence appraisal, coping, resources, and health outcome. The novelty, predictability, or uncertainty of the event, as well as its imminence and duration, can affect reactions to a stressor.[34] The type of death (sudden versus chronic illness death) may be a situational factor of importance to bereavement outcomes.[4,27-29]

Seven hypotheses derived from Lazarus's theoretical framework were tested in the present study: (1) Bereaved widowers have higher health dysfunction and lower self-rating of health than nonbereaved married controls. (2) There are differences in the ways of coping with conjugal bereavement among aged widowers who appraise their bereavement differently. (3) There is a relationship between the individual ways of coping with bereavement used by aged widowers and health. (4) There is a relationship between the varying degrees of individual resources available to aged widowers and health. (5) The use of more coping strategies (coping strength) is negatively associated with health dysfunction and positively associated with better health ratings. (6) The presence of more psychological, social, and material resources (resource strength) is negatively associated with health dysfunction and positively associated with better health ratings. (7) There are differences in appraisal of bereavement, ways of coping, individual resources, coping strength, resource strength, and health between widowers whose spouses died suddenly and those who spouses died following a chronic illness.

METHOD

Sample

The participants in this study were 59 bereaved widowers and 59 nonbereaved married men (the controls). Pastors of Catholic parishes in several midwestern cities were contacted and their assistance was sought in obtaining names of widowers and nonbereaved married men. Burial records were used to identify widowers. Widowers who were 54 or over, who perceived their bereavement as stressful, who had not remarried or were not institutionalized, and whose spouse had died 1–12 months previously were sent a letter of explanation and an invitation to participate in the study. Of the 84 widowers contacted, 25 declined participation, yielding a refusal rate of 30%.

The names of nonbereaved controls were obtained from the parish registry and church records. The controls were married and had not experienced the death of a close relative or friend within the past year. It is important to note that this may be relatively brief amount of time, since bereavement adjustments can last many years for some individuals. The researcher believed, however, that it was a reasonable amount of time for most persons to work through the grieving process. Also, none of the control participants had lost a prior spouse through death. Controls were matched by age and religion with the bereaved.

Widowers ranged in age from 54 to 86 ($M = 71.1$ years, $SD = 7.94$), and controls ranged in age from 54 to 85 ($M = 71.1$ years, $SD = 7.93$). All widowers and controls were white and Catholic. Sixty-five percent of the widowers and 80% of the controls had completed high school or had a higher level of education. Incomes ranged from $3,000 to over $11,000 a year, with 93% of the widowers and 98% of the controls reporting an income over $7,000. The widowers had been bereaved from 35 to 364 days ($M = 189$ days, $SD = 102.90$) at the time of the interview. The spouses of 31% of the widowers had died a sudden death while 69% had suffered death following a chronic illness. The widowers had cared for their spouses before death from 0 to 6,570 days ($M = 596$ days, $SD = 1233.38$).

Procedure

Within one week after receiving the letter of explanation and invitation, potential participants were contacted by telephone. For widowers who consented to participate, a home interview was scheduled. At that time, the researcher or a trained research specialist administered the structured interview, which included the Appraisal of Bereavement Questionnaire, the Ways of Coping Checklist, the Assessment of Resources, the Sickness Impact Profile, the Self-rating of Health Questionnaire, and a demographic data form. The questionnaires were administered randomly to control for order effects. Interviews with bereaved participants ranged from 1 to 3 hours. One hour was needed for completion of the questionnaires; however, many respondents had concerns or questions about bereavement or grieving that were addressed by the interviewer following completion of the questionnaires. The controls were interviewed after the widowers, since controls were matched to them on age and religion. The interview for controls ranged from 30 to 45 minutes and included random order administration of the Sickness Impact Profile and the Self-rating of Health Questionnaire and the filling out of the demographic data form.

To assess appraisal of bereavement, widowers were asked to chose one of three statements which reflected how they perceived their bereavement. Choosing "a harmful loss without other losses" meant that the widower perceived the spouse's death as a great personal loss but believed there were no other bereavement-related losses, fears, or problems he could not handle. Widowers who reported "other anticipated threats" believed they would not be able to manage and viewed bereavement as a loss accompanied by many anticipated losses, fears, and problems. Widowers who appraised their bereavement as "a challenge" viewed widowhood as a growth experience and were determined to overcome or master the loss.

Folkman and Lazarus's[36] Ways of Coping Checklist was used to measure coping. This 68-item instrument consists of behavioral and cognitive coping strategies a person might use in a specific stressful situation. The respondent answers yes or no to items which are classified into overall problem-focused and emotion-focused coping categories or into seven different ways of coping, namely, problem-focused, wishful thinking, mixed (help-seeking/avoidance), growth, minimizes threat, seeks social support, and self-blame. Scoring involved summing the number of ways of coping answered yes for each subscale. A coping strength score was obtained by adding the total number of coping strategies used by the respondent, including both desirable and less desirable ones. Cronbach alphas in the present study for the subscales were as follows: overall problem-focused (α = .56), overall emotion-focused (α = .74), problem-focused (α = .37), wishful thinking (α = .72), mixed (α = .58), growth (α = .49), minimizes threat (α = .47), seeks social support (α = .34), and self-blame (α = .56). Reliabilities were lower than those based on data from a community sample who coped with the stressful events of daily living[36] and may reflect differences in the samples investigated. It is possible that coping is situation-specific[35] and using coping scales developed from a factor analysis of coping responses to a different type of stressor may be inappropriate for bereavement.

The Assessment of Resources (AR) instrument was developed from items drawn from the research and theoretical literature relative to psychological, social, and material factors which may affect the bereavement outcome. Resources were described earlier in this chapter. The AR was scored based on the extent to which each individual resource was present. Resource strength was the sum of the scores on the 16 items of the AR. Additional information on the AR instrument is reported elsewhere.[47]

Health was defined in terms of physical and psychosocial dysfunction and an overall subjective health rating. The physical and psychosocial dimension subscales of the Gilson, Bergner, Bobbitt, and Carter,[48] Sickness Impact Profile (SIP) were used. The SIP is a behaviorally based measure of sickness-related dysfunction and it provides a reliable and valid measure of health functioning. Items address everyday activities and reflect the person's perception of his or her performance of these activities. Subjects respond to only those items that describe them today and are related to their health. The physical dimension score is calculated by adding the scale values for each item checked within categories for this dimension, dividing by the maximum possible dysfunction score for these categories, and multiplying by 100. The psychosocial dimension score is obtained in a similar manner. For both dimensions, the larger the percentage score, the greater the impairment of health functioning. Additional information on the SIP, including reliability data, is presented elsewhere.[47]

A self-rating of overall health was obtained using a Cantril ladder.[49] This ladder consists of an equal interval 10-point scale ranging from 0 (lack of health) to 9 (perfect health). Engle and Graney,[50] using an adapted version of the Cantril ladder with more than 400 elderly subjects, reported a reliability of .60. Subjects were asked to rate their present health. The higher the score, the better the health.

The type of death was assessed by asking respondents to answer a single item: "Was your spouse's death sudden or following a chronic illness?" In addition, respondents were asked to state the cause of death and to describe in detail the circumstances surrounding the death, thereby permitting the researcher to confirm the accuracy of the type of death. The distinction between sudden death and chronic illness death was not contingent on a specific medical condition. The major differentiating factor was the history of the illness causing death. A sudden death occurred without warning from or prior knowledge of a chronic health condition. A chronic illness death was any health problem supported by multiple occurrences or hospitalizations. No participants had difficulty classifying his spouse's death as either a sudden or chronic illness death. However, 10 of the widowers reported that the death was a chronic illness death but sudden; that is, the wife had a history of one or more chronic illnesses which had been getting worse, but the husband did not expect her to die so quickly. These ten widowers were classified as having experienced a chronic illness death of a spouse.

RESULTS

Descriptive data analysis indicated that the sample was a relatively healthy group of widowers and nonbereaved married men. The widowers' mean physical and psychosocial dysfunction scores and health rating were 7.69% (SD = 8.84), 13.60% (SD = 10.28), and 6.02 (SD = 1.72) respectively. For the controls, the mean physical and psychosocial dysfunction scores and health rating were 4.68% (SD = 7.27), 4.69% (SD = 8.12), and 6.34 (SD = 1.92) respectively. Maximum possible scores were 100% physical and 100% psychosocial dysfunction. A score of 9 was the highest possible self-rating of health and indicated perfect overall health. The mode on the SIP measures for both bereaved and control respondents was 0% dysfunction. On self-rating of health, the mode was 5 for widowers and 7 for controls. The SIP physical and SIP psychosocial dysfunction scores for widowers were significantly correlated ($r = .70, p < .001$). Widowers' health rating scores were significantly related to SIP physical ($r = -.51, p < .001$) and SIP psychosocial ($r = -.47, p < .001$) dysfunction scores. For control participants, the SIP physical and psychosocial dysfunction scores were significantly correlated ($r .51, p < .001$), and the health rating scores were significantly associated with physical ($r = -.58, p < .001$) and psychosocial ($r = -.39, p < .01$) dysfunction scores.

The first hypothesis, that bereaved widowers will have higher health dysfunction and lower self-rating of health than nonbereaved married control participants, was partially supported. Significant differences were found between bereaved and controls on physical and psychosocial dysfunction. Widowers had higher physical [$t(116) = 2.02, p < .05$] and psychosocial [$t(116) = 5.22, p < .001$] dysfunction than matched controls. There were no significant differences, however, in self-rating of health [$t(116) = -.96, p = .34$].

The second hypothesis, that there are differences in coping by widowers who appraised their bereavement differently, was not supported. Thirty widowers (50.8%) appraised their bereavement as a challenge, while 22 (37.3%) perceived it as a harmful loss without other losses. Seven widowers (11.9%) reported that they would not be able to manage and viewed their bereavement as having other anticipated threats. The three appraisal groups did not differ in their use of problem-focused [$F(2, 56) = .13, p = .88$], wishful thinking [$F(2, 56) = 1.01, p = .37$], mixed [$F(2, 56) = 2.37, p = .10$], growth [$F(2, 56) = .95, p = .39$], minimizes threat [$F(2, 56) = .42, p = .66$], seeks social support [$F(2, 56) = .36, p = .70$], self-blame [$F(2, 56) = 2.55, p = .09$], overall emotion-focused [$F(2, 56) = 1.09, p = .34$], or overall problem-focused [$F(2, 56) = .63, p = .54$] coping.

The third hypothesis, that there is a relationship between ways of coping and health, was not supported. The Pearson product-moment coefficients of ways of coping with the health measures are presented in Table 1. The only exception to this lack of support was that the more self-blame coping used by widowers, the higher their psychosocial dysfunction. Physical health dysfunction and self-rating of health were not significantly associated with any of the ways of coping. Because only 1 of the 33 statistical tests was significant, this finding may be due to chance and therefore should be noted with caution.

The fourth hypothesis, which focused on the relationship between individual resources and health, was partially supported. The Pearson correlation coefficients and biserial coefficients for this hypothesis are presented in Table 2. Biserial correlation coefficients are used when one variable is measured on a nominal scale but has an underlying continuity and is normally distributed and the other variable is measured on at least an interval scale. Biserial correlation coefficients were calculated for resources which had dichotomous responses. The more the widowers believed that they were in control of their bereavement and the closer they had felt to the spouse, the lower their physical and psychosocial dysfunction. Absence of ambivalent feelings toward the deceased spouse was significantly related to lower

TABLE 1   Pearson Correlation Coefficients of Ways of Coping, Coping Strength, and Resource Strength with Health Measures

Ways of coping	Physical dysfunction (r)	Psychosocial dysfunction (r)	Self-rating of health (r)
Problem focused	−.07	−.18	−.14
Wishful thinking	.10	.25	−.14
Mixed	.11	.21	−.13
Growth	−.16	−.08	.06
Minimizes threat	.24	.12	−.09
Seeks social support	−.01	−.01	−.09
Self-blame	.06	.28*	−.19
Overall emotion-focused	−.16	−.11	−.21
Overall problem-focused	.18	.25	−.02
Coping strength	.08	.16	−.17
Resource strength	−.12	−.17	.12

*p < .05, two-tailed.

psychosocial dysfunction. Closeness to the spouse, absence of ambivalent feelings, and adequacy of finances were significantly related to better self-rating of health. There was a trend for control over bereavement to be associated with better self-ratings of health ($r = .21, p = .10$).

The fifth hypothesis, which focused on the relationship between total number of coping strategies used by widowers and health, and the sixth hypothesis, which posited a relationship between total amount of resources and health, were not supported for any of the health measures (see Table 1). Use of greater numbers of coping strategies and perception of more resources were not significantly related to lower psychosocial and physical health dysfunction or better health rating.

TABLE 2   Pearson and Biserial Correlation Coefficients of Resources with Health Measures

Resources	Physical dysfunction (r)	Psychosocial dysfunction (r)	Self-rating of health (r)
Social support	−.11	−.15	.12
Rituals practiced	−.06	−.22	.05
Religious beliefs	.12	−.00	.05
Lets out emotions	−.07	−.06	−.03
Control over bereavement	−.30*	−.36**	.21
Closeness to spouse	.31*	.28*	−.30*
Dependency on spouse	.10	−.11	.02
Disagreements/conflicts with spouse	−.19	−.11	.19
Ambivalent feelings toward spouse	−.25	−.40†	.26*
		r_{bis}	
Information on grieving/widowhood	.10	.16	−.08
Previous experiences with losses	.02	−.06	−.08
Anticipatory grieving	.16	.18	.05
Good prior mental-emotional health	−.14	−.15	−.04
No other losses with bereavement	−.14	−.17	−.01
Death not preventable	−.15	−.11	.10
Adequacy of finances	−.09	−.00	.23*

*p < .05. **p < .01. †p ≤ .001, two-tailed.

Additional one-way ANOVAs were done to examine differences among appraisal groups on dysfunction, health ratings, coping strength, and resource strength. The Scheffé procedure, used because of unequal cell sizes for appraisal groups, showed that widowers with other anticipated threats had higher psychosocial dysfunction [$F(2, 56) = 3.68, p < .05$] and physical dysfunction [$F(2, 56) = 3.31, p < .05$] than the other two appraisal groups. Appraisal groups did not significantly differ in self-health rating [$F(2, 56) = 1.42, p = .25$], coping strength [$F(2, 56) = 1.13, p = .33$], and resource strength [$F(2, 56) = .96, p = .39$].

The seventh hypothesis, that there are differences in appraisal, coping, resources, coping strength, resource strength, and health between widowers whose spouses died suddenly and those whose spouses died following a chronic illness, was partially supported. Widowers whose spouses died following a chronic illness more often appraised their bereavement as a harmful loss or a challenge, while widowers whose spouses died suddenly more frequently appraised their bereavement as having other anticipated threats [$X^2(2, N = 59) = 6.95, p < .05$]. In Table 3, the means, standard deviations, and t-test results on the ways of coping, coping strength, resource strength, and health scores for type of death are presented.

There were differences in several ways of coping for type of death. Widowers whose spouses had died suddenly used more problem-focused, wishful thinking, self-blame, overall emotion-focused, and overall problem-focused coping as well as higher numbers of coping strategies than widowers whose spouses had died following a chronic illness. There were also differences in two of the resources. Widowers whose spouses died following a chronic illness reported receiving more social support [$X^2(1, N = 59) = 6.55, p < .05$] as well as more opportunity for constructive anticipatory grieving [$X^2(1, N = 59) = 14.38, p < .0001$] than those whose spouses had died suddenly. These two groups of men did not differ significantly in resource strength.

There were no statistically significant differences in physical or psychosocial dysfunction or health rating between these two groups of men. However, there was a trend toward higher psychosocial dysfunction ($r = -.22, p = .09$) and lower health rating ($r = .22, p = .09$) for widowers whose spouses had died suddenly.

In summary, widowers had significantly higher physical and psychosocial health dysfunction but not a lower health rating than nonbereaved controls. Appraisal groups did not differ in their use of ways of coping; however, the type of death was related to the coping strategies used. Widowers whose spouses had died suddenly used more problem-focused, wishful thinking, self-blame, overall emotion-focused, and overall problem-focused coping and more coping strategies than widowers whose spouse had died following a chronic illness. There were significant differences in appraisal, social support, and opportunity for anticipatory grieving but no differences in health or resource strength between these two groups of men.

Use of more self-blame coping was significantly related to higher psychosocial dysfunction. No other ways of coping were significantly related to health. Control over bereavement, more closeness to the spouse, absence of ambivalent feelings toward the deceased, and adequate finances were significantly related to health. Use of higher numbers of coping strategies and higher amounts of re-

TABLE 3   Means, Standard Deviations, and T-Test Analysis on the Ways of Coping, Coping Strength, Resource Strength, and Health Scores for Widowers Whose Spouses Died a Sudden Death versus a Chronic Illness Death

Subscale	Sudden death (n = 18)		Chronic illness death (n = 41)		
	M	SD	M	SD	T
Problem focused	6.33	2.09	5.22	1.80	2.09*
Wishful thinking	13.28	3.16	10.66	3.40	2.78**
Mixed	3.06	2.24	2.34	1.74	1.33
Growth	3.67	1.88	3.24	1.59	.89
Minimizes threat	3.72	1.67	3.54	1.38	.45
Seeks social support	2.61	.70	2.49	.71	.62
Self-blame	1.17	.99	.54	.81	2.57**
Overall emotion-focused	22.06	5.89	18.27	4.56	2.68**
Overall problem-focused	11.11	2.85	9.51	2.86	1.98*
Coping strength	33.83	8.16	28.02	6.56	2.90**
Resource strength	27.21	3.45	28.57	3.10	− 1.51
Physical dysfunction	9.94	9.06	6.70	8.67	1.30
Psychosocial dysfunction	16.99	9.25	12.11	10.46	1.71
Self-rating of health	5.44	1.72	6.27	1.67	− 1.73

Note. df = 57.
*p < .05. **p < .01.

sources were not related to less dysfunction or better health rating, contrary to what was predicted. Finally, widowers who appraised their bereavement as having other anticipated threats had higher psychosocial and physical dysfunction than the other appraisal groups.

DISCUSSION

Nonbereaved married controls had less physical and psychosocial dysfunction than widowers, confirming that bereavement is a stressful event which influences both physical and psychosocial health. These findings are in agreement with prior research findings which showed that the bereaved are at greater risk for morbidity than the nonbereaved.[7,10,16,17] No significant differences were found between widowers and controls on self-ratings of health. One explanation is that the widowers' ratings of health were inflated because they expected their health to be worse than they actually found it to be following bereavement. Relative to what they anticipated, their overall health was not so bad. While self-rating of health was significantly correlated with the dysfunction measures, it was only significantly related to a few variables, namely, closeness to spouse, absence of ambivalent feelings, and adequate finances. Several factors may have been responsible for there being so few significant findings for the self-rating of health measure. When men were rating their health, they often did so in terms of their age or compared themselves to friends who were their age. Some older men expected to be in imperfect health and to have several health problems because of their age, and they often rated their health at the lower end of the scale. Other widowers may have heard that they were supposed to be in poorer health because of bereavement, and this may have influenced their health ratings. Some widowers also evaluated themselves primarily in terms of physical health while others took into consideration both physical and mental health when rating overall health. Thus, it is important to specify physical health or psychological health or both when asking individuals to rate their health. Also, it may be that it takes a longer time for bereavement to impact on physical health because ill effects resulting from changes in nutrition, exercise patterns, and roles take time to develop. Additional research is necessary to further clarify and explain why the statistically significant findings for the self-rating of health measure were so limited.

A major premise advanced by Lazarus is that the type of appraisal influences coping: Higher degrees of threat appraisal lead to inadequate solutions to stressors while more adaptive, reality-oriented forms of coping are more likely to occur when a threat is mild. Findings from the present study do not provide support for this premise. Widowers with other anticipated threats, the highest threat appraisal group, used types and amounts of coping similar to widowers who appraised their bereavement as a challenge or without other losses. Lack of significant differences in coping by widowers who appraised their bereavement differently may be due to the low Cronbach alphas on the ways of coping. Also, that there were only a small number of subjects and so many categories of coping may have contributed to nonsignificant findings. Appraisal and coping are processes which can change over time. A longitudinal investigation is needed to sort out ongoing relationships, such as the influence of appraisals on the use of specific coping strategies, which can result in reappraisal of bereavement and also, as a consequence, in changed coping strategies.

Coping appears to be a reflection of the type of death, which seems to influence the degree of threat appraisal. Widowers whose spouses died suddenly used more problem-focused, wishful thinking, self-blame, overall emotion-focused, and overall problem-focused coping and more coping strategies than widowers whose spouses died following a chronic illness. The former more often appraised their bereavement as having other anticipated threats while the latter appraised their bereavement more as a challenge or a loss without other losses. Higher threat appraisal may cause widowers whose spouses died suddenly to need to use more ways of coping to manage their bereavement. These findings suggest that this group experiences more stress with which they must cope. It may be that widowers whose spouses died after a chronic illness death have had time to develop a repertoire of coping strategies to help them to manage prior to and after bereavement. In the case of a sudden death, spouses would not have had this preparation time to develop or muster their coping strategies to help them deal with the stress of bereavement.

Widowers whose spouses died following a chronic illness might have had more helpful social supports and more opportunity for constructive anticipatory grieving than those whose spouses died suddenly. Helpful social supports and opportunity for anticipatory grieving may have reduced the threat of loss and facilitated adaptation to bereavement. Social support may reduce the loneliness associated with the loss and provide guidance, confidants, and instrumental assistance (e.g., help with cooking and cleaning) that may reduce the threat of bereavement.[26,51] In addition, social interactions with significant others are important for stabilizing the self-concept,[52] which in turn might impact on outcomes to bereavement. Anticipatory grieving has been found to have adaptational value for the bereaved.[4,27] As one widower stated, "Her sickness brought us closer together. It wasn't too much of a surprise. I saw her go downhill. It was a blessing she went [as painlessly] as she did." For this widower, forewarning of the death gave him time to prepare for the loss, begin to work through grief, and provide his wife with extra attention and special care, which brought them closer together. Findings from the present study suggest that support and anticipatory grief may be beneficial, in that there was a trend for widowers whose spouses died following a chronic illness to have less psychosocial dysfunction and higher health ratings than those whose spouses died suddenly. Research is needed on the specific anticipatory behaviors that are engaged in by widowed persons and how each affects outcome. For example, it might not be reasonable to assume that anticipatory grief could reduce feelings of loneliness that emerge several months later. More detailed research is needed on the resources of those whose spouses die suddenly or following a chronic illness and the influence of these resources on their health.

Findings suggested that widowers who appraised their bereavement as a harmful loss associated with other anticipated threats had more physical and psychosocial health dysfunction than did other widowers. This finding is in agreement with Lazarus's theoretical premise that types of appraisal influence health. Lazarus infers that adequacy of coping in threat reduction is reflected in the health outcome (defined in terms of functioning, morale, and somatic health). However, the length of time required for coping to affect health has not been posited or evaluated. The higher psychosocial dysfunction of widowers who perceived other anticipated threats suggests that their greater use of self-blame coping may not be adequate in reducing or eliminating the threats associated with bereavement. Use of more self-blame coping was characteristic of widowers who felt guilty. Guilt feelings arose from not showing enough affection to the spouse, not insisting that the spouse see a physician, not helping out enough at home, not contacting friends who attended the funeral, and not being able to fulfill the roles and responsibilities previously fulfilled by the spouse.

No statistically significant relationships were found between coping strength and the health measures. These findings may be due to little variability in responses to coping items by widowers in the three appraisal groups. Also, use of more coping strategies might be the result of more problems or of coping strategies not working. The low to moderate reliabilities on the coping scales and subscales suggest that findings on ways of coping need to be viewed as tentative until additional findings are provided through future research.

There was some evidence that presence of resources decreased the degree of threat perceived. Belief in control over bereavement, a relationship with the spouse characterized by closeness and no ambivalent feelings, and adequate finances were related to lower health dysfunction or better health rating. However, correlations between these resources and the health measures were weak to moderate. Most of the other resources were not significantly associated with the health measures. Two factors may account for the low and nonsignificant correlations: (1) a healthy sample of widowers (as evidenced by the low mean and modal dysfunction scores) and (2) the type of measurement instrument used to assess resources. The AR instrument consisted to 16 items, with 1 item for each resource. A single item to measure a construct allows only an approximate or rough measurement. Correlations between resources and the health measures might be greater with a less healthy sample of subjects and a multiple-item, Likert-scale instrument to measure resources. In addition, little variability in responses on a few resource items, such as previous experiences with losses through death, may have contributed to the absence of significant findings. Lack of full support for most of the hypotheses may also have been due to the small number of subjects.

Presence of more resources was not significantly associated with less health dysfunction or better self-rating. One explanation for this finding may be that the men did not vary in the numbers of resources available to them. There were no statistically significant differences in the resource strengths of the appraisal groups. For this reason, it may be difficult to find widowers with more resources having less dysfunction than men with fewer resources.

Practical Implications

These findings have practical implications for professionals and clinicians caring for widowers. One function of supportive caregivers is to help individuals cope. Findings from the present study suggest that the ways of coping employed by widowers are reflections of the type of death of the wife. Higher threat may be associated with the sudden death of a spouse; the suddenness may be associated with less adaptive ways of coping, such as self-blame. Those who assist the bereaved need to be aware that differences in appraisal, social support, and opportunity for anticipatory grieving may also vary for the types of death. Bereavement counseling which addresses adaptive ways to cope with bereavement may help widowers. Those who work with the bereaved need to be sensitive and receptive to the difficulty some widowers may have in expressing their feelings of guilt and grief, since our society so often expects men to hide their emotions and show a "stiff upper lip." Helping men to realistically examine guilt feelings and understand that guilt is a normal part of grief can be beneficial. Caregivers can encourage and support widowers while they learn new roles and assume more responsibility. Helping widowers be patient when learning new skills can help decrease their anxiety. Mobilizing resources may also be helpful. For example, it may be beneficial to foster control over bereavement by supporting widowers' participation in experiences which indicate their potential for control, such as learning to drive a car, taking night school courses on financial or home management, or reading books by persons who have successfully coped with bereavement.

The findings suggest that the sudden death of a spouse, appraisal of bereavement as having other anticipated threats, limited belief in one's control over bereavement, ambivalent feelings toward the spouse, minimal closeness to the spouse, and inadequate finances may place widowers at risk for morbidity following bereavement. Awareness of these and other risk factors will help professionals pinpoint widowers most prone to stress and illness following conjugal loss.

REFERENCES

1. Holmes, T. H., & Rahe, R. H. (1967). The social readjustment of rating scale. *Journal of Psychosomatic Research, 2,* 213–218.
2. Bornstein, P. E., Clayton, P. J., Halikas, J. A., Maurice, W. L., & Robins, E. (1973). The depression of widowhood after thirteen months. *British Journal of Psychiatry, 122,* 561–566.
3. Clayton, P. J., Halikas, J. A., & Maurice, W. L. (1972). The depression of widowhood. *British Journal of Psychiatry, 120,* 71–78.
4. Glick, J. O., Weiss, R. S., & Parkes, C. M. (1974). *The first year of bereavement.* New York: John Wiley & Sons.

5. Jacobs, S., & Ostfeld, A. (1977). An epidemiological review of the mortality of bereavement. *Psychosomatic Medicine, 39,* 344–357.
6. Kaprio, J., Koskenvuo, M., & Rita, H. (1987). Mortality after bereavement: A prospective study of 95,647 widowed persons. *American Journal of Public Health, 77,* 283–287.
7. Parkes, C. M., & Brown, R. J. (1972). Health after bereavement: A controlled study of young Boston widows and widowers. *Psychosomatic Medicine, 34,* 449–461.
8. Rees, W. D., & Lutkins, S. G. (1967). Mortality of bereavement. *British Medical Journal, 4,* 13–16.
9. Berkson, J. (1962). Mortality and marital status. *American Journal of Public Health, 52,* 1318–1329.
10. Epstein, G. E., Weitz, L., Roback, H., & McKee, E. (1975). Research on bereavement: A selective and critical review. *Comprehensive Psychiatry, 16,* 537–546.
11. Kraus, A. S., & Lilienfeld, A. M. (1959). Some epidemiological aspects of the high mortality rate in the young widowed group. *Journal of Chronic Disease, 10,* 207–217.
12. Young, M., Benjamin, B., & Wallis, C. (1963). The mortality of widowers. *Lancet, 1,* 454–456.
13. Parkes, C. M. (1985). Bereavement. *British Journal of Psychiatry, 146,* 11–17.
14. Stroebe, W., Stroebe, M. S., Gergen, K. J., & Gergen, M. (1982). The effects of bereavement on mortality: A social psychological analysis. In J. R. Eiser (Ed.), *Social psychology and behavioral medicine.* New York: John Wiley & Sons.
15. Gerber, I., Wiener, A., Battin, D., & Arkin, A. (1975). Brief therapy for the aged bereaved. In B. Schoenberg (Ed.), *Psychosocial aspects of bereavement.* New York: Columbia University Press.
16. Gallagher, D. E., Breckenridge, J. N., Thompson, L. W., & Peterson, J. A. (1983). Effects of bereavement on indicators of mental health in elderly widows and widowers. *Journal of Gerontology, 38,* 565–571.
17. Thompson, L. W., Breckenridge, J. N., Gallagher, D. E., & Peterson, J. A. (1984). Effects of bereavement on self-perceptions of physical health in elderly widows and widowers. *Journal of Gerontology, 39,* 309–314.
18. Clayton, P. J. (1982). Bereavement. In E. S. Paykel (Ed.), *Handbook of affective disorders.* New York: Guilford Press.
19. Niemi, T. (1979). The mortality of male old-age pensioners following spouse's death. *Scandinavian Journal of Social Medicine, 7,* 115–117.
20. Stroebe, M. S., & Stroebe, W. (1983). Who suffers more? Sex differences in health risks for the widowed. *Psychological Bulletin, 93,* 279–301.
21. Helsing, K. J., & Szklo, M. (1981). Mortality after bereavement. *American Journal of Epidemiology, 114,* 41–52.
22. Gerber, I., Rusalem, R., Hannon, N., Battin, D., & Arkin, A. (1975). Anticipatory grief and aged widows and widowers. *Journal of Gerontology, 30,* 225–229.
23. Berardo, F. M. (1970). Survivorship and social isolation: The case of the aged widower. *The Family Coordinator, 19,* 11–25.
24. Parkes, C. M., Murray, B. B., & Fitzgerald, R. G. (1969). Broken heart: A statistical study of increased mortality among widows. *British Medical Journal, 1,* 740–743.
25. Lund, D. A., Caserta, M. S., & Dimond, M. F. (1986). Gender differences through two years of bereavement among the elderly. *The Gerontologist, 26,* 314–320.
26. Clark, P. G., Siviski, R. W., & Weiner, R. (1986). Coping strategies of widowers in the first year. *Family Relations, 35,* 425–430.
27. Carey, R. G. (1977). The widowed: A year later. *Journal of Counseling Psychology, 24,* 125–131.
28. Ball, J. F. (1976). Widow's grief: The impact of age and mode of death. *Omega, 7,* 307–333.
29. Lundin, T. (1984). Long-term outcome of bereavement. *British Journal of Psychiatry, 145,* 424–428.
30. Parkes, C. M., & Weiss, R. S. (1983). *Recovery from bereavement.* New York: Basic Books.
31. Sanders, C. M. (1982–1983). Effects of sudden vs. chronic illness death on bereavement outcome. *Omega, 13,* 227–241.
32. Lundin, T. (1984). Morbidity following sudden and unexpected bereavement. *British Journal of Psychiatry, 144,* 84–88.
33. Clayton, P. J., Halikas, J. A., Maurice, W. L., & Robins, E. (1973). Anticipatory grief and widowhood. *British Journal of Psychiatry, 122,* 47–51.
34. Lazarus, R. S. (1966). *Psychological stress and the coping process.* New York: McGraw-Hill.
35. Lazarus, R. S., & Folkman, S. (1984). *Stress, appraisal, and coping.* New York: Springer.
36. Folkman, S., & Lazarus, R. S. (1980). An analysis of coping in a middle-aged community sample. *Journal of Health and Social Behavior, 21,* 219–239.

37. Maddison, D., & Walker, W. L. (1967). Factors affecting the outcome of conjugal bereavement. *British Journal of Psychiatry, 113,* 1057–1067.
38. Bowlby, J. (1980). *Attachment and loss: Loss, sadness and depression.* New York: Basic Books.
39. Heyman, D. K., & Gianturco, D. T. (1973). Long-term adaptation by the elderly to bereavement. *Journal of Gerontology, 28,* 359–362.
40. Silverman, P. (1979). *Widow-to-widow program: Final report to the National Institute of Mental Health* (Administration on Aging, Microfiche No. CF 001 273). Rockville, MD: U.S. Department of Health, Education and Welfare.
41. Blank, R. H. (1969). Mourning. In A. H. Kutscher (Ed.), *Death and bereavement* (pp. 204–206). Springfield, IL: Charles C. Thomas.
42. Bugen, L. A. (1977). Human grief: A model for prediction and intervention. *American Journal of Orthopsychiatry, 47,* 196–207.
43. Barry, M. (1973). The prolonged grief reaction. *Mayo Clinic Proceedings, 48,* 329–335.
44. Dimond, M. F. (1981). Bereavement and the elderly: A critical review with implications for nursing practice and research. *Journal of Advanced Nursing, 6,* 461–470.
45. Morgan, L. A. (1976). A re-examination of widowhood and morale. *Journal of Gerontology, 31,* 687–695.
46. Johnson, R. L., Lund, D. A., & Dimond, M. F. (1986). Stress, self-esteem and coping during bereavement among the elderly. *Social Psychology Quarterly, 49,* 273–279.
47. Gass, K. A. (1987). The health of conjugally bereaved older widows: The role of appraisal, coping and resources. *Research in Nursing and Health, 10,* 39–47.
48. Gilson, B. S., Bergner, M., Bobbitt, R. A., & Carter, W. (1978). *The SIP: Final development and testing, 1975–1978.* Seattle, WA: University of Washington, Department of Health and Community Medicine.
49. Palmore, E., & Luikart, C. (1972). Health and social factors related to life-satisfaction. *Journal of Health and Social Behavior, 13,* 68–80.
50. Engle, V. F., & Graney, M. J. (1985–1986). Self assessed and functional health of older women. *International Journal of Aging and Human Development, 22,* 301–313.
51. Berardo, F. M. (1985). Social networks and life preservation. *Death Studies, 9,* 37–50.
52. Lund, D. A., Caserta, M. S., & Dimond, M. F. (1986). Impact of bereavement on the self-conceptions of older surviving spouses. *Symbolic Interaction, 9,* 235–244.

9

Use of Select Coping Strategies during Late-Life Spousal Bereavement

Dolores Gallagher, Steven Lovett, Patricia Hanley-Dunn, and Larry W. Thompson

This chapter explores the reported frequency of use and the helpfulness of 12 common cognitive, behavioral, emotional, and avoidance coping strategies used over a 2½-year period by older men and women to assist in adapting to a spouse's death. Few gender differences were found, although several significant differences were noted regarding which strategies were used most frequently and rated as most helpful across time. Contrary to expectations, specific coping strategies contributed only a small amount of explained variance to mental health outcome measures (e.g., depression). Further research is needed on the impact of other aspects of the coping process (e.g., religious faith) on physical and mental health end points for the elderly bereaved.

One of the major stressors of later life is spousal bereavement[1] yet systematic investigations of bereavement have tended to exclude older adults, particularly males—a point made by Lund, Caserta, and Dimond[2] in their paper on gender differences. The few previously reported studies investigating spousal bereavement in elders have focused on the emotional and psychosocial responses of the bereaved. A study by Gallagher, Breckenridge, Thompson, and Peterson[3] examining the effects of spousal bereavement on older adults (aged 55 and above) found that widows and widowers do experience more psychological distress approximately 2 months after their loss than do nonbereaved, age-matched controls. Elevated depression, grief, global severity of psychological distress, and poorer perceived mental health functioning characterized the bereaved. There was no significant bereavement by sex interaction in perceived distress, although women in both groups reported greater distress than men. Other researchers have reported

This research was supported in part by a grant from the National Institute of Aging (R01 AGO1959) to Larry W. Thompson, principal investigator.

both elevated mortality and poorer health outcomes for middle-aged males[4] and widowers whose spouses had suffered from a long-term chronic illness.[5]

Lund, Caserta, and Dimond[2] followed 192 individuals aged 50–93 for 2 years following the death of the spouse. Data from six time points indicated that there were no differences between males and females in their psychological and social responses to bereavement. Individuals gradually improved over time, but there was no clear evidence of the specific stages of grieving postulated by others.[6] Additionally, the bereaved reported relatively high levels of psychological strength and coping during those periods when they were also reporting high levels of emotional distress. The authors suggested that these seemingly inconsistent results may reflect the multidimensional nature of the bereavement experience. The bereaved are exposed to many distressing reminders of their loss but may also be developing feelings of competence and strength as a result of managing the many practical daily problems in living which can arise following the death of a spouse.

Previously published studies of spousal bereavement in older adults have contained relatively little information about the specific coping strategies individuals use to manage their grief.[7] In fact, very little systematic investigation of older adults' methods of coping with stressful life events has been reported. Folkman, Lazarus, Pimley, and Novacek[8] recently reported on a cross-sectional study investigating the types of stresses and coping strategies common to 75 younger married couples (mean age approximately 40 years) and 141 older adults (mean age approximately 68 years) living in the community. They found that older adults rated more stressors as unchangeable and therefore made more frequent use of emotion-focused coping strategies, such as distancing oneself from a stressor, accepting responsibility for the problem, and positively reappraising the problem, than did younger adults. Older adults also reported greater use of escape-avoidance strategies such as wishing the problem would go away. Younger adults rated more of their stressors as changeable and consequently reported more frequent use of problem-focused strategies designed to directly eliminate or control the stressors they encountered. Few differences in the coping strategies used were noted between the men and women studied. Males did report keeping their feelings to themselves more than females. Females were more likely to reappraise a stressful situation in a positive way than were males. These findings were consistent across age groups.

The present chapter describes the frequency and helpfulness of a set of 12 coping strategies used by older widowed adults to adapt to their grief during the $2^1/_2$ years following the death of the spouse. These data are part of a larger continuing longitudinal investigation of elders' ways of coping with spousal bereavement that includes indices of social support and the role of religion and faith in the coping process. Based on the findings of Folkman et al.[8] it was predicted that bereaved older adults would more frequently use emotion-focused rather than problem-focused coping strategies. It was also hypothesized that gender differences in types of coping strategies used would be minimal and related to the tendency of men to express their emotions less frequently than women. Although it would seem that effective use of coping strategies would lead to reduced psychological distress, the findings of Lund et al.[2] indicate that high levels of distress and positive coping efforts may coexist in bereaved elders. Stage theories of grief would predict that different profiles of coping would emerge as the grief process unfolds. Lund et al.,[2] however, found that such predictors were not supported with respect to psychological distress, and the same may be true for coping responses.

METHOD

Subjects

Participants for the bereaved sample were obtained by sending letters inviting participation in the study to 2,450 spouses of individuals aged 55 or older according to death certificates of the Los Angeles County Health Department. The letters were sent within 2 to 4 weeks of the reported death. There was a 30% response rate to the mailings ($n = 735$); of the respondents, 211 individuals (113 women and 98 men) met the age criteria and lived within a predetermined distance from the research center (the distance was set to identify those within easy reach for home interviews). A comparison sample of 163 individuals (78 women and 85 men) age 55 and over who were currently married or, if single, had not lost a spouse through death or divorce within the past 5 years was recruited from senior centers, residential facilities for elders, and the Emeriti Center mailing list of the University of Southern California. An extensive analysis of participants' background variables has been presented elsewhere.[3] (Chapter 2 in this book also reports on findings from this study.)

Procedure

Participants completed in-home interviews and a battery of self-report questionnaires at four time points: approximately 2 months after initial contact T_1; 6 months after initial contact T_2; 12 months after initial contact T_3; and 30 months after initial contact T_4. Interviews were conducted by trained research assistants and took between 60 and 90 minutes to complete. Self-report packets were returned by the participant within one week of the interview.

Measures

In the repeated interviews, both bereaved and nonbereaved participants were asked about 12 specific coping strategies that could be used to assist in adapting to a spouses's death. These were logically derived from the coping literature at that time.[9,10] They were conceptually grouped into cognitive, behavioral, emotional, or avoidant types of strategies. The cognitive strategies were (1) making use of encouraging self-talk, (2) trying to make sense of the death (looking for purpose), and (3) reflecting on past memories about the deceased. The behavioral strategies were (1) seeking information about the grief process and (2) keeping busy. The emotional strategies were (1) expressing sadness about the loss and (2) feeling as if "in contact" with the deceased. The avoidant strategies were (1) increasing the use of alcohol, (2) taking pills or tranquilizers, (3) changing eating behaviors (perhaps as a result of a change in appetite), (4) increasing the amount of sleep, and (5) staying away from people and activities. For each of these coping strategies, respondents gave two ratings: (1) They rated how often they had used the coping mechanism following the spouse's death on a Likert scale from 1 to 7 (1 indicating most frequent use and 7 meant they had not employed the technique), and (2) the respondents who used a given coping strategy also rated how helpful it had been on a Likert scale from 1 to 7 (1 was "very helpful" and 7 was "not at all helpful").

Dependent or outcome measures focusing on mental health functioning included (1) current level of grief intensity as measured by the total score on the Texas Revised Inventory of Grief (TRIG),[11] (2) depression, using the Beck Depression Inventory (BDI),[12] (3) global severity rating from the Brief Symptom Inventory (BSI),[13] which is a general measure of emotional distress and psychopathology; and (4) an overall self-rating of current mental health (1 = "I feel very troubled and bad about myself most of the time," 7 = "I feel good about myself most of the time").

In addition, there were sections in the interview devoted to a description of the person's social support network, use of social involvement and social activities to cope, and the role of religious faith and religious practices in adaptation. Other dependent variables of interest included perceived physical health status, medication usage, and mortality. In this chapter data are presented only for the specific coping strategies described above and only with regard to their relationship to measures of mental health functioning at each time point.

Because of problems obtaining compliance at T_2 and the subsequent small samples available at that time, T_2 data were dropped from the analyses that follow, which are based on measures at T_1, T_3, and T_4.

RESULTS

Changes in Coping Over Time

To assess changes over time in the frequency of these coping strategies by male and female bereaved, separate 2 (male vs. female) × 3 (times of measurement: T_1, T_3, and T_4) repeated measures analyses of variance were performed on each coping strategy variable. Means and standard deviations for each coping variable, by gender, time, frequency of use, and helpfulness, are found in Tables 1 and 2. Note that helpfulness rating of 7 (i.e., not at all helpful) were assigned to coping techniques that were not used (i.e., given a frequency rating of 7) by a subject. There were significant main effects for time of measurement on the frequency of use of only the following three strategies:

1. expressing sadness ($F = 16.6, p < .001, N = 145$), with subjects at T_1 and T_3 showing significantly more frequency in the use of this mechanism than they did by T_4.
2. seeking a purpose in the death ($F = 6.13, p < .003, N = 146$), with respondents using this strategy significantly more at T_1 than they did at T_3 or T_4.
3. reflecting on past memories ($F = 10.9, p < .001, N = 147$), with the bereaved utilizing it significantly more at T_1 and T_4 than at T_3.

Changes in the amount of helpfulness over time for each of the coping strategies were also examined. There was a significant main effect for the helpfulness of expressing sadness ($F = 7.20, p < .001, N = 97$). Respondents found this to be significantly less helpful by T_4 than they did at T_1 and T_3. There was also a significant main effect for the reported helpfulness of self-talk ($F = 4.4, p < .016 N = 61$), where it was less helpful at T_4 than at T_1.

TABLE 1 Means and Standard Deviations of Frequency and Helpfulness of Selected Coping Strategies for Older Bereaved Men over Time[a]

Coping strategies	T_1		T_3		T_4	
	M	SD	M	SD	M	SD
Cognitive						
Self-talk						
Frequency	4.7	2.5	5.0	2.6	4.4	2.1
Helpfulness	2.6	1.7	2.1	1.3	3.3	2.1
Looking for purpose						
Frequency	4.3	2.5	4.9	2.4	4.6	2.4
Helpfulness	2.8	1.7	2.8	2.3	3.3	2.6
Past memories						
Frequency	2.9	1.9	3.6	2.1	2.9	1.8
Helpfulness	3.2	1.9	3.1	1.9	3.3	2.0
Behavioral						
Keeping busy						
Frequency	3.3	2.3	5.1	2.4	4.1	2.4
Helpfulness	2.6	1.6	2.2	1.2	3.0	2.4
Information gathering						
Frequency	5.9	1.8	5.7	1.9	6.2	1.4
Helpfulness	3.7	2.3	2.0	1.0	4.7	2.0
Emotional						
Expressed sadness						
Frequency	3.9	2.4	4.7	2.2	5.0	1.7
Helpfulness	2.8	1.8	3.3	1.8	3.7	2.2
Felt contact						
Frequency	3.3	1.9	3.1	1.7	2.8	2.1
Helpfulness	2.8	2.0	3.8	2.2	2.9	2.2
Avoidant[b]						
Alcohol use	—	—	7.0	.99	6.5	1.1
Tranquilizer use	—	—	7.1	.73	6.9	.39
Eating changes	—	—	5.7	2.2	6.4	1.7
Sleep changes	—	—	7.0	.89	6.6	1.2
Avoiding people	—	—	6.7	1.3	6.4	1.4

[a]The sample size varied at each time point, from a low of 60 to the complete sample of 211; repeated measures analyses of variance were based on subjects with complete data at all three points.

[b]Helpfulness was not measured for these strategies, nor was information on their frequency at T_1.

An overall gender difference occurred for only the frequency of use of the self-talk strategy. A significant main effect for sex was observed ($F = 4.7, p < .031$), with older women ($M = 3.0$) utilizing this technique more than older men ($M = 4.7$). This sex difference was also observed on a combined "cognitive coping" variable created by summing and averaging the three cognitive items ($F = 4.03, p < .05, N = 144$). That is, in general the women employed cognitive coping strategies more frequently than did the men.

A sex by time interaction was observed only for frequency of use of keeping busy ($F = 4.16, p < .018, N = 146$). Men used this strategy most often at T_1 and least often at T_3. Women did not vary over time in the frequency of use of this strategy, and they used it significantly more often than men at about 1 year (T_3) after the spouse's death (means were 4.0 and 5.1 respectively). There were no significant interaction effects for any of the helpfulness items.

In short, fewer differences (over time or between men and women) were

TABLE 2   Means and Standard Deviations of Frequency and Helpfulness of Selected Coping Strategies for Older Bereaved Women over Time[a]

Coping strategies	T_1		T_3		T_4	
	M	SD	M	SD	M	SD
Cognitive						
Self-talk						
Frequency	4.0	2.6	4.3	2.3	3.8	2.2
Helpfulness	2.4	1.4	2.2	1.2	2.5	1.7
Looking for purpose						
Frequency	3.7	2.6	4.8	2.3	4.5	2.4
Helpfulness	2.6	2.1	3.1	1.9	2.8	2.2
Past memories						
Frequency	2.6	1.8	3.3	1.9	2.7	1.5
Helpfulness	2.9	2.1	3.1	1.8	2.3	1.8
Behavioral						
Keeping busy						
Frequency	3.4	2.4	4.0	2.4	4.0	2.4
Helpfulness	2.4	1.7	2.6	1.5	2.7	2.2
Information gathering						
Frequency	5.8	1.8	5.6	1.9	5.7	1.6
Helpfulness	3.5	2.1	3.2	1.9	3.8	2.3
Emotional						
Expressed sadness						
Frequency	3.9	1.9	4.7	1.7	4.9	1.8
Helpfulness	3.1	1.7	3.7	1.9	4.0	2.2
Felt contact						
Frequency	2.2	1.3	2.8	1.6	3.3	2.2
Helpfulness	1.7	1.1	2.3	1.9	2.8	2.2
Avoidant[b]						
Alcohol use	—	—	7.0	.56	6.6	.94
Tranquilizer use	—	—	6.7	1.2	6.6	.94
Eating changes	—	—	5.4	2.2	5.7	1.8
Sleep changes	—	—	6.5	1.4	6.5	1.1
Avoiding people	—	—	6.7	1.2	6.4	1.4

[a]The sample size varied at each time point, from a low of 60 to the complete sample of 211; repeated measures analyses of variance were based upon subjects with complete data at all three points.
[b]Helpfulness was not measured for these strategies, nor was information on their frequency at T_1.

observed than had been anticipated, although those that were found are intuitively reasonable (e.g., expressing sadness was much less frequently used and was less helpful 2½ years after the spouse's death than immediately after or at the first anniversary). It is interesting to note that women seem to use cognitive strategies more than men, while men prefer keeping generally busy as they recover from grief.

Relationship between Coping Strategies and Emotional Distress

Pearson correlations were calculated between outcome measures at T_1, T_3, and T_4 and the number of positive and avoidant coping strategies reportedly used at the same time points. The correlations are presented in Table 3. In general, greater levels of distress were associated with the use of more positive and avoidant coping strategies, especially for the measure of grief. Interestingly, the relationships between depression and general symptoms and the number of positive coping strategies used were nonsignificant at T_3 but they became significant again at T_4. Avoidant strategies were not assessed at T_1 but larger correlations were observed for depression, general symptoms, and self-reported mental health at T_4 than at T_3. Conversely, the positive relationship between grief and use of avoidant strategies at T_3 was not evident at T_4.

A clearer picture of the relationship between outcome and the subjects' coping efforts can be obtained by utilizing information about the perceived helpfulness of specific strategies. In the present study, strategies not used by a subject were considered to be not helpful and those used were given a helpfulness rating from 1 (very helpful) to 7 (not helpful) by the subject.

To evaluate the impact of specific coping strategies on the four mental health outcome measures, simultaneous multiple regression analyses were performed using the helpfulness ratings of the seven coping strategies for each of the three times of measurement, with the ratings separated by sex.

Two Months after Bereavement

At T_1 when the respondents were very recently bereaved, the helpfulness ratings of the seven coping strategies were found to constitute a significant set of predictors for level of grief for both males [$N = 89$; $R^2 = .18$, $F(7, 81) = 2.53$, $p < .02$] and females [$N = 106$; $R^2 = .22$, $F(7, 98) = 4.07$, $p < .001$]. Significance tests for the individual predictors revealed that the helpfulness of expressing sadness and trying to find meaning in the death were uniquely associated with the level of grief. Expressing sadness was reported to be most helpful by both males (beta weight $= -.25$, partial correlation $= -.25$) and females (beta weight $= -.35$, partial correlation $= -.35$) experiencing intense grief. Conversely, high levels of grief were associated with lower perceptions of the helpfulness of trying to find meaning in the death for both males (beta weight $= .29$, partial correlation $= .29$) and females (beta weight $= .29$, partial correlation $= .28$).

Using the intensity of depression (BDI) as the dependent variable and the items reflecting helpfulness of coping as predictor variables, none of the coping variables individually predicted a significant portion of the variance for males. For females ($N = 106$), the only significant relationship [$R^2 = .145$, $F(7, 98) = 2.38$,

TABLE 3   Pearson Correlations between Outcome Measures at T_1, T_3, and T_4 and the Total Number of Positive and Avoidant Coping Strategies Used at T_1, T_3, and T_4

Outcome	Positive coping			Avoidant coping[a]		
	T_1	T_3	T_4	T_1	T_3	T_4
Grief	.60****	.49****	.41****	—	.36****	.10
Depression	.25***	.08	.20*	—	.12	.32***
Symptom inventory[b]	.20**	.07	.29**	—	.19*	.31***
Mental health rating	.40****	.12	.15	—	.20*	.35****

[a]Avoidant coping strategies were not assessed at T_1 (2 months).
[b]BSI.
*$p < .05$. **$p < .01$. ***$p < .001$. ****$p < .0001$.

$p < .027$] was "trying to find meaning in the death" (beta weight = .23, partial correlation = .22), indicating that the more depressed the respondent, the less helpful they found this strategy.

Twelve Months and 30 Months after Bereavement

For data analyses at 1 year and 30 months (T_3 and T_4), summary scores were computed for each set of coping strategies (cognitive, behavioral, emotional, and avoidant), thus reducing the number of predictor variables from 12 to 4. This was done to reduce the chance of spurious significant results due to a greater number of statistical tests and a smaller sample size at these later times. At 1 year, men ($N = 63$) with higher levels of grief continued to find expressing sadness helpful [$R^2 = .27$, $F(5, 57) = 4.30$, $p < .002$, beta weight = $-.31$, partial correlation = $-.29$], as did the women ($N = 98$) in this group [$R^2 = .13$, $F(5, 92) = 2.69$, $p < .03$, beta weight = $-.34$, partial correlation = $-.32$]. No other coping strategies were significantly related to the outcome measures at 1 year.

At 30 months, men with higher levels of depression reported high levels of helpfulness for seeking information about adjusting to a loss [$R^2 = .32$, $F(5,39) = 3.72$, $p < .007$; beta weight = $-.38$, partial correlation = $-.36$]. For bereaved women, depression scores at 30 months were unrelated to the coping helpfulness variable. Finally, using the global severity score of the BSI as the dependent variable, the only significant relationship was found for the males ($N = 45$), with the helpfulness of seeking information about the grief process being higher among the men reporting greater levels of emotional distress [$R^2 = .44$, $F(5, 39) = 6.13$, $p < .001$, beta weight = $-.42$; partial correlation = $-.42$]. The self-rating of overall mental health did not show a significant relationship to any of the predictor variables at any of the three times for either sex.

In summary, these analyses indicate that very few of the coping strategies examined were uniquely associated with the specific mental health outcome measures employed in this study and those that were significant varied over time in their meaning and degree of importance. Individuals reporting the greatest distress on all outcome measures tended to use the greatest number of positive and avoidant coping strategies at T_1 and T_4. These relationships did not appear at T_3 however. Multiple regression analyses using coping variables which incorporated subjects' perceptions of the helpfulness of specific strategies revealed similar differences over time as well as across outcome measures. Intensity of grief at T_1 and T_3 was predicted by the perceived helpfulness of expressing sadness; level of depression was higher among older women trying to find meaning in the death (at T_1 only); and global emotional or psychological distress was related to seeking information about grief for men (at T_3 only). The lack of a consistent pattern of results in these multiple regression analyses suggests that use of adequate and varied coping strategies does not, in itself, seem to guard against intense grief, feelings of depression, or global emotional distress. Alternatively, "good copers" may be persons who can permit themselves to experience sadness and emotional upset caused by grief while still maintaining a variety of cognitive and behavioral skills in their daily repertoires.

DISCUSSION

This study investigated the role of several specific coping strategies that older bereaved individuals used to deal with their distress over the course of the bereavement period. Data were analyzed from the 2-month, 12-month, and 30-month measurement times in this longitudinal study. Coping strategies used were separated into primarily cognitive, behavioral, emotional, and avoidant techniques. Changes over time and gender differences were examined as they related to how frequently each respondent used a particular strategy and how helpful he or she thought each coping style had been at each time period. In addition, our distinction between the actual coping strategies used and the emotional outcome allowed us to investigate the relationship between what the respondents did to cope with their grief and the degree of emotional distress they experienced.

Several changes over time were observed in this sample. First, as might be expected, the frequency of the use of expressing sadness decreased at 30 months; this strategy was also rated as less helpful at 30 months than it had been at 2 months and 12 months. This finding is consistent with the literature on the final phases of grief work [6,14] indicating that at 30 months identity reconstruction was well under way.

Second, the strategy of seeking to find a purpose in the death was more frequently used at 2 months than at 12 or 30 months. Again, this finding is consistent with Parkes' formulation[6] according to which Phase II is a time when most individuals seek a meaning for the death.

Third, an interesting curvilinear relationship was observed in the frequency of use of reflecting on past memories, with the respondents reporting that they used this cognitive coping strategy more at 2 months and 30 months than they did at 12 months. Since 12 months generally marks the end of Phase II of grief work, it seems likely that this is a time when a conscious decision is being made to spend less time dwelling on the death and more time investing in new meanings and relationships. By 30 months, some acceptance of the loss will have occurred and reflective memories may be very comfortable at this time. Finally, respondents stated that they found the use of self-talk as a coping strategy significantly more helpful early on in the bereavement process than they did at 30 months.

Generally consistent with Lund et al.,[2] only a few gender differences were observed in the frequency of use of specific coping techniques. Women, more than men, tended to use more cognitively oriented coping strategies across time. In particular, they used more encouraging self-talk than did men. The men in our sample showed significant changes over time in their use of the behavioral strategy of keeping busy, using this coping strategy most at 2 months, and least at 12 months. Women, on the other hand, were very consistent over time in the use of this strategy, so that at 12 months, when the men were not employing it very often, the women were frequently using this technique. Although this finding appears somewhat puzzling at first, Berardo[15] reported that men tend to suppress their emotional responses in favor of action-oriented behaviors; thus, men might be staying busy at 2 months to suppress their more emotional responses, but the energy for maintaining this posture may lag by 12 months. The fact that men are again utilizing the strategy of keeping busy more than women at 30 months is consistent with existing sex-role behavior patterns. Contrary to our predictions and those of Folkman et al.,[8] the older adults in this sample did not use more emotion-focused than problem-focused coping strategies at any of the three times of measurement.

Avoidant coping strategies (alcohol use, tranquilizers, changes in eating behaviors, increased sleep, avoiding people), while used infrequently in our sample, were positively correlated with subjective distress at each time of measurement. While not assessed at 2 months, the use of these strategies was greater at 12 months postdeath and showed the expected decline at 30 months postdeath. No gender differences were observed in these variables except for a trend in changes in eating behaviors; women stated they changed eating behaviors more frequently than did men at 30 months.

Regression analyses, designed to evaluate the variance accounted for in four different mental health outcome measures by the predictor (coping) variables, failed to reveal any discernible pattern of results in the data. Intensity of grief, level of depression, overall psychological distress, and self-rated mental health were not consistently related to the frequency of use or the helpfulness of any of the four types of coping strategies studied at any of the three times of measurement, although some relationships were found for some of the measures. For example, at both 2 and 12 months after the spouse's death, intensity of grief was predicted by expression of sadness for both the men and women in this sample; however, level of depression was not clearly related to frequency of use of cognitive or behavioral coping strategies at any measurement time. These results are in general agreement with those of Lund et al.,[2] suggesting that, for elders at least, use of flexible and adaptive coping strategies can coexist with significant grief and psychological distress which may reflect the multidimensional nature of the bereavement process.

Taken together, these data indicate that older persons adapting to a spouse's death make frequent use of a variety of coping strategies and find them to be more or less helpful at different points in the grief process. Further, most of these various strategies are used irrespective of gender. There were few consistent relationships found between coping and level of psychological distress, suggesting that elders may be both adaptive and distressed after a spouse's death. The generalizability of these findings may be limited, however, for this was a well-educated sample with average psychological distress scores (on depression and related measures) in nonclinical ranges. The picture may be quite different for those elders who are seriously depressed, evidencing other forms of psychopathology, or from a less advantaged sociodemographic background. Study of the impact of sociodemographic and individual difference variables on the coping process is needed. It is also necessary to evaluate the effects of other types of coping methods (e.g., activity-oriented or spiritually oriented coping) to see if a clearer relationship might then emerge between ways of coping and degree of psychological distress.

REFERENCES

1. Osterweis, M., Solomon, F., & Green, M. (1984). *Bereavement: Reactions, consequences and care*. Washington DC: National Academy Press.
2. Lund, D. A., Caserta, M. S., & Dimond, M. F. (1986). Gender differences through two years of bereavement among the elderly. *The Geronotologist, 26*, 314–320.
3. Gallagher, D. E., Breckenridge, J. N., Thompson, L. W., & Peterson, J. A. (1983). Effects of bereavement on indicators of mental health in elderly widows and widowers. *Journal of Gerontology, 38*, 565–571.

 4. Stroebe, M. S., & Strobe, W. (1983). Who suffers more? Sex differences in health risks of the widowed. *Psychological Bulletin, 93,* 279–301.
 5. Gerber, I., Rusalem, P., Hannon, N., Battin, D., & Arkin, A. (1975) Anticipatory grief of aged widows and widowers. *Journal of Gerontology, 30,* 225–229.
 6. Parkes, C. M. (1972). *Bereavement: Studies of grief in adult life.* New York: International Universities Press.
 7. Gallagher, D. E., & Thompson, L. W. (in press). Bereavement and adjustment disorders. In E. Busse and D. Blazer (Eds.),*Handbook of geriatric psychiatry* (2nd ed). Washington, DC: American Psychiatric Association.
 8. Folkman, S., Lazarus, R. S., Pimley, S., & Novacek, J. (1987). Age differences in stress and coping processes. *Psychology and Aging, 2,* 171–184.
 9. Billings, A., & Moos, R. H. (1981). The role of coping responses and social resources in attenuating the impact of stressful life events. *Journal of Behavioral Medicine, 4,* 139–157.
10. Pearlin, L., & Schooler, C. (1978). The structure of coping. *Journal of Health and Social Behavior, 19,* 2–21.
11. Faschingbauer, T. R. (1981). *Texas revised inventory of grief manual.* Houston, TX: Honeycomb Publishing.
12. Beck, A. T., Ward, C., Mendelson, M., Mock, J., & Erbaugh, J. (1961). An inventory for measuring depression. *Archives of General Psychiatry, 4,* 53–63.
13. Derogatis, L. (1977) *Brief symptom inventory: Administration, scoring, and procedures manual.* Baltimore, MD: Clinical Psychometric Research.
14. Lopata, H. Z. (1975). On widowhood: Grief work and identity reconstruction. *Journal of Geriatric Psychiatry, 8,* 41–55.
15. Berardo, F. (1970). Survivorship and social isolation: The case of the aged widower. *The Family Coordinator, 19,* 11–25.

10

Advice on the Adjustment to Loss from Bereaved Older Adults: An Examination of Resources and Outcomes

Michael S. Caserta, Jan Van Pelt, and Dale A. Lund

One hundred and seventy-one bereaved older adults were classified as giving advice that was individual-oriented (48.6%), other-oriented (22.2%), or a mixture (29.2%) as to how others in a similar situation should manage the loss of a spouse. Those whose advice was individual-oriented tended to be older and married longer. All three groups had similar socioeconomic and support resources available to them, and there were no major differences in outcomes over a 2-year period. The mixture group reported the lowest amount of avoiding social contacts over 2 years and greater increases in perceived coping ability over the 1st year. Implications are discussed.

Those who experience conjugal bereavement will often find many aspects of life being affected. First and foremost is the emotional adjustment to the loss of one's spouse, which can result in many outcomes, such as shock, confusion, guilt, and anger.[1-3] Research has also documented that depression levels can be elevated for a period of time for some bereaved persons.[4] Other issues include adaption to being single again in a "coupled" society[5,6] and the problem of loneliness.[7] Finally, the bereaved also find themselves confronting new tasks never before addressed because they were handled by the deceased spouse.[8] These often include grocery shopping, checkbook balancing, home repairs, and yardwork.[7]

Because people differ in what is particularly problematic for them, their strategies to manage grief also vary. Such strategies include keeping oneself occupied, developing new skills, increasing social participation, reestablishing social

An earlier version of this chapter was presented at the Annual Meeting of the American Society on Aging, Salt Lake City, Utah, March 1987.

The bereavement study was funded by a grant from the National Institute on Aging (R01 AG02193). Staff support was also provided by the Intermountain West Long Term Care Gerontology Center at the University of Utah.

linkages, and engaging in meaningful, ongoing projects and activities.[1,9,10] Some strategies have been found to be associated with poor outcomes. These include self-blame, refusal to express feelings in front of others or to openly acknowledge the loss, avoiding reminders of the deceased, and the use of alcohol.[11-13]

According to Dimond,[14] why some older people manage bereavement more successfully than others may be a matter of access to adequate and appropriate resources, for example, emotional support, information, material aids, services, and new social contacts. Several authors have reported on the importance of children, family, friends, neighbors, and clergy in providing social and emotional support to the bereaved.[8,15,16] The family can help widowed persons through phone calls and visits and by keeping them busy.[8] A unique support task that can be performed by neighbors is to maintain face-to-face contact with the bereaved.[17] Religious and spiritual beliefs that involve faith in powers outside of the self facilitate coping.[16] Sanders[3] also found that religious supports were seen as important sources of strength.

It is equally important to note, however, that many of these potential resources do not inherently lead to better outcomes. In fact, some writers have suggested that negative consequences might result from some of these resources. For example, certain religious beliefs concerning the existence of a life after death might create anxiety, because the surviving spouse assumes that the deceased is watching and evaluating the survivor's actions. Expectations from family and friends might compete with those of the bereaved and, therefore, generate additional stress. Researchers cannot assume that available resources always lead to positive outcomes; each individual's circumstances and experiences vary considerably.

One of the most useful resources available to bereaved individuals could be recommendations from other bereaved individuals based on how they confronted their situation. The majority of popular literature on the crisis of bereavement has focused on personal accounts of formerly bereaved persons in dealing with the loss of a loved one. Included in their guidelines are the following: (1) Understand that grieving is a process where one adjusts in one's own way; (2) do not blame God; and (3) be aware of the importance of close friendships, courage, patience, resilience, self-esteem, and growth for achieving a new life.[18-23] As for the practical management of grief-related problems, advice is given on settling the estate of the deceased, insurance matters, taxes, arranging a daily schedule, and resolving social security issues.[24-26] One of the most obvious by-products of bereavement support groups and widow-to-widow programs is the exchange of such information.[13,27-30]

There is a variety of advice that can be given and an equal number of strategies that can potentially be employed. Where it cannot be definitely assumed that what the bereaved advise is what they actually have done, their advice at least indicates what they perceive to be successful strategies. It is reasonable to assume that their perceptions are somehow related to experiences they had in their bereavement.

Rigdon, Clayton, and Dimond[31] formulated a typology of advice that ultimately fell into two unidimensional categories. *Being individual* largely consists of attitudes that each person must grieve in his or her own way because it is believed that everyone's situation may be different. Advice, therefore, that is individual-oriented emphasizes the importance of having the bereaved make their own decisions, allowing them time to adjust, and at times letting them rely on their faith.

Alternatively, advice that entails accepting social invitations, offering assistance to and from others, and talking with others is what Rigdon et al.[31] termed *being involved with others*. This other-oriented approach to managing grief is similar to the individual-oriented approach in that both require initiative on the part of the bereaved. The main difference between the two is the reciprocity that is apparent in the other-oriented approach but noticeably lacking in the individual-oriented approach.

Rigdon et al.[31] finally noted that some advice can encompass elements of both approaches, the most common such advice being to keep busy. In other words, one can keep busy by being involved in solitary activities or by being involved with others, or both.

It is not entirely clear, however, which strategies consistently lead to better outcomes in the long run (although there have been suggestions in the literature linking keeping busy and social reparticipation with better coping).[1,9] The next research questions to be investigated therefore, should concern the factors that influence the advice offered by bereaved elders in order to determine if specific strategies result in more positive outcomes.

The specific research questions addressed in this chapter are the following:

1. What type of advice is most prevalent among bereaved older adults?
2. What factors influence the type of advice given?
3. What type of advice is associated with better outcomes?

METHODS

Sample and Procedure

The data utilized in this investigation were part of a longitudinal descriptive study of bereavement among the elderly that was completed in 1983 in the Salt Lake City metropolitan area (the University of Utah study). Recently bereaved spouses aged 50 and over were identified by using local newspaper obituaries. More detail on the methodology of the study can be found in Caserta et al.,[32] Lund et al.,[7] and in chapters 1 and 6 of this book. The total sample consisted of 192 bereaved older adults.

All respondents were asked to complete questionnaires at six times during the first 2 years of bereavement: 3 to 4 weeks (T_1), 2 months (T_2), 6 months (T_3), 1 year (T_4), 18 months (T_5), and 2 years (T_6) after the death of the spouse. With the exception of the demographic variables, all six questionnaires were essentially the same. Thirty-two (16.7%) of the participants completed five of the six questionnaires and 108 (56.3%) completed all six questionnaires. Twenty-eight (14.6%) discontinued or dropped out of the study because they were too busy, were too ill, lacked interest in the project, or had moved away. Four males and 5 females (4.7%) died during the 2nd year of the study.

Instruments

Questionnaires at each time period included two standardized scales and a variety of single-item assessments. The two standardized instruments were the

Self-Rating Depression Scale[33] and the Life Satisfaction Index-A.[34] The respondents also were asked to indicate both the presence and intensity of 26 bereavement-related feelings. Their responses were recorded on a five-point Likert scale (ranging from "never had" to "very strong"). A series of 16 bereavement-related behaviors were presented in a similar Likert format, with response categories ranging from "never did this" to "most of the time." Items included on these two lists were generated from the general bereavement and grief literature but primarily from the Harvard bereavement study.[1] The items ranged from such early grief behaviors as shock, confusion, crying, and review of the death event to such later behaviors as confidence, pride, learning to do new things, and making new friends. In addition to these checklists, each questionnaire obtained self-reported ratings for perceived stress, coping, health, and self-esteem measured by seven-point, single-item statements.

Information was also obtained pertaining to network size and the qualitative aspects of the respondents' support network, such as the frequency and ease of contact with members, the degree of closeness to them they felt, and the amount of mutual confiding and helping that occurred. Demographic information, including age, sex, years married, education, and income, was also recorded.

Categorization of Advice

At each time period, the respondents were asked, "Is there any advice that you would give someone else in a situation similar to yours?" This question was left open-ended to capture as much information as possible. The responses from each time period were then grouped together for each respondent. Three judges who were experts in aging and bereavement and had backgrounds in health and the social sciences independently classified each respondent as giving primarily individual-oriented advice, other-oriented advice, or a mixture according to how all the responses from the six times were taken together. The purpose was to derive what general kinds of advice the bereaved person had given over the 2 years.

For instance, if a person was judged to be individual-oriented in their advice, responses such as the following were pervasive throughout all six measurements:

• Take one day at a time.
• Everyone must make their own adjustments to the death.
• Take care of yourself and forget the rest.
• Pray.

On the other hand, other-oriented advice was exemplified by the following kinds of statements:

• Get involved with others and do things for people.
• Be with people and make friends.
• Accept love and help from others.

Finally, in cases where advice was mixed, the respondents may have given individual-oriented advice at first and then other-oriented advice subsequently, or vice versa. However, the advice may have been a mixture at all time periods. The following are examples of mixed advice:

• You should find comfort in mourning. Keep busy. Talk with people.
• Get involved in work, hobbies, or people.

TABLE 1   Demographic Characteristics of Bereaved by Mode of Advice Given

Characteristic	Individual oriented (n = 83)	Other oriented (n = 38)	Mixed (n = 50)
Mean age (SD)*	69.2 (8.5)	65.0 (5.7)	66.3 (7.7)
Mean years married (SD)*	43.0 (12.1)	35.3 (13.0)	37.7 (15.0)
Female	75.9%	68.4%	78.0%
High school graduates	72.3%	81.6%	88.0%
Annual income ≥ $10,000	51.4%	55.6%	54.2%

*p < .01 according to F-ratio derived from one-way analyses of variance.

- Keep busy. Do things you've always wanted to do. Keep former friends.

A respondent was classified as a particular kind of advice giver if at least two of the three judges agreed on a category. There was unanimous agreement on 44% of the cases and two out of the three judges agreed on an additional 53%, yielding a final agreement rate of 97%. On seven cases where there was no initial agreement, the judges met again, and after further examination of the responses and the criteria, they were able to agree on what category of advice to assign the respondents. Two were categorized as individual-oriented, two as other-oriented, and three as mixed advice givers.

RESULTS

Eighty-nine percent (N = 171) of the sample provided responses sufficient to be placed into one of the three categories of advice. Eighty-three (48.6%) of the respondents gave advice that was individual-oriented over the two years, 38 (22.2%) gave advice that was largely other-directed, while 50 (29.2%) gave advice that was a mixture.

Tests were conducted to determine demographic differences among the three groups, the results of which are presented in Table 1. Analyses of variance revealed that those who gave individual-oriented advice were significantly older (M = 69.2, SD = 8.5) than the other two groups [F (2, 168) = 4.52, p = .01]. Those who gave other-oriented advice had a mean age of 65.0 (SD = 5.7) while those who gave mixed advice had a mean age of 66.3 (SD = 7.7). It is also noteworthy that 25.3% of the individual-oriented advice givers were 75 years of age or older, as compared to only 5.3% of the other-oriented and 14% of the mixed advice givers.

It was also found that the individual-oriented advice givers were married significantly longer (M = 43.0, SD = 12.1) to their deceased spouses than were the other-oriented (M = 35.3, SD = 13.0) and the mixed (M = 37.7, SD = 15.0), advice givers [F (2, 168) = 5.30, p < .01]. This finding, however, is most likely related to the age differences found among the three groups. Years married, as expected, was found to be strongly correlated with the age of respondent (r = .51, p < .001).

The groups were more similar regarding sex, education, and income. The majority of each group consisted of women and high school graduates. Although there were fewer women in the group of other-oriented advice givers and fewer high school graduates in the group of individual-oriented advice givers, no statistical differences were observed with respect to these variables. Household income was also apparently not a factor, for slightly more than half of each group had an annual household income of $10,000 or more.

Further evidence of the similarities among these groups is that their support resources were almost identical. The data presented in Table 2 indicate, especially for the individual-oriented and other-oriented groups, that social networks were of equivalent size. While it appears that the mixed advice group had on the average larger networks, the differences were not statistically significant because of the wide variability that was found on this characteristic. The differences become even less apparent 1 year following the spouse's death. Even greater similarities were observed regarding frequency and ease of contact with network members. For the most part, respondents in all groups reported their networks as being contacted very easily and quite often.

Repeated measures tests were conducted on the variables described in the methods section to examine how the groups differed at each time period as well as how they changed over the 2 years. The effect of age was controlled for in the analyses. While changes over time were observed for the sample as a whole on many variables, in only two instances were statistically significant effects associated with the type of advice offered.

Statistical differences at T_1 were observed among the three groups with respect to the frequency of avoiding social contacts $[F(2, 86) = 3.47, p < .05]$. Time, both as a main effect as well as interactively with advice mode, was not statistically significant. As illustrated in Fig. 1, the differences observed at T_1 were maintained throughout the remaining 2 years. Interestingly, while the frequency of avoiding social contacts was quite low for the whole sample, the individual-oriented group and the other-oriented group remained virtually the same throughout the study period. This may be contrary to what is normally expected for this type of variable. The lowest frequency of avoidance was observed for the mixed advice group over the 2 years.

There was a difference in the way the three groups perceived how they were coping over the 2 years. While they were not initially statistically different at the baseline measurement, an interaction effect was observed between advice category and time $[F (10, 196) = 2.22 \, p = .01]$. This essentially means that not all the groups changed over time in the same fashion. Figure 2 graphically depicts the perceived coping scores of the three groups over the six measurement times. Consistent with the results of the analysis, the three groups were within 0.3 points of each other at T_1 (3–4 weeks). Additionally, the coping levels of the three groups remained quite high. With a few minor fluctuations, those in the individual-oriented group and those in the other-oriented group remained relatively constant over time. On the other hand, those who tended to give mixed advice steadily increased (though in small increments) with each measurement until 1 year after the death of the spouse; then they returned to their initial level over the 2nd year. It is interesting to note that the final measurement for each group (2 years) was identical to the baseline measurement at 3–4 weeks following the spouse's death.

In general, the type of advice that was given over 2 years was not statistically related to many of the major outcomes that were measured. The three groups were very similar in depression levels. No group had mean scores that indicated clinical symptomatology at any point during the 2 years. The highest mean score observed was 40.2 (individual-oriented group at 3–4 weeks). Furthermore, while the levels noticeably decreased over 2 years the levels of all three groups declined

TABLE 2   Mode of Advice over Two Years by Selected Indicators of Social Support (Mean Scores)

Advice mode	Time periods					
	3–4 Weeks	2 Months	6 Months	1 Year	18 Months	2 Years
Network size						
Individual-oriented	15.5	15.0	14.6	18.9	18.5	17.9
Other-oriented	14.6	15.4	14.0	17.7	20.1	18.3
Mixed	19.7	21.1	18.5	19.8	24.5	20.6
Frequency of contact[a]						
Individual-oriented	3.8	4.1	4.1	4.3	3.9	4.0
Other-oriented	3.9	4.0	4.3	4.1	4.0	3.9
Mixed	4.2	4.0	4.3	4.2	4.0	4.1
Ease of contact[b]						
Individual-oriented	4.8	4.7	4.9	4.8	4.6	4.6
Other-oriented	4.7	4.9	4.8	4.7	4.5	4.7
Mixed	4.7	4.8	4.7	4.9	4.7	4.6

[a]1 = never; 5 = very often.
[b]1 = very difficult; 5 = very easy.

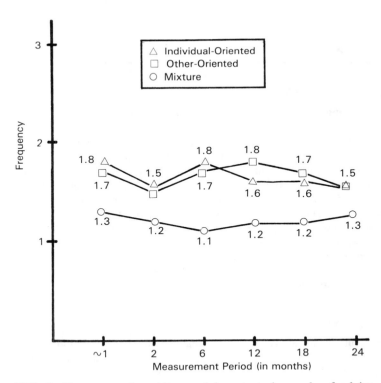

FIG. 1   Frequency of avoiding social contacts by mode of advice given over two years.

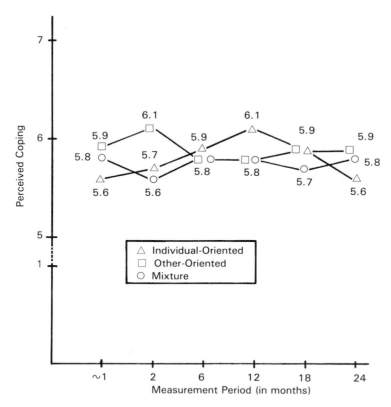

FIG. 2   Perceived coping by mode of advice given over two years.

in a similar way (an average of 0.4 point for each measurement time). This was also true of the stress associated with the death. While the levels decreased with time (an average of 0.3 to 0.5 points from T_1 to T_6), the decline was no more noticeable for any particular group of advice givers. The groups demonstrated even greater stability in terms of life satisfaction and self-esteem, reporting levels of similar magnitude and showing little change over time. For the most part, mean life satisfaction scores ranged from 13 to 14 for each group throughout the 2 years, while mean self-esteem remained between 5.3 and 5.8 for each group. Finally, with the exception of avoiding social contacts and perceived coping, no effects attributable to the type of advice given were observed on the other bereavement-related feelings and behaviors that were examined.

DISCUSSION

The respondents in this study showed a greater tendency to give individual-oriented advice, whether alone or in conjunction with advice to engage in activities involving others. Strategies which were strictly other-oriented were followed by the smallest number of respondents in this sample. One possible explanation is the age of the respondents.

Age was related to the type of advice that was given. It appears that a cohort effect may be operating, where those who are what gerontologists term *old-old* place greater emphasis on the individual resources such as self-reliance in managing a loss. Had this study not focused solely on bereaved elders, there may have been a greater prevalence of other-oriented advice than was observed.

It is more important, however, to emphasize the similarities, which were more abundant than the differences. For the most part, specific advice on how to manage the loss of one's spouse was not predictive of the major outcomes often measured in bereavement research. For instance, no indication was found that those who were more depressed offered any particular kind of advice that was different than those who were less depressed. This also was generally true of the variety of feelings experienced in grief and behaviors often associated with bereavement. Independent of the strategies that the bereaved recommended, many of them at one time or another cried, expressed some anger and even perhaps guilt, and had periods of numbness, coldness, and other related emotions common with bereavement. At the same time, no one particular type of advice was associated with many of the possible positive outcomes, such as feeling confident and proud of how one had managed the situation.

Interestingly, differences that were observed focused on those whose advice was mixed. Although the effect was often minimal, this group perceived themselves as coping more successfully through the 1st year. During the 2nd year, however, that effect gradually disappeared. This suggests that an advice strategy consisting of a mixture of recommendations may at least be associated with a slight but steady improvement in a person's ability to cope with the spouse's death early in the bereavement process. It must also be acknowledged that the other two strategies were not necessarily associated with poor perceived coping but rather with little or no change in perceived coping over a 2-year period.

The mixed advice group also reported the least avoidance of social contacts—an effect which remained constant over 2 years. While no group reported high levels of avoidance, it is nonetheless surprising that those whose advice was primarily other-oriented were no different than those whose strategy was individual-oriented. This suggests that the mixed advice group perceived the value of being with others while acknowledging the importance of drawing on one's own inner strength as well. This group most often stated that keeping busy was important to them, which may partially explain their willingness to incorporate others in their lives in addition to engaging in solitary activities. This mixture may have helped them to cope. Again, it must be emphasized that no group excessively avoided social contact—even those whose advice was individual-oriented.

Another major conclusion of this study was that many resources were similarly available and did not notably impact the advice that the bereaved persons gave. For example, all three groups had similar access to social resources. Although support networks may be very helpful in some ways, the individual-oriented respondents still believed that the best strategy for dealing with a loss does not necessarily have to involve other people. Others, particularly the younger respondents, saw the people around them as potentially helpful in the adjustment process.

It is therefore quite clear that strategies of advice are mostly determined by what the bereaved themselves perceive as their unique needs. No one best way to manage all the aspects associated with the devastation that comes from the death of a spouse was suggested. Provided a bereaved person has a full range of resources available, the strategies which the person finds most comfortable seem to work best for that person.

Future research into this topic should focus on whether more specific suggestions from bereaved older adults are associated with any outcome or the availability of a particular resource. For instance, the reliance on faith may have a different effect than simply "taking one day at a time." Both are individual-oriented strategies, but the activities involved may be quite different. A similar case could be made regarding getting involved with others. Activities involving family members may be associated with different outcomes as compared with getting involved with friends or church groups or doing volunteer work.

Finally, it is important to document how closely advice given is correlated with the strategy that is actually followed. In this way, it would be easier to discern if a given strategy is advised because it differs from another strategy used unsuccessfully or because it itself was used and was perceived to be helpful. This would lend more clarity to the findings presented here as well as provide a better understanding of the relationship between strategies that are pursued and bereavement outcomes.

REFERENCES

1. Glick, I., Weiss, R. S., & Parkes, C. M. (1974). *The first year of bereavement.* New York: John Wiley & Sons.
2. Sanders, C. M. (1980). A comparison of adult bereavement in the death of a spouse, child, and parent. *Omega, 10,* 303–322.
3. Sanders, C. M. (1980). Comparison of younger and older spouses in bereavement outcomes. *Omega, 11,* 217–232.
4. Gallagher, D. E., Breckinridge, J. N., Thompson, L. W., & Peterson, J. A. (1983). Effects of bereavement on indicators of mental health in elderly. *Journal of Gerontology, 38,* 565–571.
5. Osterweis, M., Solomon, F., & Green, M. (1984). *Bereavement: Reactions, consequences and care.* Washington, DC: National Academy Press.
6. Saunders, J. M. (1981). A process of bereavement resolution: Uncoupled identity. *Western Journal of Nursing Research, 3,* 319–332.
7. Lund, D. A., Caserta, M. S., & Dimond, M. F. (1986). Gender differences through two years of bereavement among the elderly. *The Gerontologist, 26,* 314–320.
8. Carey, R. G. (1979). Weathering widowhood: Problems and adjustments of the widowed during the first year. *Omega, 10,* 163–174.
9. Lund, D. A., Dimond, M. F., Caserta, M. S., Johnson, R. J., Poulton, J. L., & Connelly, J. R. (1985). Identifying elderly with coping difficulties after two years of bereavement. *Omega, 16,* 213–224.
10. Rubinstein, R. L. (1986). The construction of a day by elderly widowers. *International Journal of Aging and Human Development, 23,* 161–173.
11. Bowlby, J. (1980). *Attachment and loss: Vol. III. Loss, sadness and depression.* New York: Basic Books.
12. Gass, K. A. (1987) The health of conjugally bereaved older widows: The role of appraisal, coping and resources. *Research in Nursing and Health, 10,* 39–47.
13. Silverman, P. (1985). *Widow-to-widow,* New York: Springer.
14. Dimond, M. F. (1981). Bereavement and the elderly: A critical review with implications for nursing practice and research. *Journal of Advanced Nursing, 6,* 461–470.
15. Lopata, H. Z. (1977). The meaning of friendship in widowhood. In L. Troll, J. Israel, & K. Israel (Eds.), *Looking ahead: A woman's guide to the problems and joys of growing older.* (pp. 93–105) Englewood Cliffs, NJ: Prentice-Hall.
16. Richter, J. M. (1984). Crisis of mate loss in the elderly. *Advances in Nursing Science, 6,* 45–54.
17. O'Bryant, S. (1985). Neighbor's support of older widows who live alone in their own homes. *The Gerontologist, 25,* 305–310.

18. Claypool, J. (1974). *Tracks of a fellow stranger: How to handle grief.* Waco, TX: Key Word Books.
19. Grollman, E. A. (1977). *Living when a loved one has died.* Boston: Beacon Press.
20. Kushner, H. S. (1983). *When bad things happen to good people.* New York: Avon Books.
21. Peterson, J. A., & Briley, M. P. (1977). *Widows and widowhood: A creative approach to being alone.* Chicago: Follett Publishing.
22. Stearns, A. K. (1984). *Living through personal crisis.* Chicago: Thomas More Press.
23. Tatelbaum, J. (1980). *The courage to grieve.* New York: Harper & Row.
24. Glenn, J. B. (1984). *Are you prepared to be alone?* New York: Carlton Press.
25. Loewinshohn, R. J. (1979). *Survival handbook for widows (and for relatives and friends who want to understand).* Chicago: Follett Publishing.
26. Yates, M. (1976). *Coping: A survival manual for women alone.* Englewood Cliffs, NJ: Prentice-Hall.
27. Lieberman, M. A., & Borman, L. D. (1981). The impact of self-help groups on widows' mental health. *National Reporter, 4,* 2–6.
28. Parham, I., Romajik, M., Priddy, M., & Wenzel, C. (1980). Widowhood peer counseling. *Aging, 303-304* (May-June), 42–46.
29. Rogers, J., Vachon, M. L. S., Lyall, W. A., Sheldon, A., & Freeman, S. J. J. (1980). A self-help program for widows as an independent community service. *Hospital and Community Psychiatry, 31,* 844–847.
30. Vachon, M. L. S., Lyall, W. A., Rogers, J., Freedman-Letofsky, K., & Freeman, S. J. J. (1980). A controlled study of self-help interventions for widows. *American Journal of Psychiatry, 137,* 1380–1384.
31. Rigdon, I. S., Clayton, B. G., & Dimond, M. F. (1987). Toward a theory of helpfulness for the elderly bereaved: An invitation to a new life. *Advances in Nursing Science, 9*(2), 32–43.
32. Caserta, M. S., Lund, D. A., & Dimond, M. F. (1985). Assessing interviewer effects in a longitudinal study of bereaved elderly adults. *Journal of Gerontology, 40,* 637–640.
33. Zung, W. (1965). A self-rating depression scale. *Archives of General Psychiatry, 12,* 63–70.
34. Neugarten, B., Havinghurst, R., & Tobin, S. (1961). The measurement of life satisfaction. *Journal of Gerontology, 16,* 123–143.

11

Competencies, Tasks of Daily Living, and Adjustments to Spousal Bereavement in Later Life

Dale A. Lund, Michael S. Caserta, Margaret F. Dimond, and Susan K. Shaffer

This chapter reports on data obtained from 339 bereaved spouses between the ages of 50 and 89 who were participating in a larger bereavement study designed to test the effectiveness of different types of self-help groups. Additional mailed questionnaires were completed by 208 of the same participants to address some of the specific research questions related to task abilities and deficiencies.

The majority of respondents reported that they had learned at least one new task, but even more of them said they would like to learn other new skills. Men were more likely to learn through trial and error and women were more likely to learn from a relative. Also, most of the bereaved reported that having learned new skills helped them in several ways and that skill deficiencies made their coping more difficult. Perceived competencies were found to be significantly correlated with all eight indicators of bereavement adjustment with high competencies being associated with more favorable outcomes. Suggestions for future research and practical skill-training interventions are discussed.

The focus of this chapter is on the important role that an individual's competencies in performing the basic tasks of daily living can have on the adjustment process following the death of a spouse. Being able to carry out the many mundane tasks of daily life is particularly salient when spousal bereavement is experienced in later life, because physical and cognitive declines due to aging are more likely to impair functional abilities. Older bereaved spouses are confronted with daily lives which might be radically different from the routines developed over many years of married life. A bereaved individual's personal pattern of behavior fre-

Revision of a paper presented at the Annual Meeting of the Gerontological Society of America, Washington, D.C., November 1987. The bereavement intervention study was funded by a grant from the National Institute of Aging (RO1 AG06244).

quently reflects a prior division of labor, where each spouse had become responsible for completing specific tasks which contributed to the overall maintenance of the household and functioning within the larger society. Over long periods of time, each spouse may have become highly proficient at several tasks at the expense of becoming less skilled in other activities.

In addition to providing the underlying rationale for focusing on competencies, this chapter will present the results of a study designed to address four specific research questions related to competencies and bereavement. They include an identification of specific competency deficiencies and how they influence the adjustment process.

WHY FOCUS ON COMPETENCIES?

There are numerous reasons why research on bereavement would benefit from a focus on individuals' competencies. Several specific reasons will be discussed as they relate to three general categories. The first category deals with the desire to utilize the existing literature on the broader area of stress and coping. There are already theories and models within this body of literature, as well as research findings, that suggest a prominent role for personal competencies. The second category of reasons has to do with the nature of the bereavement process and the relevance of competencies. The third category is based on the assumption that competencies are learned and therefore amenable to interventions for reducing and possibly preventing some bereavement adjustment difficulties.

Stress, Coping, and Competencies

There is a rich and extensive body of literature on stress and coping resources which suggests and in some cases confirms a positive relationship between personal competencies and a variety of indicators of well-being. Although *competency* can be defined in different ways, it generally refers to a person's abilities to successfully manage, control, or meet the demands of changing environmental conditions. Competencies can include the social skills, knowledge, previous experience, and specific instrumental behavioral skills necessary to perform the many tasks of daily living. Franks and Marolla[1] defined competencies as the successful performance in meeting demands for achievement that usually require instrumental skills in adapting to the environment. The interplay between the person and environmental factors has been well stated in Lawton's[2] competency and environmental press theory and Kahana's[3] congruence model of person-environment interaction. Both views imply that the environment makes variable levels of demands on people and that personal competencies are necessary to maintain a level of balance so that needs can continue to be met and the press of events will not overwhelm the person. Lawton suggests that the environment has a great impact on low-competency people and that behavior and affect deteriorate when the press of events exceeds competencies. Similarly, Kahana indicates that person-environment congruence leads to positive mental states and satisfied needs, whereas incongruence is likely to result in negative mental health.

There is considerable consensus in the stress and coping literature that competency is an important resource for successful adjustment to negative life events.[1-14] Included among many of these reports is a common emphasis on the pragmatic skills necessary to deal with very specific problems. For example, Little[12] indicated that being able to accomplish in-home personal projects was associated with a person's quality of life, including health status. Kanner, Coyne, Schaefer, and Lazarus[9] reported that the inability to manage and resolve daily hassles was more predictive of subsequent psychological symptoms than major life events. Libet and Lewinsohn[11] found that deficiencies in social skills increased the likelihood of depression. Part of the reason competency influences these adjustment outcomes is that people who are more competent are more capable of making diverse coping responses,[11] are likely to make a greater number of coping attempts,[14] and will be active agents in making things happen.[1] In short, they have a valuable coping resource to utilize in stressful, demanding situations.

If competencies in dealing with daily tasks can improve coping abilities and impact a variety of well-being outcomes, it is imperative that research begin to examine the role that competency plays within the bereavement process. The death of a spouse has been acknowledged as one of the most stressful and disruptive events that can occur within a person's life, but very little research evidence exists concerning the extent to which competencies can influence the course of bereavement adjustments.

Competencies and Bereavement

Another personal coping resource, self-esteem, has been found to be associated with adjustment to bereavement. We reported in another article[15] that low self-esteem resulted in significantly greater coping difficulty over time. Not only was it the most predictive variable, but it was relatively stable over the first 2 years of bereavement. The stability of self-esteem was further documented when the comparison was made between bereaved and matched nonbereaved older adults and no bereavement effects were observed. The relevance of this finding to possible preventive coping interventions is discussed later in this chapter. Pearlin and Schooler[13] also reported that self-esteem and mastery in dealing with the environment can reduce the impact of strain.

Self-esteem is usually regarded as the self-evaluative and affective component of a person's overall self-concept.[16] It includes the positive and negative views that someone has of him- or herself. Perceived competencies are similar to self-esteem in that both involve perceptions of the self, are part of a person's self-concept, and can be considered as personal coping resources. Perceived competencies do not require evaluative judgments (i.e., being good or bad at something), because they focus more specifically on the extent to which people feel that they are capable of doing something. Perceived competencies and self-esteem are likely to have a reciprocal influence, since recognizing personal competencies can increase positive feelings about oneself and those positive assessments can motivate one to be more competent. If self-esteem is related to perceived competencies and, as already has been shown, it impacts adjustments, then there is considerable reason to investigate the potentially important influence of competencies on outcomes as well.

A second reason for further examination of competencies is that the lack of ability to perform tasks of daily living is a common complaint among older bereaved spouses. Again, from our research as well as others, it is clear that many people in the older age cohorts today are deficient in specific skills and their deficiencies are generally consistent with the differentiated sex role socialization process described in the sociology literature.[17] Older men have greater difficulty with home maintenance, meal preparation, laundry, and shopping, whereas older women are less prepared to do home repairs and yardwork and maintain household finances and automobiles. In an earlier study, when we asked our bereaved respondents (in an open-ended format) what their single greatest difficulty was, the second most common answer referred to problems related to tasks of daily living.[18] (Loneliness was the most common and continuing difficulty.) Although numerous scholars and investigators[19-32] have noted that bereaved persons have difficulty performing these mundane tasks, very few have focused primarily on how these deficiencies might adversely impact other bereavement adjustments. A few noteworthy exceptions include Stephenson[33] (who reported that being unable to care adequately for oneself leads to more rapid health declines), Ben-Sira[34] (who indicated that control of resources and resource enhancement improves bereavement readjustments), Gass[35] (who found that feeling in control over bereavement was associated with better psychosocial adjustment and less physical dysfunction), Hogstel[36] (who reported that widowers lacking experience in household tasks felt less useful and more lonely), and Amaral[37] (who found that disruptions in daily living correlated with greater depression, anxiety, and severity of new illnesses). Collectively, the bereavement literature illustrates the commonality of problems with daily living, but there is a considerable void in knowing which specific tasks are the most problematic and how strongly competencies are associated with other bereavement adjustments. Both of these gaps are addressed in the study reported on later in this chapter.

Two other facts about the bereavement process which contribute to the desirability of examining competencies are that many older widowed persons worry about becoming functionally dependent upon others and that grief work itself depletes energy resources. Freud[38] pointed out many years ago that grieving requires mental work which often results in physical exhaustion. Reliving past experiences and circumstances surrounding the death, crying, feeling guilt about not having done more for the deceased, attempting to discover a reason for the death, and worrying about how one will be able to do all of the tasks that the deceased spouse had done can lead to physical and emotional exhaustion. If personal competencies are seriously lacking, the exhaustion may worsen over time or the grieving person may have to spend an excessive amount of time trying to get the tasks accomplished. In either case, deficiencies in daily competencies may result in diversions from the necessary grief work, in extreme exhaustion, or both. It is possible that being competent in performing these basic tasks might minimize the fatigue resulting from worries about tasks and dependency and allow more energy for the emotional expression of grief. Also, those who lack skills in meal preparation are likely to have a greater risk of not eating well and of experiencing the subsequent negative health consequences. For these reasons, it is likely that competencies would be helpful personal coping resources, even in the early part of the bereavement process.

Other aspects of the bereavement process which are relevant to competencies stem directly from the advice of bereaved elders to others who might find themselves in a similar situation. Again, people who are more competent are better able to follow such advice. When we asked the bereaved respondents what advice they would give to others, the most common answers, aside from expressing their reluctance because bereavement is an individual experience, were to take 1 day at a time and to keep busy. Many of the bereaved described feeling overwhelmed at the prospect of having to manage their lives over the coming years, months, and days—even just 1 day. Apparently it was more manageable for them to think only about the present day, to determine what needed to be accomplished, to set realistic coping goals, and to do the best they could that specific day. Others even suggested that a daylong perspective was too overwhelming and that it was better to divide the day into smaller and more manageable parts. For example, some recommended trying to cope as well as one could in the morning, doing the same for the afternoon, and then again in the evening. This is similar to the notion of a "personal project," which Little[12] described as being important to a person's quality of life. By setting practical and realistic goals, such as projects that need to be accomplished during small parts of each day, the bereavement process might become less overwhelming. This might be done by expecting oneself to get out of bed, shower, and eat breakfast by a particular time. These projects or activities might be followed by others, such as completing specific household chores, making phone calls, shopping, going on a walk, visiting a friend, working at a hobby, or reading a chapter in a book. The overall rationale of this advice was not to divert attention away from the reality of the situation but to make each day more manageable.

As indicated earlier, people with greater competencies are less likely to be overwhelmed by the prospect of preparing a meal, changing a furnace filter, cleaning an air conditioner, or shopping at a grocery store. They might be more likely to continue breaking each day into smaller units if they identify specific tasks and are successful at completing them. Sanders[39] reported that when bereaved persons accomplished some tasks, they felt more competent. Social learning theorists claim that setting goals and not accomplishing them results in fewer attempts in the future. Conversely, being competent at a specific task will lead to greater success in accomplishing it, which will consequently make the person more capable of taking one day at a time.

Closely related to this is the advice to keep busy. Rubinstein[40] reported that the ability to fill days constructively with meaningful activities is essential to the adjustment to bereavement. Again, in our earlier study the respondents were usually clear in distinguishing busy activity from avoiding the reality of the loss situation. The important point was that long periods of inactivity only seemed to make matters worse. For many, when they became more active and filled their vacant time with purposeful activities, they felt better about themselves and believed that they were managing much better. People who are competent at a greater number of tasks have more opportunities to be busy or at least to be busy doing things at which they will be successful.

One final consideration concerning the bereavement process which brings to light the relevancy of personal competencies is the role of social support and social interactions. Because bereavement adjustments in later life frequently require some degree of both formal and informal support services, it is important that the services be available and that the bereaved know how to access them. As a number of experts[19,20,23,29] have pointed out, bereaved persons are confronted with numerous tasks that require the assistance of others. Such tasks include filling out forms for insurance, Social Security, and wills, shopping, learning how to drive an automobile, and learning how to balance a checkbook and to do other financial chores. Glick, Weiss, and Parkes[21] mentioned the importance of developing new skills specifically to deal more effectively with problems related to the many bureaucracies. Barrett and Schneweis[19] suggest that these service needs persist for many years and they argue that it is a myth that only the recently widowed need help.

It is apparent that not all bereaved older adults have access to informal assistance, as it is common for some widowers to hire assistance with these tasks.[41] When these situations arise, it is important to know what help and resources are available and how to access them.[42] Even when informal social supports are available, they may not be sufficient to resolve the difficulty without accessing more formal services. For example, someone may need home health care services for assistance that the deceased spouse previously provided. Although family and friends might provide emotional and financial assistance, they may not have the time to help with health care needs. It should be noted, however, that family and friends typically provide considerable help to the bereaved[41,43,44] by performing the tasks themselves, teaching the bereaved, or helping the bereaved access the appropriate formal services.

Even though social supports provide assistance in the bereavement adjustment process,[45] personal competencies are needed to fill in the gaps or to facilitate the effectiveness of the support resources. People who are quite competent and have greater diversity in their skills are much less likely to need assistance, because they are capable of meeting more of their own needs. The contacts with their informal support networks also are likely to be less demanding and exhausting; therefore, these networks will be less subject to depletion over long periods of time. When support persons are required to become involved in numerous tasks, especially on a daily basis, they can become fatigued, dissatisfied, and less willing and able to continue with their assistance. There also is the related issue of older adults not wanting to be dependent on others. It is certainly possible, for example, that a parent-adult child relationship might be adversely affected when the bereaved parent becomes increasingly dependent on the adult child, for the relationship ceases to be egalitarian or reciprocal and comes to be characterized by dependency. Again, competencies on the part of older bereaved adults might help to ensure that their relationships with those in their informal social networks remain egalitarian, satisfying, and intact.

Competencies and Interventions

The third category of reasons for focusing on personal competencies is based on the assumption that they can be learned, or at least improved, and therefore are amenable to interventions. Because tasks of daily life are by themselves problematic, interventions aimed at improving competencies can directly minimize a major source of difficulty. Furthermore, if competencies are associated with other coping difficulties, then interventions designed to enhance competencies are likely to improve other adjustment outcomes as well. Recognizing this dual purpose of competency-based bereavement interventions should result in an additional option for practical assistance. Traditional self-help groups provide excellent opportunities for expression, sharing, companionship, and social interaction. One-to-one counseling interventions offer opportunities for introspection, resolving emotional and psychological discomfort, and self-expression. Formal community services might help provide meals, transportation, and economic support. Competency-enhancing interventions, however, would add significantly to the intervention options and would help to fill a void in needed assistance.

One final consideration for examining competencies is the increased potential for preventing unnecessary difficulties coping with bereavement. There is no reason to wait for the death of a spouse to become more effective in managing the tasks of daily life. Interventions for self-expression do not have the same degree of potential for prevention that competency interventions have, because the death event must occur for the self-expression to be relevant. Although bereaved persons might learn from others or through trial and error how to accomplish some of these daily tasks, it is important to recognize that many of them can be learned prior to bereavement and may help to reduce some of the stress and difficulty that follows.

Research Questions

The remainder of this chapter deals with the results of a study which examined the personal competencies and bereavement adjustments of a sample of older adults. The primary concerns were to identify specific tasks with which older adults have difficulty, to discover how they learn to do new tasks, and to determine how competencies impact other bereavement outcomes. Four specific research questions are addressed:

1. Which new tasks of daily living do most bereaved older adults learn to accomplish after the death of the spouse and how do they learn them?
2. What benefits do bereaved older adults perceive from learning to perform new tasks of daily living?
3. Which tasks of daily living do recently bereaved spouses desire to learn how to perform?
4. To what extent do perceived competencies in performing tasks of daily living influence bereavement adjustments?

METHODS

The data for this investigation were part of a larger intervention study designed to assess the effectiveness of self-help groups on the adjustment process of older bereaved spouses. The type of leader (widow or professional) and duration of the groups (8 weeks or 1 year) were examined to determine which type of format was most effective. A total of 26 self-help groups were formed which represented the four different combinations of the intervention formats. In addition, there was a control group which received no intervention. Other information regarding the purpose, methodology, and practical problems of this larger study can be found in Chapter 15.

Sample and Procedure

Recently bereaved spouses over the age of 50 were identified through newspaper obituaries and were randomly assigned into one of the four intervention condition groups or the control group. Questionnaires were hand delivered 2 months after the death event to those who agreed to participate. Three hundred thirty-nine people (241 assigned to intervention condition groups and 98 to the control group) returned the T_1 questionnaires. This full sample of 242 women (71.4%) and 97 men was used to address research question 4, because the competencies scale and the other bereavement outcome measures were included in the questionnaire. These respondents ranged in age from 50 to 89 years ($M = 67.5$, $SD = 8.5$), were fairly well educated (85% high school graduates), were primarily Caucasian (98.8%), and were generally not employed outside the home (76.3%). The larger study also utilized three follow-up questionnaire assessments to examine changes due to the intervention conditions over the course of 2 years.

Because the larger study did not specifically deal with the first three research questions (which concern new skills that were learned and how they were learned), a special onetime questionnaire concerning these issues was prepared and mailed to the 339 bereaved spouses between the T_1 and T_2 (8 week follow-up) data-gathering times. This survey was completed at a mean of 8.8 months following the spouse's death. Therefore, the sample used to answer the first three research questions consists of the 208 (61.4%) persons who returned this separate question-naire. The characteristics of this smaller sample were almost identical to those in the larger study, with 72.1% female ($N = 150$) and 27.9% male ($N = 58$). No statistical differences were found between the two samples relative to age, employ-ment, and ethnicity.

Instruments

The T_1 questionnaire in the larger study took 30–45 minutes to complete. It elicited information regarding sociodemographics, the circumstances and causes of the spouse's death, social support, and several indicators of how well the surviving spouse was adjusting to the bereavement situation. These indicators included the 13 Likert-type items in the Revised Texas Inventory of Grief,[46] which assesses the extent to which grief is being resolved; the 20-item Geriatric Depression Scale,[47] which has a dichotomous choice format; the 13 Likert-type items in the Life Satisfaction Index (LSI-Z);[48] and the Rosenberg self-esteem scale.[49] All of the scales have been used widely and have sound psychometric properties. Five single-item self-report measures also were used as indicators of other aspects of the adjustment process. Respondents were asked to describe on scales from 1 (low or poor) to 5 (high or excellent) their current levels of stress, loneliness, health, nutrition, and overall coping ability.

Also included in the T_1 questionnaire was a perceived competencies scale that was modified from one used by two of the investigators in a previous study of older caregivers.[50] The version used in the present study eliminated those items that were too specific to a caregiving situation and therefore difficult to apply to a bereaved population. The scale consists of 25 items, each identifying a particular skill for which the respondents were asked to rate their perceived abilities (1 = no ability, 2 = some ability, 3 = great ability). Items ranged from instrumental activities, such as driving a car, balancing a checkbook, and planning meals, to more psychosocial skills, such as assertiveness, adaptability to change, and the ability to express oneself to others. A factor analysis yielded three subscales. The items comprising each factor and their associated factor loadings are presented in Table 1. The three subscales have been named Social and Interpersonal Skills ($\alpha = .86$), Instrumental Skills ($\alpha = .80$), and the Ability to Set Priorities and to Identify and Utilize Resources ($\alpha = .83$). A shortened name for this last factor could be Resource Identification Skills. Two items that did not satisfactorily load on any factor were "driving a car" and "doing minor repairs." They were there-fore not included in the total competence scale. The Cronbach alpha on the com-plete scale was .92.

Correlations also were computed for each of the relationships among the three subscales and the total competency score. Table 2 shows that all of the

TABLE 1   Competence Subscales

Items	Factor loadings
Social and interpersonal skills[a]	
Understand others' communications	.76
Anticipate others' reactions	.74
Recognize interpersonal problems	.69
Exercise self-control	.50
Express thoughts and feelings	.46
Cope with failure	.42
Adapt to changes	.40
Be assertive	.40
Maintain sense of humor	.31
Instrumental skills[b]	
Perform and endure physical activity	.64
Keep household clean	.64
Plan things in advance	.61
Use public facilities	.49
Use public transportation	.49
Organize time	.46
Concentrate	.41
Plan and cook meals	.33
Resource identification skills[c]	
Utilize sources of help	.85
Identify resources	.74
Meet own leisure needs	.52
Set goals objectively	.43
Manage finances	.39
Do math problems (e.g., balance checkbook)	.31

[a]Cronbach alpha = .86. [b]Cronbach alpha = .80. [c]Cronbach alpha = .83.

correlations were in the expected positive direction and were quite high, with the lowest ($r = .64$) for the relationship between instrumental and resource identification skills. These correlations indicate that the three categories of competency skills occur together in similar degrees. That is, people who perceived themselves as having good interpersonal skills also were likely to report that they had good instrumental skills and were more able to identify resources to fill their needs. Conversely, people with low competency scores in one category had low scores in the other two categories.

The separate skills survey consisted primarily of a list of 94 tasks of daily living that was generated by a review of the literature and a panel of 16 people (13 Gerontology Center staff and 3 widowed persons). The tasks included using com-

TABLE 2   Intercorrelations among Competency Subscales and Total Scores

	Interpersonal skills	Instrumental skills	Resource identification skills	Total competency
Interpersonal skills	—	.66	.69	.91
Instrumental skills	—	—	.64	.87
Resource identification skills	—	—	—	.86

Note. For all Pearson correlations, $p < .0001$.

mon household appliances and yard and lawn tools; maintaining financial records, household appliances, automobiles, and utilities; and knowing how to access resources, prepare meals, and clean house. For each of the 94 skills, the respondents were asked if they possessed the skill or could accomplish the task, if they had learned the skill after the spouse's death (for skills possessed), and if they would like to acquire the skill (for skills possessed). Additionally, those who had learned to do new tasks after the spouse's death were asked how they had learned these new skills (trial and error, from a friend or relative, by paying someone, or from some other source) and what benefits did they perceive from learning them (felt better about self, was more independent, kept busier, dealt better with grief, got along better with others, or other benefits). All respondents were asked if the lack of skills adversely affected their coping with bereavement; they were given four answer choices ranging from "no, it had not made it more difficult" to "yes, a lot more difficult." The findings presented in this chapter are based on self-reported measures and data obtained at only one time period; therefore, they should be regarded with some caution. Time series or longitudinal designs with multiple sources of information are needed to delineate more clearly the causal nature of some relationships that we examined. Self-selection into the study also is problematic, because we do not have comparable measures on all the study variables for those who decided not to participate.

RESULTS

The first research question asked which new tasks of daily living were learned during the first several months of bereavement. Because an age cohort effect has likely contributed to differential skills among older men and women, many of the statistical analyses were done separately by gender. It is highly likely that older bereaved men would be learning different tasks than older bereaved women. Tables 3 and 4 provide a rank ordering of the most common skills that participants in the study had learned since the spouse's death. Table 3 lists the skills that the men had learned and Table 4 lists those for the women. The mean age of the 58 males was 69.7 years and the mean for the 150 females was 66.4 years.

Our data indicated that women were more likely than men to learn at least one of these new tasks. One hundred thirteen women (75.3%) and 39 men (67.2%) responded in the questionnaires that they had learned new tasks, but 12 of these men and 30 of these women did not identify which specific tasks they had learned. The data in Tables 3 and 4 report the frequencies and percentages based on the full sample of men and women. Because we could not determine the exact number of tasks that the 12 men and 30 women had learned, the mean number of tasks learned is based on the 27 men and 83 women who identified at least one specific new task. Again, the bereaved women had learned slightly more new tasks ($M = 6.7$, range = 1–30) than the men ($M = 5.0$, range = 1–21). These differences, however, were not statistically significant.

According to Table 3, the most common skills that the males had learned were related primarily to cooking and household cleaning. Approximately 26% of the full sample of men had learned to cook for only one person, 21% had learned general cooking skills, and 19% had learned how to do their laundry. The next most common skills learned by these men were household cleaning, operating washing machines, grocery shopping, operating clothes dryers, preparing a specific food item, filing various claim forms, and transferring auto and house titles.

Table 4 shows that, as expected, bereaved women had learned almost a completely different set of skills than their male counterparts. The only skills that had been learned by both groups were filing various claim forms and transferring auto and house titles. These two tasks were the most commonly learned by the women, followed by filling the automobile gas tank, maintaining furnace filters, setting up or closing a will or an estate, knowing when to service the car, and making the house more secure. It is clear that bereaved males were learning to do the tasks that women in their age cohort were more skilled at and, conversely, the women were learning to do the tasks that the men had typically performed.

The second part of the first research question dealt with how the respondents had learned to do most of these new tasks. Respondents were asked to select answers from the five choices shown in Table 5. Some of the respondents selected more than one answer, so the totals for the sources of help exceed the identified sample sizes for both men and women. Among the men who learned new tasks, most indicated that they had learned them on their own (66.7%), many had help from a relative (41.0%), and some checked the category "other" (17.9%). Very few reported they had been helped by a friend or had paid someone (combined 7.7%). Of the women who had learned to perform new tasks, most had been helped by a relative (59.3%) and many had learned on their own (42.9%). Unlike the men, many of the women had paid for assistance (32.7%) or were helped by a friend (27.4%). In order to test for significant differences between the sources of help for men and women, each source was treated as a separate variable and a chi-square test for association was computed. These results confirm that men were significantly more likely to learn on their own and women were more likely to be helped by a friend and to pay someone for help.

The second research question was investigated by asking the bereaved per-

TABLE 3 Frequency of Most Common Skills Learned by Bereaved Males following the Spouse's Death ($N = 58$)

Specific need learned	N	%
Learning to cook for only one person	15	25.9%
General cooking	12	20.7
Laundry	11	19.0
Household cleaning	9	15.5
Using and maintaining washing machine	8	13.8
Learning more about grocery shopping	8	13.8
Ironing	7	12.1
Using and maintaining clothes dryer	6	10.3
Learn how to prepare or cook a specific food item or meal	5	8.6
Filing insurance, Medicare, Medicaid, and Social Security claims	5	8.6
Transferring auto and house titles	5	8.6
Mending clothes	4	6.9
Learning about general nutrition and proper diet	4	6.9
Using and maintaining vacuum cleaners	3	5.2
Balancing a checkbook (monthly)	3	5.2
Paying bills	3	5.2
Setting up or closing a will or an estate	3	5.2
Selecting a lawyer	3	5.2

TABLE 4 Frequency of Most Common Skills Learned by Bereaved Females following the Spouse's Death ($N = 150$)

Specific need learned	N	%
Transferring auto and house titles	36	24.0%
Filing insurance, Medicare, Medicaid, and Social Security claims	24	16.0
Filling the gas tank	24	16.0
Changing/cleaning furnace filters	20	13.3
Setting up or closing a will or an estate	20	13.3
Knowing when to service auto	19	12.7
Learning how to make the house more secure	18	12.0
Winterizing the home	17	11.3
How to make better use of financial resources	17	11.3
Locating where to turn electricity, water, and gas on and off	16	10.7
Doing general lawn care	16	10.7
Balancing a checkbook (monthly)	15	10.0
Paying bills	15	10.0
Winterizing the auto	15	10.0
Operating a lawn mower	14	9.3
Knowing where to service auto	14	9.3

sons if learning new tasks had helped them in any of six different ways. Again, the respondents could select more than one answer. Bereaved men selected a mean of 2.2 answers and bereaved women a mean of 2.3. The most common perceived benefits for the men were keeping busy (63.2%), followed closely by feeling better about self (57.9%), being more independent (47.4%), dealing better with their grief (34.2%), and getting along better with others (15.8%). Bereaved women differed statistically from their male counterparts in that the benefit most

TABLE 5 Sources and Perceived Benefits of Learning New Skills among Older Bereaved Spouses

	Males		Females		
	N	%	N	%	Chi-square
Method/source of learning[a]	(N = 39)		(N = 113)		
Trial and error by myself	26	66.7	48	42.9	5.64*
Learned or helped by a friend	2	5.1	31	27.4	7.23**
Learned or helped by a relative	16	41.0	67	59.3	3.20
Learned or helped by paying someone	1	2.6	37	32.7	12.52**
Other	7	17.9	7	6.2	3.49
Perceived benefits[a]	(N = 38)		(N = 106)		
Feel better about myself	22	57.9	57	53.8	0.06
Be more independent	18	47.4	88	83.0	16.51**
Keep busy	24	63.2	47	44.3	3.25
Deal better with the grief	13	34.2	31	29.2	0.13
Get along better with others	6	15.8	13	12.3	0.07
Other	1	2.6	7	6.6	0.25
Did lack of skills impact coping?	(N = 40)		(N = 117)		
Yes, a lot more difficult	4	10.0	22	18.8	2.08
Yes, somewhat more difficult	15	37.5	37	31.6	
Yes, but only a little bit more difficult	9	22.5	29	24.8	
No, it hasn't made it more difficult	12	30.0	29	24.8	

[a]Respondents could select more than one answer category.
*$p < .05$. **$p < .01$.

TABLE 6   Frequency of Most Common Needs Identified by Bereaved Males ($N = 58$)

Specific need	N	%
Setting up a living will	18	31.0%
Setting up or closing a will or an estate	17	29.3
Learning how to cook for only one person	16	27.6
Learning about general nutrition and proper diet	14	24.1
General cooking	12	20.7
Senior centers (access)	12	20.7
Finding groups with common social interests	12	20.7
How to make better use of financial resources	11	19.0
Learning more about general legal issues	11	19.0
Learn tips on how to save money (e.g., using coupons, best buys, etc.)	11	19.0
Selecting a lawyer	10	17.2
Filing insurance, Medicare, Medicaid, and Social Security claims	9	15.5
Organizing and maintaining financial files	8	13.8
Filling out tax forms	8	13.8
Learning new health exercises	8	13.8
Laundry	7	12.1
Ironing	7	12.1
Using and maintaining microwave ovens	7	12.1
Using and maintaining computers	7	12.1
Transferring auto and house titles	7	12.1
Learning about medications	7	12.1

commonly cited by them was being more independent (83%). They were similar to men in reporting that learning new tasks helped them feel better about themselves (53.8%), keep busy (44.3%), deal better with their grief (29.2%), and get along better with others (12.3%). These data clearly show that both bereaved males and females realized several important benefits from learning to do new tasks of daily living.

Although it was not a major research question, all respondents also were asked if not being able to do some of the tasks had made it more difficult to cope with the spouse's death. Seventy percent of the men and 75.2% of the women reported that their lack of certain skills had made coping more difficult. According to the data in Table 5, about 48% of the men and 50% of the women indicated that it had made it either somewhat or a lot more difficult. None of the differences between the men and women were statistically significant.

The purpose of research question 3 was to identify specific tasks that the bereaved would want to learn if a training program were made available to them. Most of the men (72.4%) and women (86.7%) in the full samples reported that they would like to learn at least one of the 94 tasks listed in the questionnaire. The women identified more such tasks ($M = 12.8$) than the men ($M = 8.4$). Tables 6 and 7 report the frequencies and percentages based on the full samples of 58 men and 150 women. For bereaved men, the most common needs or tasks were learning how to set up a living will (31.0%), how to set up or close a will or an estate (29.3%), how to cook for only one person (27.6%), how to follow good nutrition and diet (24.1%), and how to do general cooking (20.7%). Also near the top of the list were learning about senior centers and finding groups with common social interests (each 20.7%). As expected, at the top of the list for the bereaved women

TABLE 7   Frequency of Most Common Needs Identified by Bereaved Females (N = 150)

Specific need	N	%
Doing minor plumbing	62	41.3%
Doing minor electrical repairs	60	40.0
Locating where to turn electricity, water, and gas on and off	49	32.7
Finding groups with common social interests	48	32.0
Doing minor repairs on appliances	46	30.7
Learning more about general legal issues	46	30.7
Maintaining furnace	45	30.0
Setting up a living will	43	28.7
Learning to use a video recorder with the TV	42	28.0
Filing insurance, Medicare, Medicaid, and Social Security claims	39	26.0
Checking auto tire pressure	39	26.0
Knowing when to service auto	39	26.0
Filling out tax forms	37	24.7
How to make better use of financial resources	35	23.3
Learning about medications	35	23.3
Educational programs (e.g., community schools, university and college courses)	34	22.7
Doing general auto maintenance	33	22.0
Knowing where to service auto	33	22.0
Learning how to cook for only one person	32	21.3
Winterizing the auto	32	21.3

were learning home repairs such as minor plumbing (41.3%) and electrical work (40.0%), and locating where to turn on and off the electricity, water, and gas for household use (32.7%). Although these women did not specifically mention senior centers, they wanted to learn about groups with common social interests (32.0%). A variety of additional skills were needed regarding legal issues, filing claim forms, and servicing automobiles. Some of the women (21.3%) wanted to learn how to cook for only one person. Both men (12.1%) and women (23.3%) wanted to learn more about medications. A detailed review of these needed skills reveals that they are diverse, they are numerous, and, most important, they are behaviors that can be learned through practical interventions.

The final research question, perhaps the most important of the four, deals with the potential influence that perceived competencies might have on several indicators of bereavement adjustments. As indicated earlier, the data used for this research question were taken from the T_1 assessment in the larger study in order (1) to use a larger sample of respondents, (2) to use the perceived competency scale, and (3) to use measures where the independent variable was not assessed some time after the dependent variables (in this particular case, all variables were assessed at the same time).

While it previously had been established that self-esteem was predictive of bereavement outcomes,[15] in this study a strong relationship between self-esteem and competencies was found (r = .67, p < .001). The relationships between the competency measures (interpersonal, instrumental, and resource subscales as well as the total competency scores) and eight indicators of bereavement adjustment are provided in Table 8. The most noteworthy finding from all of these Pearson correlations was that all of them were statistically significant and in the expected direction (i.e., with high perceived-competency scores associated with more favorable bereavement adjustments). With only two exceptions, the strongest associations were between the total competencies scores and the outcomes. The two exceptions were the relationships between resource skills and loneliness ($r = -.27$) and between instrumental skills and perceived health ($r = .47$). The mean correlation of the total competencies score with the eight adjustment indicators was .40, indicating at least moderately strong relationships. The strongest correlations using the total competencies scores were found with depression ($r = -.68$), life satisfaction ($r = .53$), perceived coping ($r = .43$), and perceived health ($r = .43$); the weakest relationship was found with perceived stress ($r = -.19$).

With respect to the three subscales, all had mean correlations of .35 with the eight bereavement outcome measures. High interpersonal skills were most strongly associated with low depression ($r = -.62$), high life satisfaction ($r = .48$), and high perceived coping ($r = .40$). High instrumental skills were similarly associated with the same three adjustment measures but also were strongly related to positive perceptions of health ($r = .47$). Having high resource identification skills was most strongly associated with low depression ($r = -.61$) and high life satisfaction ($r = .47$).

In order to identify possible effects of age, sex, and education on competencies, we tested for these statistical relationships. Age and sex did not have direct effects on the total competencies scores, but males were unexpectedly found to have slightly higher interpersonal skill scores and older people had slightly lower instrumental skill scores. Education was related to the competency measures ($r = .11-.15$), with high education scores associated with slightly greater perceived competencies.

DISCUSSION AND CONCLUSIONS

The general conclusion of this chapter, based on the data analyses performed, is that perceived competencies and the actual ability to complete the numerous tasks of daily life are very relevant to understanding adjustments to spousal bereavement in later life. Although most of the older bereaved men and women were quite resourceful in learning how to accomplish new tasks, many indicated that they were deficient in several important tasks and that they believed their deficiencies had made the adjustment process more difficult. Our findings revealed

TABLE 8   Relationships between Competency Scales and Indicators of Bereavement Adjustment

Indicators of bereavement adjustment	Interpersonal skills	Instrumental skills	Resource identification skills	Total competency
Grief	−.28	−.26	−.28	−.31
Depression	−.62	−.58	−.61	−.68
Life satisfaction	.48	.44	.47	.53
Perceived stress	−.17	−.14	−.19	−.19
Perceived coping	.40	.40	.34	.43
Loneliness	−.23	−.21	−.27	−.26
Perceived health	.31	.47	.38	.43
Perceived nutrition	.32	.30	.24	.33

Note. All correlations are beyond $p < .01$.

that competencies were associated with more favorable bereavement adjustments on all eight indicators. Therefore, competencies were associated with psychological, physical, emotional, and social outcomes.

In the literature and conceptual sections presented earlier in this chapter, we outlined several reasons why competencies might facilitate bereavement adjustments. The present analyses were not done to prove or disprove any of the claims made; however, many of the findings were consistent with our assumptions and expectations. For example, those who had learned to do new tasks reported that they felt better about themselves, were more independent, kept busy, and dealt better with their grief; some indicated that they were also helped by being able to get along better with others. Conversely, most of the bereaved who were deficient in abilities to accomplish some tasks said that their inabilities had made their coping more difficult. It is quite possible that perceived competencies and actual task abilities also influence bereavement adjustments indirectly by facilitating behaviors and attitudes that encourage more favorable outcomes. Those who are competent in performing the many tasks of daily life and are aware of their abilities might be more motivated, skilled, persistent, and confident in their efforts to cope with the most stressful event of their lives.

Not only was our study consistent with the literature, which indicated that older men and women have differential skills regarding many of the tasks of daily living, but we were able to identify which specific skills men and women were generally able to learn on their own or through help from others and which ones they had not learned even 9 months after the spouse's death. Also, the study identified several skill deficiencies that bereaved men and women had in common, such as regarding legal and social needs. It was valuable to learn that some relatives had been quite helpful in teaching the participants (particularly the women) how to do many of these tasks and also that men were more likely to rely on trial and error. Nearly one-third of the women, however, reported that they had paid someone for assistance with these tasks.

These findings are pertinent to those who are interested in developing practical interventions for older bereaved spouses. A substantial number of the respondents stated they would appreciate having opportunities to learn many of these skills so that they could more effectively manage their daily lives. Nearly all of the skills that they wanted to learn could be taught relatively easy in one-to-one or group situations. Some of the tasks, such as legal and health care tasks, would require the use of trained professionals, but most of them would not. In fact, many older widowed persons would be capable of serving as teachers or trainers of others, which in turn would likely promote their own self-esteem, competencies, and social life. These suggestions are obviously not being made for the first time. What is being newly recommended is that such interventions can be based upon scientific and theoretical grounds, since they relate to widely acknowledged theories of coping, self-esteem, competencies, stress, self-efficacy, and environmental press. Interventions designed to provide practical skill training to older bereaved persons should be accepted and encouraged by the scientific community. Among other reasons, they offer considerable promise for facilitating positive adjustments to bereavement, can be designed to fit the constraints of controlled research investigations, and can be guided by and contribute to a variety of theoretical models and perspectives. Perhaps the best reason, however, is simply that many bereaved spouses want to learn new skills so they can use them in their daily lives.

REFERENCES

1. Franks, D. D., & Marolla, J. (1982). Efficacious action and social approval as interacting dimensions of self-esteem: A tentative formulation through construct validation. *Sociometry, 19*, 324–341.
2. Lawton, M. P. (1986). *Environment and aging*. Albany, NY: Center for the Study of Aging.
3. Kahana, E. (1982). A congruence model of person-environment interaction. In M. P. Lawton, P. G. Windley, & T. O. Byerts (Eds.), *Aging and the environment: Theoretical approaches* (pp. 97–121). New York: Springer.
4. Bandura, A. (1982). Self-efficacy mechanism in human agency. *American Psychologist, 37*, 122–147.
5. Billings, A. G., & Moos, R. H. (1981). The role of coping responses and social resources in attenuating the stress of life events. *Journal of Behavioral Medicine, 4*, 139–157.
6. Caplan, G. (1981). Mastery of stress: Psychosocial aspects. *American Journal of Psychiatry, 138*, 413–420.
7. Cohen, S., & McKay, G. (1984). Social support, stress and the buffering hypothesis: A theoretical analysis. In A. Baum, J. E. Singer, & S. E. Taylor (Eds.), *Stressful life events and their contexts*. New York: Prodist.
8. Holahan, C. K., Holahan, C. J., & Belk, S. S. (1984). Adjustment in aging: The roles of life stress, hassles, and self-efficacy. *Health Psychology, 3*, 315–328.
9. Kanner, A. D., Coyne, J. C., Schaefer, C., & Lazarus, R. S. (1981). Comparison of two modes of stress measurement: Daily hassles and uplifts versus major life events. *Journal of Behavioral Medicine, 4*, 1–39.
10. Folkman, S., Lazarus, R. S., Gruen, R. J., & Delongis, A. (1986). Appraisal, coping, health status, and psychological symptoms. *Journal of Personality and Social Psychology, 50*, 571–579.
11. Libet, J. M., & Lewinsohn, P. M. (1973). Concept of social skill with special reference to the behavior of depressed persons. *Journal of Consulting and Clinical Psychology, 40*, 304–312.
12. Little, B. R. (1983). Personal projects: A rationale and method for investigation. *Environment and Behavior, 15*, 273–309.
13. Pearlin, L., & Schooler, C. (1978). The structure of coping. *Journal of Health and Social Behavior, 19*, 2–21.
14. Rodin, J., & Langer, E. (1980). The decline of control and the fall of self-esteem. *Journal of Social Issues, 36*, 12–29.
15. Lund, D. A., Dimond, M. F., Caserta, M. S., Johnson, R. J., Poulton, J. L., & Connelly, J. R. (1985–1986). Identifying elderly with coping difficulties after two years of bereavement. *Omega, 16*, 213–224.
16. Lund, D. A., Caserta, M. S. Dimond, M. F., & Gray, R. M. (1986). Impact of bereavement on self-conceptions of older surviving spouses. *Symbolic Interaction, 9*, 235–244.
17. Robertson, I. (1987). *Sociology (3rd ed.)* . New York: Worth.
18. Lund, D. A., Caserta, M. S., & Dimond, M. F. (1986). Gender differences through two years of bereavement among the elderly. *The Gerontologist, 26*, 314–320.
19. Barrett, C. J., & Schneweis, K. M. (1980–1981). An empirical search for stages of widowhood. *Omega, 11*, 97–104.
20. Carey, R. G. (1979–1980). Weathering widowhood: Problems and adjustments of the widowed during the first year. *Omega, 10*, 163–174.
21. Glick, I. O., Weiss, R. S., & Parkes, C. M. (1974). *The first year of bereavement*. New York: John Wiley & Sons.
22. Kahana, E. F., & Kiyak, H. A. (1980). The older woman: Impact of widowhood and living arrangements on service needs. *Journal of Gerontological Social Work, 3*, 17–29.
23. Osterweis, M., Solomon, F., & Green, M. (Eds.). (1984). *Bereavement: Reactions, consequences, and care*. Washington, DC: National Academy Press.
24. Parkes, C. M. (1987). *Bereavement: Studies of grief in adult life*. Madison, CT: International Universities Press.
25. Rando, T. A. (Ed.). (1986). *Loss and anticipatory grief*. Lexington, MA: D. C. Heath.
26. Raphael, B. (1983). *The anatomy of bereavement*. New York: Basic Books.
27. Weizman, S. G., & Kamm, P. (1985). *About mourning: Support and guidance for the bereaved*. New York: Human Sciences Press.
28. Schlesinger, B. (1980). Widows and widowers in New Zealand: General information. *Journal of Comparative Family Studies, 11*, 49–55.
29. Shuchter, S. R., & Zisook, S. (1986). Treatment of spousal bereavement: A multidimensional approach. *Psychiatry Annals, 16*, 295–305.

30. Silverman, P. R. (1986). *Widow-to-widow*. New York: Springer.
31. Simos, B. G. (1979). *A time to grieve: Loss as a universal human experience*. New York: Family Service Association of America.
32. Worden, W. J. (1982). *Grief counseling and grief therapy: A handbook for the mental health practitioner*. New York: Springer.
33. Stephenson, J. S. (1985). *Death, grief, and mourning: Individual and social realities*. New York: Free Press.
34. Ben-Sira, Z. (1983). Loss, stress and readjustment: The structure of coping with bereavement and disability. *Social Science and Medicine, 17,* 1619–1632.
35. Gass, K. A. (1987). The health of conjugally bereaved older widows: The role of appraisal, coping and resources. *Research in Nursing and Health, 10,* 39–47.
36. Hogstel, M. O. (1985). Older widowers: A small group with special needs. *Geriatric Nursing, 1,* 24–26.
37. Amaral, P. (1981). *The impact of upheaval in daily living on adjustment to bereavement*. Paper presented at the 34th Annual Scientific Meeting of the Gerontological Society of America, Toronto.
38. Freud, S. (1963). *Mourning and melancholia*. In P. Rieff (Ed.), *Sigmund Freud: General psychological theory*. New York: Collier Books. (Original work published 1917).
39. Sanders, C. M. (1980–1981). Comparison of younger and older spouses in bereavement outcome. *Omega, 11,* 217–232.
40. Rubinstein, R. L. (1983). *The construction of a day by elderly widowers*. Paper presented at the 36th Annual Scientific Meeting of the Gerontological Society of America, San Francisco.
41. Clark, P. G., Siviski, R. W., & Weiner, R. (1986). Coping strategies of widowers in the first year. *Family Relations, 35,* 425–430.
42. Vachon, M. S., Lyall, W. L., Rogers, J., Freedman-Letofsky, K., & Freeman, S. J. (1980). A controlled study of self-help intervention for widows. *American Journal of Psychiatry, 137,* 1380–1384.
43. Roberto, K. A., & Scott, J. P. (1984–1985). Friendship patterns among older women. *International Journal of Aging and Human Development, 19,* 1–10.
44. Roberto, K. A., & Scott, J. P. (1986). Confronting widowhood: The influence of informal supports. *American Behavioral Scientist, 29,* 497–511.
45. Dimond, M. F., Lund, D. A., & Caserta, M. S. (1987). The role of social support in the first two years of bereavement in an elderly sample. *The Gerontologist, 27,* 599–604.
46. Faschingbauer, T. R. (1981). *Texas revised inventory of grief manual*. Houston, TX: Honeycomb Press.
47. Sheikh, J. I., & Yesavage, J. A. (1986). Geriatric depression scale (GDS): Recent evidence and development of a shorter version. In T. L. Brink (Ed.), *Clinical gerontology: A guide to assessment and intervention* (pp. 165–174). New York: Haworth Press.
48. Wood, V., Wylie, M. L., & Sheafor, B. (1969). An analysis of a short self-report measure of life satisfaction: Correlation with rater judgments. *Journal of Gerontology, 24,* 465–469.
49. Rosenberg, M. (1965). *Society and the adolescent self-image*. Princeton, NJ: Princeton University Press.
50. Caserta, M. S., Connelly, J. R., Lund, D. A., & Poulton, J. L. (1987). Older adult caregivers of developmentally disabled household members: Service needs and fulfillment. *Journal of Gerontological Social Work, 10,* 35–50.

Comparisons of Widowhood and Divorce

The findings presented in the previous chapters have helped to explain why some people cope more effectively with bereavement and why others continue to have major difficulties 2 and 3 years later—in some instances, probably for the remainder of their lives. Social support and other external coping resources can alleviate some of the less desirable bereavement outcomes for some of the spouses, but personal coping resources such as competencies, perceived control over the situation, and ability to carry out activities of daily living appear to be even more influential. These conclusions are reviewed in greater detail in Chapter 16.

Some theorists and research investigators have argued that the death of a spouse has similarities with other life events that are considered major losses, and that by examining each situation within the broader context of losses, we will obtain a clearer understanding of how to cope with each situation. The three chapters in Part III are intended to help identify what might be common and unique to two kinds of major loss in later life: the loss of a spouse through death and through divorce. The findings from these comparative studies will have implications for future research and interventions. If the two kinds of loss are experienced similarly, result in common outcomes, and are influenced by the same factors, then generalizations from one kind of loss to the other would be more acceptable and beneficial. However, because this type of comparative research is even less developed than research on bereavement itself, we need to be exceptionally cautious in not going beyond what the data suggest.

12

Management and Outcomes of Loss in Later Life: A Comparison of Bereavement and Divorce

Judy Farnsworth, Dale A. Lund, and Marjorie A. Pett

The purpose of this study was to identify similarities and differences in the experiences of recently widowed and divorced adults aged 50 and older. A sample of 110 widowed individuals drawn from the Dimond and Lund (University of Utah) longitudinal study of bereavement was compared with a sample of 109 divorced individuals obtained through a study by the faculty of the Division of Psychosocial Nursing, College of Nursing, University of Utah. Data were gathered on five global measures constructed from a series of bereavement-related feelings and behaviors and on measures of depression and life satisfaction. Widowed and divorced participants experienced similar feelings of emotional shock, helplessness and avoidance, and grief. Both samples felt relatively positive about their psychological strength and coping and were similar in terms of their overall life satisfaction. Divorced participants had significantly more difficulty with anger, guilt, and confusion, while widowed participants were significantly more depressed. Possible explanations for the observed differences between the two samples are discussed.

The lives of older adults are often characterized by loss. Two kinds of loss that have the potential to be especially poignant are the loss of a spouse through death and through divorce. The death of a spouse is commonly assumed to be the most traumatic life event experienced by older adults. It is estimated that each year 800,000 Americans over the age of 50 will become widowed[1] and that the percentage of the widowed population increases with age.[2] Divorce also is a stressful life

Data on the bereaved sample were obtained from a study funded by the National Institute of Aging (RO1 AG02193) and the data on the divorced sample were obtained through a study by the faculty of the Division of Psychosocial Nursing, College of Nursing, University of Utah.

An earlier version of this chapter was presented at the Annual Meeting of the Gerontological Society of America, Washington, D.C., November 1987.

event and frequently is compared to the loss of a spouse by death.[3-8] Despite societal norms, dependencies, guilt, financial reality, loyalty, and the tendency to sustain marital liaisons, an increase in divorce rates among older adults is anticipated.[9-11]

Divorce and bereavement experiences can affect a person physically, emotionally, socially, and economically.[12-13] The impact affects the gamut of life experiences, from the specific events of daily living, the attitudinal and behavioral dimensions that cut across personality, work, family, and other relationships, to general life goals. Some experts suggest that the resolution of the loss for both divorced and widowed individuals requires that emotional bonds with the lost partner be dissolved. Identification with the role of husband or wife needs to be disbanded and everyday routines and habits that existed between the partners need to end.[14] Not only must the loss be faced and life rearranged without the partner, but the unique dimensions of the self that were specifically tied to the relationship must be changed. As new interactions are developed and a reorientation and reintegration of the personality or "inner image" occurs,[4,15] the individual enters into what Sullivan[16] calls the "new life." Examining the experiences of older adults who have recently been widowed or divorced will contribute to a clearer delineation of the features unique to each of these new life situations.

The symbolic interactionist perspective was used in this investigation to facilitate an understanding of the dynamic forces which impact divorced and widowed older adults and to explain how people reconstruct their lives following such profound threats to their self-concepts and existing life circumstances. The theory is especially relevant to widowhood and divorce in later life, because it makes "the self" central to an understanding of behavior. It assumes that the individual's past, present, and future roles can be incorporated into the self-concept, thereby recognizing the blend of dynamic and static features of these two loss situations. It views the self as having consistent and stable elements from past relationships while being flexible enough to be modified by changes in social interactions. Changes in self-concept occur with the altered social relationships that result from the departure of a family member. Thus the theory provides a framework to examine management and adjustment processes that are utilized to construct new patterns of living without the family member.

RESEARCH QUESTIONS

The purpose of this study was to identify similarities and differences in how widowhood and divorce are experienced by older individuals. Specific research questions were as follows: Do widowed and divorced individuals differ in their management of the loss? Do widowed and divorced individuals differ on specific outcome measures of loss?

METHODS

Widowed Sample

A sample of 110 widowed individuals was drawn from the Dimond and Lund (University of Utah) longitudinal study of bereavement, which is described in other publications and in Chapters 1 and 10 of this book. The larger study examined 192 bereaved older adults over the 2 years following the spouse's death. The sample consisted of recently bereaved individuals over the age of 50 who had been identified through newspaper obituaries.

The respondents completed questionnaires at six times: 3 to 4 weeks, 2 months, 6 months, 1 year, 18 months, and 2 years. With the exception of the demographic variables, all six questionnaires were essentially the same. Other articles by Lund, Dimond, and Caserta[17-19] provide more detail about sample and methodological issues.

Divorced Sample

The data for the 109 individuals in the older divorced sample were part of an ongoing study of biopsychosocial factors affecting adjustment to loss among older divorced adults conducted by the Division of Psychosocial Nursing, College of Nursing, University of Utah. The sample consisted of recently divorced individuals over the age of 50 who had been identified through the official certificates of divorce registered with the Utah State Department of Health. If both divorcing partners met the criteria and each agreed to take part in the project, both individuals were included in the research. There were 14 divorced pairs included in the study.

Thirty-four percent ($N = 131$) of the 390 potential participants could not be reached despite a follow-up letter and numerous attempts to contact them by phone. Sixteen percent ($N = 63$) refused to participate and 22% did not meet the criteria for participation (e.g., they had remarried, were too young, or did not live in the area). The most common reasons given for refusal were that the respondent was not interested or felt too uncomfortable about the interview. One hundred and eleven respondents (28%) completed the interview, but only 109 were used in the analyses described in this paper because of the matching procedures. There were no statistical differences in the length of marriage between those who participated in the study ($M = 29.7$, $SD = 6.9$) and the nonparticipants [$M = 29.5$, $SD = 8.5$; $t(388) = 1.73$, $p > .10$] or in the length of separation [participants = 24.8, $SD = 11.1$; nonparticipants = 22.1, $SD = 13.8$; $t(388) = 1.81$, $p > .05$]. The nonparticipants were significantly older ($M = 57.2$, $SD = 8.6$) than the participants [$M = 55.8$, $SD = 4.9$; $t(388) = 4.19$, $p > .01$]. There was, however, no available information regarding the well-being of the nonparticipants.

Data were collected through personal interviews. The interview packet contained consent forms, an interview schedule of structured and unstructured questions, and a number of standardized measures of subjecting well-being.

Matching Procedures

To ensure that the two samples were similar with respect to age, sex, and time since loss and to maximize the possible sample sizes, they were matched in the following manner. First, the divorced and widowed samples were made more homogeneous by including only those who were from 50 to 69 years of age. This was necessary because many of the widowed respondents were over age 69 and the majority of the divorced respondents were under age 69. Application of the age criterion resulted in samples of 109 divorced and 110 widowed persons.

Next, because the widowed respondents were interviewed six times, it was necessary to select one specific data collection period for each of them which would most closely approximate the time period when data were collected from

TABLE 1   Gender and Time Since Loss for the Divorced and Widowed Samples

	Time since loss				
Samples	6 Months	1 Year	18 Months	2 Years	Totals
Divorced					
Males	15	9	9	11	44
Females	17	14	10	24	65
Widowed					
Males	6	3	4	5	18
Females	24	20	14	34	92
Totals	62	46	37	74	219

those in the divorced sample. To do so, the divorced respondents were subdivided into four subgroups according to time since divorce. The time periods used in subdividing were similar to the data collection times in the bereavement study: 1 to 6 months, 7 to 12 months, 13 to 18 months, 19 to 24 months. At the same time, the gender of the respondents was considered so that the two samples had similar time periods for males and females. The data periods for widowed respondents were selected in a proportion similar to those for males and females in the divorced sample. The specific data collection times for each widowed respondent were chosen from the 6-, 12-, 18-, and 24-month data collection times. Table 1 shows the breakdown of gender and the amount of time since the loss for both samples.

Respondent Characteristics

WIDOWED SAMPLE

Because most of the men in the larger bereavement study were over the age of 69, fewer of them were utilized in the present widowed sample. As a result, only 18 (16.4%) of those in the widowed sample were men. The age of the widowed sample range from 50 to 69 years ($M = 62.5$, $SD = 4.8$). The widowed respondents had been married from 6 to 52 years, with a mean of 35 years ($SD = 11.8$). Three of them had been married twice. The majority (94.5%) were white, Latter-Day Saints (70%), and high school graduates (84%).

Most (65 or 59.1%) of the widowed were not working. Their average annual income was between $6,225 and $12,499. They had a wide range of incomes; for instance, in 1982, 2 were below $3,724 and 10 had annual incomes of $37,350 or more. Seventy-one (64.5%) reported that their incomes were adequate; only 15 (13.6%) reported that their incomes were more than adequate.

DIVORCED SAMPLE

The sample of 109 divorced respondents in the study were interviewed during the summer of 1986. Forty-four (40.4%) of the divorced respondents were males and 65 (59.6%) were females. The ages of the divorced respondents ranged from 50 to 66 years ($M = 55.5$, $SD = 4.4$). The divorced respondents had been married from 13 to 44 years to their former spouses. The mean number of years married was 29.5 ($SD = 6.9$). Twenty participants had been married twice and 2 had been married three times. The majority (95.4%) were white, Latter-Day Saints (59.6%), and nearly all of them had graduated from high school (92%).

Two-thirds (73 or 67%) of the divorced participants were working full-time. Their average annual income was between $12,500 and $24,999. Like the widowed sample, they had a wide range of incomes, with 2 divorced respondents having incomes below $3,724 and 16 having incomes of $37,350 or more. Fifty-three (48.6%) reported that their incomes were more than adequate.

COMPARISON OF DIVORCED AND WIDOWED SAMPLES

Of the 109 divorced and 110 widowed individuals in this study, the majority were white (95%), female (71.7%), and Latter-Day Saints (62.5%). There were significant differences between the divorced and widowed respondents in their ages, the length of their marriages, their education, and their perceptions of the adequacy of their incomes. Widowed respondents (M = 62.5, SD = 4.8) were significantly older than the divorced respondents [M = 55.5, SD = 4.4, $t(217)$ = 11.20, p < .001]. The widowed had been married an average of 35 years (SD = 11.8), while the divorced respondents had been married an average of 29.5 years [SD = 6.9, $t(217)$ = 4.28, p < .001]. The divorced respondents, however, had more formal education [$t(217)$ = 3.22, p < .001] and were more frequently employed [$\chi^2(2)$ = 67.81, p < .001]. There were no significant differences between the incomes of the widowed and divorced after the widowed participant's incomes were adjusted by the amount of inflation,[20] 24.5% between 1981 and 1986 when the data for the widowed and divorced samples were collected [$t(207)$ = 1.74, p > .05].

Instruments

The ways that the widowed and divorced respondents managed the loss of their spouses was assessed by their self-reports of the feelings and behaviors that they experienced on a day-to-day basis. The interview schedule for the larger bereavement study contained a series of single-item indicators about a variety of loss-related feelings and behaviors. There were 26 loss-related feelings and 16 loss-related behaviors. Responses were recorded on five-point Likert scales with response categories for the feelings ranging from "never had" to "very strong" and response categories for the behaviors ranging from "never did this" to "most of the time." Items included on these lists were generated primarily from the Harvard bereavement study by Glick, Weiss, and Parkes.[21] The items ranged from such early grief characteristics as shock, confusion, crying, and review of the death event to such later experiences as confidence, pride, learning to do new things, and making new friends. In addition to these checklists, each questionnaire contained self-reported ratings for perceived stress, coping, and self-esteem measured by seven-point single-item statements.

All of the items were factor analyzed into five global scales. Seven of the items did not satisfactorily load on any of the factors and were eliminated. The five global scales and their corresponding Cronbach's alpha coefficients were as follows: emotional shock (.82), helplessness/avoidance (.77), psychological strength/coping (.78), anger/guilt/confusion (.66), and grief (.64). More detail about methodological and scaling issues can be found elsewhere.[19]

For the purposes of this study, two additional items—"visit the grave" and "angry at doctor"—were eliminated from the scales because they were not appropriate in the divorce situation. Each of the five scales and their specific items are presented below.

1. *Emotional shock*
   - Dazed
   - Numb
   - Shock
   - Feeling alone
   - Panic
   - Cold
   - Disbelief
   - Emptiness
   - Perceived stress
2. *Helplessness/avoidance*
   - Avoid social contacts
   - Take sleeping pills/tranquilizers
   - Feel like a burden to others
   - Helplessness
   - Irritability
   - Feel like crying
   - Unsure if O.K. to cry
   - Wish I were dead
   - Avoid reminders of spouse
3. *Anger/guilt/confusion*
   - Guilt
   - Angry at spouse
   - Confused
   - Afraid of nervous breakdown
   - Blame self for spouse's death
   - Try to find reason for death
4. *Grief*
   - Talk to spouse
   - Learn to do new things
   - Cry
   - Look for spouse in places enjoyed together
   - Talk to others about spouse
   - Go over circumstances of spouse's death
5. *Psychological strength/coping*
   - Feel strong/capable
   - Proud of how managed
   - Confident
   - Perceived coping
   - Self-esteem
   - Amazed at strength
   - Feel different from others

Cronbach alpha coefficients for the revised scales of the subsample of widowed individuals were as follows: emotional shock (.84), helplessness/avoidance (.73), psychological strength/coping (.77), anger/guilt/confusion (.69), and grief (.67). High scores on each subscale indicated high levels of the respective dimension: A high score on the grief scale means high grief or grief that remains unresolved.

Some of the items were reworded to make them appropriate to the experiences of those who were divorced. For example, "blame self for spouse's death" was modified to read "blame self for divorce." Cronbach alpha coefficients for the sample of divorced individuals were as follows: emotional shock (.80), helplessness/avoidance (.72), psychological strength/coping (.73), anger/guilt/confusion (.74), and grief (.52).

The outcome measures of the loss experiences focused on two well-accepted and standardized scales[22-25] which have been used to assess a person's subjective well-being. The Life Satisfaction Index-A (LSI-A)[26] was used to assess life satisfaction and the Self-Rating Depression Scale (SDS), developed by Zung,[27] was used for assessing depression levels. Both scales consist of 20 items, with either dichotomous (LSI-A) or four-point Likert response categories (SDS). The LSI-A could range from 0 to 20 (high) and the SDS from 20 to 80 (high). These measures of well-being are also reviewed in Chapter 1.

FINDINGS

Management of Loss

Considering the possible range of scores for each of the feelings and behaviors reflecting the management of the loss, both the divorced and widowed participants scored highest on the psychological strength/coping dimension (see Table 2). The mean scores for the participants in each of the four time periods exceeded the midpoint of 23.5 (7 = low, 39 = high), with standard deviations ranging from 5.8 to 6.9. The psychological strength/coping dimension included feelings of strength, confidence, and pride in the management of situations. The scores were consistently high regardless of the time since loss, suggesting that the respondents in both samples felt relatively positive about their psychological strength and coping.

The scores on the emotional shock, helplessness/avoidance, and grief subscales were in the moderate range for both samples. Widowed participants who responded 6 months after bereavement reported greater difficulty with shock, helplessness/avoidance, and grief than the other widowed respondents who reported at 12, 18, or 24 months. For the divorced subjects, however, difficulty with shock, helplessness/avoidance, and grief remained fairly constant across the different time periods. These data suggest that the impact of divorce is likely to have a more sustained affect on the divorcee than the impact of bereavement on the widowed individual. Also, while the death of a spouse might result in greater emotional difficulties early on, the divorced older adult is more likely to experience similar emotional difficulties 18 to 24 months later.

The most obvious difference between the divorced and widowed samples was on the anger/guilt/confusion scale, with the divorced participants reporting significantly more difficulty [$t(194) = 8.80$, $p < .0001$]. This difference was noted between the samples regardless of how much time had passed since the loss. There also was a slight trend of declining difficulty over time for the widowed sample. It should be pointed out, however, that the mean scores for the divorced respondents did not reach the midpoint of the possible range in scores (18.5; where 6 = low and 30 = high) at any time period, which suggests that their anger, guilt, and confusion were not excessive (see Table 2). The mean scores for the widows

TABLE 2 Comparison of Divorced and Widowed Samples on Measures of the Management of Loss Controlling for Time Since Loss

Outcome measures and samples	6 Months M(SD)	n	12 Months M(SD)	n	18 Months M(SD)	n	24 Months M(SD)	n
Emotional shock (9 = low, 47 = high)								
Divorced	21.6(7.7)	29	19.6(6.4)	23	22.2(7.4)	17	23.0(8.9)	28
Widowed	24.5(6.7)	28	19.6(6.8)	22	20.4(7.4)	18	19.9(7.1)	37
Helplessness/avoidance (9 = low, 45 = high)								
Divorced	17.6(6.8)	28	17.1(5.0)	20	16.0(3.8)	15	17.9(6.2)	30
Widowed	17.5(5.0)	28	14.9(4.1)	20	15.7(6.1)	16	15.4(5.3)	37
Anger/guilt/confusion (6 = low, 30 = high)								
Divorced	15.2(5.8)	27	12.8(3.0)	19	14.5(4.1)	17	14.2(4.6)	33
Widowed	10.8(3.8)	26	8.8(3.0)	21	9.1(3.4)	17	8.3(2.7)	36
Grief (6 = low, 30 = high)								
Divorced	15.8(4.4)	28	14.4(3.6)	20	15.3(3.3)	18	15.1(3.9)	34
Widowed	17.2(3.8)	25	15.8(4.0)	21	16.0(4.0)	16	14.1(4.1)	37
Psychological strength/coping (7 = low, 39 = high)								
Divorced	25.7(6.9)	26	27.0(5.4)	21	28.2(5.8)	18	27.6(5.0)	32
Widowed	25.6(4.8)	26	27.3(5.1)	21	29.1(5.9)	17	26.5(5.7)	37

were very low, which suggests that they experienced little anger, guilt, and confusion.

Subjective Well-Being Outcomes

Table 3 shows that the full widowed sample was significantly more depressed than the divorced sample [$t(206)$ = 3.67, p < .0001], with similar differences at each of the four time periods. Zung[27] suggested that raw scores below 40 for the SDS were within the normal range and were not indicative of psychopathology. Kitchell, Barnes, Veith, Okimoto, and Raskind[24] recommended that the cutoff raw score for normal older adults be increased to 48. Therefore, although the widowed individuals were more depressed, the mean scores for both samples at each of the time periods were below these cutoff scores. The depression scores were highest for both samples when data were collected within the first six months, with slight declines for the two middle data periods followed by a slight increase among those interviewed at 2 years following the loss.

The LSI-A mean scores averaged 13.7 for the widowed sample and 13.3 for the divorced sample. This difference was not statistically significant. The widows who responded 6 months after bereavement had a lower mean score (11.8) than widows who participated at the other time periods (M = 14.4 to 14.6). The mean scores for the divorced persons ranged from 12.3 at the 6 month time period to 14.4 at the 18 month time period (see Table 3). Therefore, the divorced and widowed samples were similar in terms of overall life satisfaction, with a trend toward higher scores as time passed. Also, it should be noted that these scores are similar or slightly higher than those reported by other researchers utilizing samples of older adults living in the community. Neugarten, Havighurst, and Tobin[26] reported a mean score of 12.4; Adams,[28] 12.5; and Wood, Wylie, and Sheafor,[29] 11.6.

DISCUSSION

The greater intensity of anger, guilt, and confusion experienced by divorced individuals may have been caused by several factors. The feelings may be a product of the feedback divorced individuals receive from others. Divorce is stigmatized and there is the possibility that the messages others send may contain elements of anger, rebuke, and blame. Even if the communication of others does not contain any such elements, the anger, guilt, and confusion the divorced individual experiences might result from the individual's own stigmatization of divorce learned from earlier experiences. Another possibility is that the demographic differences between the divorced and widowed samples (divorcees slightly younger) might reflect a cohort or "generational" difference. For example, the socialization of the younger individuals may have encouraged them to acknowledge their feelings of anger, guilt, and confusion more openly. They may be more willing to question life circumstances, accept responsibility, and live with ambiguity.

The greater degree of depression experienced by the widowed participants might be attributed to some of the differences in the ages, education, employment, and incomes between the two samples. The older widowed individuals may have had more physical ailments, some of which could have been confounded with some of the somatic symptoms of depression (e.g., constipation and rapid heart rate). Also, because of slightly less education and employment, the older widowed

TABLE 3   Subjective Well-Being Outcome Measures of Divorced and Widowed Samples Controlling for Time Since Loss

Outcome measures and samples	6 Months		12 Months		18 Months		24 Months	
	M(SD)	n	M(SD)	n	M(SD)	n	M(SD)	n
Zung Self-Rating Depression Scale (20 = low, 80 = high)								
Divorced	34.9(10.5)	30	33.5(10.1)	22	28.9(8.7)	18	31.1(7.3)	34
Widowed	39.6(8.0)	29	33.7(8.0)	20	35.9(9.2)	18	37.3(10.3)	37
Life Satisfaction Index-A (0 = low, 20 = high)								
Divorced	12.3(3.9)	31	12.8(3.9)	23	14.4(3.4)	19	13.9(3.3)	34
Widowed	11.8(4.0)	30	14.4(3.3)	19	14.6(4.1)	16	14.6(4.3)	38

individuals might have had less access to resources, such as people and health care. The lack of resources may have preempted the opportunities widowed individuals might have used to maximize their health. On the other hand, more education and employment may have allowed divorced individuals to effectively garner more resources and enabled them to maximize their health.

Because age, education, income, and other sociodemographic characteristics were not found to be predictive of bereavement outcomes in the larger bereavement study with roughly the same sample,[30] it is more likely that the differences in depression are due to the loss situations. The symbolic interactionist perspective may offer an explanation for these differences. Widowed individuals, for example, may receive more feedback from important others that focuses on the bleakness of their situation. This type of feedback might facilitate feelings of depression. Conversely, the widowed are offered more clearly defined sets of behavioral guides to cope with their adverse situation. Funerals are held, friends visit, and it is acceptable to cry; other behavioral guides are provided to the widowed which in turn might reduce some feelings of confusion.

Also, it may be more socially acceptable for divorced individuals to be angry at their spouses than for widowed individuals to harbor or express such feelings. The divorced person may be made to feel responsible for the divorce, thereby making the loss more of a guilt-producing experience. The anger that widowed individuals may feel toward the deceased or toward their situation may be directed elsewhere, perhaps toward the self. Because a hallmark of depression is self-accusation,[31-33] feelings of anger, guilt, confusion, and depression experienced by divorced and widowed individuals may be different manifestations of the same dynamic. That is, the observed differences between the reactions of divorced and widowed individuals to the loss may be a result of social custom and a reflection of the conduct that is approved and rewarded by society. Death may not negate the anger, only the response. A likely problem for the widowed, therefore, is that death produces anger and guilt but society suppresses the emotions it creates.

Nevertheless, the expressions by divorced individuals of greater anger, guilt, and confusion may be a necessary step in the divorced individual's finalization of the marriage. Hostility, mingled with regret or uncertainty, is an externalization of the loss of a spouse, of the failure of the marriage as an ongoing relationship, and of the failure of the individuals involved to "make it work." The depression expressed in greater degree by widowed individuals might be viewed both as internalization of hostility towards the spouse for dying and as fear for the future.

It is important to note that although both divorce and widowhood involve significant losses, the participants in this study were most resourceful and resilient in managing their difficulties. In fact, while they experienced emotional upheaval, anger, depression, and grief over the loss, they also reported strength, pride, and confidence in their ability to handle the loss. It is apparent that a broad range of positive and negative experiences accompany both loss situations.

REFERENCES

1. Jacobs, S., & Ostfeld, A. (1977). An epidemiological review of the mortality of bereavement. *Psychosomatic Medicine, 39*, 344–357.
2. U. S. Bureau of the Census. (1980). *Census of population: Vol. 1. Characteristics of the population* (Chap. D). Washington, DC.

3. Crosby, J., Gage, B., & Raymond, M. (1983). The grief resolution process in divorce. *Journal of Divorce, 7*(1), 3–18.
4. Gut, E. (1974). Some aspects of adult mourning. *Omega, 5,* 323–342.
5. Jacobson, G. (1983). *The multiple crises of marital separation and divorce.* New York: Grune & Stratton.
6. Parkes, C. M. (1972). *Bereavement: Studies of grief in adult life.* New York: International Universities Press.
7. Schwartz, L., & Kaslow, F. (1985). Widows and divorcees: The same or different? *The American Journal of Family Therapy, 13*(4), 72–76.
8. Weiss, R. (1979). *Going it alone: The family life and social situation of the single parents.* New York: Basic Books.
9. Chiriboga, D. (1982). An examination of life events as possible antecedents to change. *Journal of Gerontology, 37,* 595–601.
10. DeShane, M., & Brown-Wilson, K. (1981). Divorce in later life: A call for research. *Journal of Divorce, 4*(4), 81–92.
11. Uhlenberg, P., & Myers, M. (1981). Divorce and the elderly. *The Gerontologist, 21,* 276–282.
12. Rice, J. K., & Rice, D. G. (1986). *Living through divorce: A developmental approach to divorce therapy.* New York: Guilford Press.
13. Shuchter, S. R., & Zisook, S. (1986). Treatment of spousal bereavement: A multidimensional approach. *Psychiatric Annals, 16,* 295–305.
14. Hagestad, G., & Smyer, M. (1982). Dissolving long-term relationships: Patterns of divorcing in middle age. In S. Duck (Ed.), *Personal relationships 4: Dissolving personal relationships* (pp. 155–187). New York: Academic Press.
15. Charmaz, K. (1980). *The social reality of death: Death in contemporary America.* Reading, MA: Addison-Wesley.
16. Sullivan, H. S. (1956). *Clinical studies in psychiatry.* New York: W. W. Norton.
17. Caserta, M. S., Lund, D. A., & Dimond, M. F. (1985). Assessing interviewer effects in a longitudinal study of bereaved elderly adults. *Journal of Gerontology, 40,* 637–640.
18. Dimond, M. F., Lund, D. A., & Caserta, M. S. (1987). The role of social support in the first two years of bereavement. *The Gerontologist, 27,* 599–604.
19. Lund, D. A., Caserta, M. S., & Dimond, M. F. (1986). Gender differences through two years of bereavement among the elderly. *The Gerontologist, 26,* 314–320.
20. *Economic indicators.* (1987, February). Prepared for the Joint Economic Committee by the Council of Economic Advisers. Washington, DC: U.S. Government Printing Office.
21. Glick, I., Weiss, R., & Parkes, C. (1974). *The first year of bereavement.* New York: John Wiley & Sons.
22. Jegede, R. (1976). Psychometric properties of the Self-Rating Depression Scale (SDS). *The Journal of Psychology, 93,* 27–30.
23. Kane, R. A., & Kane, R. L. (1981). *Assessing the elderly: A practical guide to measurement.* Lexington, MA: D.C. Health.
24. Kitchell, M., Barnes, R., Veith, R., Okimoto, J., & Raskind, M. (1982). Screening for depression in hospitalized geriatric medical patients. *Journal of the American Geriatrics Society, 30,* 174–177.
25. Mangen, D. J., & Peterson, W. A. (Eds.). (1982). *Clinical and social psychology: Research instrument in social gerontology* (Vol. 1). Minneapolis: University of Minnesota Press.
26. Neugarten, B., Havighurst, R., & Tobin, S. (1961). The measurement of life satisfaction. *Journal of Gerontology, 16*(2), 134–143.
27. Zung, W. (1965). A self-rating depression scale. *Archives of General Psychiatry, 12,* 63–70.
28. Adams, D. (1969). Analysis of a life satisfaction index. *Journal of Gerontology, 24,* 470–474.
29. Wood, V., Wylie, M., & Sheafor, B. (1969). An analysis of a short self-report measure of life satisfaction: Correlation with rater judgements. *Journal of Gerontology, 24,* 465–469.
30. Lund, D. A., Dimond, M. F., & Caserta, M. S. (1985). Identifying elderly with coping difficulties after two years of bereavement. *Omega, 16,* 213–224.
31. Danesh, H. B. (1977). Anger and fear. *American Journal of Psychiatry, 134,* 1109–1112.
32. Freud, S. (1917). Mourning and melancholia. *SE, 14,* 243–258.
33. Melges, F. T., & DeMaso, D. R. (1980). Grief-resolution therapy: Reliving, revising, and revisiting. *American Journal of Psychotherapy, 34*(1), 51–61.

13

Independence and Social and Psychological Adjustment in Widowhood and Divorce

Gay C. Kitson and Mary Joan Roach

This study develops measures of social adjustment and independence and then examines the relationship between marital status, independence, and social and psychological adjustment in widowhood and divorce. The data are from samples of 188 widows and 188 divorcées from Cuyahoga County (metropolitan Cleveland), Ohio, matched by age, race, and median income of census tract. Social and psychological adjustment were, as hypothesized, positively associated. Widows reported significantly more difficulties on the social adjustment scale than did divorcées, and they felt less independent. Partial correlations suggest that compared to widows, much of the psychological distress divorcées experience is due to difficulties in performing social roles. The loss of the spouse may account for much of the distress of the widows.

After a greater focus on psychological adjustment to widowhood and divorce,[1-4] more attention is now being paid to social adjustment.[5-8] Social adjustment is defined here as functioning adequately in the role responsibilities of daily life—home, family, work, and leisure time—while psychological adjustment is defined as being relatively free of symptoms of psychological distress. In this chapter, we shall explore the relationship between social and psychological adjustment in age, race, and median income of census tract matched samples of widows and divorcées.

Although various aspects of adjustment to widowhood or divorce have been assessed, few studies have simultaneously looked at adjustment to these two kinds of events.[9] This despite the fact that theoretical similarities in adjustment to the two kind of event have been noted at least since the work of Willard Waller in

The research reported upon in this chapter was supported by the National Institute of Aging grant no. MHO4561.

1930.[13-15] Both kinds of event involve loss of the spouse and loss of status as individuals shift from the married status to the divorced or widowed status.

Comparative work on adjustment to widowhood and divorce is hampered by the differing age distributions for the two kinds of event. Divorce is more likely to occur at young ages and widowhood at older ages.[16] As a result, special steps need to be taken to study subjects of comparable ages so that any differences between the two groups are due to status, not age.

Lazarus and Folkman[17] point out that much of the research on social functioning has used rating scales based on clinical or community definitions of normal social functioning. The problem with such scales is that they assume that the ability to perform roles should be the same regardless of the situation. The result of such analyses is that individuals who are faced with a crisis always seem to have impaired functioning when in fact they may be functioning quite well given the situation. Therefore, it is necessary to measure social functioning from the point of view of the person experiencing the stressor and within the context of the situation he or she is facing in order to determine how well or poorly the individual is coping compared to others faced with the same or a similar situation.[18]

While psychological and social adjustment are likely to be correlated, it is unclear which dimension plays the greater role. That is, do health disturbances precipitated by widowhood and divorce lead to problems in functioning in social roles or do changes in social roles resulting from the absence of the spouse lead to health difficulties? Some research on social functioning suggests that the psychological distress precipitated by a crisis impairs an individual's ability to perform social roles.[19-22] Robert Weiss[13] suggests that recently separated or divorced individuals may not see any purpose to performing daily tasks because they are so distressed as a result of losing their spouses. They may leave tasks undone or do them haphazardly. In a Boston study of the first year of bereavement, Glick, Weiss, and Parkes[23] found young widowed persons to be socially isolated and feeling lonely and depressed, which made it difficult for them to socialize with old friends or to form new relationships. These data suggest that psychological distress precipitates difficulties in social adjustment.

In contradiction to the research discussed above, which views impaired social functioning as an outcome of the psychological distress associated with the loss of a spouse, other research takes the position that a change in marital status requires a reassessment and readjustment of roles. Role readjustment involves role conflict and role strain, which in turn produces psychological distress.[11,24-25] Such an approach suggests that psychological distress may be the result of the inability to function normally in a new role.

The ability to handle social roles may be hampered for some widows and divorcées because women have not generally been encouraged to be independent in their thoughts and actions.[26] This leads to a feeling of not being able to cope on one's own. Feeling independent can be a resource that helps a person to cope with difficult situations.[17,26] It is also likely that if a woman feels more confident of her abilities to cope, she will have less difficulty with role changes than if she is more uncertain of her abilities.

In assessing health status, it has been assumed that adjusting to divorce is more difficult than adjusting to widowhood.[2,27] However, a recent report of age, race, and census tract, matched samples of widows and divorcées indicated there were greater psychological adjustment difficulties for widows than for divorcées 3 months after the death of the spouse or filing for divorce.[28] There are few data available to suggest whether widows or divorcées will have more difficulty with social roles early in the process of adjusting to the loss of the spouse or which group will feel more independent. However, if there is a relationship between social and psychological adjustment, then we might expect that widows, who have been shown to have higher levels of psychological distress than divorcées, will also have more difficulties with social roles. It is also likely that a divorcée will feel more independent than a widow. Women are more likely to file for divorce than men.[29-31] As a result, many women facing divorce will have given some thought to the tasks that they will have to perform on their own and will feel, despite perhaps some trepidation, that they can cope on their own. A widow, on the other hand, may be less likely to have thought through some of these issues as a result of having had little warning of her husband's death, being preoccupied coping with his illness, or ignoring or denying that his death is imminent. Further- more, if death had not intervened, the widow might not have had to face the issue of her independence. Thus, widows may feel less independent than divorcées.

HYPOTHESES

Based on the discussion above of the differing ways in which social and psychological adjustment and independence may be related, the following hypoth- eses are proposed:

1. Widows will have more difficulty performing social roles than will divorcées.
2. Divorcées will feel more independent than will widows.
3. Women who feel less independent will have more difficulty with social roles.
4. Greater psychological distress will be associated with more difficulty with so- cial roles.
5. Independence will be associated with fewer symptoms of psychological stress.
6. If role strain leads to psychological adjustment difficulties, controlling for so- cial roles will reduce the amount of psychological distress that divorced and widowed women report.
7. If psychological distress reduces a divorced or widowed woman's sense of independence and increases the difficulties she has in performing social roles, then controlling for psychological distress will reduce the relationship between social roles and her feelings of dependence.
8. If feeling unable to cope on one's own is associated with adjustment difficul- ties, controlling for independence will reduce the association between psycho- logical distress and difficulties with social roles.

METHODS

For both the widowed and divorced samples, the names of the women stud- ied were collected from public records. For the divorcées, the records were from the Domestic Relations Division of the Cuyahoga County Court of Common Pleas. For the widows, the death certificates of their spouses were used. It was decided to talk with widows 3 months after the death of their spouses. Based on the experi- ence of other researchers, who generally report low response rates for bereave- ment studies that start in the 1st or 2nd month after the death of the spouse,[6,8,32] 3 months after death was chosen in an attempt to maximize the response rate. We reasoned that the death was still a recent experience but not so fresh as to make women reluctant to talk. The data were collected from February 1985 to February 1986 by women interviewers matched to the subjects, where possible, by age and race.

To be eligible for this interview, subjects had to have resided in Cuyahoga County, Ohio, at the time of the spouse's death, thereby excluding some persons who were referred to Cleveland medical centers from other counties or states. They also had to be living in the four-county Standard Metropolitan Statistical Area (SMSA) at the time of the interview and to be English speaking. (Twenty-one divorcées and 10 widows had moved from the four-county area and 3 widows and 1 divorcée were not English speaking.)

Divorcées were matched to widows on age, race, and median income of census tract of residence. To insure the inclusion of younger and older subjects and to match on age, the samples were stratified into those aged 44 and under and those 45 to 62. Age 62 was used as a cutoff for inclusion in the study to avoid confusion about bereavement and retirement issues. With the exception of ages 18–19 and 60–62, each of the age groups was further divided into 5-year intervals. This was done in an attempt to even out the age range in order to avoid the bunching of cases in the middle years. Generally, the subjects were matched on age within 3 years of one another, but in a small number of cases the differences were as much as 5 years. This means that a widow aged 42 who was similar to a 47-year-old divorcée on race and median income of census tract might have been matched to her. The result is that the cell frequencies on the matching variables are close to one another but not the same. Given the differing distributions of widowhood and divorce, with more women widowed in later years and more women divorced in younger years, the most difficult age categories to fill were the youngest widows and oldest divorcées. It was the filling of these categories which stretched out the data collection period. Subjects were also matched on median income of census tract of residence (plus or minus $5,000) and race. In five cases, the widows and divorcées differ in race but are similar in age and median income of census tract.

The completion rate for the 353 widows eligible for study was 56.9%; 201 women agreed to be interviewed, 87 (24.6%) refused, 38 (10.8%) were not contacted despite repeated efforts, 26 (7.4%) had moved without leaving a forwarding address, and 1 (.002%) had died. Of the 288 widows actually contacted, 69.8% agreed to be interviewed and 30.2% refused. By age, 95 widows (47.3%) were age 44 or under and 106 (52.7%) were age 45 or older.

Including replacements, 419 divorcées were eligible for study. For these women, the completion rate was 44.9%, 188 agreed to be interviewed, 134 (32.0%) refused, 57 (13.6%) were not contacted despite repeated efforts, 39 (9.3%) had moved without leaving a forwarding address, and 1 (.002%) had died. For those divorcées actually contacted, the response rate was 58.3% and the refusal rate was 41.6%. By age, 93 divorced women (49.5%) were age 44 or younger and 95 (50.5%) were age 45 or older.

Because of the time and expense involved in the matching procedure, only 188 of the 201 widows had a match. It took an average of 2.2 attempts per match to obtain 188 divorcées matched by age, race, and median income of census tract to 188 widows. It was much more difficult to match blacks than whites. It took an average of 4.3 attempts to match a black divorcée to a black widow, compared with an average of 1.8 attempts to match a white divorcée to a white widow.

The use of public records allows for demographic comparisons between those who completed the interview and those who did not. Although a useful source, such records do create some problems in analysis, since, for example, only the age of husband was on the death records and our concern is the age of the wife. Wives are generally younger than their husbands.[33] Similarly, with divorce records, race is not listed, so that estimates of the race of potential subjects had to be made based on the census tract of residence and other available information.

Among the widows, there were no significant differences in the completion rate by cause of death of the spouse (accidental versus natural). There were significant differences in the completion rate by age of spouse, race of spouse, and median income of census tract of residence. Widows whose husbands were aged 55 to 62 were more likely to refuse while women age 54 and under were more difficult to locate. Those who lived in census tracts with the lowest median income (under $5,000) and the next to lowest income ($5,000 to $9,999) were less likely to be interviewed. This was because many had moved and left no forwarding address. They were three times as likely to be unlocatable as those with higher incomes. When they were contacted, they were less likely to refuse than those with higher incomes. Blacks were also less likely to participate, again because they were more likely to have moved rather than because they were more likely to refuse.

For the divorcées, there were no significant differences in completion rate by age of the respondent, age of the spouse, or median income of census tract of residence. The completion rate did vary significantly by race, with blacks less likely to participate than whites. Two earlier Cleveland surveys, also using divorce court records, reported significant differences in completion rates by race.[34-35]

Overall, the completion rate was significantly higher for widows than for divorcées; that is, more of the widows contacted agreed to participate than in the case of the divorcées ($\chi^2 = 11.1$, 1 df, $p < .001$). These data suggest that widows and divorcées who were more settled would be more likely to have replied. The result is that the distress levels reported may be lower than would be expected if all the subjects were contacted, since moving is an additional stressor which might increase adjustment difficulties.

Both the widowed and divorced samples compare favorably in their completion rates to other recent public records-based studies. These include the 47% completion rate for women in the Boston bereavement study,[23] the 30% response rate in a Los Angeles County study,[36] the 30% response rate in a San Diego county study,[8] and the 40% completion rate in a Salt Lake City study collected through newspaper death notices.[32]

The completion rate for the divorced with replacements was slightly lower than for divorced women in an earlier suburban Cleveland study in which no replacements were used (49.6%).[29,34] But it was still substantially better than other recently completed studies that were based totally or partially on divorce court records and did not include replacements, for example, a 33.3% completion rate in a San Francisco-Oakland study[37] and a 22.9% completion rate in a Centre County (Pennsylvania) study based mostly on court records.[31,38]

Comparisons of background characteristics of the widowed and divorced samples indicated no statistically significant differences between the two groups on age, race, family social class (as measured by the Hollingshead Index of Social Position),[39] or income during the last year of marriage. Thus, the samples are comparable in their background characteristics, as they were designed to be. Nevertheless, an alternative explanation for the results is that the divorced are even less representative of the total divorced population than are the widowed. In the analyses that follow, findings are only reported for those 188 widows for whom divorcée matches were available.

Measures

DEPENDENT VARIABLES

Psychological status was assessed by the following measures: the Brief Symptom inventory (BSI)[40] and the Zung Self-Rating Depression Scale (SDS).[41] The BSI is scored in response to the question "In the past two weeks, how much were you bothered by . . ." Scores for the items range from 1 ("not at all"), to 4 ("extremely"). Subjects were asked to fill out these items themselves at the end of the interview. In addition to a 53-item global scale score, nine subscale scores were produced: somatization, obsessive-compulsive behaviors, interpersonal sensitivity, depression, anxiety, hostility, phobic anxiety, paranoid ideation, and psychoticism. The alpha reliability for the global, or total, scale score for the BSI was the same for the widows, for the divorcées, and for the total sample combined (.94). The reliability for the subscales ranged from a low of .69 for widows (hostility and obsessive-compulsive behaviors) and a low of .73 for divorcées (phobic anxiety) to a high of .90 for widows (anxiety) and a high of .88 for divorcées (obsessive-compulsive behaviors and depressive symptoms).* Because of the importance of depressive symptoms for the widowed and divorced, two measures of depression were used. The second measure was the SDS. It consists of 20 items, scored from 1 ("none") to 4 ("most of the time") in response to the statement, "Please tell me whether you feel this way . . ." The alpha reliability of the scale was .87 for widows, .83 for divorcées, and .86 for the combined samples, which is the most stable, heterogeneous estimate.

INDEPENDENT VARIABLES

The measure of social roles developed for this study consists of eight items assessing various activities of everyday life, including housework, cooking, and social activities outside of the home. The items were scored in response to the question, "Would you please tell me how difficult these tasks are for you, on a scale of 1 to 5, with '1' meaning 'not very difficult' to '5' meaning 'very difficult'?" The items were as follows: "Taking care of my home"; "preparing meals"; "working effectively"; "getting out of the house and doing things"; "finding time to do things I enjoy"; "dating"; "doing social activities with others"; doing things with my children."

The items do assess a common domain, as indicated by the alpha reliability score for the eight items, which was .74 for widows, .75 for divorcées, and .76 for

---

*The alpha reliability scores for the BSI scales for the widows, the divorcées, and the combined sample respectively are as follows: somatization (.85, .85, .84); interpersonal sensitivity (.77, .87, .83); anxiety (.90, .87, .89); obsessive-compulsive behaviors (.69, .81, .76); depressive symptoms (.89, .88, .88); hostility (.69, .81, .76); paranoid ideation (.71, ,84, .79); phobic anxiety (.79, .73, .79); psyschoticism (.76, .78, .76).

the combined sample. Scores on the summed scale range from 8 to 40, with a high score on the scale indicating greater difficulty with tasks. The similarity of the alpha reliability scores for widows and divorcées indicates that it is possible, as hypothesized, to assess difficulties in performing social functions in the two groups using the same measure.

Independence and dependence are viewed as important elements in a person's ability to cope with changes in his or her life.[6] For this study, five items were developed to assess a woman's sense of her ability to act independently in taking care of herself. They are scored on a five-point scale, from 1 ("not at all my feelings") to 5 ("very much my feelings"). The five items were these: "I generally do a good job of taking care of myself"; "Despite the changes in my life, I feel I can do something positive about it"; "My sense of self has been stronger since my husband's death"; "I find being on my own gives me a sense of freedom"; "I enjoy being my own boss." The alpha reliability of the independence measure was .68 for widows, .59 for divorcées, and .63 for the combined sample. While the reliability of the measure is not especially strong, it is adequate. A high score on the scale indicates a strong sense of independence.

Measures of demographic characteristics included age, race, level of education, and income expected for the coming year. We reasoned that income for the first year after the husband's death or divorce was a better measure of the subject's current situation than income in the last year of marriage. The effects of these variables were controlled to determine if they changed any of the findings. Marital status was coded as a dummy variable, with 0 = widow and 1 = divorcée.

FINDINGS

Social Adjustment and Independence Scales

The distribution of the social adjustment and independence scale scores by tertiles for widows and divorcées is displayed in Table 1. As hypothesized, widows had significantly higher mean scores on the social role scale than did divorcées. Only 38.3% of the divorcées reported moderate to high difficulty doing daily tasks, while 55.5% of the widows reported this.

As hypothesized, divorcées had significantly higher mean scores on the independence scale than did widows. Few of the women in either group had low scores on the scale, but divorcées were substantially more likely than widows to have high scores. Divorcées felt more independent and able to cope on their own than did widows.

Contrary to the hypothesis that widows and divorcées who felt less independent would also have more difficulty performing social roles, the two variables were not significantly associated in both groups. The Pearson zero order correlation between independence and social roles was significant for widows ($r = -.14$, $p < .05$) but not for divorcées ($r = -.08$, NS). Although the correlation was not strong for widows, this finding suggests that these variables may not behave the same way for widows and divorcées. To explore how the variables perform in the two samples, we shall first examine the relationships between psychological adjustment, social roles, and independence for the total sample and then for the widowed and divorced samples separately.

TABLE 1 Distribution of Scores on Social Roles and Independent Scales for Widows and Divorcées at Three Months Postloss

Scale scores	Widows	Divorcées
Difficulty with social roles		
Low difficulty (scores 8–17)	44.5%	61.7%
Moderate difficulty (scores 18–29)	45.0%	33.5%
High difficulty (scores 30–40)	10.5%	4.8%
Total	100.0%	100.0%
n	200	188
Mean score[a]	19.3	16.8
Standard deviation*	7.4	7.0
Degree of independence		
Low independence (scores 5–11)	4.5%	1.1%
Moderate independence (scores 12–18)	36.0%	12.3%
High independence (scores 19–25)	59.5%	86.6%
Total	100.0%	100.0%
n	200	187
Mean score[b]	19.1	22.4
Standard deviation**	4.3	3.1

[a]$t = 2.8$, 386 *df.*
[b]$t = 8.5$, 385 *df.*
*$p < .01$. **$p < .001$.

Relationships among Social and Psychological Adjustment and Independence for the Total Sample

Table 2 displays correlations of social roles and independence with psychological adjustment for the combined sample of widows and divorcées. These data illustrate, first, that social and psychological adjustment were, as hypothesized, positively associated. The greater the number of difficulties in performing social roles, the more the symptoms of psychological difficulty women experienced on all 11 indicators of distress. Respondents who had difficulty performing social roles had more somatic complaints, scored high on interpersonal sensitivity, were

TABLE 2 Social Roles, Independence, and Psychological Adjustment: Zero Order Pearson Correlation Coefficients for the Combined Sample of Widows and Divorcées ($n = 376$)

Indicators of psychological adjustment	Social roles (r)	Independence (r)
Somatization	.47*	−.20*
Interpersonal sensitivity	.49*	−.10
Anxiety	.54*	−.25*
Obsessive-compulsive behaviors	.54*	−.24*
Depression	.55*	−.30*
Phobic anxiety	.48*	−.27*
Psychoticism	.57*	−.24*
Hostility	.42*	−.08
Paranoid ideation	.40*	−.08
Global brief symptom inventory	.60*	−.25*
Zung depression inventory	.53*	−.31*

*$p < .001$

anxious, reported obsessive-compulsive behaviors, were depressed, scored high on the psychoticism index, and reported more symptoms of phobic anxiety, hostility, and paranoia. The global scale (the summary BSI), and the SDS were also positively associated with difficulties in social adjustment. Also as hypothesized, women who felt more independent had fewer symptoms of psychological distress. All but 3 of the 11 correlations were statistically significant. There were no significant effects of independence on these variables: interpersonal sensitivity, hostility, and paranoid ideation. The correlations of independence with the psychological adjustment variables, although highly significant, were not as strong or numerous as those between social roles and psychological distress. Less variance in psychological distress was accounted for by independence than by the social roles variable.

Our next step was to determine whether difficulties with social roles and feeling independent accounted for psychological difficulties or whether psychological difficulties accounted for social adjustment problems and a lack of feeling independent. In Table 3, the partial correlations between marital status, psychological status, social roles, and independence are displayed. The zero order correlations between marital status and social and psychological adjustment and independence are provided in column 1 of the table. As can be seen, widows were significantly more distressed than divorcées on virtually all of the measures. If the introduction of a control variable accounts for variance in a relationship between two variables, the partial correlation will decrease from what it was as a zero order association. If the relationship increases, the control variable is suppressing, or masking, the effects of the other two variables. For example, in column 1 marital status and depression, with a correlation of $-.28$, were significantly correlated with one another. With a control for social roles (column 2), the relationship was reduced to $-.22$. The relationship is still statistically significant, but we can conclude that difficulty in performing social roles accounts for some of the relationship between marital status and depression, with widows continuing to have more symptoms of depression than divorcées.

As displayed in column 2, the associations between marital status and psychological distress were reduced somewhat from the zero order associations when a control was introduced for social roles. Only one of these correlations was reduced to insignificance by introduction of the control variable: the association between marital status and somatization. When a widow had trouble with social roles, she also had more somatic complaints, but when the effect of social roles was controlled, there was no significant difference between widows and divorcées in somatic complaints.

For divorcées, paranoid feelings may be masked by the ability to perform social roles. When the effects of social roles were removed, divorcées reported more paranoid ideation than did widows. Despite the reductions in symptoms, when the effects of difficulty with roles were removed, widows were more distressed than divorcées. Overall, widows were still significantly more distressed than divorcées in 7 of the 11 relationships. It is, therefore, not simply difficulty with social roles that accounts for the greater distress of the widows.

Next we examine what happens when controls are introduced for the psychological adjustment indicators. As shown in column 1, the zero order correlation between marital status and social roles was $-.17$, $(p = .001)$. If psychological symptoms influence role behavior, the relationship between marital status and

TABLE 3 Marital Status, Social Roles, Independence, and Psychological Adjustment: Zero Order and Partial Correlations Coefficients for the Combined Sample of Widows and Divorcées

Indicators for social roles, independence, and psychological adjustment	Marital status (r)	Partial correlations (n = 376)		
		Control for social roles: Marital status and psychological adjustment	Control for psychological adjustment: Marital status and social roles	Control for psychological adjustment: Marital status and independence
Social roles	−.17***	—	—	—
Independence	.24***	—	—	—
Depression	−.28***	−.22***	−.03	.17***
Obsessive-compulsive behaviors	−.19***	−.13**	−.09	.20***
Anxiety	−.25***	−.19***	−.06	.19***
Hostility	−.07	.00	−.16*	.23***
Somatization	−.15**	−.09	−.13*	.21***
Interpersonal sensitivity	−.03	.05	−.18***	.24***
Phobic anxiety	−.24***	−.19***	−.09	.19***
Paranoid ideation	.06	.13**	−.21***	.24***
Psychoticism	−.19***	−.11*	−.09	.20***
Global brief symptom inventory	−.20***	−.13**	−.08	.29***
Zung depression inventory	−.30***	−.25***	−.02	.16**

*p < .05. **p < .01. ***p < .001

176

social roles should decrease when the psychological symptom variables are controlled. For the most part, this was the case. Nine of the 11 relationships were reduced, in seven cases to insignificance. For only two variables, paranoid ideation and interpersonal sensitivity, did the relationships increase. When paranoid feelings and sensitivity to the comments of others were controlled, the difficulty some widows were having with social roles became even clearer.

The zero order Pearson correlations between marital status and psychological status were stronger than those between marital status and social roles. As a result, more relationships were reduced to insignificance when a control was introduced for psychological status than when a control was introduced for social roles. Overall, the actual amount of variance explained by the controls (the squared zero order correlations minus the squared partial correlations) was quite similar in columns 2 and 3. We cannot conclude, therefore, whether social roles or psychological status accounts for more of the variance in the partial correlations for the combined sample. Each plays a role. Difficulty with social roles increases psychological distress and psychological distress increases difficulties in role performance.

The impact of psychological distress was greater on the relationship between marital status and social roles than it was on the relationship between marital status and independence. The zero order correlation between marital status and independence was .24 ($p < .001$). In column 4, all of the relationships between marital status and independence remained highly significant when psychological symptoms were controlled. There are virtually no differences in the correlations with and without controls. A feeling of independence was less influenced by psychological distress than was the performance of social roles. Independence may be a trait, or style of behavior, that is relatively impervious to the impact of a crisis. Women who felt independent before the husband's death or before the divorce was filed may simply incorporate whatever additional changes they must make into their perceptions of themselves after these events.

Widows and Divorcées Examined as Separate Samples

When we examined above the whole sample by marital status, we saw that widows generally reported more problems with social roles and felt less independent than divorcées on the items developed. Our next task is to determine how these items perform for widows and divorcées separately. It was hypothesized that widows and divorcées would react similarly. We have already seen, however, that social roles and independence were not significantly associated for divorcées but were for widows.

In Table 4, correlations between independence, social roles, and psychological symptoms are displayed for widows and divorcées separately. The social roles and independence scales performed similarly for widows and divorcées when these two measures were correlated with psychological symptoms. Women in both samples who had more difficulty with social roles and felt less independent had higher scores on all 11 psychological symptoms scales. For both groups of women, social roles explained more variance in distress than did independence.

Looked at as separate samples, the correlations between the measures of independence and social roles and psychological symptoms were actually somewhat stronger for divorcées than widows. The only items for which the correla-

TABLE 4   Marital Status, Social Roles, Independence and Psychological Adjustment for Widows and Divorcées: Zero Order Pearson Correlations

Indicators of psychological adjustment	Widows (n = 188)		Divorcées (n = 188)	
	Independence (r)	Social roles (r)	Independence (r)	Social roles (r)
Depression	−.22**	.60***	−.33***	.41***
Obsessive-compulsive behaviors	−.22**	.48***	−.18*	.46***
Anxiety	−.19*	.48***	−.24***	.49***
Hostility	−.07	.39***	−.10	.42***
Somatization	−.18*	.32***	−.20**	.47***
Interpersonal sensitivity	−.05	.41***	−.21***	.47***
Phobic anxiety	−.22**	.37***	−.25***	.40***
Paranoid ideation	−.08	.35***	−.17*	.40***
Psychoticism	−.19**	.46***	−.28***	.54***
Global brief symptom inventory	−.21**	.53***	−.26***	.54***
Zung depression inventory	−.21**	.55***	−.42***	.45***

*$p < .05$. **$p < .01$. ***$p < .001$.

tions were higher for widows were the two depression measures and obsessive-compulsive behaviors for the social roles scale and obsessive-compulsive behaviors for the independence scale. In all other cases, the correlations were stronger for divorcées. This means that while the widows, compared with the divorcées, were more distressed psychologically, felt less independent, and had more difficulty with social roles, independence and social roles accounted for more of the variance in psychological symptoms for divorced than for widowed women. In other words, a widow who felt independent and able to cope with her social roles still had more unexplained psychological distress than did a divorcée with similar scores on the scales. Other variables than those examined account for a substantial portion of the distress the widows were experiencing. We might speculate that these variables are likely to be related to the acute phase of the crisis of the spouse's death.

Our next task is to determine how the scales perform for the two samples when the effects of the other key measures are controlled, When the variance in psychological distress that is accounted for by social roles was controlled for widows and divorcées, as indicated in columns 1 and 4 of Table 5, the relationship between independence and psychological status was reduced for both groups. However, the reductions were greater for divorcées than widows. Among the widows, the 8 significant zero order correlations between independence and psychological distress in Table 4 were reduced to 5 marginally significant ones in Table 5, but for the divorcées, the 10 significant associations in Table 4 were reduced to 4. From these data, we conclude that difficulty in performing social roles created more psychological adjustment problems for the divorcées than for the widows studied.

In both samples, a control for independence did not reduce the relationship between social roles and psychological distress as much as the control for social roles reduced the relationship between independence and psychological status. The percentage point reduction in the correlations is 0 to 1 points in columns 2 and 5 of Table 5, (controlling for independence) compared with the zero order correlations in Table 4. This is in contrast to the 4 to 6 point reduction in columns 1 and 4 of Table 5 (controlling for social roles). The correlations between social roles and psychological adjustment continued to be highly significant. Thus, independence was of less importance than role functioning in influencing psychological adjustment for recently widowed and divorced women.

Columns 3 and 6 of Table 5 indicate the impact of controlling for the various measures of psychological adjustment on the relationship between independence and social roles. As noted above, there was no significant association between independence and social roles for divorcées ($r = -.08$), but there was a minimally significant association for widows ($r = -.14$, $p < .05$). Here, control for psychological symptoms reduced this association to insignificance for widows and also reduced the already small correlations for divorcées. Once the impact of psychological distress was accounted for, there was no relationship between independence and social roles for either group. The sense of dependence and difficulty in social roles that widows experienced was due to their high levels of psychological distress. Divorcées who had lower scores on psychological distress also experienced less difficulty with social roles and felt more independent.

Introducing controls for the variables age, race, education, and income, either singly or together, did not influence the relationships reported above; the findings, therefore, are not displayed. The patterns of adjustment difficulties observed in Table 5 are not due to differences in the effects of demographic factors in the two samples.

DISCUSSION

In this chapter the development of scales to assess difficulties in the performance of social roles and in attitudes toward independence have been described. The scales can successfully be used with widows and divorcées. As hypothesized, social roles and independence are both associated with psychological adjustment. Those having more difficulties in the performance of social roles and those who are more dependent have more symptoms of psychological distress. As expected, widows have more difficulty with social roles and feel less independent than do divorcées. Contrary to expectations, when the effects of psychological distress are controlled, independence and social roles are not significantly associated for either widows or divorcées.

In a cross-sectional study, it is difficult to determine causation. As a result, it is unclear whether difficulties with social roles, independence, or psychological symptoms play the more important role in adjustment difficulties 3 months after the death of the spouse or filing for divorce. Partial correlations can help to explore causation by determining which of the factors plays a greater role in the relationships. In these analyses, however, psychological adjustment and social roles accounted for similar amounts of variance when they were introduced as control variables. As a result, a conclusion cannot be made about the relative importance of the two variables. It is clear, however, that both variables are more important than independence in these samples. Difficulty with social roles produces some of the psychological distress that divorced and widowed women experience, while psychological distress also makes it difficult for them to perform some social roles. Although widows generally reported more difficulties with social roles and greater psychological distress than did divorcées, more of the vari-

TABLE 5 Marital Status, Social Roles, Independence, and Psychological Adjustment for Widows and

Indicators of psychological adjustment	Widows ($n = 188$)		
	1 Control for social roles: Independence and psychological adjustment	2 Control for independence: Social roles and psychological adjustment	3 Control for psychological adjustment: Independence and social roles
Depression	−.17*	.58**	−.01
Obsessive-compulsive behaviors	−.17*	.46**	−.05
Anxiety	−.14	.46**	.04
Hostility	−.01	.38**	−.13
Somatization	−.14	.31**	−.09
Interpersonal sensitivity	.01	.41**	−.13
Phobic anxiety	−.18*	.35**	−.07
Paranoid ideation	−.03	.34**	−.12
Psychoticism	−.14	.45**	−.07
Global brief symptom inventory	−.16*	.52**	−.04*
Zung depression inventory	−.16*	.54**	−.03*

*$p < .05$. **$p < .001$.

ance in the distress of the divorcées is accounted for by difficulties in social roles. The psychological distress of the widows is due in part to problems with social roles, but less so than for the divorcées. Part of the distress widows experience may be due to the generally "unwilled"[42] departure of the spouse more so than for the divorced women. Even with a lingering death, there is apparently still shock and distress at the loss (see Chapter 14). If death had not intervened, the couple would presumably still be together. As a result, the fact of the loss of the spouse was distress producing regardless of whether the woman was also experiencing trouble with social roles. For divorcées, on the other hand, the loss of the spouse was generally "willed." The women knew the relationship would end and were likely to have planned for it. However, even planned changes can require adjustment.[43,44] In these data, the causes of the distress experienced by the divorcées were clearer than for the widows. If a divorced woman had difficulties with certain of her social roles, those difficulties more directly influenced her feelings of well-being than was true for widows.

These data lend support to the "role strain" explanation of the distress experienced by the divorcées. The changes in their roles brought about by the divorce created psychological difficulties for them. For widows, on the other hand, the event itself—the death of the spouse or some other characteristics that we have not examined here—was a major contributor to the psychological distress they were experiencing. There are some longitudinal data to suggest that psychological difficulties clear more rapidly than do difficulties in social adjustment for both widowed and divorced persons.[5,8] We might expect that over time the role performance of the widows studied will become more like that of the divorcées as the shock of the death of the spouse decreases.

Although we do not have comparable data in this study on the adjustment of

Divorcées: Partial Correlations

Divorcées (n = 188)		
4 Control for social roles: Independence and psychological adjustment	5 Control for independence: Social roles and psychological adjustment	6 Control for psychological adjustment: Independence and social roles
−.24**	.41**	−.07
−.06	.45**	—
−.11	.49**	.04
.03	.41**	−.04
−.07	.47**	.01
−.09	.46**	.02
−.15*	.39**	.02
−.06	.40**	−.01
−.14*	.54**	.08
−.12	.54**	.08
−.33**	.46**	.14

men after widowhood or divorce, they may have even greater difficulty than women. In fact, some data suggest that although divorced and widowed men and women are at greater risk for physical and psychological morbidity than married or single ones, it is divorced and widowed men whose mortality risks are greater.[45,46] The performance of social tasks such as housekeeping, food preparation, shopping, and arranging social activities is more commonly the domain of women. Women's performance of many of these tasks may actually have become fairly automatic. It is possible that these social abilities make adjustment easier for women than men. The data for women in this study support this line of thought, and a similar explanation has been advanced by Helsing and Szklo[45] for men.

NEXT STEPS?

These data suggest that self-help programs for widowed and divorced persons that focus on helping them learn about unfamiliar tasks or roles that they feel uncertain about performing may be especially useful. It would also be helpful if future research were able to compare and contrast scores on independence, social roles, and psychological symptoms by gender. Men may feel more independent than women but may also have more difficulty in performing social roles.

Explorations of other factors that impact on psychological adjustment are also needed. These might include measures that examine the difference in the meaning of the loss of the spouse for widows and divorcées and the extent to which widows experience even a death after a lingering illness as a shock. Finally, although a measure of independence has been developed for this study, the alpha reliability for this measure is not particularly strong. Future efforts might be aimed at writing additional items to strengthen this measure. Because of the relative weakness of this measure compared to the other measures used, feeling independent may play a more important role than we have been able to assess. The findings also suggest that problems with social and psychological adjustment are somewhat different for widows and divorcées, at least in the first three months after the end of a marriage. The distress experienced by widows seems to be more associated with the loss of spouse and the distress experienced by divorcées seems to be more associated with difficulty with social roles. For each group of women, feeling independent and able to cope on one's own makes psychological adjustment easier.

REFERENCES

1. Bachrach, L. L. (1975). *Marital status and mental disorder: An analytical review.* (DHEW Publication No. 75-217). Washington, DC: U.S. Government Printing Office.
2. Bloom, B. L., Asher, S. J., & White, S. W. (1978). Marital disruption as a stressor: A review and analysis. *Psychological Bulletin, 85,* 867–894.
3. Clayton, P. J. (1979). The sequelae and nonsequelae of conjugal bereavement. *American Journal of Psychiatry, 136,* 1530–1534.
4. Osterweis, M., Solomon, F., & Green, M. (1984). *Bereavement: Reactions, consequences, and care.* (1984). Washington, DC: National Academy Press.
5. Bloom, B. L., Hodges, W. F., Kern, M. B., & McFadden, S. C. (1985). A preventive intervention program for the newly separated: Final evaluations. *American Journal of Orthopsychiatry, 55,* 9–26.
6. Parkes, C. M., & Weiss, R. S. (1983). *Recovery from bereavement.* New York: Basic Books.
7. Raschke, H. J. (1977). The role of social participation in postseparation and postdivorce. *Journal of Divorce, 1,* 129–140.
8. Zisook, S., & Shuchter, S. R. (1986). The first four years of widowhood. *Psychiatric Annals, 16,* 289–294.
9. Kitson, G. C., Babri, K. B., Roach, M. J., & Placidi, K. S. (in press). Adjustment to widowhood and divorce: A review. *Journal of Family Issues.*
10. Waller, W. (1930). *The old love and the new: Divorce and readjustment.* New York: Horace & Liveright. (Reprinted by Carbondale, IL: University of Southern Illinois Press, 1967).
11. Goode, W. J. (1956). *After divorce.* Glencoe, IL: The Free Press.
12. Jacobson, G. (1982). *The multiple crises of marital separation and divorce.* New York: Grune & Stratton.
13. Weiss, R. S. (1975). *Marital separation.* New York: Basic Books.
14. Weiss, R. S. (1979). *Going it alone: The family life and social situation of the single parent.* New York: Basic Books.
15. Winch, R. F. (1971). *The modern family* (3rd ed.). New York: Holt, Rinehart, & Winston.
16. U. S. Bureau of the Census. 1986. *Current Population Reports, Series P-20, No. 418. Marital status and living arrangements: March 1986.* Washington DC: U.S. Government Printing Office.
17. Lazarus, R. S., & Folkman, S. (1984). *Stress, appraisal, and coping.* New York: Springer.
18. McDowell, I., & Newell, C. (1987). *Measuring health: A guide to rating scales and questionnaires.* New York: Oxford University Press.
19. Pearlin, L. I., & Johnson, J. L. (1977). Marital status, life-strains and depression. *American Sociological Review, 42,* 704–715.
20. Pett, M. G. (1982). Predictors of satisfactory social adjustment of divorced single parents. *Journal of Divorce, 5,* 1–17.
21. Spanier, G. B., & Casto, R. F. (1979). Adjustment to separation and divorce: An analysis of 50 case studies. *Journal of Divorce, 2,* 241–235.
22. Woodward, J. C., Zabel, J. and DeCosta, C., (1980). Loneliness and divorce. *Journal of Divorce, 4,* 73–82.
23. Glick, I. O., Weiss, R. S., & Parkes, C. M. (1974). *The first year of bereavement.* New York: John Wiley & Sons.
24. McPhee, J. T. (1984). Ambiguity and change in the post-divorce family: Toward a model of divorce adjustment. *Journal of Divorce, 8,* 1–15.

25. Thoits, P. A. (1983). Multiple identities and psychological well-being: Reformulation and test of the social isolation hypothesis. *American Sociological Review, 48,* 174–187.
26. Lopata, H. Z. (1979). *Women as widows.* New York: Elsevier.
27. Verbrugge, L. M. (1979). Marital status and health. *Journal of Marriage and the Family, 41,* 267–284.
28. Kitson, G. C., Roach, M. J., Babri, K. B., & Zyzanski, S. J. (1987). *Health status in age matched samples of widows and divorcees.* Unpublished manuscript.
29. Kitson, G. C., with Holmes, W. M. (in press). *Portrait of divorce.* New York: Guilford Press.
30. Dixon, R. B., & Weitzman, L. J. (1982). When husbands file for divorce. *Journal of Marriage and the Family, 44,* 103–115.
31. Spanier, G. B., & Thompson, L. (1984). *Parting: The aftermath of separation and divorce.* Beverly Hills, CA: Sage.
32. Lund, D. A., Caserta, M. S., & Dimond, M. F. (1986). Gender differences through two years of bereavement among the elderly. *The Gerontologist, 26,* 315–320.
33. Glick, P. C., & Norton, A. J. (1979). *Marrying, divorcing and living together in the U.S. today.* (Population Bulletin 32). Washington, DC: Population Reference Bureau. (Originally published in 1977).
34. Kitson, G. C. (1982). Attachment to the spouse in divorce: A scale and its application. *Journal of Marriage and the Family, 44,* 379–393.
35. Kitson, G. C, & Langlie, J. K. (1984). Couples who file for divorce but change their minds. *American Journal of Orthopsychiatry, 54,* 469–489.
36. Gallagher, D. E., Breckenridge, J. N., Thompson, L. W., & Peterson, J. A. (1983). Effects of bereavement on indicators of mental health in elderly widows and widowers. *Journal of Gerontology, 38,* 565–571.
37. Chiriboga, D. A., Roberts, J., & Stein, J. A. (1978). Psychological well-being during marital separation. *Journal of Divorce, 2,* 21–36.
38. Spanier, G. B., & Anderson, E. A. (1979). The impact of the legal system on adjustment to marital separation. *Journal of Marriage and the Family, 41,* 605–613.
39. Hollingshead, A. B. 1957. *Two factor index of social class measurement.* New Haven CT: Yale University (Mimeograph).
40. Derogatis, L. R. (1977). *SCL-90: Administration, scoring, and procedures manual-1 for the r(e-vised) version and other instruments of the psychopathology rating scale series.* Baltimore: Johns Hopkins University School of Medicine.
41. Zung, W. W. K. (1965). A self-rating depression scale. *Archives of General Psychiatry, 12,* 63–70.
42. Blau, Z. S. (1973). *Old age in a changing society.* New York: New Viewpoints, Franklin-Watts.
43. Dohrenwend, B. S., Krasnoff, L., Askenasy, A. R., & Dohrenwend, B. P., (1978). Exemplification of a method for scaling life events: The PERI life events scale. *Journal of Health and Social Behavior, 19,* 205–229.
44. Holmes, T. H., & Rahe, R. H. (1976). The social readjustment rating scale. *Journal of Psychosomatic Research, 11,* 213–218.
45. Helsing, K. J., & Szklo, M. (1981). Mortality after bereavement. *American Journal of Epidemiology, 114,* 41–52.
46. Riessman, C. K., & Gerstel, N. (1985). Marital dissolution and health: Do males or females have greater risk? *Social Science and Medicine, 20,* 627–635.

14

Impact of Forewarning on Adjustment to Widowhood and Divorce

Mary Joan Roach and Gay C. Kitson

This paper explores the relationship between forewarning, or anticipatory grief, and psychological adjustment to widowhood and divorce. It has been assumed that being forewarned that a loss is going to occur will prompt an individual to prepare, which will help him or her accept the loss and therefore exhibit less psychological distress after the death than those without preparation. Samples of 188 widows and 188 divorcées from Cuyahoga County (metropolitan Cleveland), Ohio, matched by age, race, and median income of census tract, were interviewed to examine the impact of various forewarning measures on adjustment to widowhood and divorce. Analyses were conducted on the total, widowed, and divorced samples to explore the similarities and differences in the effects of forewarning on adjustment. The results indicate that none of the measures of forewarning affected all measures of psychological adjustment for the widows and only one measure of forewarning affected two measures of psychological adjustment for the divorcées. From these data, we cannot conclude that forewarning of the loss of a spouse results in less difficulty in adjustment.

The concept of forewarning, or anticipatory grief, has been part of the study of bereavement at least since Freud's[1] discussion of mourning and melancholia in 1917. Anticipatory grief refers to the process of anticipating the loss of a person and preparing psychologically for the event.[2] Forewarning is thought to reduce psychological distress after a death and to facilitate adjustment. The underlying assumption is that being forewarned that a loss is going to occur prompts an individual to make preparations which will help him or her accept the loss and

An earlier version of this chapter was read at the meetings of the National Council on Family Relations, Atlanta, Georgia, November 1987. The research reported on in this chapter was supported by National Institute on Aging grant no. MH04561.

therefore resolve grief with less difficulty. Even though the concept of anticipatory grief has been in the literature for many years, little empirical research has actually investigated the effects of forewarning on psychological distress among individuals who are experiencing a major loss. The focus of this chapter is on how forewarning affects the psychological adjustment of women who have lost their spouses through death or divorce.

Widowhood and divorce are two kinds of events which involve the loss of a spouse and the end of a primary relationship. Holmes and Rahe[3] found that these two kinds of life events are among the most difficult to which to adjust. If forewarning of a loss gives an individual the time needed to prepare, then we should expect that it will influence how well a widow or divorcée adjusts psychologically. The literature on the effects of forewarning on subsequent distress, however, suggests that having the time to prepare for a loss does not necessarily mean the individual will prepare for the event or that the outcome of anticipatory grief is better psychological adjustment. Clayton, Halikas, Maurice, and Robins,[4] in a retrospective study of 109 widows and widowers (mean age of 61 years), found that anticipating the death of a spouse (i.e., where the spouse was ill over 6 months) only had a positive effect on immediate postmortem depression. The effect did not last, and, within 1 year, those experiencing anticipatory grief were no different from those who had no forewarning (see also references 5 and 6). Blanchard, Blanchard, and Becker,[7] in a retrospective study of 30 young widows (age 45 or younger), found no difference in symptoms of depression, with the exception of suicidal thoughts, between those widows whose husbands died after being ill for 1 day or less and those widows whose husbands died after being ill for longer than 1 day. On the other hand, a few studies have shown that forewarning does help to reduce the negative psychological effects of loss. For example, Ball[8] studied 80 widows aged 18 to 75 whose spouses had died of an illness or accident in Sacramento County, California, and she found that anticipatory grief did mitigate overall grief reactions. She also found that young widows (aged 18 to 46) with no anticipatory grief (i.e., death occurred less than 5 days from the onset of illness) had higher grief responses than any other group. Ball used an overall grief measure that included psychological distress variables (i.e., loss of appetite, restlessness, and sleeping problems) and one indicator of a standard grief reaction (hallucinations about the spouse). Her findings support the work of Glick, Weiss, and Parkes[9] and Parkes and Weiss,[10] who suggested that when a loss is not anticipated (i.e., the illness began less than 2 weeks before death), it is more difficult for the individual to regain full psychological functioning. Psychological functioning was measured by the emotional state of the widowed person, including measures of both psychological distress and grief.

For an older individual, the loss of a spouse through death is an expected loss (or as Neugarten[11] described it, an "on-time" event), especially so for women who are aware that they have longer life expectancies than their mates. Therefore, it has been suggested that, in later life, having knowledge that one's spouse is likely to die within a specified period of time will make adjustment to the death less difficult. This is because the elderly go through mental preparations for the death regardless of prior knowledge about the eventuality of the death.[12] Conversely, for younger individuals, forewarning may have an effect because the event is untimely; they may not otherwise even think to prepare for the eventual loss. In this context, forewarning could have a positive effect on the

adjustment process for younger women. Given these considerations, it is important to study the impact of forewarning in a sample with both younger and older
widows in order to understand the relationship between forewarning and psychological adjustment.

With regard to the divorced, some literature suggests that forewarning of the
divorce may impede rather than improve adjustment to the event. Wise[13] argues
that long separations before a divorce increase psychological distress due to the
continued attachment one spouse feels toward the other (see also reference 14).
Spanier and Casto,[15] however, using a sample of men and women aged 21 to 65
years, found that sudden or unexpected separation resulted in lower initial levels of
adjustment to the divorce. Sudden separation was measured by the perception of
the respondents.

Hagestad and Smyer[16] argue that unscheduled transitions, such as divorce,
do not allow an individual to prepare for the event and therefore increase the
negative effects of the transition. They also argue that in the case of divorce, the
partner who has control over the divorce process will have the time to prepare for
the event; therefore, adjustment to the divorce will be easier for him or her than
for the partner who had little or no control over the event. Control over the event
was operationalized by the partner who suggested the divorce or initiated the legal
proceedings for the divorce.

With both divorce and spousal bereavement, age may play a role in understanding the relationship between forewarning and adjustment. In a study done in
Quebec of 427 older female devorcées (mean age 50.1 years) who had been married over 20 years before they divorced, Deckert and Langelier[17] found that these
women reported that the divorce was more stressful than their bad marriages.
They argue that women who are older and have been married for a long period of
time are so closely tied to the role of the wife that adjusting to the role of divorcée
is very difficult. They also found that the decision to divorce was made over a long
period of time (2 years or longer), which meant that the women had time to
prepare for their loss; therefore, adjustment should have been easier. They found,
however, that adjustment was difficult even with a long period of forewarning. On
the other hand, Blanchard, Blanchard and Becker[7] found that sudden death widows
who had been married for shorter periods of time had more severe depressive
symptoms initially than those who had been married for longer periods of time.
These findings suggest that length of marriage as well as age may play a role in the
relationship between forewarning and adjustment.

As this review indicates, studies of both widowhood and divorce vary in the
definitions they use of forewarning, the measures used to assess difficulties in
adjustment, and the measures used to assess longevity. Studies employing the age
of the widow as a measure of forewarning have produced different findings from
those using the length of marriage in exploring the association between forewarning and psychological adjustment to widowhood and divorce. Virtually no data we
are aware of compare and contrast the impact of forewarning on adjustment to
both widowhood and divorce. We might expect a greater impact of forewarning for
widows, since divorcées may have had a long period of awareness of problems in
the relationship even though the thought of divorce may not have become conscious.

Based upon the limited relevant research, we propose the following hypotheses:

1. Less time of forewarning will be associated with greater psychological distress for both widows and divorcées.
2. Age will have a positive association with forewarning for both widows and divorcées, with older age associated with a longer period of forewarning.
3. Longer lengths of marriage will be associated with longer periods of forewarning for both widows and divorcées.
4. Accidential deaths will be associated with less forewarning and divorces filed by the spouse will be associated with less forewarning.
5. Psychological distress will be greatest for young widows without any forewarning of the death of the spouse, next greatest for young widows with warning and then older widows.
6. Psychological distress will be greatest for older divorcées whose divorces occurred with no forewarning, next greatest for older divorcées with forewarning and then younger divorcées.
7. The more the preparation for the death or divorce, the less the psychological distress a widow or divorce will experience.

METHODS

Sample

The data on which this chapter is based are from samples of 201 widows and 188 divorcées matched by age, race, and median income of census tract in Cuyahoga County (metropolitan Cleveland), Ohio. The samples were composed by using death and divorce records. The women were interviewed approximately 3 months after the death of the spouse or the spouse's filing for divorce. The methodology is described in chapter 13 of this volume.

Our measures of forewarning are based on retrospective reports of women whose spouse had die or for whom a divorce filing was on record. It was decided to talk with widows 3 months after the death of the spouse. For women whose husbands died with little or no warning, there was probably little time to prepare for the loss of the spouse. For others, however, there was longer knowledge of the seriousness of the spouse's condition. For divorcées, it was decided that the most comparable date from publicly available records was to use 3 months from date of filing as the point of interview. In some cases, the couple might have been separated for some time before filing for divorce; in others, the decision to file for divorce was more sudden. There is no economical way to draw a representative sample of divorced persons by separation date, because there is no notification of when a couple separates, (just as there is no public notification of when an illness begins, only of when a person dies).

Measures

FOREWARNING

Because relatively little research has been done on the effects of forewarning on psychological distress, in particular, comparing and contrasting widows and divorcées it was decided to look at a variety of measures of forewarning to determine if forewarning is associated with distress and which measure has the greatest effect. The first measure of forewarning was "length of time between the start of illness and the death of the spouse" for widows [00 (less than 1 month) to 119 (15 years or more), $M = 40.3$] and the "length of time between suggesting a divorce and filing for it" for the divorced women [00 (less than one month) to 93 (7 years and 9 months), $M = 23.4$]. These two forewarning measures are comparable for widows and divorcées, since in each case the time between the start of the illness to death or between suggesting a divorce and actually filing is fairly open-ended. The reality of the termination of the relationship is still perhaps only dimly perceived.

A second measure of forewarning to be used in examining the combined sample of widows and divorcées was calculated by using the divorcées variable "length of time between separation and divorce filing" and the widows' measure "length of time between knowledge of the seriousness of the illness and the death of the spouse" in a combined measure. Replies ranged from 00 (less than 1 month) to 85 (85 months, or 7 years and 1 month). For the combined sample, $M = 13.8$; for the widowed sample, $M = 13.6$; for the divorced sample, $M = 14.1$. We reasoned that the point at which it became known that the illness would lead to death or that the relationship was bad enough to lead to separation was when women were likely to become consciously aware of the seriousness of the illness and the threat to the continuity of the relationship. Therefore, this combined forewarning measure allowed us to run analyses using the total sample to see if there was an effect of forewarning on marital status and to analyze the differences between the two groups.

We also decided to utilize two other measures of forewarning for the divorced sample for which we had no comparable measures for the widows. These two measures were the "length of time between suggesting the divorce and receiving the divorce decree" [00 (less than 1 month) to 96 (96 months, or 8 years, or more), $M = 25.0$] and the "length of time between filing and receiving the decree" [00 (less than 1 month) to 24 (24 months), $M = 10.7$]. Our study focus was divorces or dissolutions of marriage filed 3 months prior to interview, but some of the suits selected for interview were countersuits to earlier filings, which explains the variability in length of time between filing and receiving the decree. Sixteen women (8%) had not received their final decrees at the time of the interview; therefore, they were excluded from the computation of these two variables.

Preparations

With forewarning, a person not only has the opportunity to become psychologically prepared for the event but also has the time to make the necessary preparations that should help adjustment afterwards. We decided to look at preparations (i.e., activities the widows and divorcées did to better position themselves for the loss of the spouse). Each respondent was asked about 11 activities. "Did you do any of these: Change your appearance; meet some new people; go back to school; update your job skills; get a job; change jobs; learn about your legal rights; read about the experience of other women who are widowed/divorced; build a nest egg; learn about finances; work more hours?" The response categories for each item were as follows: "Before the illness/accident or decision to divorce; during the illness or during the decision; since the death or filing, plan to; had no plans." Only preparations before and during the illness or decision to divorce will be examined here. Both preparation variables were calculated by counting, first, all those preparations the respondent did either before the illness or decision to divorce and, second, those done during the illness or decision to divorce. The "before" and "during" preparation variables each had possible ranges of 0 to 11. These two measures were used, because individuals who divorce may make such preparations, either consciously or unconsciously, before actually reaching the decision period. This behavior should be different from that of the widows, for whom such activities might be more a part of normal life span development before the husband's illness.

Divorcées are significantly more likely than widows to have made preparations before the decision to divorce or the illness started and during the decision or illness period. Preparations before the illness or decision to divorce had a mean score of .8 for the widows and 1.5 for the divorcées (t = 4.18, df = 374, p < .001). Preparing during the illness or decision to divorce had a mean score of .4 for widows and .8 for divorcées (t = 3.27, df = 374, p < .001). For both samples, relatively little preparation was done prior to the death or divorce decision, with even less preparation done during the period of the illness or decision to divorce. These data suggest that forewarning may have relatively little impact on preparation.

DEPENDENT VARIABLES

Psychological distress was measured by the Brief Symptom Inventory (BSI)[18] and the Zung Self-Rating Depression Scale (SDS).[19] The BSI is scored in response to the question, "In the past two weeks, how much were you bothered by . . ." Scores range from 1 (not at all) to 4 (extremely). Subjects filled out these items themselves at the end of the interview. High scores indicate more distress. In addition to the 53-item Global Scale Score, 9 subscale scores were produced: somatization, obsessive-compulsive behaviors, interpersonal sensitivity, depression, anxiety, hostility, phobic anxiety, paranoid ideation, and psychoticism. The second measure of psychological distress was the SDS. It consists of 20 items, scored from 1 (none) to 4 (most of the time) in response to the statement, "Please tell me whether you feel this way . . ." High scores indicate more depression. Reliabilities for these measures are discussed in Chapter 13.

INDEPENDENT VARIABLES

Authors vary in using age[4,7,8] and length of marriage[16,17] as indicators of longevity of relationships, so it is unclear whether it is the low likelihood of the end of a relationship at young ages or the shortness of the relationship that makes lack of forewarning a problem. We shall look at the relationship between age and length of marriage and the measures of forewarning. Age is coded in years and length of marriage is coded in years from date of marriage to the death of the spouse or filing for divorce. Marital status is coded "0" for widows and "1" for divorcées. The zero order Pearson correlation between age and length of marriage was .62 for divorcées (p < .001) and .75 for widows (p < .001). Although highly significant associations, they still leave some unexplained variances between age and marriage.

Three other variables were used as controls: length of time between the death of or divorce from the spouse and the interview (codes range from 3 to 12 months); income [coded from 1 (under $5,000) to 9 ($50,000 and over)]; and social class as measured by the Index of Social Position [a low score indicates upper class (Class I) and a high score indicates lower class (Class V)].[20] These variables were thought to influence psychological distress; therefore, we wanted to control their effects so that they would not confound the results and lead to the wrong conclusions.

CHARACTERISTICS OF THE EVENT AND RESPONSES

Whether the death was accidental or natural and who suggested the divorce (did the respondent or the spouse or was it a mutual decision?) were considered to be relatively similar measures of the characteristics of the loss event. An accidental death offers no forewarning of the event,[10] and having the spouse suggest the idea of the divorce offers less opportunity for forewarning, which has been found to be associated with greater psychological distress.[21] On the other hand, the majority of natural deaths involve some forewarning, and having the respondent suggest or mutually agree to the divorce also implies forewarning. Type of death and who suggested the divorce were each coded "0" for natural death and for suggestion of the divorce by the respondent or mutual agreement and coded "1" for accidental death and for the spouse's suggestion. For widows there were 22 accidental deaths and for divorcées there were 53 instances in which the spouse suggested the divorce.

In the analyses that follow, the widowed sample is reduced to the 188 women for whom there was a divorced woman matched by age, race, and median income of census tract.

RESULTS

The first hypothesis, that forewarning would be associated with psychological distress for both widows and divorcées, was not supported. Forewarning, as measured by length of knowledge of the seriousness of the illness for the widowed and the length of separation for the divorced, had no significant effect on psychological distress, including the global BSI scores, the nine subscales, and the SDS (Table 1). By comparing the results for the total sample and the widowed and divorced samples, we find that the direction of the associations were the same for all samples. Virtually all of the associations were small and negative, meaning that there was an insignificant trend toward less forewarning being associated with greater psychological distress. These findings indicate that forewarning was not a major determinant of psychological distress for the widowed or divorced women in this metropolitan Cleveland sample.

As an additional test of this first hypothesis, separate analyses were done for widows and divorcées on the other measures of forewarning (length of illness for widows and length of time between suggesting and filing for divorce for divorced women) to see if these measures affected psychological distress (Table 2). Length of illness was not significantly associated with any of the psychological distress measures for widows. One of the forewarning measures has a small effect on two measures of psychological distress for divorcées. A longer time between filing for the divorce and obtaining the decree was associated with lower feelings of hostility and fewer symptoms of anxiety. Thus, for many divorced women, anger and anxiety fade as time passes. The idea of a divorce apparently became less anxiety provoking the longer the person had to think about it. These two findings lend some slight support to the hypothesis that forewarning affects psychological adjustment for divorcées. But because support was found on only 2 of 44 tests [11

TABLE 1   Pearson Zero Order Correlations for Psychological Responses to Loss for the Total, Widowed, and Divorced Samples

Psychological responses to loss	Total sample: Forewarning[a] (n = 376)	Widows: Length of knowledge of illness (n = 188)	Divorcées: Length of separation (n = 188)
Brief Symptom Inventory (BSI) subscales			
Depression	−.03	−.05	−.00
Obsessive-compulsive behaviors	−.02	−.01	−.05
Anxiety	−.03	−.04	−.02
Hostility	.00	−.04	.04
Somatization	−.04	−.03	−.06
Interpersonal sensitivity	−.05	−.03	−.08
Phobic anxiety	−.05	−.07	−.01
Psychoticism	−.06	−.09	−.01
Paranoid ideation	.00	−.01	.02
Global Brief Symptom Inventory (BSI)	−.04	−.05	−.02
Self-Rating Depression Scale (SDS)	−.08	−.07	−.10

[a]Length of knowledge of seriousness of illness and length of separation.

psychological variables and 4 forewarning measures for the divorced (see Tables 1 and 2)], we conclude that forewarning had little effect on psychological distress in the divorced sample. None of the associations between the measures of forewarning and psychological distress in either Table 1 or 2 was significant for widows. Overall, the forewarning measures were not significantly associated with psychological distress.

The findings on the relationship between the measures of forewarning and the measures of psychological distress were not affected when controls were introduced for length of time between the death of the spouse or filing for the divorce and the interview; for social class; and for income. As a result, these analyses are not presented here. In summary, there was virtually no support in these data for the hypothesis suggesting that psychological distress was associated with forewarning.

Since various definitions of forewarning have been used in past bereavement research,[7-10] we decided to analyze our data from widows using these definitions of suddenness of death. Four analyses were conducted. One used 1 day or less as a measure of sudden death; the next used less than 5 days; the third used 2 weeks or less; and the last used 6 months or less. The results showed no significant relationships between forewarning and any of the psychological adjustment measures; therefore, they are not reported in a table. What these analyses indicate was that in these data, forewarning, no matter how defined, does not affect psychological adjustment to the death of a spouse.

The second hypothesis was that older widows and divorcées would have longer periods of forewarning and the fourth hypothesis was that longer length of marriage would be associated with longer periods of forewarning. Both hypothesis were supported. Older widows and divorcées did have longer periods of forewarning than did younger widows and divorcées (see Table 2). Deckert and Langelier[17] have suggested that older divorcées may have been aware of difficulties in the marriage for a long period of time, particularly when forewarning is measured by the amount of time between filing and decree. For the widowed, the likelihood of a

TABLE 2   Pearson Zero Order Correlations for the Widowed and Divorced Samples for Psychological Responses to Loss, Sociodemographic and Event Characteristics, and Forewarning

Psychological responses to loss, sociodemographic characteristics and event characteristics	Widows (n = 188) Length of illness	Divorcées (n = 188)		
		Time between suggestion and filing	Time between suggestion and decree	Time between filing and decree
Brief Symptom Inventory (BSI) subscales				
Depression	.01	.09	.02	− .11
Obsessive-compulsive behaviors	.03	.02	− .06	− .06
Anxiety	.01	.03	− .03	− .16*
Hostility	− .01	.08	− .01	− .16*
Somatization	.04	− .06	− .07	− .15
Interpersonal sensitivity	− .02	.05	− .04	− .04
Phobic anxiety	− .06	− .03	− .03	− .12
Psychoticism	− .03	.13	.05	− .07
Paranoid ideation	.02	.10	.03	− .04
Global Brief Symptom Inventory	.00	.05	− .02	− .10
Self-Rating Depression Scale (SDS)	.00	− .02	− .06	− .09
Sociodemographic characteristics				
Age	.14*	.19**	.26**	.43***
Length of marriage	.14*	.19**	.22**	.28***
Event characteristics				
Anticipated death/who suggested divorce	− .31***	− .16*	− .08	.01

*p < .05. **p < .01. ***p < .001.

chronic illness increases with age, as does the likelihood of death; therefore, older women may have been aware of the possibility of death of the spouse for longer periods of time.

Table 2 also indicates that longer marriages did have significantly longer forewarning periods for both widows and divorcées. Therefore, the third hypothesis is supported. Older women and women who had been married for longer periods of time had more time to prepare for the death or divorce than women who were younger or briefly married. There was no difference in the strength of the association with forewarning by age or length of marriage for the widows, but two of the three forewarning correlations were stronger for age than for length of marriage for the divorced women. This suggests that it may be age rather than length of marriage which is the more important dimension.

The fourth hypothesis was that accidental deaths and the spouse's decision to divorce would result in shorter forewarning. This hypothesis was supported. For widows, length of forewarning is associated with the type of death. This means that an accidental death, as an unanticipated event, was less likely to give the widow time to prepare for the death. Age had a positive relationship with forewarning, indicating that older widows had longer periods of forewarning than younger widows. Accidents are the leading cause of death among the young,[22] while the likelihood of chronic illness increases with age.

Table 2 also shows that length of time between suggesting a divorce and filing was associated with who suggested the divorce. When the suggestion was made solely by the husband, the wife was less likely to have time to prepare for the divorce. The correlations between forewarning as measured by the time between suggestion and decree and between filing and decree were not associated with who suggested the divorce.

The fifth hypothesis was that psychological distress would be the greatest for young widows without any forewarning, next greatest for young widows with warning and then older widows. Table 3 presents the zero order Pearson correlations for psychological responses and event characteristics by the widow's sociodemographic characteristics.

For the widowed, the untimeliness of the death as measured by age and length of marriage was significantly associated with psychological distress. As expected, the correlations were negative, meaning that younger widows and those married a shorter period of time exhibited significantly greater psychological distress than their older counterparts.

As indicated in Table 2, age and length of marriage were also associated with the degree of forewarning for widows, with younger women and women who were married for a shorter period of time more likely to report less forewarning. Partial correlation analyses were conducted to determine the relative influence of length of marriage and age on forewarning and its relationship with psychological distress. Comparing columns 1 and 3 in Table 3, we find that when forewarning is controlled, the associations between age and psychological distress for widows

TABLE 3 Pearson Zero Order and Partial Correlations for the Widowed Samples for Age, Length of Marriage, Event Characteristics, and Psychological Symptom Measures ($n = 188$)

Psychological responses to loss and event characteristics	Age of respondent	Length of marriage	Control for forewarning: Age	Control for forewarning: Length of marriage
Brief Symptom Inventory (BSI) subscales				
Depression	−.11	−.09	−.11	−.08
Obsessive-compulsive behaviors	−.08	−.06	−.08	−.06
Anxiety	−.20**	−.13	−.20**	−.13
Hostility	−.30***	−.26***	−.30**	−.26***
Somatization	−.13	−.06	−.12	−.06
Interpersonal sensitivity	−.26***	−.21**	−.26***	−.21**
Phobic anxiety	−.25***	−.14*	−.24***	−.13
Psychoticism	−.29	−.21**	−.29***	−.19*
Paranoid ideation	−.27***	−.38***	−.27***	−.38***
Global Brief Symptom Inventory	−.24***	−.18*	−.23***	−.17*
Self-Rating Depression Scale (SDS)	−.14	−.07	−.13	−.06
Event characteristics				
Anticipated death/who suggested divorce	−.21**	−.23**	−.19**	−.20**

*$p < .05$. **$p < .01$. ***$p < .001$.

remained unchanged. This means that forewarning did not help to explain why younger widows have higher psychological distress than older widows. Looking at columns 2 and 4 in Table 3, we also find that the relationships between length of marriage and psychological distress were virtually unchanged when length of forewarning was controlled. Therefore, length of marriage did not explain why widows who have been married for shorter periods of time exhibit higher levels of psychological distress than widows married for longer periods of time. Overall, this part of the analysis indicated that age of the widow directly affected psychological distress regardless of the length of forewarning or length of marriage.

The sixth hypothesis was that, among divorcées, psychological distress would be greatest for older divorcées whose divorces occurred with no forewarning, next greatest for older divorcées with forewarning and then younger divorcées. This hypothesis was not supported. Age was significantly associated with psychological distress, with *younger divorcées* more distressed than older divorcees (Table 4). There were no significant association between length of marriage and the psychological distress measures among the divorced women.

As shown in Table 2, age and length of marriage had positive associations with forewarning; older divorcées who had been married for a long period of time had longer forewarning periods but distress was less for them than for those who were younger. When forewarning is controlled, the relationships between age and distress and length of marriage and distress remain (see Table 4). As with the widows, forewarning does not help explain the relationships between age and distress and length of marriage and distress for the divorced women. The data from Tables 3 and 4 suggest that it may not be the degree of warning a person has of a death or divorce that makes adjustment more or less difficult, but rather when that death or divorce occurs in the life cycle.

The seventh hypothesis was that the more preparation a person had made for death or divorce, the less the psychological distress after the event occurred. For widows, the greater the number of preparations made before the husband's illness, the less the psychological distress after death (Table 5). These women, presumably as part of their own life cycle development, were interested in making changes in themselves or in their careers. These activities may have added to a woman's sense of herself as a person and as having an identity in addition to being a "wife" or "spouse." Such efforts may then help her cope better with her spouse's death, because part of the distress people experience may be due to the loss of a role as well as the loss of a spouse. For divorcées, none of the associations between preparations and psychological distress were significant. It may be that the divorced went through the motions of preparing, but their preoccupation with feelings about the divorce overrode the positive effects these preparations might otherwise have had on their adjustment.

The number of preparations made during the illness or during the decision to divorce showed no significant relationships to the psychological distress measures for widows or divorcées (see Table 5). The longer the period of forewarning, however, the greater the number of preparations during the illness ($r = .18, p < .05$) or during the period of the decision to divorce ($r = .17, p < .05$). For widows, activities aimed at self-improvement helped to reduce psychological distress attributed to the loss of the spouse even if these activities were not consciously done to prepare for the loss. On the other hand, activities done when the woman knew her husband was ill did not help to reduce subsequent psychological

TABLE 4   Pearson Zero Order and Partial Correlations for the Divorced Sample for Age, Length of Marriage, Event Characteristics, and Psychological Symptom Measures ($n = 188$)

Measures of psychological symptoms controlled for and event characteristics	Age of respondent	Length of marriage	Control for forewarning: Age	Control for forewarning: Length of marriage
Brief Symptom Inventory (BSI) subscales				
Depression	−.05	−.02	−.05	−.02
Obsessive-compulsive behaviors	−.17*	−.03	−.17*	−.03
Anxiety	−.17*	−.04	−.17*	−.03
Hostility	−.15*	−.03	−.16*	−.03
Somatization	−.11	.03	−.10	.03
Interpersonal sensitivity	−.13	−.04	−.12	−.03
Phobic anxiety	−.19**	−.14	−.19*	−.14
Psychoticism	−.13	−.04	−.13	−.04
Paranoid ideation	−.17*	−.06	−.18*	−.06
Global Brief Symptom Inventory	−.15*	−.03	−.15	−.03
Self-Rating Depression Scale (SDS)	.03	.09	.05	−.10
Event characteristics				
Anticipated death/who suggested divorce	.01	−.09	.01	−.09

$*p < .05.$ $**p < .01.$

distress. Preparations made before or during the decision to divorce showed no relationship with distress for the divorced.

To see if preparations could account for the differences in distress levels between widows and divorcées, partial correlations between marital status and distress were conducted controlling for the number of preparations made. The results indicated that the widows' psychological distress levels were partially due to lack of preparation. A widow who prepares herself both before and during her spouse's illness will experience less psychological distress after his death than a widow who made no preparations. Preparations made before the illness had a greater effect on widows' psychological distress than preparations during the illness. This can be seen in the greater decrease in the relationship between marital status and distress when preparations before the illness were controlled as compared with controlling for preparations during the illness (Table 6).

DISCUSSION

There has been little research on life cycle differences in adjustment for the divorced or the widowed. Those studies that have explored this issue[10,16,17] have used truncated samples; that is, they have not employed samples that included younger and older persons. Our data included both younger and older women. The hypothesis that, for widows, death at a young age is more distressing than death in later years was supported, but there was no support for the expectation that divorce at an older age would be more difficult than divorce at a younger age. It therefore appears that, as with widows, young persons whose marriages end in divorce expected and hoped that their relationships would continue and were dis-

TABLE 5 Pearson Zero Order Correlations for Number of Preparations, Psychological Responses, and Forewarning for Widows and Divorcées

Psychological responses to loss and forewarning measures	Number of preparations before		Number of preparations during	
	Illness/accident (widows, $n = 188$)	Decision to file (divorcées, $n = 188$)	Illness/accident (widows, $n = 188$)	Decision to file (divorcées, $n = 188$)
Brief Symptom Inventory (BSI) subscales				
Depression	−.26***	.08	−.08	.05
Obsessive-compulsive behaviors	−.19**	.08	−.06	.03
Anxiety	−.23**	.12	−.05	.13
Hostility	−.10	.16	.00	.07
Somatization	−.18*	.05	−.09	.02
Interpersonal sensitivity	−.25***	.04	−.12	.04
Phobic anxiety	−.20**	.02	−.12	−.01
Psychoticism	−.22**	.04	−.08	−.03
Paranoid ideation	−.14	.15	−.02	−.00
Brief Symptom Inventory	−.24***	.08	−.08	.04
Self-Rating Depression Scale (SDS)	−.23**	−.07	−.01	−.04
Forewarning				
Forewarning	.13	.16*	−.18	.17*
Length of illness	.10	—	.24***	—
Time between suggestion and filing	—	.11	—	.07
Time between suggestion and decree	—	.07	—	.03
Time between filing and decree	—	−.10	—	−.02

$*p < .05. **p < .01. ***p < .001.$

197

TABLE 6 **Pearson Zero Order and Partial Correlations for Marital Status, Psychological Responses, Number of Preparations before and during Illness or Decision to Divorce for the Total Sample ($n = 376$)**

Psychological responses to loss	Marital status	Control for preparations before illness or decision to divorce Marital status	Control for preparations during illness or decision to divorce: Marital status
Psychological distress subscales			
Depression	−.28***	−.25***	−.27***
Obsessive-compulsive behaviors	−.19**	−.18**	−.19
Anxiety	−.25***	−.23***	−.25***
Hostility	−.07	−.07	−.08
Somatization	−.15**	−.14	−.14
Interpersonal sensivity	−.03	−.01	−.02
Phobic anxiety	−.24***	−.22***	−.23***
Psychoticism	−.19**	−.17**	−.17**
Paranoid ideation	.06	.04	.06
Global Brief Symptom Inventory	−.20**	−.19**	−.20**
Self-Rating Depression Scale (SDS)	−.30***	−.26***	−.29***

*$p < .05$. **$p < .01$. ***$p < .001$.

tressed when they did not. Older divorcées were more likely than younger divorcées to be aware that something was amiss in the marriage for a longer period of time. This may make the loss less distressing psychologically.

Although older women and those married longer were less psychologically distressed than younger women, forewarning had no effect on the psychological adjustment of widows or divorcées to the loss of the spouse. Knowing that death was imminent or that a marriage might end did not help to reduce the psychological distress that occurred when the marriage actually ended. This supports the argument put forth by Glick, Weiss, and Parkes[9] that even when a widow had knowledge of her husband's imminent death, the reality of that death actually occurring produced the same psychological distress as it would have if the widow had no prior knowledge. It may be that there is still the feeling of hope that a "miracle" will happen until the moment of death, and this would not facilitate a reduction in psychological distress to the event. For the divorcée, a similar hypothesis can be put forth. Until the final decree is granted, there may still be hope that the couple can "save" the marriage.

For the divorced, a longer time between filing for divorce and the final decree resulted in lower levels of anxiety and hostility. The longer time seems to have allowed a divorcée to work through some of her uncertainty about the future and her anger at the situation. This result is interesting given that the time between filing and decree seems to be decreasing with the use of no-fault divorce on the increase. The outcome of this change in divorce laws may be efficiency, but the change may also increase initial levels of psychological distress from some divorced persons.

Although being forewarned of the death of the spouse did not affect psychological symptoms, widows who had actively prepared for the future by seeking education or employment *before* the husband became ill exhibited lower levels of psychological distress after the spouse's death than those who did not prepare. The effects were not so great if preparations were made after the husband became ill, and there was no such effect for preparations before or during the divorce decision among the divorced women. Why preparations did not help divorced women is unclear. It may be, as Weiss[14] suggests, that longer periods of forewarning for divorcées are the result of continuing bonds of attachment. Therefore, attachment to the spouse overrides the psychological benefits of preparing for the event. Future research should focus on whether certain types of preparations are more helpful than others and which preparations are helpful for particular age groups. It would also be beneficial to look at the impact of preparations for long-term adjustment to widowhood and divorce.

Our data suggest that forewarning does not have much influence on the early stages of adjustment to either widowhood or divorce. The end of a relationship destroys hopes, desires, and plans. Despite the possibility of earlier losses being associated with illness or marital breakdown, the final loss of the spouse marks an irrevocable break. For both the young and old, things will never again be as they were.

An implication of this research for clinicians is that women need to be encouraged to learn the skills necessary to be independent regardless of their marital status. If or when women find themselves without a spouse, they must be able to function as single adults. Also, even if the woman anticipates the end of her marriage, ending a relationship can have a devastating psychological effect. Our data suggest that it should not be expected that adjustment will necessarily be quicker or easier for women who anticipate the end of the marriage through death or divorce than for those who do not.

REFERENCES

1. Freud, S. (1963). Mourning and melancholia. In P. Rieff (Ed.), *Sigmund Freud: General Psychological Theory.* (pp. 164–179). New York: Collier Books. (Original work published in 1917)
2. Raphael, B. (1983). *Anatomy of bereavement.* New York: Basic Books.
3. Holmes, T. H., and Rahe, R. H. (1967). The social readjustment rating scale. *Journal of Psychosomatic Research, 11,* 213–218.
4. Clayton, P., Halikas, R. J., Maurice, W. L., & Robins, E. (1973). Anticipatory grief and widowhood. *British Journal of Psychiatry, 122,* 47–51.
5. Clayton, P. J., Desmarais, L., & Winokur, G. (1968). A study of normal bereavement. *American Journal of Psychiatry, 125,* 168–178.
6. Maddison, D., & Viola, A. (1968). The health of widows in the year following bereavement. *Journal of Psychosomatic Research, 12,* 297–306.
7. Blanchard, C. G., Blanchard, E. B., & Becker, J. V. (1976). The young widow: Depressive symptomatology throughout the grief process. *Psychiatry, 39,* 394–399.
8. Ball, J. F. (1976–1977). Widow's grief: The impact of age and mode of death. *Omega, 7,* 307–333.
9. Glick, I. O., Weiss, R. S., & Parkes, C. M. (1974). *The first year of bereavement.* New York: John Wiley & Sons.
10. Parkes, C. M., & Weiss, R. S. (1983). *Recovery from bereavement.* New York: Basic Books.
11. Neugarten, B. (1977). Personality and aging. In J. Birren and K. W. Schaie (Eds.), *Handbook of the psychology of aging.* (pp. 626–649). New York: Van Nostrand Reinhold.
12. Hill C., Thompson, L. W., & Gallagher, D. E. (1988). The role of anticipatory bereavement in the adjustment to widowhood in older women. *The Gerontologist, 28,* 792–796.
13. Wise, M. J. (1980). The aftermath of divorce. *The American Journal of Psychoanalysis, 40,* 149–158.
14. Weiss, R. S. (1975). *Marital separation.* New York: Basic Books.

15. Spanier, G. B., & Casto, R. (1979). Adjustment to separation and divorce: An analysis of 50 case studies. *Journal of Divorce, 2,* 241–253.
16. Hagestad, G. O., & Smyer, M. A. (1982). Dissolving long-term relationships: Patterns of divorcing in middle age. In S. Duck (Ed.), *Personal relationships.* (pp. 155–188). New York: Academic Press.
17. Deckert, P., & Langelier, R. (1978). The late-divorce phenomenon: The causes and impact of ending 20-year-old or longer marriages. *Journal of Divorce, 1,* 381–390.
18. Derogatis, L. R. (1977). *SCL-90: Administration, scoring, and procedures manual-1 for the r(evised) version and other instruments of the psychopathology rating scale series.* Baltimore: Johns Hopkins University School of Medicine.
19. Zung, W. K. (1965). A self-rating depression scale. *Archives of General Psychiatry, 12,* 63–70.
20. Hollingshead, A. B. (1957). *Two factor index of social class measurement.* Unpublished manuscript, Yale University, New Haven.
21. Kitson, G. C. (1982). Attachment to the spouse in divorce: A scale and its application. *Journal of Marriage and the Family, 44,* 379–393.
22. Holinger, P. C. (1980). Violent deaths as a leading cause of mortality: An epidemiologic study of suicide, homicide, and accidents. *American Journal of Psychiatry, 137,* 472–476.

Interventions and Implications for Research

The next two chapters are an integral part of the book. Indeed, one of my own personal objectives was to disseminate research-based knowledge in a form that would be of practical value to those who desire to be more helpful to older bereaved spouses. The preceding 14 chapters have added to our knowledge about bereavement as a significant loss situation, the course of bereavement, and the factors that influence the adjustment process. One of the next steps is to turn to the application of this knowledge to the development of interventions to assist the bereaved and offer guidelines for future research.

Chapter 15 makes an important contribution by providing an example of how an intervention can be developed as part of a controlled scientific study. Additionally, it will be of practical value to those who are already engaged in doing intervention work or who are planning to do so in the future. Chapter 15 identifies some of the problems that were encountered, reviews how they were resolved, and offers suggestions on how to avoid similar problems.

Chapter 16 is perhaps the most usable of all the chapters, for it provides an integrated summary of the major findings of the nine studies reported on in the book plus other relevant research reports. The conclusions highlighted sacrifice some of the specificity and qualifying details of the various research findings in order to identify the important general trends that are common to many of the more recent research results. These conclusions are presented in a clear, succinct format and are followed by implications for interventions and future research which relate directly to the conclusions. This chapter should be particularly useful to those who want to sort through the complexities of the expanding research literature in order to develop research-based interventions, identify questions for future research, organize and supplement lectures and other presentations, or simply better understand the bereavement experiences of older surviving spouses.

15

Resolving Problems Implementing Bereavement Self-Help Groups

Dale A. Lund, David E. Redburn, Merry S. Juretich, and Michael S. Caserta

This chapter reports on the experiences of implementing 26 self-help groups for bereaved adult spouses aged 50–89 as part of a research project examining the effectiveness of groups led by widows or professionals and short-term versus long-term conditions. Time 1 questionnaires were completed by 339 respondents. The emphasis of this report, however, is on the identification and suggested resolution of practical problems related to the selection and training of group leaders, supervision of leaders, and selection of meeting sites as well as several problems related to the participants themselves.

The purpose of this chapter is to identify and review solutions to the major problems encountered in an applied research project which examined the effectiveness of 26 self-help groups for older adults who had recently experienced the death of a spouse. The targeted audience is not limited to those who plan to study bereavement self-help groups but includes professionals and nonprofessionals in a variety of community settings who are developing and implementing other types of self-help groups. The primary problem areas addressed include the selection and training of group leaders, group leader supervision, logistical problems associated with groups meetings, and problems associated with the participants themselves. In addition, recommendations will be made at the end of each section in order to permit those who conduct self-help groups in the future to avoid some of the difficulties that we encountered. Some of the problems and recommendations are unique, because our groups were part of a research project; thus there were both

Revision of a paper presented at the Annual Meeting of the American Society on Aging, Salt Lake City, Utah, March 1987. This chapter is based on a study funded by the National Institute on Aging (RO1 AG06244).

constraints and advantages that may not be present in other situations. These unique features will be noted when relevant.

REVIEW OF LITERATURE

The historical roots of the modern self-help movement have been traced to 19th and early 20th century sources. Katz and Bender,[1] for example, pointed to the rise of "Friendly Societies" in 19th century England which aided the lower classes in dealing with their adverse living conditions. They also emphasized the importance of the influence of trade unions and consumer cooperatives on the early self-help movement. Hurvitz,[2] while acknowledging the importance of these groups, also noted the contribution of some religious groups who emphasized group confession and mutual penance. One of the most important developments, however, was the founding of Alcoholics Anonymous in the 1930s. This organization was based on self-disclosure. The central ideas were that people could change, that self-disclosure was a prerequisite for change, and that those who have changed could help others to change.[3]

Gartner and Riessman[4] stated that there are over half a million different self-help groups representing nearly every disease listed by the World Health Organization. They divided self-help groups into four general categories: anonymous, ex-patient, living-with, and life transition. Anonymous groups draw members who acknowledge the existence of a problem and their need for help. Ex-patient groups deal with the residual difficulties following outpatient treatment or hospitalization. Living-with groups form auxiliary groups to the parent groups and assist those peripherally involved with the symptomatic individuals. Finally, life transition groups contain members who are undergoing similar role transitions and are seeking support from one another.

Generally, self-help groups consist of people voluntarily gathered together for a treatment or to accomplish a specific purpose,[1] with the focus on personal problems and the resolution of mutual individual needs.[5] These groups vary considerably with respect to their structure (e.g., direct service or social action),[6] degree of professional control,[3] size, homogeneity, intimacy, stability, and supportiveness.[7] Self-help groups also differ with respect to specific functions and group memberships.

According to the literature, there are many potential benefits for those who attend self-help groups. Participants can gain hope, receive new ideas for solutions, receive information on locating additional sources of help,[8] improve skills in developing social relationships, become less lonely,[9] learn new role definitions, have an audience of listeners, discover that others have similar difficulties, and receive added social support.[10] Withorn[5] has emphasized the benefits that result from a sense of belonging to a group and from feelings of fellowship and solidarity. She also pointed out that self-help groups are typically less expensive than other alternative services and treatments. Similarly, Parham, Romanuik, Priddy, and Wenzel[11] argue that self-help groups provide assistance to those who are reluctant to use the services of mental health and other professionals. They suggest that this is particularly valuable for the many elderly persons who prefer to interact with others of the same age and similar circumstances. King and Myers[12] add further to this list by noting the benefits of immediacy of help, informality, reciprocity, and the experiential base of knowledge that results from group participation in problem solving. While discussing preventive group interventions for elderly clients, Nickoley-Colquitt[13] pointed out that these interventions reflect a desire for need fulfillment with the least disruption and decentralization of service with maximum client control and responsibility.

Many of the general benefits of self-help groups are relevant to spousal bereavement situations among older adults. Group sessions can focus on ways to alleviate some of the difficulties related to the social isolation, hopelessness, and loneliness which often accompany widowhood. Our own research has clearly identified loneliness as the most commonly reported problem of older bereaved adults and it typically remains problematic for several years.[14] Self-help groups can be useful by providing opportunities to meet new people, engage in social activities, and form new friendships, thereby reducing the amount of time spent alone. In addition to loneliness, many bereaved elders, because of gender and cohort effects, experience major difficulties in managing the tasks of daily living, such as transportation, meal preparation, household cleaning, repairs, and general maintenance. Again, interactions during the meetings of self-help groups might result in sharing information about skills or where to go for help. Particularly important is that self-help groups can impact the two best predictors of how well bereaved elders are likely to cope with their situations. In our previous study, we learned that low self-esteem and not having the opportunity to express thoughts and feelings to others resulted in significantly greater coping difficulties 2 years after the spouse had died.[15] Conversely, positive self-esteem and expression of self led to more favorable outcomes. Self-help groups offer opportunities of impacting both variables by allowing the bereaved participants to talk freely to others who are often more likely than relatives and friends to be nonjudgmental listeners and to enhance their self-esteem by giving positive feedback on the accomplishments and adjustments which frequently occur during the course of bereavement and widowhood. Certainly, some bereaved elders already have high self-esteem and are in situations where self-expression occurs. For these reasons among others, self-help group participation may not be wanted or necessary. At the conclusion of our previous 2-year bereavement study, 56% of the older adults said that they would not have wanted to participate in a self-help group.[16] It should not be assumed that all bereaved older adults are eager and waiting to attend self-help groups.

The enthusiasm associated with self-help groups should be tempered by some additional words of caution. Rodolfa and Hungerford[17] argue that the self-help movement offers great promise and is still a largely untapped resource but the effectiveness of self-help groups has not yet been established by scientific study. Others suggest that little effort has been made to systematically evaluate group interventions; without this effort we see good intentions but no evidence whether the desired outcomes are achieved. Hiltz[18] has specifically stressed the importance of competent and constructive group leaders for minimizing depressing and upsetting group sessions. Groups that result only in the mutual comparison of miseries are less likely to be productive. Silverman[8] indicates that successful self-help groups do not just occur but require a great deal of organization and planning. Two additional limitations of self-help groups are that the participants of a group might become too reliant on it for support and that such groups cannot fully replace other professional and bureaucratic services.[5]

Self-help groups are not likely to be a panacea for the common personal and social problems of our urbanized society. They do, however, have potential for providing an important and useful service for many people. There is a need for more research, not only to document the effectiveness of self-help groups but to improve the ability of those who design and deliver these services. Rogers, Vachon, Lyall, Sheldon, and Freeman[19] stated that "as the concept of self-help becomes more refined, so too should the techniques and experiences of program development become more explicit and better documented." (p. 844)

The effectiveness of all self-help groups is largely based on what Riessman[20] has termed the "helper-therapy" principle. According to this principle, those who help are helped most, and because all members of a group help at some time, all benefit from the process. Despite this, the actual effectiveness of self-help groups has been largely undetermined. As late as 1977, Gartner and Riessman[21] described self-help groups as only "seemingly effective." And in 1981, Nicholey-Colquitt[13] called for a "systematic investigation of group interventions that produce reliable and valid outcomes." The use of control groups was also strongly suggested.

Such calls for investigation were due to the fact that much of the work done on effectiveness had been descriptive and anecdotal, for example, the early work by Riessman[20] and Gartner and Riessman[21,22] and the later work by Lindamood,[23] Rodolfa and Hungerford,[17] Klass and Shinners,[24] and Burnell and Burnell.[25] However, some researchers, including Vachon, Lyall, Rogers, Freedman-Letofsky, and Freeman,[26] Constantino,[27] Lieberman and Borman,[28] and Lieberman and Videka-Sherman,[29] employed more rigorous methodological strategies and found some positive outcomes of self-help group participation. What little scientific research has been done on self-help groups has not included a focus on bereavement among the elderly. Our current project was intended to help fill this void and to stimulate interest on the part of others to investigate intervention strategies that might be helpful in alleviating difficulties which result from the most stressful of all life events.

While the focus of this chapter is not on the outcomes of self-help groups, one of the goals of the overall study was to assess the relative success of the interventions. We have included the previous short review of literature because we believe that many of the practical problems can interfere with the effectiveness of self-help groups. The participants need to attend the meetings, contribute to the group processes, and experience the designed content of the intervention. Many potential obstacles must be resolved for the participants to have the opportunity to benefit from self-help groups.

DESCRIPTION OF THE RESEARCH PROJECT

The purpose of the intervention study, which is currently ongoing, is to determine the effects of four different conditions on the provision of self-help groups to facilitate the bereavement process among recently bereaved older adults aged 50 and over. The major study conditions were related to who functions as the self-help group leader (professional or widowed peer) and how long the groups last (short- or long-term). The professional group leaders had previous work experience in some type of counseling and had master's level preparation. The peer leaders were widowed females who had participated in a previous bereavement study and had made positive adjustments to their situation. The short-term groups were conducted weekly for 8 weeks; the long-term groups met for 8 weeks, followed by 10 additional monthly meetings. Twenty-six groups were organized to test the effectiveness of peer- versus professional-led groups and short- versus long-term interventions. A control group that received no intervention also was utilized in the study.

The comparisons being investigated were selected for several reasons. First, it is important to know if bereaved elders who participate in self-help groups manage their grief in a more timely or successful manner than those who do not participate. Second, because grief is not a disease process, there may be no reason to engage professionals in group work with bereaved elders if peers (other widowed persons) can do as well or better. Third, with limited and often scarce resources, it is important to determine whether short-term interventions can be as effective as long-term ones.

In order for the reader to understand the research context of the self-help intervention, it is important to provide some additional aspects of the study design. The following brief description of the methodology will also be helpful in identifying and resolving the practical problems with which we were confronted.

Data were collected from either delivered questionnaires (T_1) or mailed questionnaires (T_2 through T_4) at four points in time; the same schedule was followed for all participants regardless of their group assignment. The first questionnaire was delivered at approximately 2 months after the death of the spouse and mailed back prior to the participants' attendance at support group meetings. The personal visit at T_1 was made to further explain the study and encourage continued participation. The T_2 measures were obtained immediately after the completion of the 8 weekly self-help meetings (roughly 4–8 months postdeath). The T_3 questionnaires followed the completion of the long-term groups (roughly 14–17 months postdeath) and T_4 questionnaires were obtained at 2 years postdeath. The matched control group also was assessed at the same four time periods but received no intervention.

The questionnaires included items regarding demographics, socioeconomic status, competencies, self-esteem, and social support factors. In addition, the principal outcome measures included instruments to assess grief resolution through the Texas Revised Inventory of Grief,[30] depression,[31] life satisfaction,[32] and perceived coping, stress, and health.

Potential participants were identified from the obituaries in local newspapers. This method of identification was selected because other sources of mortality reporting were not readily available (only approximately 10% of deaths are not reported in the obituaries). The Utah Department of Health, for example, reports and tabulates mortality, but the reports it publishes are many times not completed until 3 to 12 months after the death has occurred. One of the goals of this project was to contact potential participants shortly after the death of the spouse (approximately 8 weeks).

Twenty-seven groups were formed, 14 of which were professionally led and 13 widow led. One of the professional groups met only once; subsequently all of the members decided not to attend additional meetings because of inconvenience and lack of interest. Eighteen of the groups had male members, 6 of them having just one male member. The average size of the groups was approximately six members. Several leaders, both peer and professional, led more than one group, but no one led more than three groups.

Over a period of 35 weeks, 1,487 letters were mailed to potential bereaved spouses after eliminating another 232 persons who did not have published mailing addresses. Of the total letters sent, 222 were returned and the spouse was never located; 47 spouses were planning to move to another city in the near future; 23 were too young (under age 50); 21 were deceased; 19 were already attending other support groups; and 5 did not speak or understand English. This resulted in a potential sample of 1,150 bereaved spouses who met the study criteria. Only 29.5% ($N = 339$) agreed to participate and completed the T_1 questionnaires (241 were assigned to be in one of the self-help groups and 98 were assigned to be controls and not attend a self-help group). The acceptance rate for the controls (38.0%) was higher than it was for those assigned to the self-help groups (27.0%). The most common reasons for refusal to participate were lack of interest (60.2%), illness (17.3%), busyness (11.8%), and upset (3.1%); in some cases the reasons were unclear. Because of the delay between the completion of the T_1 data and the beginning of some of the self-help groups, 66 bereaved spouses decided to discontinue their participation and therefore did not attend support group meetings. Of the 98 controls, 36 were men (36.7%) and 62 were women (63.3%), with an age range from 50 to 88 years ($M = 67.6$, $SD = 8.7$). Similarly, of the 175 who attended at least one self-help meeting, 42 were men (24.0%) and 133 were women (76.0%), with an age range from 50 to 89 years ($M = 67.3$, $SD = 8.2$). A telephone survey 1 year later of 125 randomly selected persons who refused to participate yielded no significant demographic differences between participants and nonparticipants. Those who had refused, however, reported slightly lower stress levels and fewer problems with loneliness, but also lower perceived coping abilities and lower self-reported health ratings.

As we mentioned earlier, we defined a number of important areas that we found to have the potential to cause major difficulties. In general, the categories of difficulty were selection of the group leaders, training of the leaders, subsequent group leader supervision, selecting and obtaining group meeting sites, and obtaining and maintaining the participation of the group members. Although we present the problem areas as separate entities, they are sometimes interrelated. For example, the largeness of the geographical area encompassed by the study area effected both the choice of sites and travel problems for group members. After each problem area, we have included a brief statement concerning our recommendations for minimizing the negative impact.

Problems Associated with Identifying Group Leaders

Eleven professional group leaders were recruited from graduate programs in counseling and clinical psychology, nursing, and social work. The candidates were selected using the following criteria: (1) previous counseling or group work experience (preferably with an elderly population); (2) expressed interest in facilitating the grief process of bereaved older adults; (3) commitment to complete the training sessions and the duration of the assigned group meetings; and (4) not having experienced a recent loss (i.e., death of a close friend or family member). Three of these leaders were males and eight were females. Three were recent PhDs, four were currently in PhD programs and the others were enrolled in a master's program or the gerontology certificate program at the University of Utah.

Because of the university setting, there was an adequate pool of qualified professional group leaders. However, as a result of our reliance on current graduate students, we experienced some staff turnover due to their desired mobility for employment out-of-state following graduation. One of the doctoral candidates left after conducting one group; two others became less interested in leading groups after completion of their degrees because they could earn more in private practice.

Most of the peer leader candidates were identified from bereaved elders who participated in our earlier longitudinal bereavement study at the University of Utah Gerontology Center. Consideration was given to those individuals who had worked through their own grief and had experienced some degree of satisfaction with their adjustments (based on data collected at a 4-year follow-up). Measures of depression, life satisfaction, self-esteem, stress, coping, and physical health were reviewed; 20 candidates were selected and then contacted by a letter and questionnaire to assess their level of interest in serving as peer group leaders. Seven of the 20 were eventually trained to be group leaders. All of them were women. Several men were invited but were not interested.

The task of selecting the candidates expressing an interest in being a peer group leader was twofold. The first undertaking was an assessment by interview to further determine each candidate's grief resolution, communication skills (to facilitate self-exploration and problem solving), flexibility, willingness to try new ideas and behaviors, and ability to communicate warmth and caring and to verify the candidate had a genuine desire to help. The second undertaking was to impart to each candidate a clear understanding of what the training and the actual group leading would be like. In addition to this, the peer group leaders were expected to have (1) a history of mutually satisfying interpersonal relationships and an affinity for helping others; (2) good health status; (3) mobility and available transportation; (4) an interest in facilitating the grief process of other bereaved elders; (5) a willingness to participate in the training sessions; (6) a commitment to complete the duration of the assigned group sessions; (7) a willingness to explore their own grief experience and style of coping and how this personal style affects behavior in a group process intervention.

Two other peer leaders were recruited through personal contacts and local agencies in order to cover designated geographical areas not covered in the previous study. The same qualifications were required and a similar interviewing process was followed to determine their potential as group leaders.

All of the group leaders were paid at an hourly rate ($8.50 for professionals and $5.00 for widowed peers) for their training and for the time spent preparing for, traveling to, and participating in group meetings. Although many of the peer leaders indicated that they would donate their time, we wanted to ensure a commitment to the project and decided that financial compensation would be best. Group leaders also were reimbursed at the university rate of $20^{1/2}$ cents per mile for travel related to group meetings.

We highly recommend that group leaders be carefully screened. As for using students as professional leaders, it would be best to consider expected graduation dates and the students' associated desire for greater mobility and income. Competitive wages need to be provided for these leaders to ensure their continued commitment to long-term projects. We only had one leader (a widowed peer) who generated significant criticism from the group members. Several of them reported that her particular religious views dominated the discussions and they recommended that we not ask her to lead other groups. This issue is noted again in the discussion on the supervision of group leaders. This potential problem was probably minimized in our project by having the questionnaire data on the widow leaders over a larly important for research investigations, which require adherence to more rigid time schedules for completion of groups and for data collection. Some group leaders may not perform satisfactorily, and alternates need to be readily available to keep the groups running smoothly.

Problems Associated with Training Group Leaders

All peer and professional group leaders were trained together in order to create some standardization within the group processes and because the amount of staff resources involved in the training were too extensive to train the professional and peers separately. It also proved beneficial for leaders of each type to learn from the unique experiences and acquire the unique skills of the leaders of the other type. This sharing of information was acknowledged and appreciated by the leaders on their assessments of the training program. Nine peer and 11 professional leaders received up to 30 hours of training spread out over 3 weeks. Four professional staff and two consultants made presentations or led sessions during the training. Two sessions were devoted to reviewing the purposes of the study and the restrictions required by scientific research. Several hours were spent presenting and discussing material on aging and elderly persons (including myths, theories, and losses in later life) and on what is known about the course of grief and bereavement. Common and unusual reactions were reviewed, as were and what are believed to be the predictors of adjustment. Considerable time was spent on how to manage group processes and on appropriate roles of group leaders. Included were flexible suggestions for the content of each session. Several hours of role-playing exercises and sensitivity training were used to simulate group sessions and to deal with the group leaders' feelings about death and loss.

At the conclusion of the training sessions, an evaluation survey was completed by the group leaders. Generally, the group leaders reported that all of the training components were quite helpful, that the training was adequate in preparing them to lead groups, and that their anxiety about leading groups had decreased because of the training. Four widow leaders indicated that prior to the training their anxiety was very high, but none of them described their feelings that way after the training. Also, following the training, only two group leaders said that they were unsure whether the group interventions would be helpful to the participants. These two did not actually lead groups. All of the others reported that they expected the groups to be quite or extremely helpful.

Based on the evaluation of the training and our observations of the group leaders during the training sessions, one widow leader and one professional leader were judged to be unfit to lead groups. The widow was too anxious and felt unprepared to lead a group, and the professional displayed little interest and commitment to the project.

The most difficult aspect of the training was finding times when most of the leaders could attend (usually early evenings and weekends). We recommend that others should be prepared to offer some training sessions for the entire group, but the experiential exercises should be scheduled in smaller groups. Some sessions will need to be offered more than one time, which should be anticipated and budgeted for. It also is important to make careful observations of the potential group leaders during the training sessions and use these observations in the screening process. Because our training evaluation was useful for screening purposes and also provided feedback to the presenters, we encourage others to implement similar procedures.

Problems Associated with Supervision of Group Leaders

The project staff included two coordinators who were to maintain regular ongoing contact with the trained group leaders. One served as the coordinator for the peer leaders and the other for the professional leaders. This was particularly important for the peer leaders, because all of them were inexperienced regarding group processes and a few lacked self-confidence. One of the problems that we experienced resulted from having to train all of the leaders together. The training was completed before all of the bereaved participants were identified, and, because sampling procedures necessarily covered several months, some leaders had to wait several months before they were assigned to lead a group. In the case of the professionals, some had lost interest in the project, and in the case of the widowed peers, some began to lose confidence in their ability to lead groups. Other common problems experienced by the widow leaders were that bereaved members sometimes brought friends or relatives with them, certain members dominated more passive members, and some members in short-term groups were inclined to continue meeting together after the official intervention had ended. Most of the ongoing problems for the professional leaders which required supervision involved the inappropriate aspects of the sites where their meetings were held (e.g., rooms that were too small, too warm or cold, or at inconvenient locations).

Our primary recommendation is to maintain regular ongoing contact with all group leaders, particularly the widowed peers. Although we met every several months with all of the leaders, we decided to have the peer group coordinator maintain even more frequent contact with the peer group leaders. They met as a full group almost every 4 to 5 weeks and, in most cases, the coordinator had one-to-one meetings with the leaders and numerous phone conversations. This ongoing supervision was absolutely necessary to help them manage unexpected problems as well as resolve difficulties due to the requirements of the research design. These meetings and this contact also helped to add to the leaders' commitment to the project, feelings of cohesion, and pride in their accomplishments. Considerable learning that was important to the leaders and the project investigators resulted from these sharing sessions.

Contacts with leaders were most helpful in quickly identifying bereaved participants in need of other professional services. Although this was uncommon, there were several instances where unusual situations developed which required other support services.

We highly recommend that group leaders have regular and easy access to other professionals for consultation and advice. Additionally, we suggest that group leaders maintain regular notes summarizing each group meeting. We needed these records for research purposes, such as validating attendance and providing qualitative data about the group dynamics and processes. When these group leader notes are written after each meeting and shared in a timely manner with other professional staff, they help to ensure that important problems do not go unrecognized and unresolved. They provide a wealth of information to investigators who do not attend the meetings, and they are useful records for the leaders as they try to maintain continuity from one meeting to the next.

Logistical Problems Associated with Group Meeting Sites

Several categories of potential sites for the group meetings included senior centers (both residential and day care), libraries, community multipurpose centers, hospitals, churches, and schools. A number of problems, however, arose with regard to some of these sites. Several were judged to be too noisy, particularly the multipurpose centers. Our first group met at such a center, and because of other activities which were taking place, particularly those involving children, the group experienced difficulties and found it necessary to move to another location.

Safety, heat, ventilation, adequate lighting, and convenient parking also were concerns. Barrier-free access was a requirement, because some participants had mobility difficulties. Several possible sites had rooms available, but the rooms were either to small, too large, or were unavailable at the times when participants preferred to meet.

The geographical area covered by the study was quite large. The Wasatch Front region of Utah includes the metropolitan areas of Ogden, Salt Lake City, and Provo and is about 100 miles long. Every attempt was made to locate and secure sites close to participants' homes. This proved to be a difficult task, but a number of solutions to transportation problems were found. Potential participants who indicated at the first contact that they were unable to drive were encouraged to ask a friend or relative to transport them. If this was not possible, other group members were asked to carpool. This was especially effective after the members had met at the first meeting and became better acquainted. If other arrangements could not be made, some group leaders offered to pick up members with transportation problems. These leaders were reimbursed for their mileage for this service. Most members, however, provided their own transportation. Only in a couple of cases were bereaved participants reimbursed for cab fare.

Several of the local senior centers insisted that their residents be permitted to participate if their facilities were used. This was not possible because of sampling considerations important to the research design, which required participants to be identified through newspaper obituaries rather than through more direct self-selection procedures. This would not, of course, necessarily be a problem for groups being conducted for other purposes.

We did not foresee the need to pay for the use of any sites, and therefore several desirable ones were unavailable. With or without budgetary constraints, others should try to allocate some resources for this purpose to guarantee that all sites are comfortable and convenient. In addition to being aware of the many convenience and comfort issues, our primary recommendations are to begin early to identify adequate sites, make personal visits to check them out, obtain written consent from the appropriate administrators so that turnover will not negate previous agreements, and be certain to discuss possible fees. According to our experiences, senior centers and libraries are the best sites. Some participants seemed reluctant to meet at hospitals. Organizers should be sensitive to the fact that some of the bereaved persons may have had their spouses die at the same hospital where their group is scheduled to meet.

Problems Associated with the Group Participants

Some of the groups, even though discouraged from doing this, continued to meet informally after the scheduled meetings ended. We discouraged this because our intervention was part of a research investigation and continued meetings are at odds with the study design and can impact the results of the study. That is, the short-term groups (eight weekly meetings) need to be short-term in order to compare their effectiveness with long-term groups. We could not, of course, forbid the members from postgroup association, but considerable importance was placed on appropriate closure during the group leader training sessions and in the ongoing supervision of the leaders. We found that this issue was not as problematic with the professional leaders, because of their professional training in this area. This phenomenon probably would not be an issue for lay groups, since there is no research design to jeopardize. In fact, informal meetings might well be encouraged in order to maintain the level of social support begun in the formal group meetings. In order for us to monitor the amount of contact that the members had outside of the formal meetings, we included a number of questions concerning this on the T_2, T_3, and T_4 questionnaires.

An additional issue that all who conduct self-help groups should be aware of is the potential for inappropriate commitment. Bereavement and the associated life transitions are very stressful and adjustment may take considerable amounts of time. It is possible for some members to become overly dependent on a self-help group and thus fail to make the role transitions that the group is designed to facilitate.

Because this was a research project with different treatment modalities (different numbers of meetings and different types of leaders), we did not want participants to be aware of the differences between the groups. Some members, however, did discover that other types of groups were being conducted, (e.g., when a neighbor or friend was invited to be in a different type of group). This was a problem with several short-term participants who felt that they needed additional meetings and so should be in long-term groups. They were told that it was important to the study that they remain in the same group and that we could refer them to a community-based group at the conclusion of their eight sessions. None of them, however, chose to be referred.

Another problem was the desire of several participants to bring family members or friends with them to the meetings. Again, for lay organizations running such groups this may not be as problematic. However, it was felt that such participation in the groups might alter the group processes and thus change the measured outcomes. We encouraged these participants to bring their friends or relatives with them but asked that they remain outside of the meeting room. In the end, this request was readily complied with and no extragroup persons participated.

Utah's large geographical area and the relatively small population led to other problems with regard to the formation of the groups. The population is, demographically speaking, quite young. A high birth rate and a lower than average mortality rate result in relatively few deaths. This, combined with the state's large area, meant that we encountered some difficulties in obtaining sufficient numbers of people in the various categories to begin groups.

Three major urban areas which compose the Wasatch Front region of Utah were included in the study: (1) Salt Lake City and county, (2) Ogden City and Davis and Weber counties to the north, and (3) Provo City and Utah county to the south. Approximatley 95% of Utah's 1.5 million people reside in these three areas. The potential number of participants identified per week from the obituaries ranged from 6 in Provo to 25 in Salt Lake City, with an overall mean of 14. Of course, our somewhat restrictive criteria for selecting spouse survivors—50 years of age or older and willing to attend group meetings—added further to the problem. It should be noted that these are the numbers for potential participants. Refusals and those who could not be located reduced the number of potential participants. Because other community-based bereavement groups were operating in the study area, some potential participants were already attending one of these groups. At least six other groups were identified in the Wasatch Front region. In general, the existence of other groups makes it imperative that each organization be aware of the others. The potential for competitive and turf-related problems should be anticipated and dealt with during the planning stages; among other things, cooperative arrangements are likely to develop as a result of similar commitments to help bereaved persons.

Given all of these considerations, the mean length of time between the initial contact (receipt of the introductory letter) and attendance at the first meeting was approximately 12 weeks. The mean time span between the death of the spouse and the first meeting was 23 weeks. The length of this period not only led some participants who had agreed to join a group to withdraw, but it also meant that some group leaders were unable to lead groups because their personal circumstances had changed.

Our primary recommendations for avoiding many of these problems are organizational in nature. Planning early, viewing the project from a community perspective, and paying attention to detail will facilitate a quality intervention. Careful consideration must be given to devising realistic time schedules for identifying participants, setting up meetings with other related community organizatins, and initiating group meetings soon after initial contacts are made. Again, regular ongoing meetings with the group leaders will help to identify and resolve unanticipated or unusual problems before they adversely affect the quality of the group meetings.

CONCLUSIONS

Although the study we have described is not completed and the assessment of the effectiveness of the 26 self-help groups remains in question, we are convinced that the project will be valuable. Because the self-help movement continues to generate momentum, we are likely to see many more applications and people involved in planning and leading these groups. Our scientific focus has allowed a critical inspection of our own self-help groups, which will be useful to others. We have identified many problems and a few solutions and made several recommendations. We are also convinced that good intentions do not necessarily lead to expected or desired outcomes, because good things do not just happen. In our case, we planned for several years, yet were surprised at the number and diversity of problems for which we were not fully prepared.

Perhaps one of our most important conclusions is that group leaders cannot work alone. They need experienced consultants and advisors to provide knowledge and offer suggestions concerning unusual situations, some of which are undoubtedly going to occur. We had the luxury of having a federal grant to hire a large professional staff with considerable expertise. Most of the staff had already worked together for several years, so compatible working relationships were the norm rather than the exception.

Our final recommendation to those who are planning similar bereavement self-help groups is to develop an ongoing evaluation plan; the evaluations can be used as feedback for program improvement and to document changes among the group participants. Developing evaluation plans will facilitate better preparation, clearer program objectives, and the sharing of outcomes with other interested persons. A commitment to adding an evaluation component to a new or already existing program also might force someone acting as a "one-person program" to find an interested colleague to share the problems and successes.

REFERENCES

1. Katz, A. H., & Bender, E. I. (1976). *The strength in the U.S.: Self-help groups in the modern world.* New York: New Viewpoints.
2. Hurvitz, N. (1976). The origins of peer self-help psychotherapy groups movement. *Journal of Applied Behavioral Science, 17,* 283–294.
3. Hurvitz, N. (1974). Peer self-help psychotherapy groups. In P. M. Roman and H. M. Trice (Ed.), *The sociology of psychotherapy (pp. #).* New York: Aronson.
4. Gartner, A. J., & Riessman, F. (1982). Self-help and mental health. *Hospital and Community Psychiatry, 33,* 631–635.
5. Withorn, A. (1980). Helping ourselves: The limits and potential of self-help. *Social Policy, 11,* 20–27.
6. Gussow, Z., & Tracy, G. (1976). Self-help health groups: A grassroots response to a need for services. *Journal of Applied Behavioral Science, 12,* 381–396.
7. Pilisuk, M., & Parks, S. H. (1980). Structural dimensions of social support groups. *Journal of Psychology, 106,* 157–177.
8. Silverman, P. R. (1980). *Mutual help groups: Organization and development.* Beverly Hills, CA: Sage Publications.
9. Crosby, C. (1978). A group experience for elderly, socially isolated widows. *Social Work With Groups, 1,* 345–354.
10. Hartford, M. E. (1971). *Groups in social work: Application of small group theory and research to social work practice.* New York: Columbia University Press.
11. Parham, I., Romanuik, M., Priddy, M., & Wenzel, C. (1980). Widowhood peer counseling. *Aging, 307–308,* 42–46.
12. King, S. W., & Meyers R. S. (1981). Developing self-help groups: Integrating group work and community organization stategies. *Social Development Issues, 5,* 33–46.
13. Nickoley-Colquitt, S. (1981). Preventive group interventions for elderly clients: Are they effective? *Family and Community Health, 3,* 67–85.
14. Lund, D. A., Caserta, M. S., & Dimond, M. F. (1986). Gender differences through two years of bereavement among the elderly. *Gerontological Society of America, 26,* 314–320.
15. Lund D. A., Dimond, M. F., Caserta, M. S., Johnson, R. J., Poulton, J. L., & Connelly, J. R. (1985). Identifying elderly with coping difficulties after two years of bereavement. *Omega, 16,* 213–224.
16. Dimond, M.F., Lund, D. A., & Caserta, M. S. (1987) The role of social support in the first two years of bereavement in an elderly sample. *Gerontological Society of America, 27,* 599–604.
17. Rodolfa, E. R., & Hungerford, L. (1982). Self-help groups: A referral resource for professional therapists. *Professional Psychology, 13,* 345–353.
18. Hiltz, S. R. (1975). Helping widows: Group discussions as a therapeutic technique. *The Family Coordinator, 24,* 331–336.
19. Rogers, J., Vachon, M., Lyall, W. A., Sheldon, A., & Freeman, S. J. (1980). A self-help program for widows as an independent community service. *Hospital and Community Psychiatry, 31,* 844–347.
20. Riessman, F. (1965). The "helper-therapy" principle. *Social Work, 10,* 27–32.
21. Gartner, A. J., & Riessman, F. (1979). *Self-help in the human services.* San Francisco: Jossey-Bass.
22. Gartner, A. J., & Riessman, F. (1980). *A working guide to self-help groups.* New York: Franklin Watts.
23. Lindamood, M. M. (1979). Groups for bereaved parents: How they can help. *The Journal of Family Practice, 9,* 1027–1033.

24. Klass, O., & Shirrers, B. (1983). Professional roles in a self-help group for the bereaved. *Omega, 13*, 361–375.
25. Burnell, G. M., & Burnell, A. L. (1986). The compassionate friends: A suport group for bereaved parents. *Journal of Family Practice, 22*, 295–296.
26. Vachon, M. L. S., Lyall, W. A. L., Rogers, J., Freedman-Letofsky, K., & Freeman, S. J. J. (1980). A controlled study of self-help intervention for widows. *American Journal of Psychiatry, 137*, 1380–1384.
27. Constantino, R. (1981). Bereavement crisis intervention for widows in grief and mourning. *Nursing Research, 30(6)*, 351–353.
28. Lieberman, M. A., & Borman, L. D. (1981). The impact of self-help groups on widows' mental health. *National Reporter, 4.*
29. Lieberman, M. A., & Videka-Sherman, L. (1986). The impact of self-help groups on the mental health of widows and widowers. *American Journal of Orthopsychiatry, 56*, 435–449.
30. Faschingbauer, T., Devant, R., & Zisook, S. (1977). Development of the Texas Inventory of Grief. *American Journal of Psychiatry, 134*, 696–698.
31. Yesavage, J. A., Brink, T. C., Rose, T. L., Lum, O., Huang, V., Adey, M., & Leirer, V. O. (1983). Development and validation of a geriatric depression screening scale: A preliminary report. *Journal of Psychiatry Research, 17*, 37–49.
32. Neugarten, B., Havighurst, R., & Tobin, S. (1961). The measurement of life satisfaction. *Gerontology, 16*, 134–143.

16

Conclusions about Bereavement in Later Life and Implications for Interventions and Future Research

Dale A. Lund

This chapter highlights the major findings of the preceding 15 chapters in the book along with some selected results from other investigations. Reviewed are 8 conclusions regarding the impact and course of spousal bereavement and 7 conclusions regarding factors believed to influence the adjustment process. Based on these 15 conclusions are seven implications or suggestions for interventions to assist older bereaved spouses and seven implications for future research. The conclusions and implications are provided to help serve as guidelines in understanding the current state of research-based knowledge about spousal bereavement in later life and to stimulate interest in developing appropriate interventions and conducting further research.

The nine research studies described in the preceding chapters add to our understanding of spousal bereavement in later life by revealing new findings which are contrary to what we expected, in some instances confirm what we already believed, and, finally, raise new questions. As we become increasingly more knowledgeable and more confident, we will improve our potential to predict who will have what kinds of difficulty and be able to know how and when to intervene to promote more positive adjustments. The contributing authors of this book share with others the compassionate goals of easing pain, providing comfort, and minimizing the many threats to the physical and mental health of older bereaved spouses. Our approach in this book has been to generate information which can be used for these purposes, but it is based on empirical research, which requires objectivity, standardized and systematic procedures, and replication to verify the accuracy and generalizability of the knowledge rather than relying on intuition, common sense, and good intentions. We believe that this accumulation and refinement of knowledge will lead to more innovative and successful ways to help those who are experiencing the major life transition which spousal bereavement initiates.

Because many variables and complex relationships were examined in this book, I would like to briefly summarize what I believe are the major conclusions from these and other research investigations. The summary is divided into two parts. First are eight conclusions regarding the degree of impact that bereavement has on the surviving spouse and on some features of the course of adjustment. Next is a review of seven factors believed to influence bereavement outcomes. These conclusions are then integrated within a discussion of intervention and research implications.

CONCLUSIONS REGARDING THE IMPACT AND COURSE OF BEREAVEMENT

1. Bereavement adjustments are multidimensional, in that nearly every aspect of a person's life can be affected by the loss. The studies presented in this book examined how the loss of a spouse can influence grief, depression, psychological distress, psychopathology, mental health, anxiety, hostility, anger, stress, self-esteem, interpersonal sensitivity, anomie, social roles, independence, life satisfaction, future outlook, performance of tasks of daily living, self-reported physical health, use of medications, physician visits, and mortality. Other possible dimensions include work and economics (e.g., employment status, productivity, absenteeism, and financial adequacy), religiosity and spirituality, family relationships, social participation, recreation, political opinions, and sexuality. Recognizing this multidimensionality is important, because any research on intervention efforts are likely to focus on only limited pieces of the larger bereavement context. Each project must be interpreted within its limitations and placed into the multidimensional picture by specifying its unique contributions.

2. Bereavement is a highly stressful process, but many older surviving spouses are quite resilient. In both of our bereavement studies at the University of Utah (longitudinal descriptive and self-help), we found older widowed persons reporting mean stress levels of 5.0 to 5.5 (on a scale 1–7) over 2 years and 72% agreeing that the spouse's death was the most stressful event that they had ever experienced. At the same time, they were found to have high self-reported coping abilities, with mean scores of 5.6 to 5.8 on a similar 1–7 rating scale. Interestingly, a control sample of 104 nonbereaved married older adults reported that if their spouses died, they would estimate their stress levels to be as high (5.8 to 6.0) as the bereaved spouses had reported but their mean coping ability to be somewhat lower (4.3 to 4.5) than the bereaved spouses had reported. Because we did not obtain before and after bereavement measures on the same individuals, we must be cautious in how we interpret these data. It is possible, however, that older adults are quite accurate in predicting the high degree of stress associated with the bereavement situation but tend to underestimate their coping abilities. In addition to these data, the first four chapters in this book present findings which can be interpreted as illustrating the resilience of older bereaved spouses. All four of the longitudinal studies (in California, Utah, Florida, and Nebraska) revealed evidence of considerable coping ability and of improvement over time.

3. The overall impact of bereavement on the physical and mental health of many older spouses is not as devastating as expected. This point is acknowledged with considerable reluctance, because it might be interpreted by some to imply that these people are not at risk for serious life difficulties and do not need any intervention services. These would be inappropriate assumptions, for bereavement does create major difficulties. It appears, however, that fewer people than expected are affected at the extremely negative end of the continuum. For example, using depression as an indicator of adjustment, only 5% of the bereaved in the Faletti, Gibbs, Clark, Pruchno, and Berman study (Chapter 4) had scores in the severe range and 10% to 17% were in the clinical range in the Dimond and Lund study (Chapter 1). Further evidence to support the conclusion above can be found in all nine studies described in this book, including those with divorced respondents. Self-reported health and life satisfaction were higher than expected and the various measures of distress and psychological difficulty were lower.

4. *Older bereaved spouses commonly experience simultaneously both positive and negative feelings.* This conclusion helps to explain why bereavement is highly stressful and yet depression and other indicators of mental health are not as bad as expected. I already noted that many bereaved adults are quite resilient. This could be explained in part by recognizing that while they might feel somewhat depressed, confused, and angry, they report fairly positive coping skills and feel confident and proud of how they have managed the situation. This coexistence of positive and negative feelings was revealed in a previous publication by this author[1] as well as in the bereavement study by Gallagher, Lovett, Hanley-Dunn, and Thompson (Chapter 9) and the widowhood-divorce study by Farnsworth, Lund, and Pett (Chapter 12). Gass also reported in Chapter 7 that the majority of widows (54%) and widowers (51%) in her study appraised their loss situation as a challenge, suggesting that even within the 1st year of widowhood many older adults recognize there are opportunities for individual growth.

5. *Loneliness and problems associated with the tasks of daily living are two of the most common and difficult adjustments for older bereaved spouses.* Although loneliness did not receive the amount of attention it warranted in the previous chapters, it is important to include this conclusion in this summary. Our previous longitudinal descriptive study found loneliness to be the most common answer (70%) to the question, "What has been the single greatest difficulty that you have had related to your spouse's death?"[1] Other researchers also have found loneliness to be one of the major problems associated with widowhood,[2-5] and it is particularly difficult for older persons who have contracting rather than expanding social networks, limited mobility (which restricts social activities), and few financial resources to engage in activities outside the home. Barrett and Schneweis[2] also reported that loneliness was one of the most persistent problems among those who have been widowed up to 16 years.

Because of my own research and several recent studies (described in Chapter 11), I believe that deficiencies in performing the tasks of daily living constitute one of the most serious problems. For one thing, they can impact many other bereavement adjustments, as indicated in that chapter. These deficiencies need to be recognized as constituting a major bereavement problem, because they are amenable to change through relatively simple interventions. Thus, they are deserving of greater theoretical and research attention.

6. *The course of spousal bereavement in later life might be best described as a process that is most difficult in the first several months but improves gradually, if unsteadily over time (the improvement may last for many years or, for some may never end).* The four longitudinal studies described in Chapters 1 through 4 were consistent in finding that the most intense grief-related feelings, depression, and

detrimental effects were experienced in the first few months following the loss. Although the various indictors of psychosocial adjustments show gradual improvement over time, the patterns of change reveal slight fluctuations, indicating that problems with mental and physical health are not fully resolved. Also, there is considerable evidence that some aspects of bereavement and subsequent adjustments may continue throughout a person's life. Such aspects may include loneliness, sadness, emptiness, depression, unsettled identify or social isolation. While stress levels declined among the bereaved respondents in our longitudinal descriptive study, the mean score (for 149, or 78%, of those who were in the study) was 3.3 at a 5-year follow-up assessment. This measure [from 1 (low) to 7 (high)] dealt specifically with self-reported stress due to the death of the spouse. Other researchers have reported data supporting the notion that bereavement is a long-term process.[2,5,6] It might be appropriate to question the use of conceptualizing grief as a process which culminates in resolution, because there may never be a full resolution. Some older bereaved spouses reported in our research that they do not feel they will ever "get over" their loss but that they have learned to live with it.

7. *There is a great deal of diversity in how older bereaved adults adjust to the death of the spouse.* While there are numerous experiences which are shared by many of these bereaved spouses (e.g., disbelief, sadness, loneliness, emptiness, etc.), there is considerable variation in coping strategies and how well they adjust to the loss. Chapter 7 through 11 presented findings which clearly reveal diversity in how bereavement is appraised, the availability of resources, the use of coping strategies, advice offered to others, and ability to perform tasks of daily living. Although most of the bereaved spouses were adjusting better than expected, there was a broad range on the adjustment continuum. That is, not all of them coped equally well. In addition to the findings presented in the preceding chapters, we obtained some data from our first descriptive study which illustrates very well the diversity in bereavement adjustments among different people. We used the Twenty Statements Test to measure their self-conceptions by asking them to make 20 different statements about themselves in response to the question, "Who am I?"[7-9] At the unfavorable end of the coping continuum are the following self-descriptions given by a 65-year-old widow 4 weeks after her husband died:

> I am a very lonely person. Lousy, all washed out, despondent, feel deserted, angry, hurt, hopeless, alone, mixed-up, cannot concentrate, very emotional, very tired, cry a lot, hateful, very bitter, misfit, nobody, very miserable, very much of a loner.

Two years after her husband's death, the same woman wrote:

> Concerned about myself, sick of living, miserable, angry upset with myself, really hurt inside, very unhappy, have mixed feelings, hateful, a handicapped person, sick of living by myself, tired of . . . . getting to be lazy and don't care about life, still hurting with the pain, tired of having nothing, confused, very bitter, don't like to live by myself, troubled and confused, and very mixed up and confused.

Even with support services from a local community mental health agency, this widow was quite devastated by her loss. Conversely, a 69-year-old widow made the following self-description 6 months after her husband's death:

Independent, love to keep busy, involved with three organizations, love being with people, I enjoy working in my yard, doing handwork, helping people, golfing, bowling, and my family, I feel that I'm my own person. I do generally what I want to do. I think that many of the things I do are with or for other people. I do still get lonely.

The contrast between the adjustments of these two widows is obvious in terms of their future outlook, social activities, mental and physical health, and self-perceptions.

8. *Bereavement and divorce are similar loss situations in that both can be highly disruptive to daily lives and both require similar coping strategies and adjustments; however, they differ enough that caution is required in generalizing situational factors from one loss to the other.* Chapter 12 revealed that both widowed and divorced persons experienced similar feelings of shock, helplessness, avoidance, and grief and had similar levels of life satisfaction. Kitson and Roach's research also found that both divorcées and widows had better psychological adjustment if they felt more independent (Chapter 13) and that forewarning of the loss was not a very good predictor of adjustment for either kind of loss (Chapter 14). Older bereaved spouses, however, were found to have more problems with depression while their divorced counterparts had greater difficulty with feelings of anger, guilt, and confusion (Chapter 12). Also, widows reported significantly more difficulty than divorcées with their social adjustment and they felt less independent (Chapter 13). Situational issues, such as which spouse initiated the divorce, the stigma associated with the loss, and how support networks function, need to be examined further before we can benefit from understanding the commonalities and differences in these two loss experiences.

CONCLUSIONS REGARDING FACTORS THAT INFLUENCE BEREAVEMENT ADJUSTMENTS

Studies that have examined factors believed to influence bereavement adjustments have frequently found either little or less than expected evidence to support stated hypotheses or assumptions. Some variables have had statistically significant relationships with selected outcomes, but many of the correlation coefficients or measures of association have been only slight or moderate. In a few cases, however, studies have revealed some factors which appear to have considerable promise in understanding and predicting who will have more difficulty in adjusting and how best to intervene in the process. It should also be noted that it is equally valuable to learn about insignificant relationships, even though our first inclination is to be disappointed. We need to be reminded that the scientific approach requires patience, persistence, and the cumulation of pieces of information which, when integrated, offer a unique opportunity to have greater clarity, accuracy, and confidence in our knowledge. The summary conclusions which follow are based primarily on the studies contained in this book, along with some additional findings from other relevant investigations.

1. *Older men and women share many similar bereavement experiences and adjustments.* Six of the chapters in this book which examined the influence of gender on the bereavement process emphasized more similarities than differences between men and women. For example, Thompson, Gallagher, Cover, Gilewski, and Peter-

son (Chapter 2) reported that women were more symptomatic than men but the difference was not due to bereavement. Van Zandt, Mou, and Abbott (Chapter 3) concluded that men and women had similar mental and physical health outcomes. Faletti, Gibbs, Clark, Pruchno, and Berman (Chapter 4) found that depression levels did not differ between men and women. Gass (Chapter 7) reported that gender did not influence physical and psychosocial dysfunction, appraisal of bereavement, number of coping strategies used, or amount of resources. Gallagher, Lovett, Hanley-Dunn, and Thompson (Chapter 9) found that while men were more likely to "keep busy" as a coping strategy and women were more likely to use the "self-talk" strategy, overall men and women were more similar than different. Finally, Caserta, Van Pelt, and Lund (Chapter 10) revealed that gender did not affect the advice which the respondents offered to others in similar situations.

We reported in an earlier article that gender was unrelated to all of our major indicators of bereavement adjustment.[1] Although widowers have been shown to be at greater risk than widows for mortality,[10] it is unclear why the relationship exists, and very little research on this relationship has focused on older persons. Men also are more likely than women to remarry,[11-14] but remarriage does not necessarily mean that the bereavement was easier or that the process had come to an end.[12] The primary conclusion, therefore, is that men and women will experience some aspects of grief differently, but as far as the more global indicators of loss-related feelings, mental and physical health, and social life, they have much in common.

2. *The effects of age, income, and education on bereavement adjustments among older surviving spouses have not been consistent or as strong as expected.* Because only a limited number of studies have been done on bereavement among older adults and even fewer have included respondents with a wide range in age and have focused on effects of income and education on psychosocial adjustments, it would be premature to conclude that the three demographic factors are unimportant. Presently, however, evidence for the direct impact of these variables is only slight. For some specific individuals, they might be important components of their overall circumstances, but for aggregate data and quantitative analyses, they are not as strongly related to bereavement outcomes as other variables. There is some evidence in our own data that suggests that income might have a greater influence on women than men.

In our research at the University of Utah, we have found that these three variables were statistically unrelated to almost all of our outcome measures.[15] In this volume we also reported that income and education did not affect the types of advice that the respondents would give to others. The research by Thompson, Gallagher, Cover, Gilewski, and Peterson (Chapter 2) found that age and socioeconomic status did not account for differences in bereavement symptoms, and Gass (Chapter 7) concluded that higher income was only slightly associated with less psychosocial dysfunction. However, Schuster and Butler (Chapter 5) found income to be inversely related to anomie. Faletti, Gibbs, Clark, Pruchno, and Berman (Chapter 4) reported that working respondents had more adaptive outcomes, and Roach and Kitson (Chapter 14) revealed that both bereavement and divorce were more distressing for their younger respondents.

3. *Although people from different religions practice different bereavement rituals and hold different values and beliefs concerning death, the present research evidence on older spouses shows that religion-related variables have not explained much of the diversity in long-term bereavement adjustments.* The studies described

in this book included participants from many different religions (e.g., Catholics, Protestants, Mormons, and Jews), but the conclusions of the studies appear to have many commonalities. We need to be careful in not committing an ecological fallacy (where the general traits of the group are assigned to each individual), but from the limited evidence available, there is little quantitative data to show that religion affects the major indicators of bereavement outcomes. We reported in an earlier article[16] that Mormons did not differ from non-Mormons on any of our general outcome measures but that religious participation ("keeping busy") and religiosity had some slight positive impact on psychosocial adjustments. We concluded that generally religion had little or no measurable effects. In support of continuing the study of the role of religion in bereavement adjustments are findings from two chapters. Faletti, Gibbs, Clark, Pruchno, and Berman (Chapter 4) reported that Jewish participants had significantly higher depression scores, although it is unclear whether the differences were due to bereavement. Gass (Chapter 7) stated that religious beliefs and the use of rituals should be examined further because she found some evidence that religious beliefs helped the health outcomes of widows but not widowers.

4. *Anticipation or forewarning of bereavement does not have much impact on the subsequent adjustment process for older spouses.* Again, while more research is warranted, the present evidence shows that when the loss is expected rather than sudden and unexpected, the adjustments that follow are quite similar. Faletti, Gibbs, Clark, Pruchno, and Berman (Chapter 4) reported that there were no major effects which could be attributed to sudden versus expected death situations, with the minor exception that those experiencing the sudden death of a spouse had more intense depression early in the process. Our research was similar in that anticipatory grief helped to reduce some of the early shock and confusion but afterward there was some evidence that these same spouses were having slightly more difficulty.[17] Gass (Chapter 8) found only a trend (not statistically significant) for expected death to be a slightly more favorable situation than death due to a chronic condition. Roach and Kitson (Chapter 14) concluded that although forewarning did not reduce psychological adjustment for widows or divorcées, some widows who prepared for a loss prior to the spouse's illness by seeking more education or employment had lower levels of distress. The findings in this book concerning the importance of competencies in performing tasks of daily living suggest that some specific kinds of preparation would likely help in the adjustment process, particularly if the skills are learned long before the spouse dies.

5. *Social support is moderately helpful to the adjustment process of many older bereaved spouses.* While this is a fairly positive conclusion about social support, in my opinion it is less positive than was expected. Many investigators anticipated that close supportive relationships with long-term members of a social network would be extremely helpful in alleviating much of the difficulty which accompanies bereavement. Perhaps, as Faletti, Gibbs, Clark, Pruchno, and Berman (Chapter 4) indicated, merely having a social convoy is not enough, since the convoy might not be a supportive convoy. It is probably more important to know what support networks do than to simply know about their existence and their structural characteristics. We reported in an earlier article that structural characteristics of support networks, such as size, strength of ties, and the extent to which network members known each other, were relatively unimportant predictors of bereavement coping.[18] Qualitative dimensions of the network (e.g., perceived closeness,

opportunities for self-expression, frequency of contacts, shared confidences, and mutual helping) were more influential in affecting coping outcomes, but even for these the amount of variance explained by social support was only between 4% and 14%. Also, Van Zandt, Mou, and Abbott (Chapter 3) noted in their discussion that social support among the rural bereaved adults appeared to be only slightly helpful. Thompson, Gallagher, Cover, Gilewski, and Peterson (Chapter 2) found that while more extensive social support was associated with less psychological distress, it did not account for much of the variance. Finally, Gass (Chapter 7) reported that social support was only associated with lower psychosocial dysfunction for widows but not widowers, and it did not correlate significantly with physical functioning.

One of the ways in which social support networks can be most helpful to bereaved older adults is in providing instrumental types of assistance. Gass (Chapter 8) discusses the importance of mobilizing resources to enable bereaved spouses to learn how to drive a car, manage a home, and learn new skills. The importance of receiving instrumental support from networks also was stressed in the findings reported in Chapter 11 (where family and friends were found to be helpful by providing assistance with the many tasks of daily living) and in Schuster and Butler's study (Chapter 5) on mental health after many years of widowhood. Schuster and Butler indicated that both affective and instrumental support were equally important.

Another important finding presented in this book is that early and consistent support from a person's support network can help reduce the negative impact of bereavement on mental health. The findings reported by Duran, Turner, and Lund (Chapter 6) showed that stable social support over time helps to buffer the effects of stress. Interestingly, Schuster and Butler (Chapter 5) found that the quantity of social support received early in the bereavement process was associated more strongly with later mental health than was support received later in the process. In other words, it was most important to receive social support early in the process to prevent long-term distress. This also is consistent with the earlier conclusion which emphasized the intensity of early grief experiences.

6. *Appraisal of the bereavement situation and specific coping strategies are only moderately associated with bereavement adjustments made by older surviving spouses.* Much more research is needed to document these associations, but the current evidence suggests that these variables have less impact than expected on bereavement outcomes. Gass (Chapter 7) found that widows and widowers who viewed bereavement as a harmful loss conjoined with other anticipated threats had more psychosocial dysfunction and that the widowers also had more physical dysfunction. She added that nearly all of the ways of coping were associated with greater psychosocial dysfunction for women but not for men. Self-blame was the only strategy which correlated with more psychosocial dysfunction for both men and women. Nearly all of the coping strategies were unrelated to physical functioning. Gallagher, Lovett, Hanley-Dunn, and Thompson (Chapter 9) concluded that the frequency and type of coping strategies did not predict outcome measures, with the exception that an avoidant strategy was associated with slightly more subjective distress. These investigators concluded that it is likely that bereaved spouses need to use different strategies for different problems at different times. Finally, Caserta, Van Pelt, and Lund (Chapter 10) did not find a correlation between the type of advice that the bereaved offered to others and their own out-

comes. There was a trend, however, for those who offered a mixture of both individual-oriented and other-oriented advice to have slightly better perceived coping ability and be less likely to avoid social contacts. Again, their conclusion consisted of recognizing the value of being able to use diverse coping strategies.

7. *Internal types of coping resources, such as independence, self-efficacy, self-esteem, and competency in performing tasks of daily living, appear to have considerable influence on the adjustments and outcomes which accompany the death of a spouse in later life.* While external resources, such as a person's social support network and the available community services, can alleviate some of the detrimental effects of bereavement, there is a growing body of evidence that even more important to the adjustment process are the internal resources which each individual possesses in varying degrees. By *internal* is meant that they are characteristics of the individual and are separate from what others can offer to the bereaved person. Some of the internal coping resources include independence, self-efficacy, self-esteem, and competencies in managing the many tasks of daily living. Other internal resources, such as knowledge, beliefs, attitudes, personality traits, spirituality, and previous life experiences, can be added to this list, but much less is known about their relationships with bereavement adjustments in later life.

Independence, self-efficacy, self-esteem, and competencies are highly interrelated constructs that influence one another in relatively complex ways. Most important, however, is that they all contribute to a person's ability and motivation to adapt to stressful and challenging changes in his or her life circumstances. Several chapters in this book provide evidence of the important role that these resources play in bereavement processes and outcomes. For example, Kitson and Roach found that widows and divorcées who felt independent and able to cope on their own had more ease in making psychological adjustments (Chapter 13). They also reported that widows who had sought more education and employment before the spouse's final illness experienced less psychological distress (Chapter 14). Both education and employment can increase feelings of independence. Also, in the report by Caserta, Van Pelt, and Lund we indicated that individual-oriented advice was the most common (Chapter 10). One of the most important findings in the research by Gass (Chapter 7) was that belief in control over bereavement was the only variable associated with less psychological dysfunction for both men and women. This is similar to what others refer to as *self-efficacy,* which involves the ability to use one's personal resources and skills in response to environmental demands.[19,20,21]

With respect to competencies in performing daily tasks, Faletti, Gibbs, Clark, Pruchno, and Berman (Chapter 4) reported that bereaved spouses who had shared responsibilities for both recreational and social tasks with their partners while they were married had lower depression during bereavement. This suggests that a less rigid division of labor between spouses was helpful later to the spouse that survived. Similarly, Schuster and Butler (Chapter 5) stated that widows and widowers with greater ability to carry out activities of daily living had better mental health, and our research on tasks of daily living found consistently high correlations between competencies and all eight psychosocial and health outcomes (Chapter 11). Self-esteem was added to the list of most influential internal coping resources, because in our previous longitudinal study it was the best predictor of bereavement outcomes 2 years after the loss.[15] We reported that those with more positive self-esteem measured at 3 to 4 weeks after the spouse's death had less coping difficulty nearly 2 years later. Because we found that self-esteem scores were quite stable over time and that a sample of nonbereaved matched controls had similar levels of self-esteem, it was likely that self-esteem even prior to the loss of a spouse would be a relatively good predictor of subsequent adjustments. Although more research is needed to test this causal relationship, self-esteem holds considerable promise for adding to our understanding of the bereavement process and outcomes.

Having considered 15 conclusions about the course of bereavement and factors which influence adjustments, we now turn our attention to several important implications for interventions and future research. These implications do not represent all that is needed in the future, but they do reflect many of the findings presented in this book as well as my personal opinions based on my understanding of the research literature and my own research on spousal bereavement in later life.

IMPLICATIONS AND SUGGESTIONS FOR BEREAVEMENT INTERVENTIONS

The primary assumption which underlies all of these implications is that interventions based on empirical research findings are likely to have an advantage over those which are based on compassion alone. In other words, satisfying and effective interventions should certainly have caring and humanistic goals, but successful outcomes will not automatically result from having such goals. Again, research-derived interventions have the advantage of being based on objective and controlled observations of many different people rather than on the experiences of only a few select people.

1. Many older bereaved spouses do not want or need intervention services. This point is important to recognize, because it is frequently assumed by clinicians and service providers that most older bereaved persons are depressed, socially isolated, and incapacitated by their loss. The research evidence does not support this assumption, although certainly some bereaved persons are depressed, isolated, and incapacitated. The tasks for those developing intervention services are many, and among their first should be an attempt to reach those who are at greatest risk—to seek them out rather than simply announcing the existence of the service—and encourage their participation by explaining how and why the service will be helpful. It is absolutely critical to recognize that many, perhaps most, of the potential population of older bereaved spouses will not want to participate. This can be discouraging to those who are committed to the value of their services, but their motivation to continue their efforts will probably be less adversely affected if they anticipate the lack of enthusiasm among many potential clients. For example, only 44% of the bereaved spouses who completed our first study said that they would have liked the opportunity of attending self-help groups,[22] and only 27% of those assigned to self-help groups in our second study actually agreed to participate (Chapter 15).

2. Interventions need to be available early in the bereavement process and continue over relatively long periods of time. There is a good deal of research evidence that the first several months (usually 1 to 4 months) are the most difficult and that early adjustments will influence outcomes much later. Also, because bereavement may last for many years and some people may not be ready for early interventions, it would be most helpful to have services available over long periods of time. This does not mean that the same people need to continue receiving services for many years, although some will have this need; rather, bereaved spouses should have an opportunity to participate when they are ready.

3. Because the impact of bereavement is multidimensional, it is imperative that interventions offer comprehensive and diverse services. It is unlikely that any one intervention will be capable of providing all that is needed, but each intervention should clearly identify which needs are being targeted in relation to the overall multidimensional process so that there is an awareness of what help is not being provided. For example, because the death of a spouse in later life can impact emotions, psychosocial functioning, health, family life, interpersonal relationships, work, recreation, financial situation, and many other aspects of a person's life, those designing interventions which provide primarily an opportunity for self-expression (such as self-help groups) should recognize that some dimensions are not likely to be addressed. Ideally, all communities would have available a variety of interventions or services so that each person's unique skills, resources, and circumstances could be matched to the most appropriate configuration of services. While this is unlikely, we can at least strive to offer interventions with the broadest scope of impact. Therefore, whenever possible, it would be worthwhile to impact several dimensions simultaneously by providing opportunities for self-expression and the enhancement of self-esteem; by teaching new skills to complete the tasks of daily living; by enhancing and mobilizing already existing social support networks; by providing education and assistance regarding health, nutrition, and exercise; and by encouraging social participation.

4. Various intervention formats and professionals are needed to ensure that appropriate services are available. Not all people experience bereavement in the same way; similarly, not all people will use or benefit from the same interventions. In terms of format, some people will only want to have a one-on-one type of intervention. This might be because they feel the uniqueness of their situation can be dealt with more effectively one to one or because they are reluctant to express personal and sensitive feelings in group situations. Others have reported to us that they particularly enjoyed being in a self-help group because they learned from others, recognized some commonalities in their situations, and enjoyed the socializing and friendships which developed.

Many people have skills and expertise which are well suited for helping bereaved spouses. Silverman[23] has shown that widows are quite capable of assisting the more recently bereaved and their continued involvement is highly encouraged. They can reveal to the new widows that they have been there and that they know how it feels to grieve. Also, there are important contributions that can be made by researchers, gerontologists, psychologists, psychiatrists, physicians, social workers, nurses, occupational therapists, counselors, clergy and many other professionals, including social scientists, lawyers, accountants, educators, and direct service providers. Again, because bereavement has a multidimensional impact, interventions can be developed by many different configurations of professional and trained team members. Widows and widowers can provide a sharing of experiences while other trained persons assist with legal, financial, health, spiritual, and educational issues. A multidimensional team approach is highly recommended, because it will increase the likelihood of developing interventions which address the diversity of needs and lead to overall success.

5. *Those who associate with older bereaved adults also should be recipients of interventions to help them with their own grief and to improve their ability to be effective in the support that they provide to the bereaved spouses.* These people might include family members, friends, clergy of the bereaved spouses, and all of those who work as professionals providing services to them. Careful thought about this statement should lead one to the conclusion that everyone would benefit from a better understanding of how older persons experience the death of a spouse and the subsequent adjustment process; after all, anyone of us might be put in the position of being the friend or relative of a surviving spouse—or of being a surviving spouse. Because social support networks have been found to be only moderately helpful to bereaved spouses, there is much room for improvement. It is quite possible that support network members, including service providers, could be more helpful if they learned to express their grief, were more sensitive to the difficulties and needs of the spouses, and were educated about ways to offer assistance. Some of the older bereaved participants in our studies told the interviewers that they felt disappointed in other family members, particularly in their adult children, for the lack of grief shown in their presence. Most of these adult children were experiencing grief but probably had not adequately conveyed it to the parent, or at least the parent did not recognize it. In either case, the lack of shared and communicated grief points out the potential for interventions which include at least one component where family members or close friends participate together.

6. *There is a need for additional innovative interventions to facilitate positive bereavement adjustments for older surviving spouses.* This can be accomplished by increasing the public awareness of the needs, documenting the benefits of existing interventions, encouraging new professionals to develop expertise in bereavement, and attracting experts from other disciplines and professions to make their unique contributions. Equally important is the active involvement of professionals, the bereaved spouses, and members of their support networks in the development and implementation of new bereavement programs. Creative ideas should be more plentiful when more informed people are encouraged to contribute.

7. *Interventions should include an evaluation component to assess their processes, outcomes, and overall impact.* Evaluation efforts should be made to demonstrate to others that the interventions are having the desired effects, to provide feedback necessary to the staff for making improvements in the interventions, and to help others avoid unnecessary mistakes in their interventions. Evaluation does not need to be the major component of an intervention, but it does warrant inclusion and should be incorporated into the program during the early planning stages so that project objectives are clearly delineated, intervention strategies are consistent with the objectives, and appropriate before-and-after measures can be obtained.

IMPLICATIONS AND SUGGESTIONS FOR FUTURE RESEARCH

The following implications and suggestions for further research on older bereaved spouses are based on the studies presented in this book, other relevant research, and my own personal opinions. They focus on research design issues, study samples, variables to be included, and measurement considerations.

1. *More research is needed to test the effectiveness of various types of interventions.* Such research differs from evaluating already existing programs, where the

primary purpose is to provide a service rather than to test research questions and hypotheses. Experimental designs with random assignment of subjects into treatment and control groups are strongly recommended because they provide unique opportunities to determine casual relationships and contribute to theoretical refinements which can be applied to other related situations. They also are most appropriate for identifying which aspect of an intervention is producing a specific change in the adjustment process. To date, very few controlled intervention studies have been done, but present knowledge about the bereavement process and adjustments is certainly sufficient to allow proposing interventions based on past research findings and a variety of theoretical frameworks.

2. *Longitudinal studies which have shorter intervals between measurement periods, cover a longer period of time, and begin prior to the spouse's death are needed.* Obviously, it would be ideal to obtain data from people well in advance of the bereavement event so that the actual impact of the loss could be more clearly determined. These studies would require large samples of people and substantial financial support, but the time and money would be worth the investment. The longer time periods are important because some detrimental effects of bereavement may take many years to surface as bereavement adjustments and experiences interact with other changing life circumstances. Causal relationships are easier to identify when it is clear that one variable changes prior to changes in another. Also, the long-term effects of interventions need to be assessed to identify which specific components produce the longest-lasting effects and to determine some of the cost-benefit ratios where long-term benefits can be included in the equations. Shorter intervals between measurement periods would provide more accurate assessments of the subtle and transitory characteristics of the course of bereavement. These data also would help to explain how apparently contradictory feelings and emotions can be experienced simultaneously and what factors trigger the ups and downs of the roller-coaster-like process. Several measures obtained every few days or every week would provide a greater understanding of the problems associated with daily life and how new skills are learned and used.

3. *Future studies should include early bereavement assessments.* Regardless of the study design (observational, experimental, survey, etc.), it is important that the primary study variables be assessed almost as early as possible, usually 1 to 2 months after the death. As indicated earlier, many of the most painful and intense feelings are experienced at this time, and early experiences have been relatively good predictors of subsequent adjustment. Later entry periods can be built into research designs to permit the inclusion of bereaved persons who were initially reluctant to participate.

4. *Research using large samples is desirable for the purpose of completing multivariate analyses.* Multivariate statistical analyses are needed to determine the effects of various combinations of and interactions among variables. These analyses can contribute to our ability to test complicated theoretical models and our ability to refine our predictions of bereavement outcomes. Both abilities can be used to improve the overall effectiveness of interventions by helping to identify which types of people are likely to benefit the most from which types of intervention. Multivariate analyses require relatively large samples to meet the underlying assumptions and mechanics of the statistical calculations.

5. *Heterogeneous samples and cross-cultural comparisons are needed to help identify the universal and unique features of bereavement.* Although people from

different ethnic, cultural, gender, and age groups have been examined, it is most unusual to have much of this heterogeneity built into one study. Comparisons from one study to another are difficult and limited, because the studies are usually done at different times, with different age cohorts in their samples, and use different measures, designs, and analyses. Single studies with greater heterogeneity among the samples would provide interesting data on which individual factors, (e.g., age, gender, religion, and ethnicity) and which cultural traits (e.g., norms, rituals, and values) create similarities or differences in bereavement experiences. These answers would be valuable to our understanding of bereavement as well as other common life transitions.

6. *Bereavement research on older spouses should include measures of self-esteem, self-efficacy, compentencies in tasks of daily living, social supports and other coping resources, loneliness, positive and negative feelings and experiences, and transitory aspects of the adjustment process.* While many independent and dependent variables need to be included in bereavement studies, I strongly recommend that the ones mentioned above receive extra consideration; they have all been shown to be influential or important indicators of outcomes. I have already discussed quite extensively the prominent roles that internal coping resources (e.g., self-esteem, self-efficacy, and competencies) have in affecting bereavement adjustments. Similarly, lack of social supports and other coping resources, such as community services, are important situational factors that can make some people at greater risk for unfavorable adjustments. Measures of loneliness should be included, since loneliness appears to be the most common and persistent problem that older bereaved spouses experience. Because many studies have neglected to include measures of positive feelings and behaviors (e.g., confidence, pride, learning new skills, and forming new satisfying relationships) and some research has shown that a wide continuum of positive and negative characteristics can accompany bereavement, we will gain more accurate and comprehensive knowledge if studies include measures all along the positive-negative continuum. It will also be worthwhile, particularly in intervention studies, to include measures which assess the transitory aspects of daily life, for short-term interventions are more likely to impact the daily stresses and satisfactions than they are to alter more stable constructs like life satisfaction, which requires a reassessment of one's entire life.

7. *Research should examine a broader range of predictor variables and theoretical models.* Many other social science theories need to be applied and tested and other predictor variables need to be included if there is to be any increase in the amount of variance explained in bereavement adjustments. More bereavement research should be done using continuity and disengagement theory, symbolic interactionism, cognitive dissonance theory, and environmental press, life span, self-efficacy, and appraisal models (to identify only a few examples). Additional predictor variables might include characteristics of the marital relationship, personality traits, previous life experiences, adjustments to other losses, spirituality, family environment, expectations of adult children and grandchildren, attitudes toward aging, and specific preparations for widowhood.

Knowledge about spousal bereavement among older adults is clearly in its infancy, and there is a substantial need for more research. Both innovative approaches and replication studies are desired so that we can better understand, explain, and predict bereavement adjustments. With greater confidence in our abilities to do these things, we can provide more successful interventions and improve the well-being of those who are experiencing one of the most stressful life experiences that they will ever confront.

REFERENCES

1. Lund, D. A., Caserta, M. S., & Dimond, M. F. (1986). Gender differences through two years of bereavement among the elderly. *The Gerontologist, 26*, 314–320.
2. Barrett, C. J., & Schneweis, K. M. (1980). An empirical search for stages of widowhood. *Omega, 11*, 97–104.
3. Lopata, H. Z. (1973). *Widowhood in an American city.* Cambridge, MA: Schankman Press.
4. Parkes, C. M. (1987). *Bereavement: Studies of grief in adult life.* Madison, CT: International Universities Press.
5. Carey, R. G. (1979). Weathering widowhood: Problems and adjustments of the widowed during the first year. *Omega, 10*, 163–174.
6. van Rooijen, L. (1979). Widow's bereavement: Stress and depression after 1½ years. In I. G. Sarason & C. D. Spielberger (Eds.), *Stress and anxiety.* Cambridge, MA: Winthrop.
7. Kuhn, M., & McPartland, T. S. (1954). An empirical investigation of self attitudes. *American Sociological Review, 19*, 68–76.
8. Lund, D. A., Caserta, M. S., Dimond, M. F., & Gray, R. M. (1986). Impact of bereavement on the self-conceptions of older surviving spouses. *Symbolic Interaction, 9*, 235–244.
9. Spitzer, S., Couch, C., & Stratton, J. (1971). *The assessment of self.* Iowa City: Sernoll.
10. Osterweis, M., Solomon, F., & Green, M. (1984). *Bereavement: Reactions, consequences and care.* Washington, DC: National Academy Press.
11. Cleveland, W. P., & Gianturco, D. T. (1976). Remarriage probability after widowhood: A retrospective method. *Journal of Gerontology, 31*, 99–103.
12. Burks, V. K., Lund, D. A., Gregg, C. H., & Bluhm, H. P. (1988). Bereavement and remarriage for older adults. *Death Studies, 12*, 51–60.
13. Northcott, H. C. (1984). Widowhood and remarriage trends in Canada 1956–1981. *Canadian Journal on Aging, 3*, 63–78.
14. Spanier, G. B., & Glick, P. C. (1980). Paths to remarriage. *Journal of Divorce, 3*, 283–298.
15. Lund, D. A., Dimond, M. F., Caserta, M. S., Johnson, R. J., Poulton, J. L., & Connelly, J. R. (1985). Identifying elderly with coping difficulties after two years of bereavement. *Omega, 16*, 213–224.
16. Lund, D. A., Caserta, M. S., & Dimond, M. F. (in press). A comparison of bereavement adjustments between Mormon and non-Mormon older adults. *Journal of Religion and Aging.*
17. O'Donnell, J. C. (1988). *Bereavement and the elderly: Anticipatory grief.* Unpublished thesis, University of Utah, College of Nursing.
18. Dimond, M. F., Lund, D. A., & Caserta, M. S. (1987). The role of social support in the first two years of bereavement in an elderly sample. *The Gerontologist, 27*, 519–604.
19. Bandura, A. (1977). Self-efficacy: Toward a unifying theory of behavioral change. *Psychological Review, 84*, 191–215.
20. Bandura, A. (1982). Self-efficacy mechanism in human agency. *American Psychologist, 37*, 122–145.
21. Holahan, C. K., Holahan, C. J., & Belk, S. S. (1984). Adjustment in aging: The roles of life stress, hassles, and self-efficacy. *Health Psychology, 3*, 315–328.
22. Lund, D. A., Dimond, M. F., & Juretich, M. (1985). Bereavement support groups for the elderly: Characteristics of potential participants. *Death Studies, 9*, 309–321.
23. Silverman, P. R. (1986). *Widow to widow.* New York: Springer.

Index

THE HOLY SPIRIT
IN THE
OLD TESTAMENT

THE HOLY SPIRIT
IN THE
OLD TESTAMENT

LEON J. WOOD

ZONDERVAN
PUBLISHING HOUSE
OF THE ZONDERVAN CORPORATION
GRAND RAPIDS, MICHIGAN 49506

THE HOLY SPIRIT IN THE OLD TESTAMENT
© 1976 by The Zondervan Corporation
Grand Rapids, Michigan

Fifth printing 1981

Library of Congress Cataloging in Publication Data

Wood, Leon James.
　The Holy Spirit in the Old Testament.

　(Contemporary evangelical perspectives)
　Bibliography: p.
　Includes index.
　　1.　Holy Spirit—Biblical teaching.　　2.　Bible.　O.T.
—Criticism, interpretation, etc.　　I.　Title.
BS1199.S69W66　　　231'.3　　　75-38803
　ISBN 0-310-34751-3

Printed in the United States of America

CONTENTS

PREFACE

Although many books have been written about the Holy Spirit, they have considered the subject almost exclusively a New Testament presentation. If the Old Testament is mentioned at all, it is only in passing or in the form of a comparative remark. Some writers have doubted that the Old Testament contains any sure references to the Holy Spirit and that certainly people of the time had little, if any, conception of this Third Person of the Trinity. No books to my knowledge treat the subject of the Holy Spirit in the Old Testament as such.

It is my view that the Old Testament does have some definite things to say regarding the Holy Spirit and His activity during this time. There is evidence that at least well-taught people of Israel knew of Him and recognized the need of His presence and empowerment in their lives, if they were to serve God effectively.

A question that has puzzled many Bible students concerns the spiritual renewal of people in the Old Testament. Some have doubted that true spiritual renewal existed prior to the founding of the church at Pentecost, and few have believed that the Old Testament could have included such New Testament truths as the "indwelling," "sealing," or "filling" of the Holy Spirit. This question is considered in the following pages, where it is maintained that all these truths were experienced by Old Testament saints. They did not call their experiences by these names, nor could they have defined them, but their existence is witnessed in the lives of the true believers. The one main area of work begun for the first by the Holy Spirit at Pentecost was the baptism of believers into the church and their resulting empowerment for gospel proclamation.

Another question that has caused considerable discussion concerns the possibility of ecstaticism among Israel's early prophets. Did Saul, for instance, become an ecstatic when he "prophesied" among a group of prophets and then lay in a stupor for a period of many hours (1 Sam. 19:18-24)? It is my view that ecstaticism was not practiced by

Israel's true prophets, and explanations are given for the so-called difficult passages that some scholars believe say that it was.

Finally, the subject of evil spirits, especially as related to Saul, is investigated. This is a timely topic, for many today are curious about demons and demon possession. Saul's experience has significance for this issue.

The test quoted most often is the King James Version. At times it has seemed advisable to use my own phrasing, where greater clarity is needed. Because the King James Version uses the name LORD for the personal name of God, *Yahweh* (Jehovah), I have employed this form in the discussion.

THE HOLY SPIRIT
IN THE
OLD TESTAMENT

1

IDENTIFYING THE QUESTIONS

Questions regarding the Holy Spirit are usually answered on the basis of the New Testament. This is as it should be up to a point, for the New Testament has much to say concerning the Third Person of the Godhead.[1] The Old Testament, however, also has much to say concerning the Holy Spirit, and its testimony should not be overlooked. The Bible is one book, and its two Testaments are closely related. The Old Testament provides the background and basis for New Testament truth, while the New Testament expands and enlarges on seed-forms of thought set forth in the Old Testament.

The subject of the person and work of the Holy Spirit is always important for study, for He is the Third Person of the Trinity. He indwells the Christian and gives daily guidance and enablement. In a day when there is special stress on the work of the Holy Spirit, the subject becomes even more important. And if in that stress erroneous ideas are commonly advocated, the necessity of study becomes even greater. This is the current situation as the "charismatic" movement has gained a large place in religious activity. An understanding of what both the Old and New Testaments have to say is of vital significance. Whatever the Scriptures set forth, and from whatever part, should be a primary concern for every Christian.

The subject of the work of the Holy Spirit in the Old Testament is too frequently dismissed with the assertion that He came on people at one time and later left them. This is said in contrast to the New

---

[1] Says J. E. C. Weldon (*The Revelation of the Holy Spirit*, p. 10), "The doctrine of the Holy Spirit is in a preeminent sense a doctrine of the New Testament." J. H. Raven (*The History of the Religion of Israel*, p. 164) denies that there is any distinctive reference to the Holy Spirit in the Old Testament.

Testament truth that in the church age the Christian is indwelt by the Spirit and that this is continuous. The second part of the assertion is altogether true. The Holy Spirit does continually indwell the believer in the New Testament age. And the first part is also true, up to a point. The Holy Spirit did come on people and later leave them, but the meaning of this coming on and leaving is seldom defined. Since the usage of these words is put in contrast to the fact of the New Testament Christian's being continuously indwelt, the implication is that this coming on and leaving concerned the spiritual relationship of Old Testament people to God. And this, in turn, might imply — though the statement is seldom made — that the Old Testament person could be saved and then lost, depending on whether the Holy Spirit was on him or not.

Such a conclusion, however, would not square with the biblical truth of the security of the believer. Surely Old Testament believers enjoyed eternal security, as well as believers of the New Testament time. Few students of the Bible would want to believe otherwise. But if this were true, what about the coming on and leaving of the Holy Spirit in Old Testament time?

That He did come on and leave Old Testament people is indicated numerous times. For instance, of Othniel, the first of the judges, it is said that "the Spirit of the LORD came upon him" (Judg. 3:10). Then of Saul, prior to his battle at Jabesh-gilead, it is stated that "the Spirit of God came upon" him (1 Sam. 11:6), and later, after his second rejection for the kingship, that "the Spirit of the LORD departed from" him (1 Sam. 16:14). So what does this coming on and leaving mean? In what sense did the Holy Spirit come on and leave people in Old Testament time?

Another question to consider concerns what might be called unexpected reactions of people at times when the Holy Spirit came on them. For instance, the Holy Spirit was made to come on seventy elders who were to help Moses in judging Israel during the days of wilderness travel, and when He did, all seventy began to "prophesy." Further, when two of this number continued in the activity after the others had stopped, Joshua asked Moses to make them stop also (Num. 11:16-28). What kind of activity was this "prophesying" of the seventy, that all could be involved at the same time? And what would cause Joshua to request that the two be made to stop when they wanted to continue? Still further, what relation did the coming of the Holy Spirit on these people have to this activity?

Two similar experiences happened to Saul before he became Israel's first king. At one time the "Spirit of God came upon him" so that he "prophesied" along with a "company of prophets" and is said to have become changed "into another man" as a result (1 Sam. 10:1-12). Another time "the Spirit of God" came upon him, and he not only "prophesied," but then "stripped off his clothes" and lay in this condition the remainder of that day and the following night (1 Sam. 19:23,24). Again the question arises regarding the relation between these times of the Holy Spirit's coming on Saul and the resultant prophesying activity, and also to his becoming a changed man in one instance and laying in an apparent stupor for several hours in the second.

Liberal scholars commonly view these instances as examples of ecstatic frenzy on the part of the participants. They understand the references to the Spirit to be merely indications of an emotional surge in the individuals' own personalities as they experienced these occurrences. Conservative scholars normally disagree with this explanation but have little to say regarding an alternative explanation.

There are still other questions to consider. For instance, was the Holy Spirit as active during Old Testament time as in the New? What was His part in creation? Did He play a role in bringing revelation to Old Testament prophets and others? Did He effect regeneration in people then as now? Did He indwell, fill, and seal the Old Testament saint as He does the Christian today? What did He begin doing at Pentecost that He had not been doing before that time?

Besides these, there are questions that are indirectly related to this subject. One concerns the "evil spirit" that came on Saul immediately after the Holy Spirit departed from him (1 Sam. 16:14). Who or what was this "evil spirit"? And is there any relation between what Saul experienced and that of a person controlled by demons? Jesus encountered numerous people controlled by demons in His time, and many believe people are often similarly controlled today. Another question concerns the occasion when Saul consulted the woman of a "familiar spirit" at Endor (1 Sam. 28:9-25). What transpired for Saul at this time? Did Samuel, who was called up by the woman, really appear? If so, does this give reason to believe in the authenticity of mediums and spiritists?

These and other questions logically arise and are significant in respect to the subject before us. The following discussion will consider them and suggest explanations.

2

THE IDENTITY AND WORK OF THE HOLY SPIRIT

Before entering into a discussion of the questions posed in chapter 1, there are some basic matters that call for attention. The first concerns the identity and personality of the Holy Spirit and scriptural evidence that He is indeed a true member of the Godhead as indicated.

A. The Identity and Deity of the Holy Spirit

1. **His identity.** Conservative theologians agree that the Holy Spirit is the Third Person of the Godhead: God the Father is the first; God the Son is the second; and God the Holy Spirit is the third. These distinctions — first, second, and third — are not believed to refer to rank, however, for all three persons are equal in power and honor. The terms are viewed merely as a useful way of making a distinction between the three.

The Scriptures give evidence that the three persons are to be differentiated. At the time of Christ's baptism, God the Father spoke from heaven; God the Son in His divine-human form was about to be baptized in the Jordan by John the Baptist; and God the Holy Spirit descended upon Him there in the water "like a dove" (Matt. 3:16; cf. Mark. 1:10; Luke 3:22). When Christ gave His great commission to the disciples, He instructed them, among other things, to baptize "in the name of the Father, and of the Son, and of the Holy Spirit" (Matt. 28:19). When Paul closed his second letter to the Corinthians, he did so with the benediction, "The grace of the Lord Jesus Christ, and the love of God, and the communion of the Holy Spirit, be with you all" (2 Cor. 13:14). And Peter made the same threefold distinction at the

14

beginning of his first letter, writing, "Elect according to the fore-knowledge of God the Father, through sanctification of the Spirit, unto obedience and sprinkling of the blood of Jesus Christ" (1 Peter 1:2). The Holy Spirit does have his own distinct identity among the three persons of the Trinity.

2. **His personality.** The fact that the Holy Spirit is a Person — and not merely an influence, force, or power — is important to recognize. Liberal theologians commonly speak of Him otherwise. The denial of His personality dates back even to the Monarchians and Arians of the early church, and church history has continued since to have representatives of the erroneous view. The Scriptures, however, give ample testimony that He is indeed a Person.[1]

First, characteristics true only of a personality are ascribed to Him: intelligence (John 14:26; 15:26); emotion (Isa. 63:10; Eph. 4:30); and will (Acts 16:7; 1 Cor. 12:11). Second, designations true only of a personality are ascribed to Him: the masculine pronoun *ekeinos* is used for Him (John 16:14), even though the word *spirit* (pneuma) is itself neuter; and the name *parakletos* ("Comforter" or "Counselor") is used of Him (John 14:16,26; 15:26), a term which cannot be translated "comfort" or "counsel" and so be taken as an abstract influence. Third, He is mentioned in relation to other persons in a way true only of a personality (John 16:14; Acts 15:28; 1 Peter 1:1,2; Jude 20,21). Fourth, several passages clearly distinguish Him from His own power and thus imply His personality (Luke 1:35; 4:14; Acts 10:38; Rom. 15:13; 1 Cor. 2:4). Fifth, He performs work attributable only to a personality, such as searching, knowing, speaking, revealing, convincing, commanding, striving, helping, building, inspiring, making intercession, and performing miracles (Gen. 1:2; 6:3; Luke 12:12; John 3:8; 16:8; Acts 2:4; 8:29; 13:2; 16:6,7; Rom. 8:11,26; 15:19; 1 Cor. 2:10,11; 2 Peter 1:21).

3. **His deity.** The fact that the Holy Spirit is God has already been established by showing Him to be the Third Person of the Godhead. The Scriptures give additional evidences of this truth, however, and these are worth noting.

For example, divine names are ascribed to the Holy Spirit. Peter uses the very name *God* for Him (Acts 5:3,4). The same name is

[1]For enlarged discussion, see George Smeaton, *The Doctrine of the Holy Spirit*, p. 23.

implied for Him in 1 Corinthians 3:16, where the Christian is said to be the "temple of God," because the "Spirit of God" dwells in him; see also 2 Timothy 3:16 compared with 2 Peter 1:21, and Exodus 17:7 compared with Hebrews 3:7-9. Also, divine works are effected by Him: creation (Gen. 1:2; Job 26:13; 33:4), regeneration of the sinner (John 3:5,6; Titus 3:5), and the resurrection of saints (Rom. 8:11). Then, divine attributes are ascribed to Him: omnipotence (Rom. 15:19; 1 Cor. 12:11), omniscience (Isa. 40:13,14 compared with Rom. 11:34; 1 Cor. 2:10,11), omnipresence (Ps. 139:7-10). And further, divine honor is rendered to Him (Matt. 28:19; Rom. 9:1; 2 Cor. 13:14).

B. The Work of the Holy Spirit

The Scriptures indicate that each of the divine Persons carries on a work distinct from that of the others. In general, the work of the Father is that of serving as supreme planner, author, and designer; that of the Son as worker, carrying out the directives of the Father, and especially giving revelation of the Godhead; and that of the Holy Spirit as completer or consummator, bringing to final form that which has been brought into existence by the Son at the Father's command.

This work of the Holy Spirit carries particular reference: first, in respect to natural creation, He "moved" (Gen. 1:2) on the face of the chaotic waters and in six days brought them to a complete state of order (cf. Job 26:11-14; 33:4; Ps. 104:30). And, second, in respect to recreation (regeneration) of man, He prepared the body of Christ (Luke 1:35; Heb. 10:5-7), inspired the writing of Scripture (1 Cor. 2:13; 2 Peter 1:21), formed and empowers the church (1 Cor. 3:16; 12:4-11; Eph. 2:22), and teaches and guides Christians (John 14:26; 15:26; 16:13,14; Acts 5:32).

C. Meaning of *ruah*

The word for *spirit* in the Old Testament is *ruah*, employed in its noun and verb form some 388 times. It is used to designate the human spirit, God's Holy Spirit, and several other entities such as "wind," "breath," "odor," and "space." Surprisingly, its most basic meaning seems to have been "wind."[2] It is used to mean "wind" approxi-

[2]Cf. Weldon, *The Revelation of the Holy Spirit*, p. 10. Smeaton, (*Doctrine of the Holy Spirit*, p. 19), however, says the basic idea was "living breath" and not "lifeless wind."

mately[3] 101 times (e.g., Gen. 8:1; Exod. 10:13,19), which is more than one-fourth its total times of employment, and from the idea of wind several of the other meanings find their derivations. It is rendered "breath" 18 times (e.g., Job 9:18; 15:30), and breath is wind that enters a person's lungs. From this comes the meaning "odor" used 13 times (e.g., Gen. 8:21; 27:27), odor being brought to one's attention by his breath. Another derived meaning is "space" used 6 times (e.g., Gen. 32:16; Job 41:16), and wind occupies a large space.

The relation of "wind" to "spirit" is not so easily seen, but probably is based on the idea that both are invisible. Jesus tied the two concepts together based on this similarity when speaking to Nicodemus. He referred to the wind as that which could be heard but not seen and then said, "So is every one that is born of the Spirit" (John 3:8). The Old Testament uses *ruah* for the spirit of man about eighty-four times and for the Spirit of God about ninety-seven times.

Linked closely in idea to man's spirit is the thought of an emotional response in man, and *ruah* is used in this sense about twenty-eight times. For instance, Genesis 45:27 speaks of Jacob's "spirit" reviving at the news that Joseph was still alive. The thought can hardly be that Jacob's spirit, as an entity, came back to life, but that he took on new strength in emotional outlook (see also Exod. 6:9; Num. 5:14,30). Another meaning closely linked is that of the life principle in man; *ruah* is used in this sense about eleven times. For instance, when Samson was given water miraculously by God, it is said that "his spirit came again, and he revived" (Judg. 15:19; see also 1 Sam. 30:12; Job 6:4). Then, besides these meanings, one finds the angels of God called "spirits" four times (e.g., Job 4:15; Ps. 104:4), "evil spirits" mentioned eighteen times (e.g., Judg. 9:23; 1 Sam. 16:15,16), and even the "spirit" of a beast once (Eccl. 3:21).

D. Identifying References to God's Spirit

The most important meaning for *ruah* in regard to the consideration herein is the "Spirit" of God. The interest is in studying references to God's Spirit so that the nature of His work in Old Testament time can be determined. A significant question, then, concerns how one may be sure when *ruah* is used in reference to God's Spirit.

Admittedly, there are times when the meaning of *ruah* is not

[3]The number can only be given approximately for some instances are uncertain.

definite. This is more true, however, involving instances where man, rather than God, is the subject. For instance, each Israelite who brought liberally of his material possessions for building the tabernacle is said to have been "made willing" to do this by his "spirit" (Exod. 35:21). Here "spirit" could refer to man as a spirit or to man's emotional response to the need present. It is sometimes difficult to know whether *ruah* refers to the "breath" a person breathes or to the "life principle" that keeps him alive. For example, Jeremiah speaks of the foolishness of making idols, one reason being that there is "no *ruah* in them" (Jer. 10:14; cf. 51:17). He could be referring to breath that is breathed or to the fact that idol has no "life." Still another distinction sometimes difficult to make is when *ruah* means "wind" and when it means "in vain." For instance, Isaiah cries out to God, in view of Israel's ineffectiveness as a witness to the world, "We have as it were brought forth *ruah*" (Isa. 26:18). The translation "wind" is frequently used here, but the thought quite clearly is "in vain." Israel's testimony had been empty of significance.

In respect to distinguishing between references to man's spirit and God's Spirit, however, there is really little difficulty. With almost no exception, the context shows whether God or man is the subject. Frequently, the word *ruah* will be accompanied by the following genitive *of God* or *of the* LORD. Many times a possessive pronoun, *my* or *his*, will be used with the word, with the context showing the antecedent to be God. Or if neither of these clues exist, God will be the subject of the passage in which the word appears. In the following discussion, only those passages where the distinction is clear will be used as evidence for points made. In the event any possibility of ambiguity is involved, attention will be given to showing, exegetically, that the reference is indeed to God.

A further word is in order concerning the identity of the references of *ruah*, when used in such phrases as the "Spirit of God" or "Spirit of the LORD." Did the Old Testament writers have the Third Person of the Trinity definitely in mind, or merely a power or influence of God? Paul Jewett believes it was only the latter, as he says the term *spirit* is never used in the Old Testament "to clearly imply that the Spirit is a Person distinct from the Father and the Son." Then he adds, "The Spirit of God is the divine nature viewed as vital energy."[4]

[4]"Holy Spirit," *The Zondervan Pictorial Encyclopedia of the Bible*, III (Grand Rapids: Zondervan, 1975), p. 184.

There seems reason to believe, however, that informed Old Testament people conceived of the Holy Spirit in a more advanced way than this thinking gives them credit for. No doubt they would not have been able to make a theological formulation regarding the Trinity, but still they seem to have made a distinction between the Spirit of God and God Himself and this in a way to characterize the Spirit as having qualities of personality. For instance, the psalmist writes, "Thou sendest forth thy Spirit, they are created, and thou renewest the face of the earth" (Ps. 104:30). The verb *sendest forth* is hardly applicable to merely a power or influence of God. On that basis, one would simply expect such an expression as, "Thou didst create and renew the face of the earth by thy power." A spirit which could be sent forth must be one that is distinct from the being from whom it is sent forth, and if that spirit in turn could create and renew, then an aspect of personality is implied.

Again, one day Elisha asked that a "double portion of" Elijah's "spirit" (2 Kings 2:9) be given to him. In the same context, fifty young "sons of the prophets" (training prophets) refer to the "Spirit of the LORD." The implication is that this "Spirit of the LORD" is the same as the Spirit Elisha asked from Elijah. If so, this means that the Spirit here in view was distinguished from God Himself; and since, as the context indicates, Elisha was greatly empowered when this Spirit came upon him, the aspect of personality is again implied.

Later still, Ezekiel, who speaks so frequently regarding the Spirit, refers to the Spirit either as doing something to or for him in most significant ways. For instance, in 3:12 he says, "Then the Spirit took me up" for the purpose of transporting him to the city of Tell-abib. Again in 11:1, he states, "Moreover the Spirit lifted me up and brought me unto the east gate of the LORD's house." Such language once more shows the prophet distinguishing between the Spirit of God and God Himself, and, since the Spirit thus in reference does these things either to him or for him, personality for the Spirit is again implied.

It is also important to recognize that the matter of the identity of the Holy Spirit in the Old Testament is not so much a question of what people thought regarding this member of the Godhead as it is what the intention was of God Himself who inspired the writers. His intention is indicated in numerous passages. In Genesis 1:2, where the Spirit of God is said to have moved or brooded upon the face of the

19

waters following the initial creation, certainly the meaning is that the Third Person of the Godhead so moved or brooded. Or years later, when God told Zechariah that his work was done, "Not by might nor by power but by my Spirit" (Zech. 4:6), the reference surely was to the Third Person of the Trinity as the One responsible for God's work being accomplished.[5]

E. A Comparison of the Use of *ruah* and *pneuma*

A comparison of the use of *ruah* in the Old Testament and of *pneuma* in the New Testament is noteworthy. The latter is the Greek equivalent of the former.[6] A study of how each was employed shows something of the change in basic concept that came by the time the New Testament was written.

A first matter to note is that in New Testament times the concept was used more frequently. *Pneuma* is used approximately the same total number of times (378) in the New Testament as *ruah* in the Old (388), but the New Testament is only about one-fourth as long. This means that the concept occurs roughly 4 times more frequently. Secondly, this increase is mainly in reference to God. The Spirit of God is mentioned no less than 261 times out of the total 378 occurrences of *pneuma*, well over two-thirds. A third matter is that there is a marked increase in the thought of the holiness of the Spirit. Out of these 261 references to the Spirit, 94 employ the qualifying adjective holy (*agios*)[7] for the combined idea "Holy Spirit." In contrast, the Old Testament does this only 3 times (Ps. 51:11; Isa. 63:10,11). Finally, the meaning seen to be basic and most used for *ruah* in the Old Testament, "wind," is used hardly at all. Only once is *pneuma* so translated, and that is when Jesus referred to the "wind" in comparison with the Holy Spirit (John 3:8). The parallel idea "breath" also comes to be limited to one mention (2 Thess. 2:8). In respect to man as a "spirit," the references remain about the same in number and manner of occurrences.

The main significance of these facts is clearly that, under God's direction, the thinking of New Testament believers became more occupied with the existence and importance of God's Spirit and

---

[5]See further discussion, chapter 4, pp. 32,33.

[6]Paul makes an identification of "Spirit" in the two Testaments in 2 Corinthians 4:13, as he speaks of "the same spirit" and then quotes from Psalm 116:10.

[7]In addition, Romans 1:4 uses the phrase "Spirit of holiness."

especially with the holiness of this member of the Godhead. This is not surprising, but in keeping with what has been observed. As with other scriptural doctrines, the New Testament takes up the truth of the Holy Spirit and brings it to a fuller degree of development. At the same time, however, the fact that the Old Testament does use *ruah* in reference to God's Spirit nearly one hundred times shows that the concept there cannot be overlooked. It is important therefore, to see how these references may reflect similar or different attributes and activities of the Spirit than in the New Testament.

Another significant comparison between *ruah* of the Old Testament and *pneuma* of the New concerns concepts associated with the terms. In the Old Testament, Isaiah 4:4 associates the concepts "judgment" and "burning" with the divine *ruah*, in the phrase "by the spirit of judgment and the spirit of burning."[8] Then Isaiah 11:2 speaks prophetically of Christ as one who would be anointed with "the spirit of wisdom and understanding, the spirit of counsel and might, the spirit of knowledge" (cf. Exod. 31:3). Joshua is also spoken of as being full of the "spirit of wisdom" (Deut. 34:9). As already observed, Psalm 51:11 and Isaiah 63:10,11 speak of the Spirit as the "holy spirit"; and Zecharish 12:10 refers to the "spirit of grace and supplications."

In the New Testament, the concept holy is repeated and given much greater emphasis. The concept wisdom also receives notice again; Ephesians 1:17 refers to the "spirit of wisdom." This is true also of grace; Hebrews 10:29 warns against doing "despite unto the Spirit of grace." The concepts from the Old Testament which are not repeated in the New are judgment and burning (which go together, for the latter lends stress to the former), understanding, counsel, might, knowledge, and supplications.

Several concepts, however, are mentioned in the New Testament which are not noticed in the Old. John 15:26 (cf. John 16:13) speaks of the "Spirit of truth." Romans 8:2 refers to the "Spirit of life" (cf. John 6:63). Romans 8:15 states that Christians have received the "Spirit of adoption." Romans 15:19 mentions the "power of the Spirit." Second Corinthians 4:13 declares that Christians have "the same spirit of faith." Ephesians 1:13 says that Christians are sealed with the "holy

[8]The reader should not let the noncapitalization of *spirit* in these biblical quotations influence him as to whether or not they speak of God's Spirit. The quotations are taken normally from KJV which usually capitalizes the term only when a definite indication of divinity is given, such as the use of the genitive "of God" or "of the LORD."

Spirit of promise." And Hebrews 9:14 refers to the "eternal Spirit." So, then, the New Testament alone employs the concepts life, truth, adoption, power, faith, promise, and eternal. It hardly needs discussion that the concepts which are peculiar to the Old and New Testaments, respectively, are just as the careful student of the Bible would expect in view of the nature of the two Testaments and their particular stresses of God's truth.

3

OLD TESTAMENT REFERENCES
TO THE SPIRIT

We now take notice of the more significant references made in the Old Testament to the Holy Spirit. This list will include most of the approximately one hundred mentions, all that will be of significance for discussions later in the book. We will consider them according to periods of Old Testament history.

A. Creation to the Patriarchs

The first references concern creation. Following the initial statement concerning creation, Genesis 1:2 says, "And the Spirit of God moved upon the face of the waters," thus implying that the Spirit superintended the six days of creative work that followed. Job 26:13 enlarges on the thought as it states, "By his spirit he hath garnished the heavens," and Job 33:4 quotes Elihu as saying, "The Spirit of God hath made me." Isaiah 40:13, in a creation context, asks rhetorically, "Who hath directed the Spirit of the Lord, or being his counsellor hath taught him?" Then the Spirit's continuing control and care of the creation is reflected in Job 27:3, where Job declares, "The spirit of God is in my nostrils," and also in Psalm 104:30, where animal life is particularly in view as the statement is made concerning God, "Thou sendest forth thy spirit, they are created: and thou renewest the face of the earth."

One other reference follows after the time of creation but still very early in man's experience. It is Genesis 6:3, where God says, "My spirit shall not always strive with man, for that he also is flesh." The thought is that an aspect of work, which the Holy Spirit had been carrying on until the time in view, was soon to end. No references to the Spirit occur in connection with Abraham, Isaac, or Jacob.

B. Moses to Samuel

A first reference from the time of Moses comes as God indicates that a special enablement would be given to Bezaleel, the chief craftsman to work on the tabernacle. Exodus 31:3 (cf. 35:31) says, "And I have filled him with the spirit of God, in wisdom, and in understanding, and in knowledge, and in all manner of workmanship." God wanted expert workmanship on His place of dwelling.

The Spirit is next mentioned in reference to the seventy elders who were to help Moses in judging the Israelites. The nation was moving from Sinai to Kadesh-barnea when God instructed Moses to select these men, and He said, "I will take of the spirit which is upon thee, and will put it upon them" (Num. 11:17). Then in Numbers 11:25 God is said to have done this, and when He did, the seventy began to prophesy "and did not cease." Finally all but two did stop, but Eldad and Medad continued, and then Joshua asked Moses to make them stop and Moses refused.[1]

Two later references also concern the time of Moses. Nehemiah 9:20 speaks of Israel in the wilderness and says of God, "Thou gavest also thy good spirit to instruct them, and withholdest not thy manna from their mouth." Then Isaiah 63:10,11 refers both to the people's sin at that time and to Moses' Spirit-led guidance, stating, "But they rebelled, and vexed his holy Spirit: therefore he was turned to be their enemy. . . . Then he remembered the days of old, Moses, and his people, saying, Where is he that brought them up out of the sea with the shepherd of his flock? where is he that put his holy Spirit within him?"

According to Numbers 24:2, Balaam, from far-away Mesopotamia, experienced the "spirit of God" coming upon him as he spoke of Israel's place of favor before God. And Joshua, who succeeded Moses, is twice said to have been indwelt by the Spirit. Numbers 27:18 records God's instructions to Moses, "Take thee Joshua the son of Nun, a man in whom is the spirit, and lay thine hand upon him"; and Deuteronomy 34:9 states directly, "And Joshua the son of Nun was full of the spirit of wisdom."

[1] For discussion of this "problem passage," see chap. 9, p. 93; chap. 10, p. 111; chap. 11, pp. 113,114.

The next group of passages all refer to certain of the judges as being filled by the Spirit. Four judges are said to have had this experience: Othniel, "And the Spirit of the LORD came upon him, and he judged Israel" (Judg. 3:10); Gideon, "But the Spirit of the LORD came upon Gideon, and he blew a trumpet; and Abi-ezer was gathered after him" (6:34); Jephthah, "Then the Spirit of the LORD came upon Jephthah" (11:29) after which he went on to win over the Ammonites; and Samson, "And the spirit of the LORD began to move him at times in the camp of Dan between Zorah and Eshtaol" (13:25; cf. 14:6,19; 15:14).

C. The United Monarchy

Several references occur in respect to Israel's first king, Saul — references which will be cause for considerable discussion later in the book. The first occurs in 1 Samuel 10:6,10 where, prior to his time of rule, Saul experienced the "Spirit of the LORD" come upon him and he was "turned into another man" (v. 6), as he "prophesied" along with a "company of prophets" (v. 10). A somewhat similar occasion is mentioned in 1 Samuel 19:18-24 where, after Saul had become king, he experienced the "Spirit of God" come upon him and he "stripped off his clothes" and "lay down naked" the rest of that day and the following night (vv. 23,24). In between these two occasions, just before his significant victory over the Ammonites at Jabesh-gilead, the "Spirit of God" came upon him, and he won the battle (11:6). Then in 1 Samuel 16:14, the sad indication is given, "But the Spirit of the LORD departed from Saul." In place of God's Spirit now an "evil spirit" came (16:14), with the result that Saul's rule became severely troubled and the kingdom deteriorated in strength.

The first reference to David and the Spirit comes when David was still a young man. Immediately after Samuel anointed him as Israel's next king, the indication is given that the "Spirit of the LORD came upon David from that day forward" (1 Sam. 16:13). David recognized that God's Spirit rested continually on him, as shown by numerous other references: Psalm 51:10, where David prays, "Take not thy holy spirit from me" (cf. 51:12); Psalm 139:7, where he asks, "Whither shall I go from thy spirit?"; Psalm 143:10, where he requests of God, "Teach me to do thy will; for thou art my God: thy spirit is good"; 1 Chronicles 28:12, where David gives Solomon the pattern for the projected temple, and the indication is that David had this "by the spirit"; and finally 2 Samuel 23:2, where at the close of his life, the great king looks back and says, "The Spirit of the LORD spake by me, and his word was in my tongue." One reference of another kind occurs in connection with Amassai, a chief captain of a group of fighting men who came to David when in flight from Saul. Of him it is said that "the spirit came upon" him with the result that he spoke words of loyalty and comfort to David (1 Chron. 12:18).

Only one reference in respect to Solomon is found. It occurs in Proverbs 1:23 where, speaking in behalf of God, he gives the divine admonition, "Turn you at my reproof; behold, I will pour out my spirit unto you."

D. The Divided Monarchy

The period of the divided monarchy saw a marked increase of ministry through prophets, and numerous references relate this ministry to God's Spirit. At one time the prophet Azariah gave words of encouragement to Asa, king of Judah; and 2 Chronicles 10:1 says that the "Spirit of God" came upon the prophet in doing so. Later, in the reign of Jehoshaphat, the "Spirit of the LORD" came upon the young prophet, Jahaziel, and he gave words of encouragement to this monarch (2 Chron. 20:14). And in the reign of Joash, following the death of the godly high priest, Jehoiada, the "Spirit of God" came on Zechariah, son of Jehoiada, for the purpose of warning the king and his advisers concerning sins they had committed following the death of the high priest (2 Chron. 24:20).

A few references occur in respect to Elijah and Elisha. The first comes from the lips of Obadiah, a chief assistant to King Ahab, when, on meeting Elijah, he voiced the fear that "the Spirit of the LORD" would carry Elijah away should he, Obadiah, go and tell Ahab that Elijah wanted to see him (1 Kings 18:12). A group of references come at the occasion of Elijah's transport to heaven. At the time, Elijah asked his young assistant, Elisha, what he could do for him before leaving him; the young man requested that he be given "a double portion of" Elijah's "spirit" (2 Kings 2:9). Immediately after, fifty young "sons of the prophets" (training prophets), who had observed not far away, exclaimed, "The spirit of Elijah doth rest on Elisha" (v. 15). Then the same group asked Elisha for permission to make a search for Elijah in the possible event that the "spirit of the LORD" had taken the prophet and "cast him upon some mountain, or into some valley" (v. 16).

One of the earliest writing prophets, Joel, though not speaking of himself as being filled by the Spirit, voices a significant predictive word from God: "And it shall come to pass afterward, that I will pour out my spirit upon all flesh; and your sons and your daughters shall prophesy, your old men shall dream dreams, your young men shall see visions: And also upon the servants and upon the handmaids in those days will I pour out my spirit" (Joel 2:28,29).

Hosea, prophet to the northern nation of Israel, though not speaking of himself as being Spirit-filled, indicates that prophets generally were considered to be thus characterized, as he says, "The prophet is a fool, the spiritual man is mad" (Hos. 9:7). The phrase *spiritual man* is literally "man of the spirit" (*'ish ha-ruah*), and the prophet here expressed his message in terms of popular thinking of the day.

Micah, prophet to Judah, does refer to himself as Spirit-filled, saying, "But truly I am full of power by the spirit of the LORD" (Mic. 3:8). Earlier in his book, he shows himself conscious of the Spirit's work, as he writes, "O thou that art named the house of Jacob, is the spirit of the LORD straitened?" (2:7), and again, "If a man walking in the spirit and falsehood do lie, saying . . ." (2:11).

The great Isaiah does not refer to himself as filled by the Spirit, but he has much to say regarding the Spirit, showing again a strong awareness of the Spirit's ministry. One group of passages speaks of certain attributes of the Spirit: Isaiah 4:4 refers to the "spirit of judgment" and the "spirit of burning"; 11:2 to the "spirit of wisdom and understanding, the spirit of counsel and might, the spirit of knowledge and of the fear of the LORD"; and 28:6 again to the "spirit of judgment." Another group shows Isaiah predicting that Christ, when He would come, would be controlled by the Spirit: Isaiah 11:2 states that the Spirit of the Lord would rest upon Christ; 42:1 that God would put His "spirit upon him"; and 61:1 that the "Spirit of the Lord God" would be upon Him.

A third group indicates that the people of Israel should be similarly controlled: Isaiah 30:1 warns Israel of punishment since the people did not "take counsel" of God's "spirit"; 32:15 states that Israel would suffer trouble "until the spirit be poured upon" the people from on high; 44:3 promises that in the future God would "pour" His "spirit upon" Israel's posterity that they might experience blessing; and

59:21 promises similarly that in a future time God's "spirit" would "not depart out of" Israel's "mouth, nor out of the mouth of" Israel's "seed, nor out of the mouth of" Israel's "seeds' seed . . . from henceforth and for ever."

Still a fourth group indicates that the Spirit was the true superintendent of the universe: Isaiah 34:16 states that at God's command "his spirit" would "gather" the Israelite people back to their land; 40:7 declares that "the grass withereth the flower fadeth: because the spirit of the LORD bloweth upon it"; 40:13 asks rhetorically, "Who hath directed the Spirit of the LORD?"; and 59:19, again in prediction, states that in a future day the "Spirit of the LORD" would "lift up a standard" in Israel's behalf.

Two postexilic passages should also be noticed, for they speak of these preexilic prophets as being empowered by the Spirit. Nehemiah 9:30, speaking of God, declares, "Yet many years didst thou forbear them, and testifiedst against them by thy spirit in thy prophets." And Zechariah 7:12 refers to "the words which the LORD of hosts hath sent in his spirit by the former prophets," which Israel would not obey.

E. Exilic and Postexilic Period

From the time of the Babylonian exile, Ezekiel has much to say regarding God's Spirit. One group of passages indicates that Ezekiel himself was filled by the Spirit: Ezekiel 2:2 gives his own words, "And the spirit entered into me"; 3:24 says similarly, "Then the spirit entered into me"; and 11:5 in the same vein states, "The spirit of the LORD fell upon me." In seven other passages, Ezekiel speaks of the Spirit's transporting him to another place: Ezekiel 3:12 indicates, "Then the spirit took me up"; 3:14, "So the spirit lifted me up"; 8:3, "The spirit lifted me up between the earth and the heaven"; 11:1, "The spirit lifted me up, and brought me unto the east gate of the LORD'S house"; and see also 11:24; 37:1; 43:5. Then in eight other passages, Ezekiel speaks of the Spirit's doing yet other things: Ezekiel 1:12, referring to the "four living creatures," says that "whither the spirit was to go, they went" (cf. 1:20); 1:21 says that "the spirit of the living creature was in the wheels" (cf. 10:17); 36:26,27 sets forth God's promise to Israel, "A new spirit will I put within you . . . I will put my spirit within you"; and see also 37:14 and 39:29.

From the postexilic time, three references occur. Haggai 2:5 gives God's promise to the returned exiles, "According to the word that I covenanted with you when ye came out of Egypt, so my spirit remaineth among you; fear ye not." Zechariah 14:6 states the well-known passage, "Not by might, nor by power, but by my spirit, saith the LORD of hosts." And Zechariah 12:10 refers again to the future as the promise is given, "And I will pour upon the house of David, and upon the inhabitants of Jerusalem, the spirit of grace and of supplications."

4

THE HOLY SPIRIT IN CREATION

Most theological discussions of creation ascribe the work of creation to God, without making any distinction in respect to the persons of the Godhead. Admittedly, the Old Testament itself often does this, or else it speaks of the Father as the Person primarily responsible. In the New Testament, however, there are well-known passages that show the Son's having had an important part, especially John 1:1-3 and Colossians 1:16,17. And there is ample reason for believing that the Holy Spirit played a significant role. The concern of this chapter is to investigate the nature of that role.

A. The Creation of the Universe

1. Evidence that the Holy Spirit had a part in creation.

a. **Scripture passages cited.** There are several Scripture passages that speak of the Holy Spirit's having had a part in the creative work. The most significant is Genesis 1:2, "And the Spirit of God moved upon the face of the waters." The important word here is *moved* (*merahapeth*). The Hebrew form is a piel participle, connoting continued action. The thought in view is well illustrated in Deuteronomy 32:11, where the only other piel form of the word in the Old Testament is found. In this passage God's care of Israel in the wilderness is likened to an eagle *fluttering* over her young in providing for them. The idea of the word in Genesis 1:2, then, is that the Holy Spirit "fluttered over," "took care of," "moved upon" the chaotic state of the world in the interest of bringing order and design. Since the indication comes immediately before the description of the six-day creative activity, the implication is that the work of the six days was performed by the Spirit.

30

The last half of Psalm 33:6 seems to speak similarly, the total verse reading, "By the word of the LORD were the heavens made; and all the host of them by the breath of his mouth." The word for *breath* is again *ruah,* which could well be translated "spirit." The first half of the verse probably refers to the work of the Son in creation, speaking of Him as the "word";[1] and the last half, then, should be understood to refer to the Spirit. So taken, the verse means that all the heavenly bodies were made by a combined effort of the Son and the Spirit. Job 26:13 speaks specifically of the Spirit in this creative work of the starry hosts, stating, "By his spirit he hath garnished the heavens." The word *garnished* carries the thought of beautifying or bringing to a state of order and design.

Isaiah 40:12-14 indicates by implication that the Spirit had a part in creating both the earth and the heavens. The passage first asks, "Who hath measured the waters in the hollow of his hand, and meted out heaven with the span," and then significantly puts the questions: "Who hath directed the spirit of the LORD, or being his counsellor hath taught him? With whom took he counsel and who instructed him . . . and taught him knowledge, and shewed to him the way of understanding?" The thought cannot be missed that it was the Spirit who, without need of outside instruction, did the measuring of the waters and the meting out of heaven.

Then a continuing, providential control over creation is indicated for the Spirit in three other passages. In Job 27:3, Job speaks of his own life's being maintained by the Spirit, stating, "The spirit of God is in my nostrils." In Job 33:4, Elihu similarly refers to his life's having been brought into existence by the Spirit, saying, "The spirit of God hath made me." And in Psalm 104:30, it is animal life that is primarily in view as the psalmist writes, "Thou sendest forth thy spirit, they are created: and thou renewest the face of the earth."[2]

[1]The Son is called the "Word" in John 1:1-3, using the Greek *logos,* the equivalent of the Hebrew *davar* here used, where the context again concerns creation.

[2]Besides these passages, the plural *'elohim* (God) is sometimes used as an argument that the Spirit had a part in creation. The thought is that any time *'elohim* is used to indicate the Creator, the Holy Spirit must be implied as having had a part since the plural form of the word connotes the Trinity (see, for instance, John F. Walvoord, *The Holy Spirit,* p. 39). This manner of argument, however, does not seem justified. The word *'elohim* is more likely merely a plural of importance or majesty. Numerous other Hebrew words also are commonly pluralized (for instance, life, *hayyim,* Gen. 2:7,9, et al.; blood, *damim,* Gen. 4:10,11, et al.; water, *mayim,* Gen. 1:2,6,9, et al.; heaven, *shamayim,* Gen. 1:1,8,9, et al.), all words of importance. Further, even a single false god of the heathen is called *'elohim:* for instance, Baal-zebub, the god of Ekron (2 Kings 1:2).

b. The Holy Spirit is the subject of these passages. Some expositors argue against the force of these passages, pointing out that none of them speak of the Spirit by the fuller designation, Holy Spirit. It is asserted that the passages use only such indications as "spirit of His mouth," "His spirit," "the spirit of the LORD," which they say speak of God's "spirit" only as a consciousness or power of God, not of the Third Person of the Trinity. Several arguments, however, may be raised in opposition.

First, the Old Testament elsewhere, as has been demonstrated, clearly distinguishes the Trinity in three persons — Father, Son, and Holy Spirit. If this were not true, one could see reason in the objection cited; but it is true. Further, in other Old Testament contexts, where no question exists concerning the Holy Spirit as subject, similar designations for Him are found as in these creation contexts.

Second, in the New Testament, where the specific designation "Holy Spirit" is found repeatedly, there are also numerous occasions when reference to the Holy Spirit is by similar designations as in these creation contexts. For instance, Galatians 4:6 speaks of Him as the "Spirit of his Son" and 2 Thessalonians 2:8 as the "Spirit of his mouth." If such expressions are used for the Third Person in the New Testament, one need not take them otherwise when employed in the Old Testament. And that the New Testament writers identified their "Holy Spirit" with the "Spirit of God" of the Old Testament is evident from several passages. For instance, it was their Holy Spirit whom Israel rejected as guide in the wilderness (Acts 7:51); it was their Holy Spirit who was the author of faith in Old Testament believers as well as themselves (2 Cor. 4:13); it was their Holy Spirit who gave Israel instructions for ceremonial service (Heb. 9:8); it was their Holy Spirit who gave revelation through David, Isaiah, and others (Matt. 22:43; Mark. 12:36; Acts 1:16; 28:25; Heb. 10:15); and it was their Holy Spirit who revealed beforehand concerning the "sufferings of Christ" (1 Peter 1:11) and who had moved "holy men of old" in recording all such revelation (2 Peter 1:21).[3]

Third, as already observed, the parallel clauses of Psalm 33:6 give indication to the same end. Because the first clause, "By the word of the LORD were the heavens made," refers to the Second Person, the Son, the second clause, "the host of them by the breath [spirit] of his

[3]For further discussion, see B. B. Warfield, *Biblical Doctrines*, pp. 103, 104.

32

mouth," should be taken in reference to the Third Person.

Fourth, to understand the idea of "spirit" in reference to God as merely His consciousness or power is to characterize God in finite terms, after the pattern of men. It is proper to think of man as having consciousness and power, because man is finite and complex in his constitution. But God is the great infinite Being, who is not distinguishable from His attributes. He *is* consciousness, power, love, glory, and a host of other concepts; He does not *have* them. He is not complex as finite man, but the great eternal Whole, constituting in Himself all that is true, good, and beautiful. Distinctions appropriate for Him are those made by the Scriptures, the distinctions of Father, Son, and Holy Spirit.[4]

2. The nature of the Spirit's work. In view of the passages noted above, the nature of the Spirit's work in creation can be discussed. First, however, the general character of the Spirit's work in the divine economy should again be brought to mind, for one could expect that His creative activity would be in keeping with it. It was noted to consist in the completion and bringing to a state of perfection that which the Son had previously brought to existence, according to the plan and design of the Father. This is seen illustrated in the regeneration of the sinner. The Spirit takes of the eternal life provided by the Son and imparts this to the sinner, then energizes this life so it may become increasingly dominant in the person.

The word *moved (merahapeth)* used in Genesis 1:2 is especially important in this context. It was noted to mean a "fluttering over," or "caring for," the chaotic world, like a mother bird providing for her young. The word does not, then, refer to an act of initial formation from nonexistent substance. Such an act was performed, certainly, for the world is not eternal; it was brought into existence when there was no substance from which to form it. But this act was that of the Son; He created *ex nihilo* (from nothing). The Spirit, however, quite clearly worked with what the Son had already created, fashioning it into the design planned by the Father. It was not that the Son could not have so fashioned it, nor was it that the Spirit could not have created *ex nihilo;* both Persons have adequate power. It was only that in the divine purpose, the Son was to carry the process to one state of fulfillment and the Holy Spirit to another. In terms of Scripture

[4]Similar arguments are set forth by Abraham Kuyper, *The Work of the Holy Spirit,* pp. 28,29.

division, the Son's work is the subject of Genesis 1:1, "In the beginning God created the heavens and the earth," and the Spirit's work the subject of Genesis 1:2-31, where the six days of activity are set forth.[5]

Abraham Kuyper may be right in believing that even the "germs of life" had been brought to existence by the Son, so the Spirit, in imparting life to the animate world, also had this property to use, in addition to material and immaterial substance.[6] If so, the Spirit's work consisted in shaping the many inanimate objects and then the shaping of, and impartation of life to, the animate world. More particularly, His first action was to cause light to shine upon the chaotic world (the Son had no doubt already created the principle of light). Then, in respect to the inanimate world, He divided between atmospheric water and terrestrial water, and later between this terrestrial water and soil here on earth, thus constituting solid ground, aswell as oceans, lakes, and streams. Further, in respect to the animate world, He brought together the necessary substance to fashion grass, trees, and other plant life, with its higher properties than plant life; and He did the same for human life, with its still higher properties, especially in being made in the very image of God (Gen. 1:26,27).

Because the Spirit's work did not involve creation *ex nihilo*, one should not think less of His work. It was of enormous importance. Before He began to work, the world lay in a formless mass, called in Genesis 1:2 a state of being "without form and void" (*tohu wa-bohu*); after He worked everything was fashioned into its respective, perfect form. From chaos had come order, from shapelessness design, from a nonfunctioning universe one that could operate and display the glory of God.

B. The Creation of Man in Particular

1. The Spirit brought man to existence. It has been implied that man was given his form by the Spirit, even as other aspects of creation. This follows from the fact that man was formed on the sixth

---

[5]This is understanding Genesis 1:1 to refer to the initial act of creating the world in a formless mass. Some expositors believe it to constitute a summary of all the creative work of the six days (see, for instance, B. Waltke, "The Creation Account in Genesis 1:1-3," Part II, *Bibliotheca Sacra* 132 [April-June, 1975], 136-144).

[6]Kuyper, *Work of the Holy Spirit*, p. 29.

day, and the Spirit was responsible for the work of all six days.

The fact follows also from three other lines of evidence. One is the statement of Genesis 1:26,27, where the plural pronoun is used, "Let us make man in our image, after our likeness." There is no satisfactory way of accounting for this plural except by taking it as a reference to the Trinity of God. This means that all three Persons were involved in making man after the divine image. The Father evidently planned man's design, the Son brought His constituent elements to existence, and the Holy Spirit gave him the form and nature planned.

The second line of evidence is that it is the Spirit who always is the particular Person of the Trinity who makes any contact with man that the Godhead sees necessary. This happens at man's regeneration and sanctification. The Spirit imparts the new life of regeneration and brings it to fruition. This even happened when Christ the Son became incarnate. It was the Spirit who prepared the body in the womb of the human mother, Mary (Luke 1:35), and it was the Spirit, given to Christ without measure (1 John 3:34), who directed and empowered Him in His divine-human activity (see Matt. 4:1; 12:28; Luke 2:27; 4:14,18). It is logical, then, to think of the Spirit's being the one who did the work of fashioning man into his designed state, truly an occasion of divine contact with man.

Finally, the third evidence is the direct indication of passages already noted from Job. In 27:3, Job says, "The spirit of God is in my nostrils," and in 33:4 Elihu states that "the spirit of God" had made him. Both men seem to have been referring to their own lives, but, if the Spirit was responsible for their lives, it follows that He was responsible for man's first life in Adam.

2. The work performed. Genesis 2:7 tells what the Spirit did in making man: "And the LORD God formed man of the dust of the ground, and breathed into his nostrils the breath of life; and man became a living soul." Two basic actions are indicated: a formation of man's body from material substance and the impartation of the life principle, both of which had already been brought to existence. When the life principle was imparted, the result was a "living soul," or human being. The same two actions may well have been in Elihu's mind when he said, "The Spirit of God hath made me," and "the breath of the Almighty hath given me life."

Though the life principle had already been imparted to plant and animal life, life at the same level was not necessarily now given to man. Life that plants possess enables them to perform certain functions, such as grow, make leaves, turn their flowers to the light, etc.; while the life animals possess enables them to do more complex things, such as walk, make noise, respond to actions of other life forms, etc. The life man possesses, however, enables him to do and be much more. In his doing, he has the power of self-consciousness, rational process, and spiritual awareness; in being, he is immortal — so, though his body suffers decay, man himself lives on, never to cease — and he is made in the very image of God. So, then, if the Son brought the life principle to existence in the original creation, as well as all substance, He must have done so in all its three earthly categories, and it must be that the Spirit now took of the highest category and imparted it to man. He had already used the first two in the formation of plants and animals.

Though the Spirit's work in fashioning man may be distinguished in the two parts noted, one need not believe that these two parts were separated in time of accomplishment. It is not likely that man's body was formed first and then, after an intervening period, the life principle imparted. Probably no time elapsed when one would have seen man's body lying inert on the ground, waiting for life. More likely, both actions were effected simultaneously, as one.

3. **Man as thus fashioned.** As thus given form by the Spirit, man began as a fully developed adult. He did not have to grow in physical stature, nor did he have to develop in intellectual ability or knowledge. He was never a child. No indication or implication is given that he had to grow. Rather, he was sufficiently mature to be in need of a wife. In that connection, God first instructed him to name all the kinds of animals, thus giving him opportunity to consider these other created life forms. He did this, but found no "helpmeet" (lit. "a helper corresponding to him") among them. Then God (specifically, again, the Spirit, no doubt) made woman from a part of his body. Being thus in need of a wife, he was an adult in physical and emotional make-up, and being able to name the kinds of animals, he was intellectually mature.

A most significant factor in man's formation is that he was made in the image of God. In Genesis 1:26, God is heard to say, "Let us make man in our image, after our likeness"; and in 1:27 the action is asserted, "So God created man in his own image, in the image of God created he him; male and female created he them." The two words

36

image and *likeness* are probably used synonymously for emphasis,[7] so that no distinction need be drawn between them. The meaning of the thought these were intended to convey, however, is important to identify. It may be divided into two main categories.

The first concerns man's being. Man was created a personality. That is, he was a finite replica of the infinite Personality of God. As a personality, he was essentially spiritual (as against material), and he was invisible and immortal. He was a rational and moral being, with the powers of intellect, emotion, and will. He possessed self-consciousness and the ability of self-determination. The second category concerns the intellectual and moral integrity of man's being. This revealed itself as true knowledge, righteousness, and holiness (Eph. 4:24; Col. 3:10). Man, then, was not created innocent, in a state of moral neutrality. He did not have to do something in order to *become* righteous. He was righteous as made. This seems to be implied in the term *very good* of Genesis 1:31, which refers back to all that had been fashioned, and also in the term *upright* as used in Ecclesiastes 7:29. Man was created with "knowledge" of truth, as God knew and willed it, with "righteousness" in that he acted in accordance with that truth, and with "holiness" in that he possessed a character that was itself, and desired to act, in accordance with that truth.

Another noteworthy factor true of man at his formation was that he was susceptible to the control of the Spirit who had formed him, without the hindrance of sin's influence that exists for regenerated man today. It is sometimes asserted that regenerated man lives at a higher plane of God-pleasing experience than Adam before the Fall. In one sense this is true. Adam did not yet have unlosable spiritual life; he was not eternally secure as a child of God. That is why he could lose that life, as he did, at his fall in the Garden of Eden. Regenerated man does have eternal life, received from Christ, the fully successful "Second Adam."

In respect to holiness of character, however, Adam was at a higher plane. He had no sinful nature that causes a battle within the Christian today (see Rom. 7:15-25). Because of the Fall, man's faculties and

[7]This follows from the fact that the two words elsewhere are used quite interchangeably. In Genesis 1:27 only *image* is used, in 5:1 only *likeness*, in 5:3 only *image* again, and in 9:6, both terms once more; then in the New Testament Col. 3:10 uses only *image*, while James 3:9 employs only *likeness*. The same idea seems to be in mind whichever term is employed in any of these passages.

inclinations became impaired and his passions corrupt. At regeneration, man receives the Holy Spirit, but the Spirit must come to him from without. Therefore, the Christian can hinder the work of the Holy Spirit in his life, "quenching" (1 Thess. 5:19) and "grieving" (Eph. 4:30) Him. Since Adam's personality was created morally perfect, however, the Holy Spirit could work through his natural faculties without hindrance. It was for this reason that direct communication with God was possible in the Garden of Eden (Gen. 1:28; 2:16).[8] It was natural then for man to talk with God.[9]

[8]This communication did and could continue temporarily after the Fall (Gen. 3:8-19), for there was need that man realize the seriousness of his action in eating the forbidden fruit. After that general time, however, occasions of revelation to man could only occur on a supernatural basis, and then only because, first, those contacted were regenerated on the basis of Christ's atoning work, and, second, there was need for revelation of God's truth into the realm of man.

[9]For further discussion, see Kuyper, *Work of the Holy Spirit*, pp. 34, 35.

5

OLD TESTAMENT PEOPLE ON WHOM
THE SPIRIT CAME

The Holy Spirit not only had an important part in the creation of man, but He had a vital work in respect to man thus created. As noted, most discussions of that work are based on the New Testament. When references are made to the Holy Spirit in the Old Testament, the interest is usually limited to noting that His existence is recognized in certain passages. Little is said relative to the nature of His work as manifested in these passages.

As observed in chapter 1, when the Spirit's work in the Old Testament is discussed at all, it is done usually in terms of His coming on people and leaving them. This is often taken to mean, among other things, that the Spirit, therefore, did not permanently indwell believers, as in New Testament time. Lewis Chafer, for instance, states, "The Spirit is not said to indwell all Old Testament saints who were counted as the covenant people of God," and he cites as evidence the fact that Nicodemus seemed to be at a loss to understand Christ's meaning in respect to regeneration (John 3:8-12).[1] J. Oswald Sanders states in similar vein, "On the day of Pentecost . . . the Holy Spirit came to earth to achieve man's regeneration and to fit him for life as a child of God."[2] But if the Old Testament saint was not permanently

[1] Lewis S. Chafer, *Systematic Theology*, I, pp. 407,408. For later discussion of the Nicodemus passage, see chapter 8, pp. 82-84.

[2] J. Oswald Sanders, *The Holy Spirit and His Gifts*, p. 48. Herbert Lockyer (*All the Doctrines of the Bible*, p. 68) states, as he speaks of the Holy Spirit in the Old Testament, "Yet His incoming was more of an inworking than an indwelling. Remaining among men, He did not abide with them (cf. Psalm 51:11; Haggai 2:5)." See also Walvoord, *Holy Spirit*, pp. 155,230.

indwelt by the Spirit, how was he able to remain a child of God? The New Testament is clear that believers now are preserved by the indwelling Spirit (2 Tim. 1:12; 4:18; 1 Peter 1:5). Were Old Testament saints able to keep themselves? It is not easy to believe so.

Closely related to the nature of the Spirit's work in the Old Testament is the question of the change that came at Pentecost. The Scriptures teach that the day of Pentecost, following Christ's resurrection, did mark the beginning of the church; and the Holy Spirit is definitely said to have come on its first members that day (Acts 2). Also, Christ Himself stated that when the Spirit would come these people would be empowered in a way not known before (Acts 1:8). The question rises, therefore, what kind of power did believers then receive? What did the Spirit then begin to do in and through them that He had not done before? Such terms as the following are commonly used of the Spirit's work after Pentecost: *regeneration, indwelling, sealing, filling, empowering,* and *baptism.* The question more specifically, then, is: Which, if any, of these functions were already carried on in Old Testament time by the Holy Spirit and which began only at Pentecost?[3]

An answer to these questions can only be determined after all Old Testament passages that involve the Spirit's work have been studied. Passages mainly concerned are those which speak of one or more persons' having the Spirit either come on or leave them. It will be necessary to note these passages and then make a judgment regarding the meaning in each case. In other words, the interest will be in asking in what sense the Spirit came on or left the persons concerned.

In this chapter, the interest is only in identifying the passages and occasions involved, with a brief indication of the type of work done by the Holy Spirit in each instance. The following chapter will enlarge on the type of work carried out. The people involved in these instances fall into four general classifications.

---

[3]W.B. Pope (*A Compendium of Christian Theology,* II, p. 329) speaks of the work of the Holy Spirit, following Pentecost, as follows: "His internal function is the exercise of Divine power on the heart, or within the soul: to the unconverted in infusing the grace of penitence and the power of faith, issuing in an effectual inward conversion; to the believer in renewing the soul by communication of a new spiritual life, and carrying on the entire work of sanctification." For Pope, then, both regeneration and sanctification are works solely of the New Testament age. J. D. Pentecost (*Things to Come,* p. 263) lists the following ministries of the Holy Spirit as true only in this New Testament age: baptism, indwelling, sealing, and filling.

A. Judges

The first classification is that of the judges of Israel, who were raised up by God in years preceding the introduction of Israel's monarchy. Four are said to have had the Spirit come upon them.

The first was Othniel (Judg. 3:10): "The Spirit of the LORD came [*hayah*, "was"] upon him, and he judged Israel and went out to war." The result was that the current enemy of Israel, Cushan-rishathaim of Mesopotamia, was defeated and Israel had "rest forty years" (3:11).

The second judge to have the Spirit come on him was Gideon (Judg. 6:34): "But the Spirit of the LORD came [*labash*, "clothed"] upon Gideon, and he blew a trumpet; and Abi-ezer was gathered after him." This time the result was a gathering of no less than 32,000 men from the tribes of Manasseh, Asher, Zebulun, and Naphtali to Gideon, for the purpose of fighting the enemy of Gideon's time, the Midianites (cf. 7:3).

The third judge was Jephthah (Judg. 11:29): "Then the Spirit of the LORD came [*hayah*, "was"] upon Jephthah, and he passed over Gilead. . . ." The result on this occasion was that Jephthah was enabled to gather a fighting force, as he traveled through much of the land for the purpose, and then to inflict a sound defeat on the enemy of his time, the Ammonites.

The fourth was Samson, who four times experienced the Spirit coming on him. Judges 13:25 says, "And the Spirit of the LORD began to move [*pa'am*, "impel"] him at times in the camp of Dan between Zorah and Eshtaol." This may have been the time when Samson first experienced his endowment of supernatural power. Judges 14:6 states, "And the spirit of the LORD came mightily [*tsalah*, "overpower"] upon him, and he rent him [a lion] as he would have rent a kid." Judges 14:19 says, "And the spirit of the LORD came [*tsalah*, "overpower"] upon him, and he went down to Ashkelon, and slew thirty men." And Judges 15:14 states, "And the spirit of the LORD came mightily [*tsalah*, "overpower"] upon him, and the cords that were upon his arms became as flax that was burnt with fire, and his bands loosed from off his hands." The last three times all involved actions calling for a display of great strength.

An evaluation of these texts shows that all involved empowerment for a physical activity. None of them had to do with salvation from sin in any sense, so that any of the "spiritual" concepts mentioned above (regeneration, indwelling, sealing, etc.) were involved.

B. Craftsmen

The second classification concerns men who were involved in a craft. Bezaleel was the first of these, chosen by God to work on the tabernacle. Of him, God said, "I have filled [*male'*, "fill"] him with the spirit of God, in wisdom, and in understanding, and in knowledge, and in all manner of workmanship" (Exod. 31:3; cf. 35:31). The purpose was that Bezaleel might "devise cunning works, to work in gold, and in silver, and in brass, and in cutting of stones, to set them, and in carving of timber, to work in all manner of workmanship" (31:4,5). Another skilled worker, Aholiab, was assigned to work with Bezaleel, besides others unnamed, and probably the Spirit was similarly given to all these, for God said of them, "And in the hearts of all that are wise hearted I have put wisdom, that they may make all that I have commanded" (v.6).[4]

The second craftsman was David, to whom God gave the plans for the later temple. First Chronicles 28:11,12 states, "Then David gave to Solomon his son . . . the pattern of all that he had [*hayah*, "was"] by the Spirit, of the courts of the house of the LORD." The statement that David had these plans "by the spirit" can only mean that the Spirit had controlled his thoughts in forming them. God had given the plans for the tabernacle supernaturally to Moses years·before, and so one should only expect that God would have been equally interested in giving those for the temple.

The third was Hiram, the counterpart of Bezaleel, for working on the temple. An explicit reference to the Spirit does not occur regarding him, as it does regarding Bezaleel, but the implication seems clear enough in 1 Kings 7:13,14, "And king Solomon sent and fetched Hiram out of Tyre . . . a worker in brass: and he was filled with wisdom and understanding, and cunning to work all works of brass." The verb for *filled* is *male'*, just as with Bezaleel, and it is here in the Niphal form (passive) indicating that an action was wrought upon him. In view of the context, the only likely way for him thus to be wrought upon was by being "filled" by the Spirit.

An evaluation of these occasions of the Spirit coming on people shows again an aspect of empowerment or enablement for an activity.

[4]In keeping with this are God's words as He speaks of those who should make the priestly garments, calling them "wise hearted, whom I have filled with the spirit of wisdom" (Exod. 28:3). The phrase "spirit of wisdom" is the same as used of Joshua (Deut. 34:9) and predictively of Christ (Isa. 11:2), where surely the Holy Spirit is in view.

The type of activity required of craftsmen was quite different from that involving the judges. These men did not raise armies or fight battles, yet they still performed a service. Both Bezaleel and Hiram worked with their hands in making things, and David worked with his mind in planning a building. Thus again the work of the Spirit with all three had nothing to do with salvation from sin or any of the "spiritual" concepts mentioned earlier.

C. Prophets

The third classification concerns prophets. More passages exist under this classification, and they call for more discussion than those of the prior two. It will be helpful to divide the discussion between prophets said to have been filled only temporarily and those implied to have been filled continuously.

1. Prophets filled temporarily. This first group of prophets appear to have been filled only for a particular time of activity, after the pattern of the first two groups noted. The type of activity differed, but not the temporariness of the Spirit's empowerment. The implication regarding all three is that the Spirit came upon the persons involved for the activity concerned and then left them when that activity had been completed.

The first of these prophets was Azariah, of the reign of Asa, king of Judah. Asa had just won a significant victory over Zerah the Ethiopian, and when Asa returned to Jerusalem, "the Spirit of God came [*hayah*, "was"] upon Azariah the son of Oded," and he brought a message from God to the returning victor (2 Chron. 15:1-7). The message contained words of both encouragement and advice.

The second was Jahaziel, of the reign of Asa's son and successor, Jehoshaphat. News had just reached Jehoshaphat concerning an invasion of three nations from the east, the Moabites, Ammonites, and Edomites (2 Chron. 20:1,22,23); and Jehoshaphat called for a fast in Jerusalem and there before all who gathered he offered a prayer of entreaty. In response to the prayer, "upon Jahaziel . . . came [*hayah*, "was"] the spirit of the LORD in the midst of the congregation" and he spoke a message of both encouragement and instruction, including the well-known, significant words, "The battle is not yours, but God's" (20:14-17).

The third prophet was Zechariah (not the later-writing prophet), of the reign of Joash, following the death of the godly high priest,

Jehoiada, Zechariah's father. As long as Jehoiada, Joash's adviser, had lived, the young king had done well, but after Jehoiada's death sinful counselors were able to influence him to adopt sinful ways. The result was that "the spirit of God came [*labash*, "clothed"] upon Zechariah" to give a message of rebuke to the king (2 Chron. 24:20). The king then had Zechariah stoned to death.

Fourth was the non-Israelite prophet, Balaam. Chronologically, he lived earlier than the three just considered, but because he was not an Israelite — in fact he lived far north in Mesopotamia (Deut. 23:4) — it is best to list him separately from those who were. At the time of Israel's conquest of Canaan, still before the actual crossing of the Jordan River, Balaam was summoned by the Moabite king, Balak, to come and "curse"[5] Israel. Balaam came but then pronounced blessings on the nation, rather than curses, much to Balak's disgust. After doing this three times, from three different places, Balaam began to speak more extensively concerning Israel and the blessings God had in store for this people. Before he gave these later words, the significant indication is given, "And the spirit of God came [*hayah*, "was"] upon him" (Num. 24:2).

The fifth person, Amassai, also preceded the three prophets of Israel mentioned, but he is properly considered separate from them for he was not really a prophet. He was a military man, who had led a group of fighters from the tribes of Benjamin and Judah to help David while in flight from Saul. Surprisingly, it is said of him, at the time his group came to David, that "the spirit came [*labash*, "clothed"] upon" him, with the result that he gave a message of introduction to David and promised the allegiance of his group (1 Chron. 12:18).

The activity involved for each of these five people was speaking a message for God. The Spirit of God came upon them in connection with this action, clearly enabling them in regard to it. An evaluation of the occasions, then, once more shows an aspect of empowerment or enablement for an activity. This activity had nothing to do with the salvation of the persons concerned and therefore not with any of the "spiritual" concepts in view.

2. Prophets filled continuously. The five men just discussed comprise the full list of prophets who are said to have had the Spirit come

---

[5]It was thought that such a curse would weaken the one cursed; cf. Egyptian execration texts, *Ancient Near Eastern Texts*, 2nd ed. (Princeton, NJ: Princeton University Press, 1955), pp. 328,329.

on them at the time of giving a prophetic-type message. The question immediately arises, What about the other prophets? Were they not also empowered by the Spirit? Why should these five people — two of whom were not even Israelite prophets — have been empowered, if the great prophets (like Amos, Hosea, Isaiah, Jeremiah, et al.) were not? This question, though it is only indirectly related to the particular subject at hand, calls for consideration.

The following discussion will show that these prophets were Spirit-empowered, but in a continuous manner, rather than temporarily as the five noted. It will also present a rationale for the reason why these prophets are not said to have had the Spirit come on them, as the five mentioned; and it will present further evaluation of the manner and purpose of their Spirit-empowerment.

a. Evidence that most prophets were empowered continuously. In giving evidence for continuous Spirit-empowerment for these prophets, another distinction between prophets must be made. Some of these prophets have direct indications given regarding them that they were continuously Spirit-empowered, while most do not. We will consider the former group first and show how this direct indication is presented.

1) *Prophets said to have been Spirit-empowered.* The prophets now to be discussed do not fall in the category of the five mentioned earlier, for the indication of Spirit-empowerment of the two groups is not the same in kind. This will become clear as each is considered.

The first to notice are Elijah and Elisha, both of whom ministered in the ninth century B.C., well before the first of the writing prophets. They were both of major importance, however, and the ministry of prophecy was the life occupation of each.

Evidence that both were continuously Spirit-empowered comes from the account of Elijah's transformation to heaven (2 Kings 2). Elijah, knowing that he was about to be taken from the earth-scene, asked his devoted helper, Elisha, what he could do for him before leaving him. Elisha answered with the important words, "I pray thee, let a double portion of thy spirit be upon me" (v.9). That Elisha was indeed speaking about God's Spirit in this answer is indicated by words given shortly after by fifty young prophets who had been observing. They said, "The spirit of Elijah doth rest on Elisha," and then, again, "Peradventure the spirit of the LORD hath taken" Elijah up and "cast him upon some mountain, or into some valley" (vv. 15,16).

45

This request of Elisha, that he be given a "double portion" of the Spirit that had been upon Elijah, indicates two important factors in Elisha's thinking: First, he recognized that Elijah's great work of prior days — for which God was now honoring him by this remarkable translation to heaven — had been due to the Spirit's empowerment; and, second, he now, being at the point of taking over the work in his master's place, needed to have this same special provision if he were to do so. Such thinking implies, among other things, that Elisha believed Elijah's Spirit-empowerment had been continuous and that he desired his own to be of the same kind.

Micah was one of two prophets who directly stated in his book that he was empowered by the Spirit, and he did so in words which again connote continuous filling. Micah 3:8 reads, "But truly I am full [*male'*, "fill"] of power by the spirit of the LORD." It should be noticed that Micah did not say merely, "I am being filled," or that "the Spirit of the LORD came upon me." He used the perfect form of the verb to show that the Spirit's filling had occurred sometime in the past, and the context indicates his recognition that this filling was still true of him at the time of his writing. In other words, he was aware that he was continuously filled by the Spirit.

In remarkable contrast to the other writing prophets, Ezekiel has much to say regarding his relation to God's Spirit. He thus gives indication of having been unusually conscious of his dependence on the Spirit for his work. For instance, in 2:2 he says, "The spirit entered [*bo'*, "come"] into me" with the result that he was given important instructions regarding his work. In 8:3 he says again, "The spirit lifted me up" and then brought him in vision to Jerusalem. References of this kind continue as one reads on in his book, as he speaks of the Spirit entering into him,[6] transporting him to some locality, or having some other relation to his ministry. Such consciousness of the work of the Spirit is consistent only with the fact that Ezekiel was continuously empowered by the Spirit and that he was unusually aware of it.

2) Prophets not said to have been Spirit-empowered. We now come to speak of prophets who are not said to have been empowered

---

[6]Though Ezekiel does speak of the Spirit entering into him, somewhat in parallel with statements by the five persons mentioned earlier, his manner of doing so differs from theirs in that it does not imply merely temporary infilling. And the fact that Ezekiel mentions the Spirit in so many other ways in connection with his ministry adds further evidence that he did not consider himself only temporarily filled.

by the Spirit, and this is a much larger group. It includes the great writing prophets, Isaiah, Jeremiah, Hosea, Joel, Amos, Obadiah, Jonah, Nahum, Habakkuk, Zephaniah, Haggai, Zechariah, and Malachi. Four of these do use the term *Spirit*, but not in a way to indicate His empowerment of themselves. The four are Isaiah (e.g., 4:4; 11:2; 19:14; et al.), Hosea (9:7), Haggai (2:5), and Zechariah (4:6; 7:12).

Evidence that these prophets were continuously Spirit-empowered, though not directly claiming it by statement, is found in two directions.

The first direction is that of definite statements by two postexilic writers that prophets of preexilic time were so empowered, implying that this was continuous. Zechariah is the first of the two. Writing shortly after the first return from the Babylonian captivity, he talks about sin in general of preexilic Israel, and then he speaks particularly of the people's unwillingness to hear "the words which the LORD of hosts hath sent in his spirit by the former prophets" (7:12). Nehemiah is the other one. Writing about seventy-five years after Zechariah,[7] he also speaks of the sin of preexilic Israel and in that connection says of God, "Yet many years didst thou forbear them, and testifiedst against them by thy spirit in thy prophets" (9:30). It should be recognized that neither of these men refers to any particular group of prophets; the implication is that all the well-known preexilic prophets were empowered by the Spirit in their ministry. The indication is clear that they believed this empowerment was continuous.

The other direction is that of a comparison with other important people in the life of Israel, who are indicated to have been continuously Spirit-empowered. This involved especially people who held public office. These people and the way in which Scripture shows that they were continually empowered will be considered in the next section. Now it need only be said that, if at least a few prophets and a significant number of civil officials were continuously empowered, the fact is established that God did so provide for people who held important positions, and, since prophets surely can be so classified, the probability of their empowerment becomes strong.

b. Rationale for the absence of the mention of Spirit-empowerment. We come now to consider the rationale behind this

---

[7]Zechariah wrote after 520 B.C. and Nehemiah after 445 B.C.

absence of mention concerning Spirit-empowerment by so many of the prophets. Why did they not say directly that they were so empowered, if they were? The answer lies in another distinction among the prophets that must be drawn. That is the distinction between those who have been seen as only temporarily empowered and those continuously so. Five persons, only three of whom were Israelite prophets, were seen among the first group, and all the writing prophets besides others among the second. Why should the one group have been only temporarily empowered and the other continuously?

The answer lies in a consideration of relative importance. The latter group was simply more important as prophets in God's program than the former. Because they were, they needed a continuous enablement, while the others needed special power only for an occasion. Of the three Israelite prophets in the first group (Azariah, Jahaziel, and Zechariah), none of them are mentioned in the sacred record other than the one time. It may well be that God saw each of them in need of Spirit-empowerment only for that time. The great writing prophets, however, and others like Elijah and Elisha were in constant need of special help. They were full-time prophets, occupied daily with divinely assigned tasks. Therefore they had a continuous need for Spirit-empowerment and God met them in that need.

This distinction between the two groups of prophets makes possible an answer to the first question. The reason why so many of the regular prophets did not call attention to their personal endowment with the Spirit is probably because they did not see any need to do so. They were full-time prophets and were therefore continuously Spirit-empowered. More than that, there was no time in their prophetic experience[8] when they could say, "And the spirit of God came upon me," as in the case of Azariah, Jahaziel, or Zechariah. He was continuously on them; He did not need to come on them just because they had to give a special message or perform a special mission. And the people seemed to realize this. Hosea 9:7, using language of the average person in Israel, refers to a prophet as a "spiritual man" (lit. "man of the Spirit," 'ish ha-ruah). Also, both Zechariah's (7:12) and Nehemiah's (9:30) references noted above, to

---

[8]The first coming could well have been contemporary with their call, and this coming was probably not of a nature that lent itself to a special mention.

preexilic prophets' being empowered by the Spirit, are each in the vein of knowledge commonly known and understood.

c. Evaluation. As with the first two groups, the judges and craftsmen, Spirit-empowerment for the prophets again had to do with an activity and not with an inward change of their own hearts. This was true for both those temporarily filled and those continuously filled. It is true that their work had to do more with spiritual matters than that of the first two groups. The prophets received revelation from God and delivered God's message to people, and these functions concerned spiritual truth. This was spiritual truth, however, that had to do with the relationship of others to God, rather than themselves. The Spirit did not empower prophets that they might themselves be brought into a right relationship with God.

D. Civil Administrators

The fourth classification of people is civil administrators, and evidence exists that these also enjoyed the provision of Spirit-empowerment on a continuous basis.

Taking the group historically again, the first to notice is Moses. That he was Spirit-empowered is made clear from the account of the seventy elders being similarly empowered in the wilderness. In Numbers 11:17, God is heard to say, "I will take of the spirit which is upon thee [Moses], and will put it upon them [the seventy]; and they shall bear the burden of the people with thee." It is evident that God considered Moses already to have the Spirit on him, and now the Spirit was to rest also on these helpers. One must believe, then, that Moses was Spirit-empowered continuously, and that this condition had existed for many years. One must believe also that these seventy helpers now became continuously Spirit-empowered in parallel to him. It may be noted also that Isaiah, years later, gives evidence that Moses was Spirit-empowered. In his book (63:10-12) the prophet speaks of the sin of the Israelites while in the wilderness and then refers to the "holy spirit within" Moses, "that led them by the right hand of Moses with his glorious arm."

The second to notice is Joshua, who succeeded Moses. Numbers 27:18 falls in a context in which Joshua is selected to be Israel's new leader, and here God tells Moses, "Take thee Joshua the son of Nun, a man in whom is the spirit, and lay thine hand upon him." This reference to "spirit" is sometimes taken by expositors as merely an indication of natural insight and wisdom or a higher power breathed into Joshua's soul by God,[9] but these suggestions do not do the word or its context justice. It is true that the word does not have the article, but it does not always have the article when referring to the Spirit of God (cf. 1 Chron. 12:18), and here Joshua is being selected to be Israel's next leader, in the pattern of Moses. If Moses was endowed with the Spirit, one should only expect that his successor would have to be. Then a similar indication is given in Deuteronomy 34:9, "And Joshua the son of Nun was full of the spirit of wisdom." The phrase "spirit of wisdom" is the exact phrase used prophetically of Christ in Isaiah 11:2, where reference is surely to the Holy Spirit. Christ was to be given "wisdom" by the Spirit, and so was Joshua.

Third is Israel's first king, Saul, who was also the first national ruler following Joshua.[10] In 1 Samuel 11:6, where the context concerns Saul's battle with the Ammonites at Jabesh-gilead, the significant words occur, "And the Spirit of God came (*tsalah*, "overcome") upon Saul when he heard those tidings" of the need of the people of Jabesh-gilead. The result was that he gathered a huge army and won a brilliant victory over the enemy. The occasion made possible the actual establishment of his kingdom, and he did begin to rule shortly thereafter. Then in 1 Samuel 16:14, after Saul's second rejection as king (1 Sam. 13:11-14; 15:26-28), it is said that "the Spirit of the LORD departed from Saul." If the Spirit "departed" from him at this time, it follows that the Spirit had been continuously on him previously. The logical time when that continuous empowerment began would be the occasion just mentioned of his coming on Saul prior to the Jabesh-gilead battle.

It should be noted, in passing, that the Spirit is said to have come upon Saul still earlier than this: at the time of his prophesying with the company of prophets in accordance with Samuel's prediction (1 Sam. 10:6,10). In view of the manner of this occasion, however, and also because the Spirit is said to have come on him again prior to the Jabesh-gilead battle, one may believe that this earlier occasion was only temporary.[11]

[9]For references, see J. P. Lange, *Numbers* in *A Commentary on the Holy Scriptures*, p. 156.

[10]After Joshua came the judges, but they were not national rulers in the sense of Moses, Joshua, or the kings of the monarchy. Even Samuel did not hold such an office.

[11]See discussions, chapter 10, pp. 105, 106; chapter 11, p. 114.

The last to notice is Israel's second king, the great David. In 1 Samuel 16:13, the verse immediately preceding that which tells of the Spirit's departing from Saul, the statement is made, "And the spirit of the LORD came upon David from that day forward." The last four words, "from that day forward," are particularly significant; they indicate that the young man then became continuously empowered. The occasion involved was the anointing of David by Samuel as Israel's future king, which makes the statement even more meaningful. This continuous empowerment was in anticipation of that rule, enabling him in ways appropriate until that time and then to make him the finest ruler possible.

In keeping with this thought are the words of David in Psalm 51:11: "Take not thy holy spirit from me." These words have often been misunderstood; some even believe that David was requesting that he not lose his personal salvation.[12] But David was not thinking of this; he simply did not want to lose the special Spirit-empowerment that had been his from the day of his anointing by Samuel. He had seen Saul lose his empowerment when the Holy Spirit had been taken from him — his manner of rule had rapidly deteriorated after that — and he did not want the same to happen to him. The words indicate, then, his recognition of continuous Spirit-empowerment.

Still a third statement, made by David at the close of his life, points to the same conclusion. He said "The Spirit of the LORD spake by me." David was aware at this late time, then, that the Spirit had not left him — at the time he had earlier asked in Psalm 51:11 — and that the Spirit had empowered him in his writing. Further passages to which reference could be made are: Psalms 139:7; 143:10; Matthew 22:43; Mark 12:36; Acts 1:16.

Finally, an evaluation shows that this group of people were also empowered by the Spirit for an area of service and not in respect to a personal relationship to God. They were all administrators over God's people and they were enabled that they might be effective administrators. One might argue that Saul experienced spiritual salvation at the time of the Spirit's coming on him prior to the Jabesh-gilead battle, but this is not likely. The Spirit had already come on him temporarily, as observed, and also Samuel had anointed him to be king even before that (1 Sam. 10:1). It is hard to believe that

---

[12]For instance, H. C. Leupold (*Exposition of Psalms* [Grand Rapids: Baker, 1970], p. 405) writes of this text, "In the mind of the writer the loss of the Spirit means the total loss of God's grace."

God would have directed a person to be anointed whom He did not consider to be His child at the time. Or, one might argue that David was regenerated at the time the Spirit came on him. Again, however, he had already been anointed to be Israel's next king (1 Sam. 16:13); and, further, the coincidence of the Spirit's coming on both Saul and David with their approval as Israel's king is too significant to overlook. Both experienced Spirit-empowerment, not Spirit-regeneration, at these times.

E. Other Mentions of the Spirit

The four groups of people mentioned comprise all the persons of whom it is said that the Spirit either came on or departed from them. Other references to the Spirit, as noted in chapter 3, speak of the Spirit in some other respect. For instance, in Genesis 6:3 He ceases to strive with man; in Joel 2:28,29 it is predicted that one day He would be poured out on people so that they would "prophesy," "dream dreams," and "see visions"; in Isaiah 11:2 it is predicted that the "spirit of the LORD would rest upon Christ; in Haggai 2:5 the returned exiles are assured that God's "spirit" remained among them, even as had been promised years before; and in Zechariah 4:6 Israel is instructed that God's work is done not by man's "might" or "power," but by God's "spirit."

None of these, nor any of the other passages that might be mentioned, refer to any aspect of spiritual renewal of the person concerned. They show the necessity of God's Spirit being upon people to influence them properly, yet none of them speak of imparting new life in salvation, and surely not of removing such life. No Old Testament text speaks of this activity. Whenever the Spirit is said to come on or leave a person in Old Testament time, then, the reason is found in some area of that person's activity.

6

EMPOWERMENT BY THE SPIRIT

The prior chapter has reviewed every instance in the Old Testament where one or more persons experienced the Holy Spirit's coming on or departing from them. Each was found to involve an aspect of divine empowerment for a task; none were found to involve spiritual renewal. This makes the question pertinent whether or not Old Testament people experienced spiritual renewal, and, if they did, why the Spirit is not said to have come on them for that purpose in at least some instances. This question will be investigated at some length in the following chapter. In this chapter, however, further discussion is necessary relative to aspects of empowerment granted to Old Testament people. It will be well to consider each of the four classifications in the same order as has been followed. The interest is in studying the reason why the people in these classifications needed this manner of special provision — when others did not — and the nature of that provision when given.

A. Judges

Four judges were seen to comprise the first classification: Othniel (Judg. 3:10), Gideon (6:34), Jephthah (11:29), and Samson (13:25; 14:6, 19; 15:14). Each of these had a major need for special ability at the time the Spirit is said to have come on them.

Othniel had to fight Cushan-rishathaim of Mesopotamia. Because of the sin of the Israelite people, God permitted six invasions of their land by other nations, and Cushan-rishathaim led the first one. The people of Israel were weak at the time and had no army; indeed, they were divided in thought, as each tribe lived quite to itself. Othniel himself was advanced in years[1] and, on the basis of merely natural inclinations, would have wanted no part in fighting this enemy, who had already held control in the land for eight years. Therefore, he needed special empowerment, that he might have reason for encouragement to carry out the challenge and ability for it when he did so. He would have needed first merely to raise an army and inspire men to follow him under the difficult conditions; then he would have needed to devise strategy and lead these men in a way to bring the victory necessary.

Gideon was required to fight Midianites, who had been able to raid in Israel almost unhindered for six years. These years had shown the Israelites to be in an almost hopeless condition of weakness. The Midianites had apparently allowed the Israelites the "privilege" of planting and nurturing their crops, but then each year had come in large number to seize the harvest. Few situations could hardly be more humiliating to a people. On the seventh year, however, God called Gideon to lead an army against the annual raid. At the time, Gideon was unpopular in his community (Judg. 6:15,28-30), much less a military figure in whom men of the day held confidence. There seemed to be no possibility of his even raising an army, much less leading it in battle. Therefore, it was necessary that "the spirit of the LORD" come upon him to inspire men to follow him (6:34). The result was that he was enabled to do this and then given direction for a remarkable victory.

Jephthah had to fight Ammonites, who had been able to hold the Israelites east of the Jordan under their domination for eighteen years (Judg. 10:8). These transjordan Israelites had not been involved in the earlier invasions, but now they were involved, and they felt helpless before the superior strength of the neighboring Ammonites. No doubt their weapons were few, for the enemy had been in control of their land for so many years, and their morale was even at lower tide. Finally they sought out Jephthah, who had been driven from their midst years before due to an improper birth, and asked him to solve their problem. Jephthah did so, but the odds were greatly against him in winning over so strong an enemy. He even vowed a most serious vow (11:30,31), if God would grant him victory. His

[1]He was the younger brother of Caleb (Josh. 15:17; Judg. 1:13), and Caleb was already eighty-five during the conquest under Joshua (Josh. 14:10), and at least another twenty-five years had elapsed since then. Othniel must have been no less than seventy-five or eighty years old at the time.

need of special provision by the Holy Spirit, then, was great, and God met it. It may be noted that once more the Spirit was provided even before he raised his army (11:29), indicating that he needed help already at that time.

Samson was called to "begin to deliver Israel out of the hand of the Philistines" (Judg. 13:5) and to do so by working quite alone. The Philistines held Israelites under their control longer than any of the other invaders, a total of forty years (13:1). Probably half of this time had elapsed by the time Samson was called to his assignment. God did not instruct him to raise an army to fight the enemy directly, and therefore equipped him in a unique manner that he might be able to fight alone. He was given remarkable strength. The impartation of that strength, however, and the proper employment of it — so merely selfish ends would not be served — called for the Spirit to come on him. In fact the Spirit is said to have come on him four times (13:25; 14:6,19; 15:14). Probably the first time was when the special strength was first imparted, and then the other three times — each of which involved a major display of strength — were occasions when still greater ability was needed and granted.

Each of these four judges, then, did need special empowerment to carry out their assigned tasks. The challenges in each case were great. The question arises, however, concerning the other judges, whether the tasks of these four were sufficiently greater so that they alone were Spirit-empowered. The answer is not easy. If the others were given similar provision, no indication is given of it. All did have important work to do and surely did need God's help in doing it. Whether this need was great enough to call for the coming of the Holy Spirit on them, however, cannot be answered with certainty. At least these four were enabled, and they did have unusually great need.

B. Craftsmen

Three craftsmen experienced the Spirit coming on them: Bezaleel (Exod. 31:3; 35:31), David (1 Chron. 28:11,12), and Hiram (1 Kings 7:13,14). These craftsmen had tasks to perform of a different type than that of the judges but their tasks were equally demanding.

Bezaleel was instructed to work on the tabernacle. He was to "devise cunning [carefully executed] works" laboring with "gold," "silver," "brass," "stones," and "wood." In other words, he was to do work which required unusual skill in molding, shaping, and carving figures made from these materials. The lampstand alone, to be located in the "holy place" of the tabernacle, provided an enormous challenge. It had a central shaft and six branches and was to be "one beaten work of pure gold." More than that, it was extensively carved, with each branch having a series of "knops" (spherical shapes) and "flowers," and then capped by a lamp which one may believe was to be a work of art in itself (see Exod. 25:31-37). God of course wanted the finest, because the tabernacle was to be His place of dwelling among His people. Bezaleel, no doubt, was already naturally gifted in this type of work — accounting for his selection to do the work at all — but God saw that he needed yet greater skill and provided it by this special enablement of the Spirit. As indicated in the prior chapter, Aholiab and the others who helped may also have been especially equipped, though no definite indication is given regarding them.

David had the task of designing the temple. Because this was to be God's house, taking the place of the tabernacle, its design must also[2] be of divine origin. Accordingly, there was need for David to be supernaturally directed in his thinking, and this called for special supervision by the Spirit. Thus it is stated that "David gave to Solomon his son . . . the pattern of all that he had by the spirit, of the courts of the house of the LORD (1 Chron. 28:11,12). It should be noticed that, since David had already been empowered by the Spirit on a regular basis as king — as observed in the prior chapter — this aspect of enablement was something in addition. Most likely, since the Spirit had first come on him only in respect to the kingship, the Spirit now gave special guidance also for the act of designing the building. There is no indication that He had to *come on* David again in order to enable him for this additional function.. He was already continuously on him, for the one purpose, and apparently He simply added this further purpose for the time needed to accomplish it.

The need for Hiram to be Spirit-empowered was clearly the same as for Bezaleel. He was already a skilled worker in metal and wood, recommended highly to Solomon by the King of Tyre (2 Chron. 2:7,13,14). God, however, wanting the finest work on the temple, as He had on the tabernacle, saw fit to have that skill made still greater. Accordingly, Hiram "was filled [*male'*, "filled"] with wisdom and understanding" to this end.

[2]God had given the particular design of the tabernacle to Moses on Mt. Sinai (Exod. 25-30).

C. Prophets

The reason prophets needed special empowerment by the Spirit was so they might serve in the most effective manner possible. They were important to the religious life of Israelites. One might well call them the "preachers" of their day, proclaiming God's Word to the people.

It is interesting to compare them with priests of the day in respect to Spirit-empowerment. Priests, too, were important. In fact, priests were specified and given extensive instructions in the law of Moses, while prophets were not. The latter were recognized there (Deut. 18:15-22), but not specified or given instructions. Priests, however, are never said to have had the Spirit come on them in connection with their work.[3] This is a surprising fact, and one is prompted to ask regarding the reason. The reason is probably that the function of the priests was quite routine and also well spelled out in the Law. Priests knew what they were to do and, doing it continually, did not need special enablement by the Spirit. Prophets, on the other hand, seldom knew what they might be assigned to do next, and they had no written rules by which to proceed. They had changing, challenging, and even dangerous missions to perform, and so needed special provision from God.

There was another reason why at least many of the prophets needed the special ministry of the Spirit. It was necessary in order to receive revelation from God. Priests, too, had been given a way to receive revelations from God — namely, through the use of Urim and Thummim (Exod. 28:30) — but this could only be used by the high priest of the day; ordinary priests could not approach God by this means. Many prophets, however, could and did receive revelation. The Spirit's special provision for prophets, therefore, concerned two basic needs: the provision of revelation that they might have God's information to declare to the people, and enablement in the declaration that it might be performed in the best way possible. It is well now to consider the two groups of prophets, distinguished in the prior chapter, to determine whether each was enabled in both ways or not.

1. Prophets filled temporarily. Five people were noted as filled

---

[3]Both Jahaziel (2 Chron. 20:14-17) and Zechariah (2 Chron. 24:20) were Levites, but the Spirit of God came on them in respect to a prophetic-type, rather than priestly, work.

temporarily: Azariah (2 Chron. 15:1-7), Jahaziel (20:14-17), Zechariah (24:20), Balaam (Num. 24:2), and Amassai (1 Chron. 12:18). Only the first three were observed to be Israelite prophets. The manner in which all five are said to have had the Spirit come on them indicates that it was primarily in reference to receiving God's word rather than giving it out. For instance, of Azariah it is said that "the spirit of God came upon" him, with the result that he spoke a message to Asa. The implication is clear that the Spirit came to tell Azariah what to say, and perhaps where and how to say it. But nothing is stated about the Spirit enabling him in the speaking. If He did so, the implication at least is not present.

2. Prophets filled continuously. The discussion of the prior chapter showed that most prophets — including the great writing prophets — were filled by the Spirit continuously. A further study of the passages concerning them indicates that they were Spirit-filled for both the purpose of receiving and declaring God's word. Both purposes are indicated as the specific passages are studied together.

The indication of Micah (3:8) as to his own empowerment is definitely in reference to the aspect of declaration. He said, "But truly I am full of power by the spirit of the LORD . . . to declare unto Jacob his transgression, and to Israel his sin." The important word here is *declare*. Nehemiah's reference (9:30), as he speaks of preexilic prophets who lived long before, is in the same vein. He stated that God had "testifiedst against" preexilic Israel by the "spirit in" the prophets. The significant word is *testifiedst*.

On the other hand, Ezekiel refers clearly to the aspect of revelation. In 11:5-12, for instance, he writes, "And the Spirit of the LORD fell upon me, and said unto me, Speak; Thus saith the LORD, Thus have ye said, O house of Israel: for I know the things that come into your mind, every one of them," and then the message continues. Here the Spirit came on Ezekiel to tell him what to say.

It is only logical that the Spirit would have enabled these prophets in both respects. He was on them to equip them as prophets; therefore, He would have aided them in every way necessary. He would have wanted to be involved with their reception of divine messages, and He would have wanted to enable them to deliver the messages most effectively. Ezekiel (2:2) speaks also of having the Spirit simply give him general instructions for the performance of his work, an aspect which had to do neither with the reception or declaration of a message. The full-time, important prophets, then, quite clearly were enabled to be good prophets in whatever aspect of their work this enablement might involve.

D. Civil Administrators

Civil administrators were Spirit-empowered again simply to do the job well to which they had been appointed. Civil leadership was important in the life of Israel, just as religious leadership. Four such leaders were noted in the prior chapters as being specially empowered: Moses (Num. 11:17; Isa. 63:10-12), Joshua (Num. 27:18; Deut. 34:9), Saul (1 Sam. 11:6; 16:14), and David (1 Sam. 16:13; Ps. 51:11).

Moses had the immense task of leading the Israelites from Egypt to Canaan. It was one of the greatest challenges any man has ever faced. Simply the logistical problem of moving as many as two million[4] people at one time would have been enormous. Then there was the work of organization, communication, and merely keeping the people reasonably happy and working together, without strife and discord. Besides this there were apparently endless cases of social dispute that needed to be settled (see Num. 11:10-15), which Moses for a time tried to care for himself. The task would have been enough had it continued only the sixteen (approximate) months[5] until Kadesh-barnea — when God had wanted them to move on into the land — but, due to the sin of the people at that time, it had to last for a total of forty years (Num. 14:34). One need not wonder that God saw Moses in need of continuous Spirit-empowerment.

Joshua's task was nearly as demanding. It fell to him to make conquest of Canaan, which contained an advanced, fighting people and strong, walled cities. Jericho alone, with its impregnable fortifications,[6] constituted an immense obstacle in itself. Even armies of large nations, with the most advanced military machines and weapons available, could take such a city only by prolonged siege.

[4]There were 603,550 men twenty years and older (Num. 1:46). This number must be doubled to get the number of both men and women, and then to this must be added the children. There were probably more than 2,000,000 total.

[5]Two months had elapsed in getting to Mt. Sinai (cf. Num. 33:3 with Exod. 19:1). More than eleven months had been spent at Sinai (see Num. 10:11). Then perhaps three months were spent in getting to Kadesh-barnea, in the reconnaisance of the forty days by the spies, and in the people choosing not to enter the land.

[6]For possible description, see Leon J. Wood, A Survey of Israel's History (Grand Rapids: Zondervan, 1970), pp. 173,174.

Later came the encounter with a confederacy of the leading cities of southern Canaan (Josh. 10:1-43), and later still a similar confrontation with cities of the north (11:1-14). And Joshua did not have many years in which to accomplish so much, for he was already advanced in age when he became leader.[7] Again one need not wonder that Joshua too was seen to be in need of continuous Spirit-empowerment.

Saul and David also needed special enablement. For one thing, neither possessed a background normal for kings. Saul was the first king and did not grow up in a palace situation to know how kings and courts operate. He had to learn this without ever being at a court. David did not grow up in a court either. When Saul failed as Israel's first king, God turned to David when he was only a youth who knew merely the open field where sheep grazed. This was hardly a place to learn about court life.

Another factor is that both Saul and David needed to be given self-confidence for their important tasks. This was true especially of Saul. When his servant wished to make inquiry of Samuel concerning lost animals, Saul did not want to do so. The servant had to urge him and even offer his own "fourth part of a shekel of silver" (1 Sam. 9:8) as payment to Samuel to persuade his reluctant master to make the visit. Then, later, when Saul had been selected in the midst of tribal leaders to be king (10:19-21), he could not be found by the leaders because he had hidden himself "among the stuff" (probably wagons with which the leaders had come). They had to search for him there. Saul was certainly timid by nature and hardly suitable in personality to be the leader of the new monarchy. This called for a change to be made.

David also may have been somewhat timid by nature. At least when Samuel went to Bethlehem to anoint one of Jesse's sons as Israel's next king, David did not go with the rest of the family to a general time of sacrificing. Seven sons went, but David, the youngest, remained at home to tend the family's sheep. One would think that the family would have had servants to care for the sheep, if David had really wanted to go with the others. He may, then, have been of a natural retiring nature. It is understandable that he could

---

[7]Joshua had been old enough forty years earlier to be one of the spies (Num. 13:8). He died at the age of 110 (Judg. 2:8), and the conquest could hardly have lasted more than six years (see Josh. 14:7-10). He may have been close to one hundred when he became leader.

have been, since he had seven dominant older brothers (cf. 1 Sam. 17:28).

Then, most important, both Saul and David had enormous tasks to perform. Their work as Israel's first two kings might well be compared for challenge to that of Moses and Joshua. Saul's task was to mold a disunited group of tribes into a nation. People who before had been separated from each other, both by geographical feature[8] and inter-tribal dissension,[9] had to be made to think and work together. Old grudges had to be put aside and a willingness substituted to work toward common goals. Furthermore, the people would have to begin to pay taxes. This had not been necessary during the judges period, for there had been no civil government to support.[10] Taxes are never easy to accept, especially when people have not had to pay them before. The difficulty of the task that faced Israel's first king can hardly be overemphasized.

David's task was just as great, however; in fact, it may have been even more challenging because Saul had failed as the first king. Also the Philistines were now in control of Israelite territory in greater degree than when Saul had taken over command. This was because Saul and his army had perished on Mt. Gilboa in a tragic defeat before this perennial enemy, and following this the Philistines had been able to move through the land almost at will. Ishbosheth, Saul's fourth son, who tried for a time to succeed his father as king, did not even attempt to make his capital west of the Jordan, but instead on the east side at Mahanaim (2 Sam. 2:8,9). So David not only had to do what Saul had failed to do, in respect to unifying the tribes, but he had to solve this serious Philistine problem before he could even start on the main issue. One has to say of him, also, that his task cannot be overemphasized for its size and importance.

Both Saul and David, therefore, needed special empowerment.

[8]The deep Jordan valley separated the eastern tribes from the main group, and the Esdraelon valley, running southwest from just north of Mt. Carmel, put the northern tribes in a group by themselves for much of the time.

[9]Actual civil war had broken out twice: once between Benjamin and the rest of the tribes (Judg. 20), and later between Ephraim and Jephthah's transjordan army (Judg. 11:1-6). The fact that Ephraimites at the time could not pronounce "shibboleth" in the way, apparently, that other tribes could is indicative of an advanced degree of provincialism, that doubtless was shared in varying degrees by other tribes.

[10]The Law gave no provision even for elders to receive public support, and they were the main civil officials recognized. Elders probably supported themselves, only serving in their public capacity on a part-time basis.

Neither was sufficient in himself for his God-given task. Accordingly, God sent His Spirit on both.

The fact that the Spirit in time left Saul, who failed, whereas He did not leave David, who succeeded, should not be missed. It was the existence of Spirit-empowerment, clearly, that made the difference between the reigns of each. The saddest reference to Saul in the Bible is the indication that "the spirit of the LORD departed from" him (1 Sam. 16:14). He is the only person of whom this is said. Of others, the fact is implied, since the nature of the Spirit's coming on them was only temporary in kind, but it is never stated. It is said of Saul, however, and the fact is indicative both that the Spirit had remained on him continuously until that time and also that his rule could be expected to degenerate after that departure.

Degeneration is exactly what did occur, as numerous matters give indication. It was after this departure, for instance, that Saul came under the influence of an "evil spirit" (apparently in place of God's Spirit), that he then showed himself personally incapable of combating the Philistines (1 Sam. 17:1-11), that he became bitterly and unreasonably angry at David so that this young military leader had to flee, that he unmercifully slew eighty-five priests of Nob along with their families (22:18,19), that God no longer would answer his inquiries by "dreams," "Urim," or "prophets" (28:6), that he therefore disgraced himself by resorting illegally to a woman of a familiar spirit to inquire of Samuel (28:7-25), and that he suffered the tragic, ignominious defeat before the Philistines at Mt. Gilboa and this probably because so few Israelites would longer respond to his call for battle (31:1-10).

Some discussion is in order concerning why only these four Israelite administrators — Moses, Joshua, Saul, and David — are said to have been Spirit-empowered, when others are not. Why is this not said, for instance, of the great Samuel or of Solomon, who yet ruled in the time of the united monarchy, or of the later godly kings Hezekiah or Josiah?

The answer which best commends itself is twofold: first, that these four were fully national figures, and, second, that as such they faced the most demanding tasks of any other national figures. Samuel was not a national figure. That is, he did not hold an official office; he was a prophet and judge, but he was not an officially appointed leader over Israel as Moses and Joshua were, and of course the later kings.

Solomon was a national figure, but his task as king was much less demanding than that of either Saul or David. Solomon did know the ways of the court, even from earliest life; he was not timid or shy; and he did not have the challenge of uniting a country or fighting great enemies. This does not mean his task was small, but only that it did not compare with what these four had to face. His need for Spirit-empowerment, then, was less. And if Solomon's need was less, the same surely was true for the kings of the divided monarchy. Of course, of the nineteen kings of the northern kingdom, none of them were even counted as "good" by God; they all sinned grievously in their lives and ways of rule. Of the nineteen kings of the southern kingdom, eight were considered "good," but apparently their tasks were not considered great enough to qualify.

The concluding note of this chapter must be that the purpose of the Spirit's coming on people was that of empowering them for a divinely assigned task. This was indicated in the prior chapter, and now this further inquiry into the background and circumstances involved with each case has in no way changed that conclusion. All four classifications of people — judges, craftsmen, prophets, and administrators — were thus equipped to do their work in the best proper manner. The tasks of all four groups were vitally important in God's program with His people, and He saw the need for this special provision that they were done carefully and well.

7

SPIRITUAL RENEWAL IN THE
OLD TESTAMENT

We now come to the subject of spiritual renewal in the Old Testament. The prior two chapters have investigated every instance where one or more Old Testament persons are said to have experienced the Spirit either come on or leave them. The conclusion has been definite: every instance concerned an aspect of empowerment for a task, with no instances seeming to involve spiritual renewal. The question therefore arises whether or not Old Testament people were spiritually renewed. If the Spirit is not said to have granted this renewal, did anyone experience it?

The answer is that spiritual renewal was indeed experienced, as will be shown presently. This means that the occasions of the Spirit coming on or leaving a person do not determine the answer to the question. Evidence, therefore, must be sought elsewhere. The investigation of these occasions has been important, however, to show that they do not provide evidence and to keep one from appealing to them for wrong conclusions.

The interest of the present chapter, therefore, is to consider what other evidence there may be for spiritual renewal in the Old Testament. A determination is called for first that such renewal was truly experienced and then the matter of evidence will be discussed.

A. Spiritual Renewal as Experienced in the Old Testament

1. The fact. It is not difficult to show that Old Testament people did experience spiritual renewal. All one has to do is to think of some of the great Old Testament characters to recognize this. There was

Noah, "a just man and perfect in his generations" (Gen. 6:9); Abraham, a mighty man of faith, of whom it is said that he "believed God, and it was counted unto him for righteousness" (Rom. 4:3); Moses, who esteemed "the reproach of Christ greater riches than the treasures in Egypt" (Heb. 11:26); David, who was chosen of God as "his servant" (Ps. 78:70) and whose heart was "perfect with the LORD his God" (1 Kings 15:3); the great writing prophets, whose lives were such outstanding examples of obedience; and the many others listed in the "hero" chapter, Hebrews 11, of whom it is said that "the world was not worthy" of them (Heb. 11:38). These and many more were truly people of God, who enjoyed a state of spiritual renewal in the presence of God.

2. The evidence. The evidence that spiritual renewal, or regeneration, was true of such Old Testament people lies mainly in two directions. One is that these people lived in a way possible only for those who had experienced regeneration, and the other is the avenue of logical deduction that argues back from New Testament truth. For some reason, the Old Testament itself does not speak of the matter directly. Chafer is quite correct when he asserts: "The Old Testament will be searched in vain for record of Jews passing from an unsaved to a saved state, or for any declaration about the terms upon which such a change would be secured." Then, because this is true, he states: "No positive declaration can be made" whether Old Testament people were regenerated or not.[1]

Chafer's conclusion, however, is unwarranted in view of the two lines of support mentioned. The first line alone seems sufficient, for what more telling evidence for regeneration could there be than the lives of these great Old Testament saints? How could such lives be accounted for otherwise? These people were born sinners, as any of New Testament time (Rom. 3:23). Yet they came to display the very highest in faith and obedience to God. As was noted, Noah is called "a just man and perfect in his generations" (Gen. 6:9). Abraham is actually made an example of faith for New Testament believers in Romans 4:1-25 and Galatians 3:13-18. Joseph experienced extreme cause for complaint, yet is never said to have become bitter or lost his faith in God. Many others could be named as well. Their lives were outstanding in faithfulness and dedication, and they are set forth in the Old Testament as examples to follow. Did they achieve such

[1]Chafer, *Systematic Theology*, VI, pp. 73,74.

commendable lives by their own efforts? Did they have some resource in their own nature on which they could draw that people of New Testament time do not have? The answer, of course, is that they did not. But, if not, they must have experienced an impartation of new life, just as saints of the New Testament, and this means regeneration.

The other area of evidence is that of logical deduction on the basis of New Testament truth.[2] This deduction runs as follows: The New Testament declares that all men are born lost sinners (Rom. 3:23) and that this has been true since Adam in the Garden of Eden (Rom. 5:12-21). It states that Christ is the only way of salvation from such a state of sin (John 14:6) and that the benefit He provided in His work of atonement is solely through trust in Him (John 1:12; Acts 16:31). It indicates that when one does this he experiences regeneration (Titus 3:5). Since this is the only way of salvation possible for man, and since man has been in need of this salvation since the time of Adam, it must be that Old Testament people had to be, and were, saved, or regenerated, in the same way as New Testament people.

One may object that Old Testament people could not exercise faith in Christ like those of the New Testament, since Christ had not yet lived. This is true to a point, but Paul provides the biblical answer by his reference to Abraham in Romans 4. Paul says, "Abraham believed God, and it was counted unto him for righteousness" (v. 3). The Old Testament person was counted righteous simply on the basis of believing God. By the time of Abraham, God had revealed a certain amount of information, and Abraham's responsibility was to believe that amount. By David's time, more had been revealed, and it was necessary for a person to believe that additional amount. To Isaiah was revealed definite information even regarding Christ,[3] and by his time people could, and had to, believe this also. People simply had to believe God and what He had said by their time, and, when they did, they were judged as righteous by God, which is another way of saying they were regenerated.

Still a third area of evidence may be cited. It is the effort Jesus put forth during His time on earth to bring people to a state of righteousness. This area of evidence is cited separately, for some expositors

[2]Chafer (p. 72) warns against this manner of argument, but in this instance the warning does not appear appropriate, as the argument attempts to show.

[3]To David, already, some messianic information had been revealed; for instance, see Psalm 22.

speak of Jesus' day as a sort of transition period between the Old and New Testament times, and therefore not a true exemplary period of Old Testament conditions. There were transitional aspects involved during His time, certainly, but so long as Christ had not yet died and the church had not officially begun at Pentecost, the fact and manner of regeneration must have been the same as in Old Testament time proper. The area of evidence, then, is quite admissable.

The evidence consists simply in the fact that Jesus put forth extensive effort to bring people to a belief in Himself and therefore to a condition of righteous standing in God's sight. He called the tax collector Zacchaeus down from a sycamore tree and went to dine in his house that he might prompt faith in his heart and be able to tell him, "This day is salvation come to this house" (Luke 19:1-9). He recognized the notable faith of a paralytic, brought by four men who let him down through a hole in the roof of a house, and Jesus responded by saying, "Son, be of good cheer; thy sins be forgiven thee" (Matt. 9:1-8; cf. Mark 2:3-12; Luke 5:18-26). Jesus not only healed a man at the pool of Bethesda (John 5:1-9), but later spoke the significant words to him, "Behold, thou art made whole: sin no more" (John 5:14); and that he spoke of being spiritually "whole" is made clear by his later statement to critical Jews who knew of his words, "Verily, verily, I say unto you, He that heareth my word, and believeth on him that sent me, hath everlasting life, and shall not come into condemnation; but is passed from death unto life" (John 5:24).

Two significant occasions of this kind are recorded in John 3 and 4. The latter chapter tells of Jesus' leading a sinful woman of Samaria to a saving knowledge of Himself. She wanted water from Jacob's well, but Jesus told her that whoever would believe in Him would "never thirst" again and instead have within him "a well of water springing up into everlasting life" (John 4:14). The result was that she did believe and also "many of the Samaritans of " her city of Sychar (John 4:39). The former chapter tells of Jesus' witness to the self-righteous Nicodemus. He told the well-taught Jew, "Ye must be born again" (John 3:7; cf. vv. 3,5). To be "born again" means to receive new life, in other words, be regenerated. Now Jesus would not have told this person to do something that was impossible for him,[4] and the fact that Nicodemus did experience regeneration is demonstrated by his later

---

[4]See further discussion of this passage, chapter 8, pp. 82-84.

willingness to have a part in Christ's burial (John 19:39).

These illustrations from Jesus' life show that regeneration was indeed possible — and was effected — during His time of ministry. The fact that it was, besides the first two lines of evidence noted, gives clear indication that the same was true during all Old Testament time from the Garden of Eden. Regeneration, the impartation of new life made available by the work of Christ, was experienced by Noah, Abraham, Joseph, Moses, David, and the many others of the Old Testament period. Further, since regeneration in New Testament time is effected by the Holy Spirit (Titus 3:5), it is logical to believe that He was the person of the Trinity that did the same at the earlier time. [5]

3. The reason for no explanation in the Old Testament. One may ask why the Old Testament itself does not make the fact of regeneration clear in the form of some direct statement or discussion. The truth is clearly illustrated in lives, but not declared in writing. The answer can only be that God saw fit to wait with this revelation until New Testament time. This should not be thought strange, for numerous truths are illustrated in the Old Testament which receive explanation only in the New.

For instance, the New Testament tells us that, when Adam sinned in Eden, he did so as the representative of the human race (see Rom. 5:12-21; 1 Cor. 15:22); but in the Old Testament all we have is the story of Adam's personal sin. When God came to Adam and told him he would die if he ate of the tree's fruit, He did not say, "Thou and thy posterity shalt surely die," but only, "Thou shalt surely die." A person would not know from the Old Testament alone that Adam was the federal head of the human race. [6] God saw fit to wait with an explanation regarding this basic truth — even while men were being born in sin due to Adam's fall throughout the time of the Old Testament — until New Testament time; He apparently saw fit to wait with an explanation also regarding regeneration.

[5]Kuyper (*Work of the Holy Spirit*, p. 119) speaks in this regard: "Believing Israelites were saved. Hence they must have received saving grace. And since saving grace is out of the question without an inward working of the Holy Spirit, it follows that He was the Worker of faith in Abraham as well as in ourselves." See also E. H. Johnson and H. G. Weston, *An Outline of Systematic Theology and Ecclesiology*, p. 186.

[6]Even Genesis 3:15, important as it is relative to Christ's future coming, really says nothing concerning Adam's federal headship. The most one could say of it is that the thought is there implied, but surely not stated or explained.

B. Indwelling, Sealing, and Filling Also in the Old Testament

In chapter 5, several terms were mentioned as commonly associated with the Spirit's work in the New Testament. They were *regeneration, indwelling, sealing, filling, empowering,* and *baptism.* Of these, we have thus far discussed the first, regeneration. Now we shall consider the next three to determine whether or not they also were experienced in Old Testament time. The last two will be considered separately in the last two sections of the chapter.

1. Indwelling. By *indwelling* is meant the continuedness of the Spirit's residence within the saint following the occasion of regeneration. Regeneration is a momentary act, when spiritual life is imparted to a sinner. It happens instantaneously. Indwelling, on the other hand, only begins then. It is the Spirit that enacts regeneration, and when He does He enters into the person, so that the person becomes "the temple of God" (1 Cor. 3:16,17; 2 Cor. 6:16). Indwelling means that this relation continues from that point on.

The fact that the Holy Spirit does indwell Christians is established by numerous texts: Romans 5:5; 8:11; 1 Corinthians 2:12; 6:19,20; 2 Corinthians 5:5; Galatians 4:6; 1 John 3:24; 4:13. In Romans 8:9, in fact, the statement is made, "If any man have not the Spirit of Christ, he is none of his"; and Jude 19 identifies the non-Christian as a person "having not the Spirit."

The question at issue is whether or not this indwelling of the Holy Spirit characterized saints of the Old Testament as well as of the New. Some scholars assert that it did not. John Walvoord, for instance, states, "In the Old Testament . . . the Holy Spirit did not indwell all the saints," and cites as evidence 1 Samuel 16:14 where the Spirit is said to have departed from Saul.[7] The prior discussion, in chapters 5 and 6, has shown, however, that this departure from Saul did not concern regeneration or indwelling, but only empowerment. The

---

[7] Walvoord, *The Holy Spirit*, p. 152; see also Mark G. Cambron, *Bible Doctrines,* p. 124. B. B. Warfield (*Biblical and Theological Studies*), however, says: "The Spirit of God, in the Old Testament, is not merely the immanent Spirit, the source of all the world's life and all the world's movement. . . . He is as well the indwelling Spirit of holiness in the hearts of God's children." J. B. Payne (*The Theology of the Older Testament,* p. 174) says similarly, "David, in his intimate personal communion with God, was the first to reveal the activity of the Holy Spirit as indwelling and guiding the believer," and refers especially to Psalm 143:10. He enlarges on this idea in his extended discussion of regeneration in the Old Testament; see pp. 240-45.

question of indwelling is not settled by this or similar texts, then, any more than is the question of regeneration.

On the other hand, a strong argument that Old Testament saints were indwelt may be built on the fact that they were regenerated, as shown above. It was argued that, since they were regenerated, it must have been the Holy Spirit who brought this about. Now it may be argued that, since these Old Testament saints certainly remained in a regenerated condition, it must have been the Holy Spirit who kept them so. The New Testament is clear that the Christian is incapable of keeping himself, any more than he is capable of saving himself. He must be "kept by the power of God" (1 Peter 1:5). One must ask, then, Did the Old Testament saint possess an ability for perseverance not known to the New Testament saint? The answer is clear: They did not possess such an ability and were not able to keep themselves. But, if not, they must have been kept by God, and this means, surely, the Spirit of God. One might argue that the Spirit could have kept them, whether continually indwelling them or not. Since He keeps the New Testament saint by indwelling, however, it seems reasonable to believe that He kept the Old Testament saint in the same way.

2. Sealing. Sealing means the assurance of the sinner's continued salvation, so it will not, nor cannot, be lost. The thought is closely tied to the indwelling of the Spirit, for it is His continued indwelling that makes certain the eternal security of the believer. In other words, it is the fact of the permanent indwelling of the Holy Spirit that constitutes the sealing of the believer. The Spirit, in the constancy of His indwelling the believer, is Himself the seal.

There are three New Testament passages that speak particularly of the Holy Spirit's work in sealing Christians: 2 Corinthians 1:22, "Who hath also sealed us and given the earnest of the Spirit in our hearts"; Ephesians 1:13, "After that ye believed, ye were sealed with that holy Spirit of promise"; and Ephesians 4:30, "And grieve not the holy Spirit of God, whereby ye are sealed unto the day of redemption."

In view of the discussion regarding the indwelling of Old Testament saints, the conclusion follows that they were also sealed. If the Old Testament person was continually indwelt by the Spirit, and this indwelling constitutes the sealing of the Spirit, then he was certainly sealed. There is no indication that believers of Old Testament time lost their state of spiritual renewal any more than believers of today, which means they enjoyed a condition of eternal security just as believers of the present age. This condition of eternal security is made to exist for the New Testament saint by the sealing of the Holy Spirit. Again it seems reasonable to believe that the same was true for the Old Testament saint.

3. **Filling.** The term *filling* means the control the Holy Spirit holds over the life and behavior of the believer. There is again a close relation in idea to the indwelling of the Holy Spirit, but a clear distinction exists. It is true that no person can be filled by the Spirit who is not indwelt, but a person may be indwelt without being filled. Indwelling speaks merely of the continued presence of the Spirit within the believer, without indicating anything as to the degree to which the believer is submissive to His direction and will. Even the rebellious Christian — if truly a Christian — is indwelt, for when a person once becomes a child of God, the Spirit never leaves him. Filling, however, speaks of the extent of control which the abiding Spirit has over the person.

Therefore, filling is directly related to the believer's degree of yieldedness to the will of the Spirit within him. It is quite correct to say that filling has more to do with how much of the believer the Spirit has than how much of the Spirit the believer has. Because he is indwelt by the Spirit, the believer has all of the Spirit, but it depends on the degree to which the believer is filled as to how much of him the Spirit has. In Ephesians 5:18, the filling of the Spirit is likened to drunkenness; Paul says, "And be not drunk with wine, wherein is excess; but be filled with the Spirit." The believer, in being filled, is to be under the control of the Spirit in a similar manner to which an inebriated person is under the control of drink. When the believer is not yielded, he is said to "quench" the Spirit (1 Thess. 5:19) or to "grieve" the Spirit (Eph. 4:30). The indwelling Spirit, then, does not force His will on the believer, but seeks a voluntary submission, so that His will can dominate in the believer's life. This domination is called filling.

Were Old Testament saints filled by the Spirit like New Testament saints? In view of all that has been said, it is reasonable once more to believe they were. If they were indwelt by the Spirit, certainly the Spirit desired to control their lives in the same manner that He does New Testament saints. It is likely also that the degree to which He would have been able to do so would have again depended on the degree of yieldedness of the one indwelt. This means that the degree of filling would have varied among believers, as it does today. The more dedicated persons would have been filled to a greater degree, those less dedicated to a lesser degree.

An explanation is called for in regard to this use of the word *filling*, when compared with the use of the verb *filled (male')* in the Old Testament concerning the Spirit's coming on people. For instance, it was noted earlier that God said of Bezaleel, "I have filled [*male'*] him with the spirit of God" (Exod. 31:3). The explanation is simply that these two uses of the word are not at all in the same sense. It was noted in chapter 5 that several different words are employed in the Old Testament for describing the several occasions when the Spirit came on people, and the word *fill* is one. Each of these times, no matter what word is used, speaks of a coming on the person to enable him for a task. So, then, the word *fill* as used there does not in any respect have reference to the "filling" of the believer so that he comes to be increasingly controlled by the Spirit in his life and behavior.

C. Spirit-Empowerment Also in the New Testament

The term *Spirit-empowerment* has been commonly used herein when referring to the work of the Spirit in the Old Testament. As just observed, every instance of the Spirit's either coming on or leaving an Old Testament person involved the empowering of that person for a task. Spirit-empowerment, then, has been established as a work of the Spirit in Old Testament time. The question therefore becomes pertinent whether this was true also in New Testament time. Were New Testament people Spirit-empowered?

The answer is definitely that they were, and many examples of this are set forth. For instance, Peter (Acts 4:8; cf. 4:31), like the prophets of old, is said to have been "filled with the Holy Spirit," with the result that he spoke a divinely given message to the hostile Sanhedrin. Similarly, Paul (Acts 13:9) is said to have been "filled with the Holy Spirit," to speak a strong word of rebuke to the sorcerer Elymas, who was trying to prevent the salvation of "the deputy of the country, Sergius Paulus." Both men, of course, had long been indwelt by the Holy Spirit, which means that this "filling" for a task was an additional provision for them, just as in the Old Testament. It may be noted, too, that the word *filled (pimplemi*[8]) is used for the Spirit's

[8]Greek equivalent of the Hebrew *male'*.

action toward these men, even as in the Old Testament; and, being used in this way, it should not be understood any differently. It has no relation, then, to the word *filling* as employed in the discussion above.

The New Testament gives many other examples. In 1 Corinthians 2:4, Paul speaks of his whole ministry while in Corinth as having been by "demonstration of the Spirit and of power" (meaning power which the Spirit demonstrated through him; in other words, empowerment given to him). In Acts 18:25, the preaching of Apollos in Ephesus is said to have been the result of being "fervent in the spirit" (meaning that it was made effective by the Spirit empowering him). A few other examples may simply be listed: Stephen was given the ability to look into heaven by the Spirit (Acts 7:55). Numerous people were provided with needed information by the Spirit — Peter (Acts 10:19; 11:12) Agabus (Acts 11:28; 21:11), Paul (Acts 16:6,7; 20:23), and certain disciples (Acts 21:4). Miracles were performed by the Spirit (Rom. 15:18,19). Believers were helped in their infirmities by the Spirit (Rom. 8:26). And saints are said to be taught by the Spirit (1 Cor. 2:13) and to be given gifts for ministry by the Spirit (1 Cor. 12:8-11; Heb. 2:4). Actually, there are more cases of Spirit-empowerment of believers in the New Testament than in the Old. So, like regeneration, indwelling, sealing, and filling, Spirit-empowerment was experienced in the times of both Testaments.

A further word regarding Spirit-empowerment calls for notice. It concerns the relation between the indwelling of the Spirit and empowerment by the Spirit. As indicated above, both Peter and Paul, who had long been indwelt, were especially empowered by the Spirit for speaking messages on the occasions concerned (Acts 4:8 and 13:9). This means that the two functions of the Spirit are indeed two and not one, even as indicated in earlier discussions regarding Old Testament situations. The indwelling of the Spirit concerns His permanent residence in every believer; His empowerment concerns the granting of special ability for a divinely given task. All believers, then, experience the former, but only those given particular tasks the latter. Jesus had Spirit-empowerment in mind when He told the disciples that, when they would come into dangerous situations, they should not be concerned because the "Spirit" would give them "in that same hour" what they should say (Matt. 10:19,20).

One may believe that the Spirit stands ready to give similar provision to believers today. A task suddenly confronts an individual, which he knows he cannot meet alone; an opportunity to witness to a person arises when words seem naturally to fail; an assignment to speak in a place or situation is given, for which one feels himself wholly inadequate — these and many other challenges come for the believer, and the Spirit is ready to grant special ability — as He did to an Othniel, a Bezaleel, a David, a Paul — and this should be a source of both confidence and joy for every child of God.

D. Baptism by the Spirit Began at Pentecost

The one aspect of work by the Spirit left for discussion is baptism, and this is the one aspect which did begin at Pentecost. The other aspects — regeneration, indwelling, sealing, filling, and empowerment — were common to both Testaments. There is nothing about them particularly Old Testament in kind or New Testament. The situation is different with baptism, however; it is definitely limited to the New Testament.

The reason for this is that baptism has to do with the church, and the church did not begin as a distinct organism until Pentecost. In fact, it was the baptism of believers by the Holy Spirit that inaugurated the church. It was not that the church began and then was baptized. It began when believers were baptized to form it. This happened when the Spirit came upon the believers assembled in Jerusalem on the day of Pentecost (Acts 2:1-12).

Baptism, when used in the sense here intended, has nothing to do with water. Baptism by water is an important New Testament truth, but it is quite different in subject matter than baptism by the Spirit. The truth of baptism by the Spirit is set forth in 1 Corinthians 12:13: "For by one Spirit are we all baptized into one body, whether we be Jews or Gentiles, whether we be bond or free; and have been all made to drink into one Spirit." Several other passages also make reference to it: Matthew 3:11; Mark 1:8; Luke 3:16; John 1:33; Acts 1:5; 11:16; Galatians 3:27; and Ephesians 4:5. The reader of the New Testament should notice that each of these passages which concern time preceding Pentecost speak of this baptism as yet future, while each which follow it as past.[9] This is further indication that baptism was first carried out on that day. Since the church did not exist before Pentecost, baptism could not have been carried on in Old Testament time.

The baptism of the Spirit is that work which joins Christians

[9] See Walvoord, *The Holy Spirit*, p. 139; also Cambron, *Bible Doctrines*, p. 131.

together into a common bond of church relationship. It unites them, giving them an organic oneness. It provides them with a sense of mutual love, and sets before them a common purpose. It is because of this unifying baptism that Christians, wherever they meet, feel an immediate closeness of friendship. They are of one group, a part in one grand enterprise.

When the church was first instituted at Pentecost, there was need that baptism be granted to many at one time. The idea of church is quite meaningless apart from a collection of several people. Therefore, on Pentecost, the Spirit came in baptism on an assembled group of believers, probably 120 in number (Acts 1:15). Since that time each believer is individually baptized into that body then begun. The baptism of believers as a collective group is no longer necessary, for a church already exists. Individuals need only be baptized into it and thus joined to it.

The moment of baptism is the same as the moment of regeneration; in fact, it is the same also as the moment when indwelling and sealing begin. The Holy Spirit imparts new life in regeneration, as He comes into the person to indwell him and so seal him as a permanent child of God, and at the same time baptizes him into the church body. Filling and empowerment may also occur at the same moment, but not necessarily. One should be filled then, for he should yield himself to the Spirit's will from the very first. Empowerment, however, will only come when this person is faced with a challenge calling for special strength or ability.[10]

The reason for baptism's being instituted at Pentecost — which is another way of stating the reason for the inauguration of the church — was that there was need for the spread of the gospel message. Christ had now lived and died and the good news of salvation was ready to be taken to a lost world. Through Old Testament days, God had in large part segregated His Word in Israel, until the provision for man's salvation might be made in the work of Christ. Now that this had been done, there was no longer need for segregation. The world at large should hear of the wonderful provision. No longer should there be a special people — in terms of a nation — but a universal people, without barrier or "middle wall of partition" (Eph. 2:14; cf. Gal. 3:28) between them. For this reason, a new organism was called for,

[10]One type of empowerment is an exception, empowerment for gospel proclamation, see pp. 76, 77.

established on a different basis than the nation Israel. This organism was the church. The organism needed unity, a sense of oneness, so it could recognize and present itself as a common group. This was supplied initially by the collective baptism of believers at Pentecost, and continues to be provided by a continuing baptism of individuals at the time of their regeneration.

It should be understood that the church, as used in this context, is the church universal, not local. The universal church is the organism to which all believers belong, no matter what set of denominational statements they ascribe to. The local church is an organized group of these believers holding to a particular set of such statements. There is only one universal church; there are many local churches. It is into the universal church that believers are baptized by the Spirit. For references to the universal church, see Matthew 16:18; Ephesians 1:22; 3:10,21; 5:23-32; Colossians 1:18, 24; et al.; for references to a local church, see Acts 5:11; 11:26; 1 Corinthians 11:18; 14:28,35; 16:1; Galatians 1:2; 1 Thessalonians 2:14; et al.

The last matter to notice is that baptism involves a certain aspect of empowerment for the believer. Actually, Spirit-empowerment can be distinguished in the Scriptures in varying degrees. It was noted, for instance, that Samson was regularly empowered to provide special strength; but on three occasions he is said to have had the Spirit come on him, evidently, to grant him still greater strength for the time involved. Paul, in the New Testament, certainly was continually empowered by the Spirit, but still the Spirit came on him additionally at the time of speaking to the sorcerer Elymas (Acts 13:9). Though it is true that Spirit-empowerment, as it has been discussed in the foregoing discussions, concerns occasions when the Spirit granted specific and remarkable provisions of power for tasks, it is also true that there is a degree of empowerment granted to every Christian at baptism.

Evidence for this empowerment may be taken first from logical deduction. If God brought the church to existence for the purpose of proclaiming the gospel, it is logical to believe that He would have given power to its members, when baptized into the church, to carry out that purpose. Evidence may be found, secondly, in the Scriptures themselves. This power for gospel proclamation was promised already by Christ in Luke 24:49: "Tarry ye [here] in the city of Jerusalem, until ye be endued with power from on high." Jesus again promised it in Acts 1:8, just before His ascension to heaven: "But ye shall receive power, after that the Holy Spirit is come upon you: and ye shall be witnesses unto me both in Jerusalem, and in all Judea, and in Samaria, and unto the uttermost part of the earth." Some persons, such as those called to the ministry of evangelism, no doubt have this aspect of empowerment more than others. The clear implication of these passages, however, is that all children of God have it in some degree. All, then, should realize this and make use of it. Sadly, many do not, and this can only be displeasing to the Holy Spirit who grants the power. Witnessing the gospel message is a task in which every Christian should be engaged.

8

CONFLICTS RESOLVED

A few questions naturally arise concerning the conclusions set forth in the preceding discussion and these should be answered. Also, certain Scripture passages some expositors believe are in conflict with the view need to be explored.

A. Questions Answered

Answers to some of the questions now to be posed have been touched on in the prior chapter, but they call for more discussion than was appropriate there.

1. How could Christians be "filled" with the Spirit for the first time on Pentecost? According to Acts 2:4, the Christians who were assembled together on Pentecost were "all filled with the Holy Spirit." As evidence of this filling, "there appeared unto them cloven tongues like as of fire" (Acts 2:3). The immediate result was that those filled were able to speak in tongues other than their own, so that foreign visitors (at the annual Feast of Pentecost) could understand them in their own languages. The occasion was climaxed by a sermon from Peter, with the result that "about three thousand souls" were saved (2:41).

The question concerns how believers could have been filled by the Spirit prior to this time, as previous discussions have shown, and still be said here at Pentecost to be filled for the first time. How could they have been filled already, yet now suddenly be filled for the first?

The answer involves the meaning of the word *filled*. As noted in the prior chapter, the Scriptures do not always use the word in the same way, or even in the way intended by theological discussion. It was observed at the time that the Old Testament often uses the word (*male'*) to refer to a person being empowered for a task (e.g., Bezaleel, Exod. 31:3). This use of the word was distinguished from the theological employment of *filling*, where the meaning refers to one's spiritual relationship to God. Now, in Acts 2:4, the word is used in reference to the baptism of the Spirit. The believers were baptized into the one church-body, formed at this time. It was this aspect of filling, then, that began at Pentecost. Christians were baptized into the new church, and this concept of being filled had not existed in Old Testament time. But this does not mean that believers could not have been filled prior to this, in the sense of their own spiritual relationship to God. As has been observed, they were.

These distinctions in the Spirit's work, and others that have been made, call for a related point to be clarified. When the Scriptures speak of the Spirit's coming on a person, or leaving him, this should not be understood in a spatial sense. The Spirit being God, and therefore omnipresent, cannot be spoken of as moving from one place to another, like a finite being. Finite man is either in one place or another, and has to move from one place to get to another. This is not true of the Spirit, who is present everywhere all the time. His coming on a person, then, or filling a person, must be understood in terms of an aspect of work He either begins or ceases in respect to that person. More specific language would refer to an aspect of work by the Spirit's coming on or beginning in a person, rather than the Spirit Himself doing so.

Therefore, in respect to the question at hand, one could properly answer that, prior to Pentecost, in Old Testament time, that aspect of the Spirit's work called "filling" was being carried on regularly, in which believers were being made spiritually mature, while at Pentecost that aspect of work called "baptism" was begun for the first time.

2. The Old Testament speaks only of the Spirit's work of empowerment. The question now concerns the reason why the Old Testament refers only to the empowerment of people by the Spirit, if the Spirit was also regenerating, indwelling, sealing, and filling them. Should not the fact that these other concepts are not mentioned in the Old Testament be cause enough for believing that they were not being carried on? This question has already been considered in the prior chapter (pp. 68,69) in respect to regeneration, but more needs to be said concerning indwelling, sealing, and filling.

These concepts, though not mentioned as such in the Old Testament, are there in the sense of illustration. They are not set forth in word discussion, but they are in the life-presentations of the saints involved. And, make no mistake, this is a true way of being included in the Old Testament.

Speaking first of sealing, it is there in the sense of the preservation of Old Testament saints. They did not lose their status of a righteous standing in God's sight any more than New Testament saints. They continued faithful to God in spite of temptations and sometimes extreme trials. Jacob became a more spiritual man at the close of his life than at the beginning. Even Samson, though he fell into deep sin with Delilah, came back into God's favor before his death, with his special strength restored to pull down a great Philistine temple. But how could they be kept in this spiritually approved condition apart from the work of the Holy Spirit? And the work of the Holy Spirit that so keeps a man is designated in the New Testament as sealing.

Really nothing more needs to be said regarding indwelling. This concept is implied as soon as sealing is established, for it is the indwelling of the Holy Spirit that constitutes the sealing of the Holy Spirit.

Then the concept of filling, pertaining to yieldedness of life, can be shown to exist in the Old Testament from numerous passages. For instance, in Deuteronomy 10:16, God commanded already in His law, "Circumcise therefore the foreskin of your heart, and be no more stiffnecked." In other words, the people were to put away sin from their lives and no longer rebel against God's revealed will. This means they were to have yielded lives, which indicates they were to be filled by the Spirit. Years later, Jeremish spoke in similar terms: "Circumcise yourselves to the LORD, and take away the foreskins of your heart, ye men of Judah and inhabitants of Jerusalem" (4:4). Again, he spoke of a future day when God would put His "law" in the "inward parts" of the people "and write it in their hearts," so that He would be "their God, and they" would be His "people" (31:33). The implication is that the people knew this should already be the situation, but that, since it was not, they could know a day was coming when it would be. Or, besides such passages as these, one can take evidence from the very lives of the great Old Testament saints. They lived in a manner yielded to God's will. In other words, they demonstrated that they were filled by the Spirit.

3. Did Old Testament saints recognize these truths? To what degree were Old Testament saints aware of these truths? Did they know about regeneration, indwelling, sealing, and filling? Did they understand the concept of empowerment, which is the one work the Old Testament mentions? The answer to these questions can only be that Old Testament people did not understand any of these truths in detail. In fact, formulations of them were not made until well into church history, following the time of Christ.[1]

As for the concepts — regeneration, indwelling, sealing, and filling — one can say that the ideas were to some extent recognized, though they would not have been distinguished by these names, nor could they have been defined in any detail. However, Old Testament saints surely understood the difference between a person who was a true child of God and one who was not, a difference the New Testament would speak of in terms of regeneration. Certainly also they recognized that more than their own abilities were involved in remaining true to God, a fact the New Testament would speak of in terms of indwelling and sealing. David, for instance, cried out following his sin with Bathsheba, "Create in me a clean heart, O God; and renew a right spirit within me" (Ps. 51:10), showing his recognition of dependence on God for a restoration to God's favor. And one may be sure, also, of their awareness that they were to conduct themselves in a way pleasing to God, a truth the New Testament would speak of in terms of filling. Samuel reminded Saul that "to obey" God "is better than sacrifice, and to hearken than the fat of rams" (1 Sam. 15:22).

4. The rationale for speaking only of empowerment. Still another question concerns the reason why the Old Testament speaks of the Spirit's work of empowerment, when it does not of regeneration, indwelling, sealing, or filling. What was there about the work of empowerment that called for it thus to be singled out for mention? The Scriptures do not give a definite answer, but one may be conjectured. It involves the fact that empowerment concerned service that people rendered to God, while the other concepts involved personal relationships. God evidently saw more important that man recognize the secret of successful service than the secret of a right spiritual relationship to Himself. This is not to say that service was considered more important than a right spiritual relationship. The

[1]See Earle E. Cairns, *Christianity Through the Centuries*, pp. 142-145.

Bible, in fact, lays greater stress on the latter than on the former. It is only to say that God saw man had need of realizing in greater measure where the source of his power for service lay.

God did indeed want man to remain in a right relationship with Himself, and man was admonished to this end again and again. That was the great stress of the prophets, as they urged people to put away sin and live righteously before God. The people, however, did not need to know that it was really the indwelling of the Spirit that kept them in that relationship. The need was to urge them to live in this way and the Spirit would then do His part in cooperation with them — as He does for Christians today — whether they knew of this or not.

Regarding empowerment, however, the people needed concrete encouragement. Tasks before them were simply too big and challenging without knowing that the supernatural power of the Spirit indwelt them to aid them. A clear example of this need is provided in the instance of Elisha's asking Elijah that a "double portion" of the Spirit be given to him, as he faced the challenge of continuing the work of his beloved master (2 Kings 2:9). Elijah was about to leave him. The two had been fighting God's battle together, against the provocations of the house of Ahab and Jezebel for some years, and Elisha knew that he was incapable in himself of meeting the challenge. He knew that the secret of Elijah's success, as he had led in this battle, had been the special empowerment of the Spirit, and he now wanted that same power in his own life. David echoed a similar heart-cry as he requested of God, "Take not thy holy spirit from me" (Ps. 51:11). He had seen the havoc Saul had wrought when the Spirit had been taken from him, and he wanted no repetition of this in his rule. So, then, an understanding of the empowerment of the Spirit was necessary for Old Testament leaders to have the courage and confidence needed to move ahead in the tasks divinely assigned.

B. Passages Considered

We now come to consider a few Scripture passages which some expositors believe are in conflict with conclusions that have been reached in prior discussions. A proper understanding of the passages, however, will show that they are consistent with these conclusions.

1. John 3:3-21. This first passage comes from Jesus' conversation with Nicodemus. Jesus told the learned Jew, "Except a man be born again, he cannot see the kingdom of God" (v. 3). Nicodemus immediately registered surprise and wondered if Jesus meant a man would have to "enter the second time into his mother's womb" (v. 4). When Jesus explained that this was not what He meant, Nicodemus still responded, "How can these things be?" (v. 9). Jesus appropriately replied, "Art thou a master of Israel, and knowest not these things?" (v. 10).

The conflict seen in this passage with the conclusions made herein is well expressed by Lewis Chafer as follows: "The doctrine of regeneration by the Spirit came as a surprise and bewilderment to Nicodemus."[2] In another place, Chafer enlarges on the thought by noting that, since Nicodemus was a leader in his day, Jesus' words would no doubt have been just as strange to Judaism generally.[3] His point in both places is to say that regeneration, evidently, was unknown to the Jews of Jesus' day and therefore to all of Old Testament day. Then, to account for Old Testament people being the kind of godly people they were, he says, "The Israelite began by being born into a covenant relation with Jehovah and from then on was able to continue in right relation to Jehovah through the sacrifices which were, in the event of sin, the basis of forgiveness and restoration."[4]

According to this view, Israelites were born into a right spiritual relationship with God simply by being one of Abraham's posterity and then were able to maintain this relationship through the sacrifices. This view, however, does not accord with the truth that man died spiritually in Adam in the Garden of Eden and can be saved by grace alone, on the basis of the shed blood of God's Lamb, Jesus Christ. It must, therefore, be rejected, and the surprise registered by Nicodemus be explained in quite a different way.

Nicodemus was surprised because of his lack of knowing what he should have known. Jesus implied this when He responded to him, "Art thou a master of Israel, and knowest not these things?" Nicodemus should have known of what Jesus spoke, though he may have had reason not to recognize the exact words at first, *born again*. But the Old Testament had said enough regarding the nature and importance of a changed life to which he could have quickly related these words. David was specific that God did not want sacrifices, if

[2]Chafer, *Systematic Theology*, I, p. 407.
[3]Ibid., VI, p. 73.
[4]Ibid., I, p. 408.

that was all they were, but a proper spirit, saying, "For thou desirest not sacrifice; else would I give it, thou delightest not in burnt offering. The sacrifices of God are a broken spirit: a broken and a contrite heart, O God, thou wilt not despise" (Ps. 51:16,17).

Then in Psalm 143:10, David related the Spirit to the God-pleasing life: "Teach me to do thy will; for thou art my God: thy spirit is good; lead me into the land of uprightness." David shows that he well understood what God had long before recorded in His Law: "And the LORD thy God will circumcise thine heart, and the heart of thy seed, to love the LORD thy God with all thine heart, and with all thy soul, that thou mayest live" (Deut. 30:6). Years later, in similar vein, Ezekiel rebuked the people for not living this kind of life before God and predicted a day when God would "give them one heart," and would "put a new spirit within" them, and would "take the stony heart out of their flesh, and . . . give them an heart of flesh" (11:19; cf. 36:26,27).

These passages, and many more, show that God had long wanted a change of heart on the part of his people and not merely sacrifices. But a change of heart can only come when the Holy Spirit imparts regeneration — or, as Jesus put it, when a man is "born again." Man cannot bring this about himself, whether he lived before or after the Cross. Since the Fall, man has been spiritually dead, and he must be made alive with new life by regeneration, if he is to become spiritually alive. This is the truth recognized by Old Testament writers, and it is this truth that Nicodemus should have brought to mind when Christ spoke to him. It is no wonder that Jesus rebuked him. It is true that the Old Testament does not use the term *born again* for this concept, and so if Jesus had left the discussion only with this statement one could understand at least Nicodemus' initial surprise. But Christ went on to explain what he meant by the term, and then Nicodemus had no excuse at all.

2. John 7:37-39. The second passage is found in Jesus' words at the Feast of Tabernacles (probably during His last year of ministry), when He said to the people, "If any man thirst, let him come unto me, and drink. He that believeth on me, as the scripture hath said, out of his belly shall flow rivers of living water. (But this spake he of the Spirit, which they that believe on him should receive: for the Holy Spirit was not yet given; because that Jesus was not yet glorified.)"

Here Jesus spoke of a day coming when "rivers of living water" would flow from believers to the end that thirsty men might freely drink. In explanation, John, the writer, added the note that Jesus thus spoke of the Spirit which believers "should receive" at some future time, since "the Holy Spirit was not yet given." The time in view clearly was the day of Pentecost and following, when the Holy Spirit would be given for baptizing believers into the church and empowering them for spreading the gospel. The "rivers of living water" were the words and life-influence that believers then would be able to extend to thirsty men in sin that they might have newness of life in salvation. In other words, Jesus was speaking of the day of church activity, when the gospel would go forth to a dying world. The aspect in mind, then, in which the Spirit had not yet been given, was just as has been explained above. It was the aspect manifested at Pentecost, when the Spirit did come to baptize believers into the church and empower them for gospel proclamation. The passage says nothing in respect to the Spirit's not having done other work in previous time, as discussed earlier.

3. **John 14:16,17,26; 15:26; 16:13.** The third passage consists of several references in Jesus' discourse to His disciples the evening before the Crucifixion. The references are parallel in content and significance and can well be considered together.

The general thought of them is Jesus' promise that the Holy Spirit would be sent to believers, as their "Comforter" or "Counselor" (*parakletos*), after Jesus had returned to heaven. When the Spirit came, He would remind believers of what Jesus had said while He was here (14:26; 15:26), He would instruct them concerning "things to come" (16:13), and He would remain with them "for ever" (14:16). It is generally agreed that the time in view was again the day of Pentecost. The Spirit did come, and the various matters set forth in the references did come true. Each of the matters had to do with church activity, which began then.

One statement in John 14:17 calls for further discussion. It is cited by John Walvoord in support of his view that Old Testament saints were not indwelt by the Spirit.[5] Speaking of the passage, he states, "Christ contrasts what was true before and after Pentecost in the expression, 'for he dwelleth with you, and shall be in you.' Here is the

---

[5]Walvoord, *The Church in Prophecy*, pp. 37,38: Cambron argues similarly, *Bible Doctrines*, p. 135.

theological distinction between the work of the Spirit before Pentecost and after Pentecost." He continues to explain this distinction by saying that the Spirit dwelt "*with* the saints" prior to Pentecost and "*in*" them following that time.

It is quite true that a distinction in meaning exists between the prepositions *with (para)* and *in (en)*. In brief, the distinction is that the former speaks of "being near," "alongside of," or "in the immediate proximity," and the latter of being "within." What this distinction means in reference to the Spirit's relation to the believer, however, is not easily ascertained, nor does Walvoord elaborate on it. He simply says that the latter preposition *in* speaks of "a more intimate" relationship between the Spirit and the believer,[6] and that the use of both in this one passage indicates that the Old Testament saint was not indwelt.[7]

One finds difficulty in relating the meaning of these prepositions to the Old Testament presentation of the Spirit coming on and leaving people. The idea of simply remaining near a person is not at all the same as coming on and leaving him. Furthermore, the way in which Christ used the preposition *with (para)* in this text shows that He had in mind a continuation of action in respect to it, for he employed a present perfect form of the verb *meno* ("dwelleth") along with it. The only distinction that seems to be meaningful, in respect to the implied view that Walvoord draws, is that the Old Testament believer was somehow "outer-dwelt" by the Spirit and the New Testament believer "inner-dwelt." But nowhere does either the Old or New Testament ever speak of the Spirit ministering to Old Testament saints by simply being near them, rather than within them.

It is theoretically possible that the Spirit could have ministered to Old Testament saints by working on them from without, but this thought does not appeal to one's mind as a meaningful distinction from the Spirit's New Testament activity. Why should Old Testament conditions have called only for remaining near saints, while New Testament conditions call for entering the saint? Moreover, when the Old Testament does speak of the Spirit's coming on Old Testament saints for the purpose of empowerment, it uses verbs which clearly speak of coming within them: e.g., "entering into" (*bo'*, Ezek. 2:2; 3:24), "overpowering" (*tsalah*, Judg. 14:6,19; 15:14; 1 Sam. 10:10;

---

[6]Walvoord, *The Church in Prophecy*, p. 37.
[7]He argues similarly in *The Holy Spirit*, pp. 72,73.

11:6), "clothing" (*labash*, Judg. 6:34; 1 Chron. 12:18; 2 Chron. 24:20), "being filled" (*male'*, Exod. 31:3; 35:31), and "falling upon" (*naphal*, Ezek. 11:5). None indicate the idea of simply being near or in the vicinity of.

Since Jesus did use two different prepositions, however, it follows that He did wish to convey some variant meaning. What was the difference He had in mind? The difference that seems to fit the situation best is the distinction that has been seen already — the distinction between the Spirit's work in believers before the church started and after this time. Christ was saying that the Spirit had been "with" believers in the senses that have been noted (regenerating, indwelling, sealing, filling, empowering), but that the time was near when He would additionally baptize them and then empower them in a new way for gospel proclamation.

But what did Jesus see in the use of *with* that suited this Old Testament activity, in distinction from *in* for the additional work of the New Testament? The most likely answer is that *with (para)* is probably the nearest Greek word in meaning to *in (en)* and still have a clear distinction indicated.[8] Actually, when used with the word *dwell*, as here, the preposition *para* carries a close relation to *en*. For instance, it is used several times to mean "dwelling in the same house" (see John 1:39; Acts 9:43; 18:3; 21:8). Jesus wanted to make a distinction between the Spirit's work in the Old and New Testaments — for a distinction would exist when the work of baptism began — and so a different preposition was called for; yet He needed one that was close in meaning, for a basic similarity in work would continue.

4. John 20:22. The fourth passage is found in the context where Jesus appears to the disciples in the upper room following His resurrection. He is said to have "breathed on them" and then stated, "Receive ye the Holy Spirit." The relationship between Jesus' action here and the coming of the Holy Spirit on Pentecost following is a debated question quite apart from the more basic matter considered here. It is appropriate, however, to suggest an answer, since the whole subject of Pentecostal activity is in point.

The answer most in keeping with the overall teaching of Scripture is that Jesus did not actually impart the Holy Spirit at this time, but that His action was symbolic of what would happen shortly on Pente-

[8]The preposition *eis* is still nearer to *en*, but too near to maintain a real distinction.

cost. This is evidenced by the following considerations: (1) Nothing different in the lives of the disciples is demonstrated at this time, to show that a new work of the Holy Spirit began then; (2) Jesus Himself said, following this time, "Ye shall be baptized with the Holy Spirit not many days hence" (Acts 1:5), and again, "But ye shall receive power, after that the Holy Spirit is come upon you" (Acts 1:8); and (3) on Pentecost, ten days after Christ's ascension, the Holy Spirit did come in a dramatic fashion, indicating the beginning of the church. Jesus' action and words at this earlier time, then, were a sign and pledge of what would happen. That He breathed on the disciples, prior to speaking the words, was to show them the origin of the Spirit when He would come. The Spirit would proceed from the Son, like breath was proceeding at the moment from His mouth.

5. Joel 2:28,29. The last passage to consider comes from the Old Testament. Here Joel predicted a day when the Spirit of God would be poured out on believers. He wrote, "And it shall come to pass afterward, that I will pour out my spirit upon all flesh; and your sons and your daughters shall prophesy, your old men shall dream dreams, your young men shall see visions: And also upon the servants and upon the handmaids in those days will I pour out my spirit."

The question asked regarding this passage is this: If Joel said that this action of the Spirit would occur only in a future day, then how can one say the Spirit was already at work in believers in his own time? And that Joel was indeed referring to a future day is indicated by Peter's clear indication on Pentecost that at least a partial fulfillment was then being made (Acts 2:16-18). Furthermore, it is commonly held that the complete fulfillment will not transpire until Christ's millennial reign on earth.[9]

The answer to the question lies in noting exactly what Joel predicted regarding this pouring out of the Spirit. Nothing he said concerns regeneration, indwelling, sealing, or filling. It concerns, rather, empowerment, the one aspect of work that is said in the Old Testament to have transpired at that time. He spoke of people prophesying, dreaming dreams, and seeing visions, all aspects of empowerment. The contrast in Joel's mind, then, did not concern the type of work the Spirit would do in the future, but aspects of empowerment and the number of people who would be so empowered.

[9]For discussion, see L. J. Wood, *The Bible and Future Events* (Grand Rapids: Zondervan, 1973), pp. 163, 164.

Certain of the prophets were empowered in respect to receiving revelations in some of these ways in Old Testament day, but Joel was saying that a day was coming when "all flesh," including "sons" and "daughters," "old men," "young men," and even "servants" and "handmaids," would be empowered to "prophesy," "dream dreams," and "see visions."

Peter's reference to the passage on Pentecost was to say that an aspect of this special empowerment was being experienced at that time in the believer's ability to speak in foreign tongues. The complete fulfillment will come, however, only when the millennial reign of Christ is established and the Holy Spirit will be active among believers to a degree not seen in the world before. The harmony of Joel's statement with the prior discussion exists, then, in recognizing that Joel was not speaking of no empowerment at all by the Spirit in his day, but that a day to come would see this being accomplished in far greater degree. The verse has no bearing on whether or not the Spirit indwelt Old Testament saints.

9

WERE THE EARLY PROPHETS ECSTATICS?

We now turn to a quite different area of inquiry. Its relation to the work of the Holy Spirit in the Old Testament is less direct than prior discussions, but it still is of a nature calling for investigation. This area concerns the question of ecstaticism among the prophets, particularly the early prophets in Israel's history. Many scholars believe that these prophets were ecstatics and that this was an essential characteristic if people of the day were to accept them as prophets. A comment by E. O. James is only typical: "It was this type of shamanistic behavior . . . that constituted the principal role of the professional ecstatics described in Israel as *nebi'ism* [prophetism]."[1] Other writers speak of an ability for ecstaticism as actually a badge of authority for the prophet, without which people would not have accepted them as authentic.[2]

The reason it is necessary to consider this question is that there are a few Scripture passages used to support the erroneous viewpoint, and the Holy Spirit is mentioned in them. His work thus becomes involved, and one has to ask what the nature of His work was as indicated by them. Actually, the more important of these passages have already been studied in prior discussions, but they must now be considered in respect to this matter of ecstaticism. Such questions as the following call for answer: Did the individuals concerned in these passages engage in ecstaticism? If not, how should the occasions described be understood, some of which are rather surprising in nature? And what is the correct explanation of the Holy Spirit's role as involved in them?

[1]E. O. James, *Prophecy and the Prophets,* p. 79.
[2]See N. Porteous, "Prophecy," in *Record and Revelation*, ed. H. Wheeler Robinson, for numerous references.

WERE THE EARLY PROPHETS ECSTATICS?

A. The Nature of Ecstaticism

It is essential first to understand what is meant by ecstaticism. What is this phenomenon that numerous scholars believe early prophets of Israel practiced?

The idea and pursuit of ecstaticism is believed to have originated in Asia Minor.[3] It is thought to have moved from there westward into Greece and eastward into Syria and Palestine toward the end of the second millennium B.C. Thus the Canaanites came to accept the practice, and the thinking is that Israel became influenced by them. Various forms of ecstaticism have since been found in many parts of the world, as people have sought revelation from their gods by this means. Probably Delphi in Greece, with its famous center of oracular pronouncement, was the best known of ancient ecstatic centers. E. O. James describes the activity there as follows:

> It would appear the inspired prophetess, when an oracle was demanded, arrayed herself in long robes, a golden headdress, and a wreath of laurel leaves, and drank of the sacred spring kassotis. She then, it is said, seated herself on a tripod over a vaporous cleft in a chasm of a cave below, unless she actually entered the cave to encounter the vapour, in order to attain a state of enthusiasm. In this condition she gave counsel as the mouthpiece of Apollo.[4]

Certain forms of ecstasy were carried out only as a ritualistic exercise for some festal celebration, but the type of ecstasy to which prophecy is compared was motivated by a desire for revelation. The spirit world was sought, and to that end efforts were made to gain a release from contact with the world of reality. To achieve the ecstatic state, various means were employed, including a sacred dance to rhythmic music, breathing poisonous gas, and even the use of narcotics. The thought was to have the natural powers of reason set aside so that the mind might be opened to a reception of the divine word. Accompanying this rapport with the spirit realm was normally a physical seizure, which T. H. Robinson describes as follows:

> It consists of a fit or attack which affected the whole body. Sometimes the limbs were stimulated to violent action, and wild leaping and contortions resulted. These might be more or less rhythmical and the phenomenon would present the appearance of a wild and frantic

[3]See T. J. Meek, *Hebrew Origins* (Gloucester, MA: Peter Smith, 1960), p. 155, for discussion; also William O. Oesterley and T. H. Robinson, *Hebrew Religion* 2nd ed. (Naperville, IL: Allenson, 1937), pp. 185,186.
[4]James, *The Nature and Function of Priesthood*, p. 40.

91

dance. At other times there was more or less complete constriction of the muscles, and the condition became almost cataleptic. The vocal chords were sometimes involved, noises and sounds were poured out which might be unrecognizable as human speech.[5]

Normally a priest would be on hand to interpret such utterances, for these were thought to be the speaking of the god.

This type of ecstasy, then, is what is believed to have been shared by the early Israelite prophets. The earliest of them — assigned to the day of Samuel — are thought to have assembled as bands and moved through the country offering their services. The thinking is that people would come to them, present their earnest inquiries, and these prophets would then seek the divine answer by their display of ecstatic frenzy. Because of the unusual behavior while in the ecstatic state, the prophets came to be called "madmen" (*meshuggah*).

A main argument for this view is based on a comparison with religious practices of other nations of the day. It is assumed that, because other peoples pursued this form of divine contact, Israel surely did. The conservative scholar, however, who believes that Israel was unique in its world, having been specially called to existence by God and given its laws and instructions supernaturally, places little reliance on this manner of argument. No doubt Israel borrowed some aspects of its culture from the Canaanites, but not in basic matters. Religiously, some Israelite people defected to the worship of the Canaanite god, Baal,[6] but Israel's official religious belief had been given by God through Moses already at Mt. Sinai, prior to the conquest of Canaan.

Besides this main argument, however, there are a few Scripture passages to which adherents of the view appeal, and these call for discussion. We shall first note them in their contexts and then show the argumentation that is taken from them. A refutation of this argumentation will be presented in the following chapter. There are three principal passages used, plus a few others which support them.

B. Passages Thought to Support Ecstaticism

1. The main passages. All three of the main passages have been noted in prior discussions, but not from the point of view at issue.

[5]Robinson, *Prophecy and the Prophets,* p. 31.
[6]The story of Gideon is especially indicative of this; notice particularly Judges 6:25-32.

a. Numbers 11:25-29. The first passage concerns the occasion when God appointed seventy elders to assist Moses in administering the affairs of Israel in the wilderness. Moses had become overburdened in the work, and God told him to bring forth these elders so the Spirit who was already on Moses could be placed also on them. It was observed earlier that the purpose of this sharing of the Spirit was to empower these men that they might be able to perform this work properly.

All this was done, and when the Spirit came on the group, each of them began to "prophesy" (*yithnabbe'u*),[7] apparently for some time. Finally all ceased in this action but two, Eldad and Medad, and they continued on, even running through the Israelite camp as they prophesied. They came to the notice of Joshua, who then went to Moses to urge that they be made to stop. Moses, however, mildly rebuked the younger man, as he expressed the wish that "all the LORD'S people were prophets, and that the LORD would put his spirit upon them." In this activity called prophesying, no message is said to have been spoken either by the whole group of seventy together or by Eldad and Medad.

b. 1 Samuel 10:1-13. The second passage involves Samuel's anointing of Saul as Israel's first king, and a resulting occasion of prophesying by Saul. Saul while still a young man, along with a servant, had come to Samuel to ask about lost donkeys. Samuel answered his question, but then, more importantly, poured "a vial of oil" on Saul's head and said, "Is it not because the LORD hath anointed thee to be captain over his inheritance?" (v. 1). Because of the significance of the act, and no doubt the astonishment of Saul, Samuel further told him of three events that would soon befall him as he returned on his way home, implying that their occurrence would provide evidence for Saul's validating the action just performed.

One of these predicted events concerned Saul's encounter with a "company of prophets coming down from the high place with a psaltery, and a tabret, and a pipe, and a harp, before them," who would be engaged in "prophesying" (*mithnabbe'im*, a participle, indicating continued action) at the time (v. 5). He further stated that "the spirit of the LORD" would come on Saul when he saw them and that he would then "prophesy" (*hithnabbi'tha*) also and be "turned

[7]"Prophesy" is a key word in these passages, for adherents of the view believe it means "ecstatic frenzy" each time.

into another man" (v. 6). All these events, including this last, did occur just as predicted. Saul met the "company of prophets," experienced the "spirit of God" come upon him, and then prophesied along with those he met (v. 10). In doing this, he exhibited behavior that was so different from what was customary for him that onlookers asked, "What is this that is come unto the son of Kish [Saul's father]? Is Saul also among the prophets?" (v. 11).

c. **1 Samuel 19:18-24.** This passage also concerns an occasion of prophesying by Saul. By the time involved, however, he had already served as king for most of his forty-year reign (Acts 13:21), and he was engaged in efforts to kill David, whom he recognized as a rival to his throne. He learned that David had recently fled to Samuel at Ramah[8], and he sent three groups of messengers to apprehend and return David to him. None of the groups were successful, however, for all three on coming to David found Samuel and a "company of prophets prophesying"; the result was that each group then experienced the "spirit of God" coming on them, followed by their own act of prophesying, while they remained in the company of Samuel's prophets. Finally, Saul himself went, no doubt in the heat of disgust and anger, but on the way to Ramah the "Spirit of God" came also on him and he began to "prophesy" (*yithnabbe'*), even before arriving where the others were. Later, he "stripped off his clothes"[9] and then "lay down naked all that day and all that night" (1 Sam. 19:24).

2. Supporting passages. Besides these three main passages, a few others are believed to give supporting evidence. The thought is that these additional passages show that the word *prophesy (hithnabba')* carried a wider meaning than merely "to speak for God," which most admit is its main meaning at least later in the Old Testament. This wider meaning, it is maintained, bears a significant relationship to the idea of ecstatic frenzy, and so gives further evidence that *prophesy* could mean "to be ecstatic" in the main passages. Three passages are believed to indicate the wider meaning, "raving," and three others the meaning "madness."

[8]The text says that they were at "Naioth in Ramah." Naioth means "dwelling," and so, since the group of prophets was also there, it is likely that this was the dwelling of the school over which Samuel was head: a school of prophets.

[9]*Clothes (beged)* may here stand merely for the outer robe, which encumbered one for ready movement. The word *naked ('arom)* seems to mean here only the removal of this garment as in Isaiah 20:2; Micah 1:8; and John 21:7 *(gumnos)*.

a. **The "raving" passages.** The first passage, 1 Samuel 18:10, again concerns Saul and again during the time when he was making attempts to kill David. In extreme anger one day, as an "evil spirit from God came upon" him, "he prophesied (*yithnabbe'*) in the midst of" his house, as David played the harp in his presence, and he threw a javelin at the young man to take his life. It is asserted that this use of "prophesy" can only mean an outburst of raving anger on Saul's part. In view of the circumstances, and since no message is indicated to have been spoken by Saul at the time, the assertion seems warranted.

The context of 1 Kings 18:29, the next passage under consideration, speaks of the frenzied activity of Baal prophets on Mt. Carmel. Elijah had arranged a contest with them to prove that the God of Israel, not Baal, was the one true God. The contest involved a trial of Israel's God and Baal to see which of them could send miraculous fire to ignite a prepared sacrifice. In attempting to procure fire from Baal, his prophets are said to have "cried aloud, and cut themselves after their manner with knives and lancets," and to have "leaped upon the altar" (18:26,28), but all to no avail. In carrying on this frantic activity they are said to have "prophesied" (*mithnabbe'im*, participle). That the word could be used in reference to this type of activity is asserted again to show that it had the wider meaning of "raving." Again, one has difficulty in countering this assertion.

The third passage, 1 Kings 22:10-12, does not show the "raving" idea nearly so clearly, but still it is often cited along with the first two. It concerns the occasion when four hundred prophets of King Ahab "prophesied" before Ahab and his guest at the time, King Jehoshaphat of Judah. These prophets had been asked to discover God's will regarding a projected battle with the Arameans of Damascus at Ramoth-gilead. They replied, "Go up; for the LORD shall deliver it into the hand of the king" (22:6). To add force to this message, one of the prophets, Zedekiah, "made him horns of iron: and he said, Thus saith the LORD, With these shalt thou push the Syrians, until thou have consumed them" (v. 11). Following this, the indication is made that "all the prophets prophesied [mithnabbe'im, participle]" saying, "Go up to Ramoth-gilead, and prosper: for the LORD shall deliver it into the king's hand" (v. 12).

The reason this passage does not evidence the "raving" idea like the others is because a message was involved. It is true that the action of the one prophet, Zedekiah, did exhibit some emotional excess, but still it fell far short of what the prophets of Baal demonstrated on Mt. Carmel. And no message was communicated at that time as there was here. In this instance, then, the prophesying of the four hundred may have consisted of a united presentation of what they believed was God's word to the two kings.[10] If so, there is no connotation of "raving" in the use of the word *prophesy* this time.

b. The "madness" passages. There are also three passages which are believed to show that the idea of "madness" was associated with the word *prophecy*. The three use the word *mad* in describing how certain people thought of prophets. This is believed to support the idea of ecstaticism in Israel, since, if prophets did put on ecstatic displays, it would have been natural for the idea of "madness" to have arisen in respect to them. It may be properly stated, however, that these passages do not establish the desired evidence as clearly as the first two of the former group. What they show is only that certain people — who had an anti-prophet attitude anyway — thought of prophets as "mad" men.

The first passage, 2 Kings 9:1-12, concerns a young training prophet Elisha sent north to Ramoth-gilead to anoint Jehu as king of Israel. Jehoram was still king at the time and Jehu was merely a captain in his army. Jehoram had just lost a battle with the Aramaeans of Damascus and returned wounded to Jezreel in Israel to recover. Jehu was still with the defeated Israelite army at Ramoth-gilead, where the battle had transpired, and to him there the young prophet came. He anointed the captain as instructed, told him how to proceed, and then quickly departed. Following this, one of Jehu's men asked Jehu, "Is all well?" and then added the words here in point, "Wherefore came this mad fellow [*meshugga'*] to thee?" (v. 11). Since the young man's actions had been quite proper, the characterization "mad fellow" must have resulted from the customary thinking this soldier had concerning prophets.

The weakness of evidence in the passage is found in the identity of the person who spoke of the prophet in this manner. He was a soldier in the army, and it is common for rough men of an army to have a distorted opinion regarding religious leaders. Just because this person thought of prophets as "mad" does not necessarily mean that people commonly thought of them in this way.

[10]Though their message was false, as the full story shows, they could well have believed it to be true and presented it as such.

Jeremiah 29:26, the second passage, tells of a letter which had been written by one of the captives in Babylon and sent back to Jerusalem. Shemaiah, the writer, had sent the letter as a way of opposing Jeremiah's work in Jerusalem, but somehow Jeremiah had seen it and here made reference to it. Included in the contents of the letter was the derisive remark regarding prophets, "Every man that is mad [*meshugga'*], and maketh himself a prophet." The remark shows that this Shemaiah did think of prophets as "mad" people.

The weakness of evidence here is the same as in the former instance. The person who wrote the letter and used the term *mad* concerning prophets was one who was no friend of prophets. His letter had been written for the very purpose of opposing Jeremiah, the leading prophet of the day, and no doubt he had Jeremiah especially in mind when he used the term. Again, just because a person like Shemaiah thought of Jeremiah and other prophets in this way is insufficient reason to believe that this was the attitude of people in general.

The third passage, Hosea 9:7, occurs in a context where Hosea is characterizing the wrong thinking of Israelites of the day, who were unfaithful to God (Hos. 9:1). He includes as a part in this wrong thinking the words of the people, "The prophet is a fool, the spiritual man [lit. "man of the Spirit," *'ish ha-ruah*] is mad [*meshugga'*]." The parallelism in this statement has the force of saying that prophets, being men of the Spirit, were "mad" men.

Though a much wider group of people is here shown to have had this wrong thinking, the point in issue remains unproven. Hosea was characterizing the thinking of sinful Israelites, who were opposed to God and therefore to all who stood for God and proclaimed His message. Their thinking, then, cannot be taken as that of people who were not opposed to God and His messengers, and therefore the passage cannot be used to prove that prophets were ecstatics who put on "mad" displays for people in seeking revelation from God.

C. Arguments for Ecstaticism

With the passages to which adherents of ecstaticism appeal now before us, we may consider the arguments that are drawn from them. All the arguments are based mainly on the first group of passages; other passages come into the discussion only in a supporting role. The arguments may be grouped under seven heads.

1. Argument by deduction. One argument, mentioned in passing earlier, is not based on any of these passages, but issues from logical deduction. It is that, because other nations of the day — especially the Canaanites — practiced ecstaticism, one should only expect that Israelites would have done the same. Israelites had come to settle among the ecstasy-observing Canaanites, and in such cases it is normal for an incoming people to be highly influenced by those among whom they settle. History indicates that this is even more true when the native people are further advanced in physical culture than the newcomers. This was true when Israel came into Canaan. Israel had lived in desert conditions for forty years, and before this the people had been slaves in Egypt. They had not built houses in the desert, nor had they learned to farm. Basic matters of this kind had to be learned on arriving in Canaan. Canaanites, on the other hand, were very advanced in their day. Archaeological research has shown them to have had excellent pottery, fine houses, well-laid-out towns, and strong-walled cities. It is argued, therefore, that since Israel had to learn these technical matters from Canaanites, it is logical they learned also religious matters, such as ecstaticism.

Coupled with this thinking is the belief that the word *prophesy* could mean both "raving" and "mad," as observed. Since these are both highly emotional concepts, it is thought that they add further reason for believing that Israelites did accept the idea of "ecstatic frenzy" for the word.

2. Involvement of a Canaanite-type high place. A second argument concerns the involvement of a Canaanite-type high place in one of the three main passages. The company of prophets Saul met on his return home after being anointed by Samuel was "coming down from the high place" (1 Sam. 10:5). Such a high place (*bamah*) was Canaanite in idea, and, therefore, it is argued, these prophets should be expected to have been influenced themselves by Canaanite-type practices, including ecstaticism.

3. Musical instruments were played. A third argument concerns the involvement of music in this same instance. The company of prophets Saul met are said to have come down from the high place "with a psaltery, and a tabret, and a pipe, and a harp, before them" (1 Sam. 10:5). Thus, they were playing music, and music is known to have been employed in other countries as a way of inducing the ecstatic state. The point is made that this music was likely being used for the same purpose here.

4. **Saul was "turned into another man."** A further argument is taken from Samuel's statement to Saul that, when he had contacted this company of prophets, he would be "turned into another man" (1 Sam. 10:6). Then, coupled with this statement is the later indication that, when Saul did begin to prophesy, having met the prophets, he was changed so much in behavior that onlookers were surprised and voiced the question, "Is Saul also among the prophets?" (10:11). Such a change in manner of behavior, it is alleged, can only be accounted for on the basis that Saul became ecstatically frenzied.

5. **Saul lay in an apparent stupor for many hours.** One argument is based directly on Saul's later encounter with Samuel's prophets at the time David had fled to Samuel at Ramah. In that instance, Saul not only prophesied, as on the first occasion, but then removed at least a part of his clothing and lay down in an apparent stupor "all that day and all that night" (1 Sam. 19:24). Such an action, with a resulting state of stupor, is said to be in the pattern of other ecstatics of the day and, therefore, is best explained as a demonstration of ecstatic frenzy. It is thought to be significant to the same conclusion that, due to this behavior of Saul, people were caused again to ask, "Is Saul also among the prophets?" (19:24).

6. **Involvement of the "Spirit of God."** An argument is also taken from the fact that the "Spirit of God" is said to have been involved with all three of the main instances. The seventy in the wilderness are said to have had the Spirit come on them, and both occasions involving Saul speak of the same happening regarding him. This argument is based on what the term *Spirit of God* is thought to mean, namely, a heightening of the natural god-consciousness of these men so they believed they were having rapport with the supernatural world. In other words, it is believed these references to the "Spirit of God" are references themselves to the ecstatic state in which this natural consciousness was thus heightened. To say, therefore, that the "Spirit of God" came on them is another way of saying that they became ecstatic; and, since this is asserted in all three of these instances, all three must have been occasions of ecstatic frenzy.

7. The prophesying of the seventy. The last argument is not a positive argument, as the others have been, but a reply to an objection that is anticipated to the viewpoint, in respect to the seventy in the wilderness prophesying. The objection is that, since that occasion happened before there was any contact with Canaanites, the prophesying then displayed could not have been Canaanite-type ecstaticism. The response of adherents of the view — who are mainly of the liberal, critical school — is that the story as given in Numbers is couched in language and concepts of a much later day, after Canaanite influence had been experienced. This answer is based on the view that Moses was not the author of the Pentateuch, but that it was written by numerous authors from the period of the divided kingdom and later. Therefore, the term *prophesy*, in the sense of ecstatic frenzy, could have been used by them in this story, which the authors believed happened long before in the wilderness experiences of their ancestors.

10

ISRAEL'S PROPHETS WERE NOT ECSTATICS

The belief that ecstaticism existed among Israel's prophets at any time is rejected by most conservative scholars. Adhering to the view that the Bible is the product of supernatural revelation and inspiration, they believe that prophets were specially called by God and that many were given the messages they were to preach by direct supernatural communication. They reject the idea that any true prophet sought divine communication by means of ecstatic behavior. Passages that refer to a "company of prophets" — which appear only from Samuel's time — are thought of, not as referring to a band of ecstatic, mad fellows, but to a young group of training prophets under the tutelage of Samuel. When trained, these young men no doubt went forth in the ministry of prophetism for themselves, proclaiming God's message.

Admittedly, several of the passages noted in the prior chapter show unusual meanings for the word *prophesy* and, accordingly, call for special consideration. It is believed, however, that each is subject to quite a different interpretation than what adherents of the ecstatic idea make of them. The present chapter will show this to be the case. To this end, it will be well first to give a refutation of each of the seven arguments noted for ecstaticism, and then to present positive evidence in favor of the different rendition.

A. Refutation of Arguments for Ecstaticism

In giving the refutation, we will follow the same order in respect to the arguments as observed in the prior chapter. The observations to be made regarding each are interested either in showing a fallacy in the argument concerned or else accounting for the factors on which it is based in a more plausible and Bible-centered way.

  1. Argument by deduction. The argument based on deduction from comparative religious practices of other peoples depends for its validity on the extent to which Israel followed religious customs of other peoples. On this question, even liberal scholars differ markedly. For instance, W. C. Graham states, "Little by little, in the long process of settlement, they [the Israelites] became in all but name Canaanites."[1] But William Albright writes, "Every fresh publication of Canaanite mythological texts makes the gulf between the religion of Canaan and of Israel increasingly clear."[2]

The conservative view is that Israel's similarity to other peoples in religious matters was minimal, so far as official acceptance is concerned. Religious leaders and people generally who were faithful to God did not borrow at all in any basic matters. They could not have done so, for God had revealed to them what they were to believe and practice even before entering their Promised Land. Moses had been the recipient on Mt. Sinai, and he had recorded the information in the official Law. It is true that Israelite people had become influenced by the Canaanites. Indeed, many had come to an actual worship of the false god Baal, but in this they had defected from what they had been taught.

Actually, the three main passages noted, when taken at face value (without restructuring their records to accord with liberal presuppositions), are in keeping with this viewpoint. Regarding the passage of the seventy in the wilderness, the occasion occurred prior to any Canaanite contact, as was observed. Adherents of the ecstatic viewpoint believe this was a case of ecstatic frenzy, and account for the apparent difficulty by saying the story reflects the thinking of people much later in Israel's history, when Canaanite influence had been experienced. Such an explanation, however, does not take the story at face value and also denies the Mosaic authorship of the Pentateuch; the conservative scholar cannot accept either idea.

Regarding the two passages that concern Saul and his encounters with Samuel and groups of prophets, a significant factor in both cases is that Samuel was closely related to the prophetic groups. In the

---

[1]W. C. Graham, "The Religion of the Hebrews," *Journal of Religion*, 11 (1931), 244.
[2]Albright, "Recent Progress in North Canaanite Research," *Bulletin of the American School of Oriental Research*, 70 (1938), 24.

instance recorded in 1 Samuel 10, Samuel knew beforehand when the group in question would be coming down from the high place and so was able to foretell of them to Saul. This means that he was knowledgeable of their life pattern and schedule. If they were students in his school, as suggested earlier,[3] he would have known what time their class would let out and so known where they would be and at what time. Then in the instance recorded in 1 Samuel 19, Samuel is said to have been "standing as appointed over" the group involved, and this shows not only a close relation to the group but an actual headship over it. Samuel himself, however, was directly opposed to any kind of Canaanite influence and repeatedly warned the Israelites against it (see 1 Sam. 3:11-18; 7:3-6), something even liberal critics admit. It is therefore quite unthinkable that Samuel would have associated himself with a movement that was basically Canaanite in origin and characteristic.

In respect to the lack of any message from God being spoken in these passages, when the word *prophesy* is used in them, one must admit that the word does carry a different meaning than is normal for it. But that this different meaning has to be ecstatic frenzy does not necessarily follow. It could be something else, and a suggestion will be made shortly as to what is likely.[4] Regarding the meanings "raving" and "madness," the latter has already been shown to have no argumentative value for the position, and the former is not the same thing as ecstaticism. The relationship it carries to the basic meaning of "prophesy" will be shown presently, and it is a relationship which is fully in keeping with a nonecstatic view of prophets.

2. Involvement of a Canaanite-type high place. A Canaanite-type high place was involved at the time of Saul's first meeting with the prophetic group, and it is true that such centers of worship did come into Israel as a result of Canaanite influence. Accordingly, they are regularly disapproved in the Old Testament — with the significant exception of one period of time. That was the period following the loss of the Shiloh sanctuary[5] until the building of the Jerusalem temple by Solomon, when there was no official place of worship. It was during this time when the incident happened. Consequently, that prophets

[3]See chapter 9, p. 94, n. 8.
[4]See pp. 110-112.
[5]The ark was taken from the tabernacle at Shiloh at the battle of Aphek (1 Sam. 4:11), and the tabernacle was soon moved to Nob (1 Sam. 21:1-9).

were coming down from such a high place at this time does not necessarily imply that they were Canaanite in type. Samuel, as just observed, was surely not a Canaanite-type prophet, and it was during this same general period when he even offered sacrifice at such a high place (1 Sam. 9:19).[6]

3. Musical instruments were played. The prophets Saul met coming down from the high place were playing musical instruments, and it is true that music was used at times in other countries to induce the ecstatic state. These prophets need not be thought of as using the instruments for this purpose, however. Other reasons could have been in mind, and one will be presented shortly which fits the nonecstatic explanation. In fact, the manner in which the instruments are mentioned suggests that they were not being used for an ecstatic purpose. They are referred to in connection with the prophets "coming down" from the high place, as though they were playing them as they walked along. Music that helps to induce ecstasy, however, is not music that is played while one is walking; it is music that is played while people dance in long, tiring, repeated movements, with the players either stationary or else involved themselves in the same sort of movement. The music is of a definite kind, characterized especially by a pronounced rhythm and beat. Martin Buber, himself a liberal critic, recognizes the inconsistency of the argument, as he says that ecstasy

> is not stirred up in a people of early culture by such acts as these, but by an enthusiastic singing of monotonous songs. Truly such singing is ecstatic, but it is also bound up with a strict rhythm and is accompanied by rhythmical movements of all its members.[7]

To become ecstatically frenzied requires a proper mental attitude on the part of those who wish the state. They have to be sympathetic to the idea and even want the state sufficiently to work hard at achieving it. It is not easy to become ecstatically frenzied. One must be emotionally adapted to the condition and then follow well-planned procedures over an extended period of time.

Nothing in the text suggests that these prophets were of such a

[6]Other passages mentioning a high place during this period are 1 Chronicles 16:39 and 21:29, both in reference to David's time, and 2 Chronicles 1:3,13, when Solomon sacrificed at the high place at Gibeon, where the tabernacle was then located. Each shows a favorable context.

[7]Martin Buber, *The Prophetic Faith* (New York: Macmillan, 1949), p. 63.

frame of mind. They are described merely as walking down from a high place playing the musical instruments listed. And neither can one possibly think of Saul being interested in ecstaticism. He simply met these men, and without any apparent time for preparation or prolonged activity, he began suddenly to "prophesy." Then, thinking of the second encounter with these prophets, set forth in 1 Samuel 19, Saul was at this time even a less likely prospect for ecstasy. Rather than seeking an ecstatic experience, he came in disgust and anger that three groups of messengers had not brought David to him. He was surely not sympathetic to whatever might be the situation when he found David; he wanted only to make sure the young man was arrested and, probably, that the members of the three unsuccessful groups were punished as well.

4. Saul was "turned into another man. When Samuel foretold to Saul that he would encounter the company of prophets, he informed him that at the time he would be "turned into another man." Two matters, however, show that this was not a prediction that Saul would become an ecstatic.

The first is the significant fact that Şamuel was the one who made the prediction, and he implied approval of the idea when he made it. This is directly counter to Samuel's own anti-Canaanite attitude, so evident in other parts of the story. Samuel's stress in ministry clearly was that Israelites turn from following Baal worship and return in truth to the Law of Israel's own God. This means he must have had some other thought in mind when he spoke these words.

The second matter concerns what may indeed have been in Samuel's mind. A clue comes from verse 9 of the same passage, where a parallel thought is expressed: "God gave him another heart." This notice in no way suggests a loss of self-control in ecstaticism. Rather "a new heart" connotes the idea of a new attitude, a new emotional outlook. And this thought fits well into the story. Saul had been hesitant about going to see Samuel at first (1 Sam. 9:5-10), which suggests a lack in self-confidence on his part.[8] But now Samuel had just anointed him for the kingship, and an ability to rule calls for strength in leadership. It may well be that an objection that had immediately come to Saul's mind, when earlier anointed by Samuel,

[8]Similarly, he showed timidity later when selected as king by Israelite elders at Mizpeh, even hiding himself from them at the time (1 Sam. 10:21,22). See discussion in chapter 6, p. 60.

had been this natural timidity on his part. How could he rule when he had this kind of personality? There was need, therefore, that he be shown how God could change that personality to give him the kind of confidence necessary. When the change was actually experienced, as indicated by the words, "God gave him a new heart," Saul's recognition of the fact must have been very meaningful. The change, quite clearly, was only temporary at this time yet, for it would be some time before Saul would actually rule.

5. Saul lay in a stupor many hours. In Saul's second encounter with the prophets, he not only prophesied but then took off at least some of his clothes and lay in an apparent stupor many hours. One must say that conduct of this kind is hardly normal and indicates a lack of self-control on Saul's part. Two factors again, however, show that this abnormal action could not have been the result of self-induced ecstasy.

The first is that he alone, of all who prophesied at the time, showed this response. Many others did prophesy, including the company of prophets and all three groups of messengers sent earlier to apprehend David (1 Sam. 19:20,21). At least some of these had also partially disrobed, for the word *also (gam)* is used in respect to Saul's action in doing this (19:24), but it is quite clear that no others lay down in a state of stupor. One must ask, then, if Saul's display of stupor was the result of ecstatic frenzy — which must then have been shared by these others — why did these others not act in the same way? Since they did not, it is appropriate to look for a reason that was peculiar to Saul alone.

The second factor has already been noted: Saul was a most unlikely prospect for an experience of ecstatic frenzy that day. He was angry with David to begin with, then he had sent three unsuccessful groups of messengers to apprehend him, and finally in complete disgust and frustration he had come himself. If anyone was ever a poor candidate for becoming ecstatic, Saul was the man at that time. Still he is said to have prophesied, even as the others, and this is said to have begun with him even before arriving where the others were. Another reason must exist, then, for both his prophesying and his stupor, and one will be presented under positive arguments soon to follow.

6. Involvement of the Spirit of God. The Spirit of God is said to have come upon the participants in each of the three main passages, and it is believed this is further evidence that each involved ecstaticism. This conclusion, however, is based on an understanding of the Spirit of God that is at complete variance with the rest of Scripture. Adherents of the view see it as meaning only a heightened God-consciousness of the people involved, so that they believed they were having rapport with the supernatural world. The Bible, however, makes clear that the Spirit of God is the Third Person of the Godhead. In all of these instances He was empowering the participants concerned for tasks they needed to do. When this meaning is accepted for the Spirit, any evidence for ecstaticism becomes nonexistent.

7. **The prophesying of the seventy.** Nothing in addition to what has already been said need be stated here. To account for the idea of ecstasy being involved in the story of the seventy who are said to have prophesied in the wilderness, adherents of the view have to deny Mosaic authorship to the account and make it the product of a writer from the time of the divided monarchy. No conservative scholar will admit of such a denial of biblical inspiration.

B. Positive Evidence

Not only is a refutation possible of arguments presented in favor of ecstaticism, but positive arguments may be formulated against it. The following are the more significant.

1. **The basic meaning of "prophesy."** A cornerstone in the ecstatic viewpoint is that the word *prophesy* in the Old Testament could mean "to act as an ecstatic," and that it did mean this regularly in Israel's earlier history. A study of the word, however, does not reveal this to have been a possible meaning.

The Hebrew word in view is *naba'*, used always in either the niphal or hithpael form (*nibba'* or *hithnabba'*). It is used 113 times in the Old Testament, and its derivative *nabi'* ("prophet") is used over 300 times. There is little agreement on the etymology of the word. Gesenius reflects ecstatic thinking when he sees it as a weakened form of *naba'*, "to bubble up."[9] A. R. Johnson, however, believes it comes from the Accadian *nabu*, "to speak."[10] And William Albright agrees, only takes the passive meaning, "one spoken to" or "called."[11]

[9]Gesenius, *Hebrew and Chaldee Lexicon*, trans., Tregelles, p. 525.
[10]A. R. Johnson, *The Cultic Prophet in Ancient Israel*, p. 24.
[11]Albright, *From the Stone Age to Christianity*, p. 231.

Others find its root in the Arabic *naba'a*, "to announce," and even in the Hebrew *bo'* "to come" or "enter in."[12]

Whatever the correct etymology of the word, its basic meaning is made clear by its usage in the Old Testament. That meaning is "to speak for God." Any number of passages can be cited in evidence, but a few are particularly significant and can be noted briefly.

a. Passages which indicate the basic meaning. A first to notice is Exodus 7:1: "And the LORD said unto Moses, See, I have made thee a god to Pharaoh: and Aaron thy brother shall be thy prophet." A significant background for this passage is found in Exodus 4:10-16, where Moses has objected to God's call to return to Egypt, claiming, among other things, incapability of speech. To this God has answered that He would provide Aaron to speak in his place, even being a "mouth" for Moses. Now here, in 7:1, Aaron in serving as Moses' mouth is called Moses' prophet (*nabi*). The meaning of "one speaking for another" is well illustrated.

A second is Deuteronomy 18:15-22. Here Moses has just promised that God would raise up a "Prophet" (*nabi'*) for the people, like unto himself. Then in verse 18 God adds that He will put His words in this prophet's mouth so that the prophet would "speak unto them all that" He, God, would command him. Thus, the prophet's task was to be God's spokesman.

A third is Amos 7:12-16. The text concerns Amos while in the city of Bethel, speaking against the false worship there of the golden calf and against the king, Jeroboam II. Amaziah, a priest at Bethel, rebukes Amos, telling him to go back home to Judah "and prophesy [*tinnabe'*]" there and not in Bethel. Amos replies that, though he was not a "prophet" (*nabi'*) by vocation, he was there at Bethel because God had told him, "Go, prophesy [*hinnabe'*] unto my people Israel." The meaning of "prophesy," then, is well illustrated as Amos' activity of speaking God's message to the people at Bethel.

Then a fourth type of passage is found in the many occasions when God assigned a task to a prophet. All concern the work of oral ministry. Isaiah was instructed, "Go, and tell this people" (Isa. 6:9). To Jeremiah came the words, "Go to all that I shall send thee, and whatsoever I command thee thou shalt speak" (Jer. 1:7). To Ezekiel

[12]See Harold H. Rowley, *The Servant of the Lord and Other Essays on the Old Testament* (London: Lutterworth Press, 1952), p. 97; and also Geerhardus Vos, *Biblical Theology*, pp. 209,210.

the command was, "I do send thee unto them; and thou shalt say unto them" (Ezek. 2:3,4). And then when one considers the type of work in which all prophets were engaged, it was regularly the work of proclaiming God's truth.

The basic meaning of the word is thus well established. It is only in the few passages noted in the prior chapter — out of the more than four hundred total occurrences, counting verb and noun — when it is used with variant meanings. Still, because these do exist, it is necessary to relate them to the basic idea.

b. Relation of variant meanings. Three possible variant meanings are found in these passages. One is "raving," found to be well established. A second was "madness," found to be less well based. And a third will soon be identified as "praising," again with solid evidence. A common denominator for each of the three meanings is manifest: emotional involvement. When one raves, becomes angry, or engages in praise, he becomes emotionally involved.

The probable relationship of this idea to the basic idea of "speaker for God" is not difficult to see. It is that the prophet was expected to speak for God with emotional involvement. God did not desire, nor did the people expect, that a prophet would perform his task merely as a routine duty. He was expected to proclaim God's word fervently. The act of prophesying was thought of as a vibrant work, an emotionally filled experience, a declaration of God's message with force. Because the word could be used in only its emotional connotation — as these few passages show — this aspect of emotional involvement, in the full meaning of the word, must have carried a prominent place in the thinking of the day.

It should be clearly understood, however, that this manner of emotional speaking is not at all what is meant by ecstatic frenzy. The person who practiced the latter lost all rational contact with the real world in his attempt to gain rapport with the supernatural realm. His type of activity was entirely foreign to the prophets of the Old Testament.

2. Israel's resistance to Canaanite influence. A second positive argument is that Israel displayed a remarkable resistance to Canaanite influence, rather than being susceptible to it. The ecstatic viewpoint is based on the assumption that the opposite was true. Archaeological research, however, has shown in recent years that Israel's borrowing from Canaan was surprisingly little. It is true that liberal critics of a few years ago held to the opposite idea almost without exception,[13] but in recent years this has changed. Albright was quoted earlier in this connection, and Frank Cross writes similarly: "Both their [Israel's] religion and their organization were sufficiently strong to overpower, not only the decadent Canaanites and their religion, but in time also the powerful opposition of the Philistines."[14]

The fact that Israel did present this resistance to Canaanite influence means that there had to be strong factors existent to make this true. As has been explained, it was normal for incoming people to be heavily influenced by a native populace, especially if the latter were further advanced in physical culture as was true when Israel entered Canaan. These resistance factors almost certainly were from religious sources, for Israel had only a minimum of civil government that could have provided them.[15] And certainly one of those factors — and perhaps the principal one — was found in the priestly system. Priests and Levites were numerous, were scattered evenly among the tribes in forty-eight cities (Num. 35:1-8; Josh. 21:1-41) so that a grass roots contact was possible, and they had easy access to the written Law at Shiloh which forbade Canaanite interplay. Another one, however, would surely have been the prophets. They were raised up to reinforce the work of priests and urge the people to conform their lives to that same Law. This makes the idea unthinkable that they might themselves have been of Canaanite origin or that their practices might have been borrowed from them.[16]

3. The meaning "praising." The principal question to answer, in this presentation of positive arguments, concerns the meaning of the

[13]See p. 102, n. 1, and also Abraham Kuenen, *The Religion of Israel*, I (1870), p. 235, or James Robertson, *The Early Religion of Israel*, I (Philadelphia: Westminster Press, 1903), p. 189.

[14]Frank Cross, "The Tabernacle," *Biblical Archaeologist*, 10 (1947), 16.

[15]The period when the factors would have been the most necessary was in Israel's early history, when first contact with Canaanites was made and before King David completely conquered them. In this period, the judges time, there was no head ruler over all the tribes or any one tribe; there were only elders in local communities and a few court officials, besides the unofficial (non-legally-prescribed) judges; see Wood, *A Survey of Israel's History*, pp. 192, 193 for discussion.

[16]Even Walther Eichrodt, himself a liberal, asserts this in his *Theology of the Old Testament*, pp. 328,329.

term *prophesy* as used in the three main passages used by the ecstatic adherents. The question is apt, for no message is presented in any of the three. The meaning "to speak for God," then, does not apply. Ecstatic adherents believe it means "ecstatic frenzy," but this has already been seen not to fit. The question remains, What does the term mean?

The answer is that it means "praising." Evidence that this is a possible meaning for the word is found in 1 Chronicles 25:1-3. In this passage, David is described as selecting certain people to lead in praising activity at the house of God. In verse 1 of the passage, the sons of Asaph, Heman, and Jeduthun are selected and they are said to be ones "who should prophesy [*nebbe'im*] with harps, with psalteries, and with cymbals." Then in verse 2, other men are selected and they too are said to be those "which prophesied [*ha-nibba'*, niphal participle] according to the order of the king." In verse 3, still others are selected, and of them the highly significant indication is given, "who prophesied [*ha-nibba'*, niphal participle] with a harp, to give thanks and to praise the LORD." The prophesying activity of these Levitic singers, then, consisted in rendering praise to God, as they employed "harps," "psalteries," and "cymbals", for accompaniment.

This meaning for the word fits the three passages well, in complete contrast to the idea of ecstatic frenzy. In the instance of the seventy in the wilderness (Num. 11:25-29), the thought of the use of "prophesying" would be that these seventy began to render praise to God, when the Spirit was placed upon them. Praise of this kind would not have had a direct relationship with their intended task of assisting Moses, but it would have been a natural response to the fact of their empowerment by God's Spirit for their new task of judging.

This praising activity likely was in the form of singing one or more songs of praise. That two of the number, Eldad and Medad, continued on in the activity is not strange. They probably enjoyed singing and were perhaps given to more exuberance in their joy than the others. They apparently wanted all the camp to know of their joy and so moved through the camp letting the fact be known. Some people found this offensive, and Joshua thought it his duty to report the matter to Moses. In view of this kind of activity, however, Moses' response is not surprising, as he said he would not make them cease and that he wished that "all the LORD's people were prophets" (Num. 11:29).

In the first of the two instances regarding Saul (1 Sam. 10), the thought would be that the prophets, coming down from the high place with musical instruments, were again rendering praise to God. They could well have just been dismissed from class, as noted earlier, and they could have had the custom of singing as they walked together to their place of residence. This would account for Samuel's knowing ahead of time that they would be so engaged when Saul met them. Then, as to Saul's action when he did encounter them, the thought would be that he simply joined in singing with them. The astonishment of those seeing him, when he did so, would have been due to his otherwise timid nature. They had been accustomed to seeing him standing aside watching such activity, rather than joining in with it.

In the second of the two instances regarding Saul, the thought would be similar. This time, however, the first people to become unexpectedly engaged in rendering praise would have been the three messenger groups sent by Saul to apprehend David. Coming to where Samuel's training prophets were enjoying their songfest, and experiencing the influence of the Spirit of God coming on them, each group in turn joined the prophets in the activity. The total group would have made quite a choir. Then, when Saul came later, the thought would be the same; only with him the activity of singing would have started even before he arrived (1 Sam. 19:23). How to account for Saul's wanting to sing now, when before he had been so angry, is not easy to explain, and this is true also regarding the three messenger groups, who likely were composed of hardened soldiers. The text, however, specifically mentions that on both Saul and the messengers the Spirit of God came, and this was just before the singing was undertaken. The thought, quite clearly, is that it was this coming that brought about the activity in both instances. The significance of this, as well as an explanation for Saul's lying in a stupor for several hours, will be included in the discussion of the next chapter.[17]

[17]For similar discussion by the author, see his "Ecstasy and Israel's Early Prophets," *Bulletin of the Evangelical Theological Society*, 9 (Summer 1966), 125-37.

11

THE HOLY SPIRIT AND THE
PROPHETIC EXPERIENCE

The interest now turns to the relationship of the Holy Spirit to the prophetic experience. The subject has been mentioned in general in prior discussions, but now it calls for attention for itself. We ask, in what way did the Holy Spirit empower prophets? What was the particular aspect of empowerment granted to them?

The first aspect of this question concerns the three special passages: In what way did the Spirit bring empowerment in each of these occasions? Then the broader question must be discussed: In what way did the Spirit empower prophets in the more common instances, when speaking was involved?

A. The Spirit of God in the Special Passages

The three passages considered here are again those mentioned in the prior two chapters: one concerning the seventy in the wilderness and the other two concerning Saul. Each has been seen to concern a coming of the Spirit on the people concerned. It may be noted in passing that neither the "raving" or "madness" passages (1 Sam. 18:10; 1 Kings 18:29; 22:10-12; 2 Kings 9:1-12; Jer. 29:26; Hos. 9:7) concern this coming on anyone and so do not call for notice in this connection. The aspect of empowerment involved with the first two main passages has been rather well explored, and therefore little more needs to be said regarding them; some basic questions remain concerning the third one, however. Each will be considered, to the extent necessary, in the order followed in the prior discussions.

1. **Numbers 11:25-29.** Really nothing new calls for notice regard-

ing this passage. It was seen that the empowerment of the Spirit was to equip the seventy elders for assisting Moses in judging the people. That they prophesied in giving praise to God, at the time of being so empowered, was seen to be a sort of by-product of the empowerment. They were not empowered so they would render praise; rather the act of giving praise issued from their hearts as a proper and natural result of being so empowered.

2. 1 Samuel 10:1-13. The main points to notice regarding 1 Samuel 10:1-13 have also been observed. They are that Saul's empowerment, as he met the company of prophets, was for the purpose of giving him a confident personality. The change was not intended to be permanent, for the kingship still lay several months in the future, but as a reassurance to the young man of what God could and would do when the moment for actual rule arrived. That Saul praised God in song at the time, then, was not a reason for the empowerment. It came once more as a result of the empowerment. It was a result in a different sense, however, than with the seventy. Saul did not sing merely for joy that he had been empowered, but his singing was the evidence that he had been empowered. That is, it was because he had been given a changed personality that he found himself willing and desirous of joining the prophets in song. It provided the evidence that the change had been effected.

3. 1 Samuel 19:18-24. There is more that calls for discussion regarding 1 Samuel 19:18-24, the second instance when Saul came upon singing prophets. Two main questions need to be answered: first, In what sense was Saul empowered on this occasion? and, second, What prompted Saul to lay in the stupor for a period of several hours?

a. The manner of empowerment. The manner in which Saul was empowered this time must have been different in nature both from his first time and from that of the seventy. Empowerments on those occasions concerned equipment for a task. But no task was involved in this instance. Saul had already been king for most of his forty-year reign; and the Spirit, who had empowered him for this task, had been taken from him sometime previous (1 Sam. 16:14). No hint is given that the Spirit now came on him for this purpose again. Therefore, the reason must be found in another direction.

The clue is found in the need for David's life to be spared. He was to be Israel's next king and therefore had to be kept from all attempts of Saul to kill him. First, the three messenger groups had to be turned aside in their mission. They should not be permitted to seize David and return him to the angry king. Therefore, the Spirit of God came on them to change their viewpoint regarding David. They probably were made to see him as righteous and Saul as unrighteous; this in turn could have caused them to desist in their assignment, not wanting a part in the wrong of apprehending such a one. A further purpose would have been to bring them to render praise in song, along with the praising prophets. If they should become so engaged, they would certainly no longer be interested in arresting the young man who had a part in the occasion of song.

Thus, there was an obvious need to turn Saul aside from his intentions. He was angry enough at David already, when he sent the three messenger groups. He had been thwarted several times in taking David's life by then — the last time by having his own daughter trick him (1 Sam. 19:11-17) — and he surely wanted success this time. As each messenger proved unsuccessful, he undoubtedly became more incensed, until finally he went himself. What he would have done to David, if he had succeeded in taking him at the time, is illustrated by what he actually did do to Ahimelech and eighty-four priests of Nob not long after (22:16-19). He killed all of them — merely because Ahimelech had given a little help to David in his flight from Saul — and also their defenseless wives and children, besides livestock.

God, however, was not about to let Saul have his way with the prospective king, and therefore the Spirit of God was sent upon Saul to change his attitude. A truly major change was called for. From an intensely angry man, he had to be changed to a praising man. He had to see his own messengers in a different light; he had to see Samuel's prophets and Samuel himself in their proper role; and he had to see David the way God saw him. More than this, he had to recognize that God's will was centered in the man he sought, and that it was God who was supreme in the universe and deserved all praise. He had to be brought to the place where he was willing to join in song and render that praise himself. This was a momentous change, but this is what had to be accomplished, if David was to be spared; and this is what the Spirit brought to pass. Even before Saul arrived at the scene, where the others were engaged in praising, he began himself.

This means that this entire major change in thinking was made to occur also before arriving. The reason, no doubt, was that Saul not be permitted to reach the scene and issue out angry orders before being changed.

In the case of the three messenger groups and Saul, then, one must say that the praising — and the change in manner of thinking it represented — was itself the purpose of the Spirit empowerment. Both the messengers and Saul were empowered that they would have this change of mind and therefore render praise.

b. The reason for Saul's stupor. Some have considered Saul's action in lying in a stupor, following his time of prophesying, as one of the most convincing reasons for ecstaticism on his part. What other explanation, it is asked, could there be for such an abnormal reaction?

As has been indicated, the behavior was abnormal. People do not ordinarily lie the remainder of a day and all the following night in a partially disrobed condition, without moving. It has also been observed, however, that the explanation of ecstatic frenzy does not fit the situation. Ecstatic frenzy calls for a sympathetic participant, and Saul was anything but sympathetic, naturally, to what Samuel's prophets and his own messengers were doing when he arrived. As has just been seen, it took the supernatural power of the Holy Spirit to bring about a change that was sympathetic to the idea of praising; but this thought is entirely foreign to ecstatic adherents.

There is an explanation, however, that does fit all the factors involved. It is that Saul was suddenly taken with a sense of extreme melancholy and despair. The general story is clear that Saul was given to emotional moods of this kind. The situation was of a type to bring such a mood. He had been terribly angry on setting out on this occasion. Moreover, he feared David, both because of David's talents in winning wars and because Saul recognized — without admitting the fact, no doubt — that God's own hand was on David as Israel's future king. Also, he had come upon the actual scene of his own messengers engaging in praise with Samuel's prophets, and, even more significant, David himself standing in the approving company of the great Samuel. Saul kept Samuel in high regard all his life;[1] and, therefore, that David would be in Samuel's approving company

[1]This is indicated signally by Saul's desire to speak with Samuel, following the prophet's death, and therefore asking the woman of Endor to bring Samuel up from the grave that he might do so (1 Sam. 28:7-25).

spelled all too clearly the end of Saul's hopes for the continuing rule of his family. David was clearly the favored one. As a result he was overcome with a sense of despair. Emotional excesses are subject to pendulumlike change in any case, and Saul now moved from an excess of anger and optimism to a depth of despair and pessimism. Thus drained of all emotional and physical strength, he lay down in the stupified condition for the several hours indicated.

B. The Spirit of God and the Prophetic Revelational Experience

Two main aspects in the prophetic experience have been identified in prior discussions. One is the reception of God's message, and the other the declaration of that message. The first concerns revelation, the second proclamation. This is not to say that all prophets received revelation. No doubt, many did not, but found the information they were to proclaim either in the revealed law or from what had been revealed to other prophets. Many did, however; they were told what to say and when, how, and where to say it. The present inquiry concerns the nature of this revelational experience and, more particularly, the relation of the Spirit of God to it. In what way was special empowerment involved in it?

1. An "ab extra" factor. One extreme has been avoided thus far in understanding the prophetic revelational experience: Prophets did not become ecstatically frenzied. Another extreme must also be guarded against: The prophetic experience was not merely a naturalistic one, so that the prophet's mind was no more inspired than that of a modern writer. The moment of revelation was much more than this, for in it the mind learned what it had not known before. An *ab extra* factor was involved, so that a contact with Deity was made and an event of supernatural revelation occurred. The following statements are basic to keep in mind regarding this important subject; they relate either negatively to the two extremes to be avoided or positively to the *ab extra* factor that must be recognized and stressed.

a. No indication of self-stimulation. The first statement is that no times of revelation give evidence of any form of self-stimulation being employed. Such forms were always employed by ecstatics. The music of the company of prophets in 1 Samuel 10 is often cited as such a form, but it has already been found to be explained in another and better way. Also, David's so-called sacred dance of 2 Samuel 6 has received mention by scholars in this connection, and at that time David did lead others in a procession involving leaping and dancing before the ark of God. It should be recognized, however, that David's activity had nothing to do with seeking a message from God. No revelation was then imparted. David was engaged only in bringing the ark into the city of Jerusalem. It is noteworthy, also, that David's rational processes were well under control during the whole time. He offered sacrifices, pronounced a blessing on the people, and gave everyone bread and wine before bringing the occasion to a close.

Another instance often cited as an act of self-stimulation for revelation is recorded in 2 Kings 3:15. On this occasion, Elisha the prophet called for a "minstrel" to play before him, that "the hand of the LORD" might come upon him in revelation. Elisha did desire revelation from God at this time, and it was indeed given; however, nothing else in the context fits the idea of self-stimulation for achieving an ecstatic state. The word used for *minstrel* (root, *nagan*) refers to a person who plays with some type of stringed instrument,[2] which would give a soft, soothing type of music, not wild and ecstatic. Also, the word is used in the singular, meaning that Elisha called only for one person, and one person could hardly bring stimulation sufficient to bring on ecstatic frenzy. A much more likely explanation is that Elisha simply wanted soothing music played so that he might be quieted before God — after having been visited by three great kings — and thus be brought to a mood conducive for God to reveal to him.

b. No indication of initiating the revelational experience. The second statement is that no times of revelation give an indication of any prophet initiating the revelational experience.[3] God did the initiating; the prophets simply awaited His word. This is in contrast to the high priest's use of Urim and Thummim (see Exod. 28:30; Num. 27:21; Deut. 33:8), by which he did initiate a revelational contact with God, as divinely prescribed. The pattern of the prophetic experience is illustrated nicely by Samuel's reception of revelation while still a

---

[2]The word is used fourteen times in the Old Testament — twelve definitely carry reference to one or more stringed instruments, and the other two easily could (see Ps. 68:25 and Ezek. 33:32).

[3]Eichrodt (*Theology of the Old Testament*, p. 318) speaks to this end: "Israel knows nothing of the prophet's being able thus to gain mastery over God and to force his way into the divine world."

lad (1 Sam. 3:4-14). God spoke to him one night, and Samuel thought the voice came from Eli, the high priest of the day and teacher of the young Samuel. Three times God called, and on the third time Eli realized that God was the One who was speaking and then counseled the boy accordingly. On the fourth time, Samuel said that he was ready to hear what God had to say, and God revealed the intended information. God initiated the occasion in every respect, then; Samuel did nothing to bring it about.

It is true that prophets could, and did, pray for a time of revelation. In 1 Samuel 8, Samuel asked God for counsel relative to the people's request for a king, and it was given. God, however, still controlled the revelation. Samuel could in no respect command God, but only wait for a possible response after voicing his request.

c. No indication of a frenzied state. The third statement is that there is no Scripture passage that indicates or in any way suggests that a prophet had a frenzied experience. And neither is there any passage where the experience is ever demanded by another as evidence of the prophet's authority to speak. To the contrary, numerous portions tell of times when such a demand would have been expected — if ecstaticism was considered a "badge" of authority as ecstatic adherents claim — but none of them either show it to have been displayed or demanded. For instance, it would have been natural for King David to have demanded such a "badge" of authority from the prophet Nathan, when Nathan rebuked him so pointedly for his sin with Bathsheba (2 Sam. 11,12). He did not, however, and surely nothing in the scriptural account suggests that Nathan put on an ecstatic display.

d. No indication of any loss in rational power. The fourth statement is that no passage tells of an occasion when a prophet lost his rational power in a moment of revelation. Adherents of the ecstatic idea believe that such a loss in rational consciousness was not only experienced but diligently sought by the prophet. But no case of this can be found. Instead, one finds Moses able to think quickly of reasons why he could not respond to God's call to return to Egypt, when spoken to from the burning bush (Exod. 3,4). The lad Samuel, just mentioned, could yet relate the morning after his revelation all that God had told him the night before. Isaiah, after his memorable vision in the temple, was able to think of his own unworthiness and then volunteer himself to be God's emissary to the Israelite people (Isa. 6:1-8).[4]

e. But more than human reason was necessary. The fifth statement is that the prophet's experience in revelation was more than an exercise in rational ability. Though the prophet did not experience ecstatic frenzy, he did experience an *ab extra* factor, an influence from the outside. Reason was transcended, while it still retained its natural power. There was a contact with the divine, without any negation of the human. The human mind was enabled to move beyond its finite limitations and come away from the moment knowing more than it had before.

The center of the experience was always the "word" of God. A message was communicated, and the prophet was convinced that God had spoken it. Afterwards, he would go forth and assert without hesitation, "Thus saith the LORD." And he was prepared to suffer and even die for the message thus given. Micaiah was willing to endure confinement in prison (1 Kings 22:26-28). Zechariah was prepared to die by stoning (2 Chron. 24:20,21). Jeremiah was ready to be cast into a cistern-type dungeon, intended to bring about his death (Jer. 38:4-6).[5]

2. This "ab extra" factor was a work of the Spirit of God. It was in respect to this *ab extra* factor that one finds the work of the Holy Spirit involved. He was the One responsible for it; He caused it to happen. He brought about the occasion and effected the transfer of divine information. Two forms of evidence for this may be cited.

a. Two forms of evidence. First, there are numerous times when the Spirit of God is closely associated with a revelational experience (see Num. 24:2ff.; 1 Chron. 12:18; 2 Chron. 15:1,2; 20:14ff; 24:20; Ezek. 2:2ff.; 3:24ff.; 11:5ff.). Second, it is the particular work of this Third Person of the Godhead to make such contact with man in the

[4]Stanley Cook (*The Old Testament, a Reinterpretation* [New York: Macmillan, 1936], pp. 188,189) writes in this vein: "It was the sanity of the prophets and not their manticism which made them such tremendous factors in human history."

[5]Even liberal critics are compelled to take notice of this fact. Robinson ("The Philosophy of Revelation," *Record and Revelation*, p. 314), for instance, writes, "When we would trace the most essential part of the Old Testament religion back to its most essential element, we find a man standing in the presence of God, and so wrought upon by Him that he comes away from that presence ready to declare in the teeth of all opinion and all persecution, 'Thus saith Yahweh.' "

God-related experiences that man has. The Holy Spirit is the One who brings to completion any work of grace toward man, planned by the Father and effected by the Son. And revelation of heaven-sent information is a part of that work. One passage that speaks directly of this important truth is 2 Peter 1:21: "For the prophecy came not in old time by the will of man: but holy men of God spake as they were moved by the Holy Spirit."[6] The word *moved* is from the Greek root *phero*, meaning "to move along by carrying." The last part of the verse might be translated, "as borne along by the Holy Spirit." So, then, prophecy came through the prophets as they were "borne along" by the Spirit.

    b. The nature of the Spirit's work in revelation. What now was the nature of this revelational work of the Spirit? What is meant by the term *borne along*? A study of the many times when a revelational contact with man was made shows that three factors were involved.

    The first was an appropriate occasion made such by the prophet's being in a proper attitude of mind and heart. As noticed earlier, Elisha asked that a minstrel play soothing music — probably a tune from the temple services — to help bring him to such an attitude. Apparently he recognized that his recent contact with the three kings — the heathen king of Edom, the Baal-worshiping Jehoram of Israel, and the backslidden Jehoshaphat of Judah, who otherwise was a true follower of God (2 Kings 3:9,12) — had made him an unfit recipient, so the atmosphere had to be changed if God was to reveal information to him. Daniel had been fasting and praying for three weeks when a grand heavenly messenger brought God's message to him (Dan. 10:2-6). And the apostle John, years later, states that he was "in the Spirit on the Lord's day" when he received his great revelation of the glory of the Son of God" (Rev. 1:10-16). Most occasions are not this specific, but none suggests that the prophet was not in an attitude appropriate to the nature and sacredness of the occasion.

    The second factor involved a heightening of the prophet's natural mental ability so he could understand and remember what had been said. This factor is evidenced by sheer force of logic. Heaven-sent

---

[6]Also 1 Peter 1:11 speaks similarly of prophets, saying, "Searching what, or what manner of time the Spirit of Christ which was in them did signify." It was no doubt the Holy Spirit that revealed to Joseph (Gen. 41:38,39), Daniel (Dan. 2:27-30; 5:11-14), Jeremiah (Jer. 1:9; 30:1,2), and others, though only the general term *God* or LORD is used in reference to the One in view.

information could not be distorted. God wanted it to remain unchanged from the form in which it had been disclosed. It was true, accurate, and suitable to the time concerned; it should be conveyed to people without any variation. Therefore, the human instrument was important as the conveyer, and he needed to be equipped to perform the task correctly. This means that, rather than losing rational powers at the time, the person needed to have them the sharpest possible. He needed to be inspired, with mental faculties raised to their keenest point of efficiency and his understanding and memory heightened to their finest quality. Moses was probably the most outstanding example of such an empowered person. After having been on Mt. Sinai for two periods of forty days each, he was enabled to come down and record without error all that God had told him during this extended time.

The third factor was the actual impartation of the heaven-sent information. With the prophet in a suitable attitude of mind and heart, and with his mental faculties sharpened to their finest capacity, the Spirit found the situation appropriate for inserting a message into the prophet's mind. It might be given by audible voice, as occurred with Moses at the burning bush (Exod. 3:4ff.), but more often, likely, by simply an inaudible insertion into the human mind. The prophet, in this state of heightened mental powers, would suddenly recognize that he possessed information additional to what he had known before. And with this recognition would be the realization that this information had come from God. Thus it was that the prophet was made ready to declare, as noted, "Thus saith the LORD." He had the additional information, he possessed the certainty that it had been given by God, and he was prepared to proclaim it in the face of any danger or opposition.

3. Dreams, visions, and theophanies. Besides this direct form of revelation, God also used other means of communicating with man. These means included dreams, visions, and theophanies. They were not used nearly as often as the direct method of contact, and especially not with prophets. Since they were employed, however, and to some extent with prophets, they call for at least brief consideration. The following observations are in order.

First, certain basic distinctions between them call for notice. A revelation by a dream found the recipient in a passive, nonconscious state, with the reality of what was dreamed found only in noncorporeal mental images. At the other extreme, revelation by theophany (especially, the Angel of the Lord) found the recipient in an active, conscious state, with the One revealing possessing an objective, corporeal body. Between the two, a revelation by a vision found the recipient in an active, conscious state (like the theophany), but with the reality of what was visualized existent only in noncorporeal mental images (like the dream).[7]

Second, because of these distinctions, the three forms of revelation were appropriate for different situations. The dream was more suitable for people of little or no spiritual discernment. Pharaoh of Egypt, Abimelech of Gerar, Nebuchadnezzar of Babylon, all of whom were complete pagans, were given dreams. Never did such a person receive either a vision or a theophany appearance. In a dream, the recipient was neutralized in his personality, and existed only as an inert instrument to whom information might be imparted without hindrance by an improper, paganistic response.[8] It is true that Jacob dreamed at Bethel (Gen. 28:12-15) and Joseph while still a lad (Gen. 37:5-10), and both were certainly children of God at the time; both, however, may also have been comparatively immature in spiritual matters.

On the other hand, a theophany·appearance was normally reserved only for persons of high spiritual maturity. It was an Abraham, a Joshua, a Gideon, a Manoah, and later Daniel's three friends in the fiery furnace (Dan. 3:25), as well as Daniel himself (6:22) to whom such an appearance was given. They had spiritual understanding that made them suitable respondants to this manner of personal, face-to-face contact.[9]

Visions also were employed with spiritually mature people. Abraham had a·vision (Gen. 15:1), also Nathan (1 Chron. 17:15), Ezekiel (Ezek. 1:1; 8:3), Daniel (Dan. 8:1) and others. Visions continued to occur in New Testament time, for example, Ananias (Acts 9:10), Peter (10:3,17,19), or Paul (16:9). Visions seem to have been employed more often as a manner of revelation than either the dream or the theophany.

[7]William Lee (*Inspiration of Holy Scripture*, pp. 168f.) refers to visions as experiences of ecstasy. This is a use of the term *ecstasy*, however, in a far different sense than employed by adherents of ecstatic frenzy.

[8]For discussion, see Vos, *Biblical Theology*, pp. 83-85.

[9]It is possible that the Angel's appearance to Hagar (Gen. 16:7-13) and later to Balaam (Num. 22:22-35) are exceptions to the rule, but that He did appear to them may indicate a spiritual relationship to God, on the part of both, otherwise not disclosed.

Third, though none of these three forms of revelation are ever said to have been particularly the work of the Spirit of God, this is likely. As has been seen, revelational activity fits into the general type of work carried out by the Third Person of the Trinity. It was He who effected the direct manner of revelational contact, and it is logical to believe that He was the One who did the same with these more indirect methods. That is, He sent the dream and the vision, and He even superintended in the coming of the Second Person in the theophany appearance.

C. The Spirit of God and the Prophetic Declarative Experience

The Spirit of God empowered prophetic activity not only in respect to message-reception but also message-declaration. Micah wrote, "I am full of power by the spirit . . . to declare" (3:8). Nehemiah stated that God had *warned* Israel by His "spirit" through "the prophets" (9:30). What was the nature of this aspect of the Spirit's work?

Extensive discussion is not needed here, for the answer is quite obvious. The Spirit's special empowerment would have been necessary to make the prophet's declarations the most effective. This would have involved such factors as bringing to the prophet's mind those matters which God desired him to communicate (for the prophet did proclaim much that did not come by direct revelation), an organization of these matters into a structure that would best influence and persuade listeners, some instruction regarding the most advantageous time and place to give the message, and then the actual delivery of the information so that its effect would carry the greatest weight.

The question arises whether or not this special empowerment constituted an inspiration of the prophet comparable to that enjoyed when Holy Writ was penned. Was Isaiah, for instance, inspired to the same degree when he spoke a message as when he wrote his book of prophecy? The most likely answer is that he was not. When he wrote, he was inspired to the point of infallible accuracy. What he wrote, therefore, was the very Word of God. When he spoke, however, he probably was superintended only in a way comparable to a preacher of today. It is fair to say that any servant of God, truly called to the ministry, enjoys special empowerment by the Holy Spirit. Peter was so empowered as he spoke before the Sanhedrin (Acts 4:8); the early disciples were "all filled with the Holy Spirit" to enable them to speak "the word of God with boldness" (Acts 4:31); and Paul was "filled with the Holy Spirit" to give him words to speak to Elymas the sorcerer (Acts 13:7-9). This does not mean, however, that Peter, the early disciples, or Paul spoke at these times infallibly — or that preachers today do. It means only that the Spirit of God granted — or grants — ability above that normal for the person. This is likely the degree to which Isaiah and the other prophets were empowered for oral proclamation in their day.

12

SAUL AND EVIL SPIRITS

A final subject to consider involves Saul and the realm of evil spirits. Questions concerning evil spirits are much discussed today, and this makes the consideration timely. The subject falls within the compass of this volume, for Saul experienced the coming of an "evil spirit" to influence him immediately after God's Spirit departed from him. This is stated in 1 Samuel 16:14: "But the spirit of the LORD departed from Saul, and an evil spirit from the LORD troubled him." The verse implies that the latter took the place of the former, and the fact that "the LORD" is related to both spirits in the verse suggests that this replacement was intentionally permitted by Him. Questions thus arise regarding the identity of this "evil spirit" and the reason why God permitted the replacement. One is prompted to inquire also if the second spirit was allowed to have the same influential position in respect to Saul as God's Spirit.

Still another area of inquiry concerns Saul's visit to the woman of Endor and the resulting appearance of Samuel, who had died sometime before. The subject again pertains to the spirit realm — particularly the realm of the departed dead — and is therefore timely once more and fits logically into the discussion.

A. Saul and His Evil Spirit

The time during Saul's reign when he first experienced the influence of the evil spirit may be determined approximately. His total reign lasted forty years (Acts 13:21). The evil spirit first came on him after God's true Spirit left him (1 Sam. 16:14), and this apparently occurred shortly after Samuel anointed David to take Saul's place

(16:12,13). David began to reign in Hebron soon after Saul's death, in 1010 B.C.[1] He was then thirty years old (2 Sam. 5:4), meaning that he was born in 1040 B.C. He could hardly have been less than fifteen years old at the time of his anointing (having been left to attend the family's sheep), giving a date for this event of about 1025 B.C. Since Saul had been anointed in 1050 B.C. (forty years before 1010 B.C.), he would have reigned about twenty-five years by the time God's Spirit left him and the "evil spirit" came upon him. This means he was under the influence of the latter approximately fifteen years. Since his years of greater strength as a king resulted from the Spirit's special empowerment, it follows that his better years in comparison with his weaker ones were of the same proportion.

1. **Identity of the "evil spirit."** A first question concerns the identity of Saul's "evil spirit." Who or what was it? A first fact to make clear is that it was a true spirit-type being, and not merely a bad attitude or guilty conscience, as held by some expositors.[2] The intended parallel with God's Spirit, who had just left Saul, is too apparent to see this replacement as other than a true spirit being. Besides this, the language used regarding this spirit is not satisfied by the idea merely of a guilty conscience. For instance, the spirit is said to have been "from the LORD" (1 Sam. 16:14). Also, when David would play before the king, at a time when the evil spirit would come upon him, the spirit would then leave (16:23), but a guilty conscience does not come and go in this fashion. And, further, on more than one occasion when the evil spirit came on Saul, he even seized a spear and tried to kill David at such a time of playing (18:10,11; 19:9); merely a bad conscience would not have affected the king in such a way.

But what sort of spirit being was it? There are two possibilities — either a good spirit, meaning an angel, or a bad spirit, meaning a demon sent by Satan. It, of course, could not have been God's Holy Spirit, for He had just been withdrawn from His place of empowerment in Saul's life. Of the two possibilities, it could not have been a good spirit either, for this spirit is specifically called an "evil spirit." It

[1]Following the two forty-year reigns of David and Solomon, the date of the division of the kingdom is commonly placed at 931/930 B.C.; cf. Edwin Thiele, *The Mysterious Numbers of the Hebrew Kings*, pp. 39-52, for discussion.
[2]For instance, George Caird (*Interpreter's Bible*, II [New York: Abingdon Press, 1936], p. 969) calls this spirit "a bad conscience produced by his [Saul's] own disobedience to what he believed to be the will of God, and his consequent break with the man who had been instrumental in bringing him to the throne."

must, then, have been a demon sent by Satan. The Bible is clear that Satan has a host of demons at his command (Mark 3:22-27), and this seems to have been one.

One difficulty may be noted for this conclusion. The spirit is said to have been "from the LORD" (1 Sam. 16:14). Besides this, five times a grammatical construction is employed which gives the literal meaning of either "evil spirit of God" (16:15, 16,23; 18:10) or "evil spirit of the LORD" (19:9).[3] One must ask how this spirit could have been sent by Satan if it is said to have been either "from" or "of " God.

The answer is not difficult; the spirit was sent from God in the sense that God permitted it to begin to influence Saul when God's true Spirit had been removed. This sending was passive in nature, not active. Satan was the active agent. He was the one who wanted Saul to fail as Israel's king and was all too ready to send an emissary to enhance the failure when given an opportunity. So long as God's good Spirit had been on Saul, there was no opportunity; but now there was, and God permitted Satan to use it. It must be remembered that, though Satan is extremely powerful, he can do nothing that is not permitted by God (see Job 1:9-12; 2:4-7). No doubt, God saw fit to grant the permission as a punishment for Saul's disobedience.[4]

2. The rationale for Satan's sending a demon. The reason Satan wanted to send a demon to influence Saul calls for enlargement. He did not want Saul to succeed, as just observed; but, more than that, he did not want God's nation Israel to succeed. The people had not prospered during the preceding period of the judges — no doubt also then because of Satan's influence in strategic places and ways — and he did not want a different experience for them now that a king had been installed. A prosperous people would bring admiration and inquiry on the part of neighboring countries, and this in turn would lead neighbors to learn of Israel's unique belief in one God only, in contrast to their many gods. Satan did not want this.

But a principal way in which to keep the people from prospering was to bring a hindering influence on the king. Leaders of nations are always key people. A good and wise leader will usually bring about good and prosperous conditions; a poor and unwise one will bring about unpleasant conditions. Saul, Israel's first king, was a prime

---

[3]The KJV uses the nonliteral "from" in each of these places.
[4]Says Carl F. Keil (*Old Testament Commentary, The Books of Samuel*, p. 170): "This demon is called 'an evil spirit (coming) from Jehovah,' because Jehovah had sent it as a punishment."

target for Satan's attack; to make him fail would make the new monarchical program fail at its very inception.

3. Method employed. A logical question — and one of major significance in the present day — concerns Satan's method in sending this evil emissary; or, from God's point of view, it concerns the method God permitted Satan to employ in sending this demon to influence Israel's king. Was the demon sent to "possess" Saul, as people were possessed by demons in Jesus' day? Or was he sent only in the sense of influencing the king, working from outside the personality of Saul? Certainly, demons that possessed people in Jesus' day worked from within[5] the personalities of the people involved, for Jesus is said to have cast them "out." If a definite answer is possible, it must be based on the manner of expressions used in the text regarding this spirit and Saul. Verbs and prepositions are especially important.

Perhaps the best approach to the question is to make a comparison between verbs and prepositions used in respect to this spirit's relation to Saul and those employed in respect to the relation of God's Spirit to those He empowered. Certainly one can fairly say that God's Spirit held control from within the personalities of those He empowered, and so, if similar verbs and prepositions are used regarding Saul's evil spirit, it should follow that he also held control from within Saul's personality. If these should be different, then one could doubt that this was true.[6]

The following is a list of the verbs and corresponding prepositions used relative to the Holy Spirit's coming on people:

[5]The word *within*, or *possessed*, in this context clearly means "a control over" a personality, so the demon can speak in place of the person, while using the person's voice (Matt. 8:31; Mark 4:9-12; Luke 8:30-32) and even cause him to commit acts of self-destruction (Matt. 17:15; Mark 9:18-22; Luke 9:39-42). Working from "without" seems to be limited to acting by persuasion, much as Satan with Eve in the Garden of Eden. Persuasion can be a powerful tool, especially in the hands of Satan and his hosts, but it falls short of actual control.

[6]This is not to say that God's Spirit holds control over saints exactly like demons over people they possessed. He does hold control, for He indwells the person, keeps him eternally secure, and empowers him for work (none of which fits the idea of mere outward persuasion). The Spirit does this, however, in full cooperation with the person, so that the person can even hinder His work (Eph. 4:30; 1 Thess. 5:19). No doubt, many cases of demon possession find the person working in cooperation with the demon also (mediums, for instance, people of "familiar spirits"), but it would be difficult to maintain that every case of demon possession in the New Testament involved the same. Demons may not have permitted possessed persons to enjoy the same cooperative factor that the Holy Spirit does.

Passage	Person Involved	Verb Used	Preposition Used
Exod. 31:3; 35:31	Bezaleel	fill, *male'*	with, *be* (both times)
Num. 11:17	Seventy elders	put, *sim*	upon, *'al*
11:25,26	Seventy elders	rest, *nuah*	upon, *'al* (both times)
24:2	Balaam	was, *hayah*	upon, *'al*
Deut. 34:9	Joshua	was full, *male'*	none used
Judg. 3:10	Othniel	was, *hayah*	upon, *'al*
6:34	Gideon	clothed, *labash*	none used
11:29	Jephthah	was, *hayah*	upon, *'al*
13:25	Samson	move, *pa'am*	none used
14:6,19 15:14	Samson	overpower, *tsalah*	upon, *'al* (three times)
1 Sam. 10:6,10	Saul	overpower *tsalah*	upon, *'al* (both times)
11:6	Saul	overpower *tsalah*	upon *'al*
16:13	David	overpower *tsalah*	unto, *'el*
19:20,23	Saul's messengers	was, *hayah*	upon, *'al* (both times)
2 Kings 2:15	Elisha	rests, *nuah*	upon, *'al*
1 Chron. 12:18	Amassai	clothed, *labash*	none used
2 Chron. 15:1	Azariah	was, *hayah*	upon *'al*
20:14	Jahaziel	was, *hayah*	upon *'al*
24:20	Zechariah	clothed, *labash*	none used
Isa. 11:2	Christ	rest, *nuah*	upon, *'al*
32:15	Israel	pour out, *'arah*	upon, *'al*
42:1	Christ	give, *nathan*	upon, *'al*
44:3	Israel	pour out, *yatsaq*	upon, *'al*
61:1	Christ	is (understood), *hayah*	upon, *'al*
Ezek. 2:2; 3:24	Ezekiel	come, *bo'*	in, *be* (both times)
11:5	Ezekiel	fall, *naphal*	upon, *'al*
36:27	Israel	give, *nathan*	in, *be*
Joel 2:28	Israel	pour out, *shaphak*	upon, *'al*

Zech. 12:10	Israel	pour out, shaphak	upon, 'al

Summary:

Verbs	Times Used
was, *hayah*	8
overpower, *tsalah*	7
rest, *nuah*	4
fill, *male*'; clothe, *labash*	3
give, *nathan;* come, *bo';* pour out, *shaphak*	2
put, *sim;* move, *pa'am;* pour out, *'arah;* pour out, *yatsaq;* fall, *naphal*	1

Prepositions	
upon, *'al*	25
with, in, *be*	5
unto, *'el*	1
no preposition used	5

The following is a similar list of the verbs and prepositions used relative to an "evil spirit" coming in contact with people:[7]

Passage	Person Involved	Verb Used	Preposition Used
1 Sam. 16:14,15	Saul	terrify, *ba'ath*	none used (both times)
16:16	Saul	in being, *hayah*	upon, *'al*
16:23	Saul	in being, *hayah*	unto, *'el*
18:10	Saul	overpower, *tsalah*	unto, *'el*
19:9	Saul	was, *hayah*	unto, *'el*

Summary:

Verbs	Times Used
terrify, *ba'ath*	2

[7]Two other passages speak of an evil spirit, Judges 9:23 and 1 Kings 22:23. Neither is parallel in kind to those regarding Saul and so are omitted here. Neither would change the conclusions made, if they were.

in being, *hayah*	2
overpower, *tsalah;* was, *hayah*	1

Prepositions

unto, *'el*	3
upon, *'al*	1
no preposition used	2

A study of these tabulations leads one to the following conclusions:

a. Verbs connote control by the Holy Spirit. Several of the verbs used regarding God's Spirit connote the idea of taking control of a person, working from "within." This is true mainly of the verbs *fill, clothe, rest upon, come in,* and *move. Overpower* probably also should be put in this group, especially because it is used with *upon.* The others used — *was, give, put, pour out,* and *fall* – speak of contact but not necessarily of control-type contact.

b. Verbs do not connote control by the evil spirit. In contrast, no verbs used in regard to the evil spirit speak of a similar inner control. *Terrify* shows a strong response on Saul's part, but it does not imply whether the cause came from outside his personality or from within. *In being* and *was,* both from *hayah,* are equally noncommittal, as was noted in respect to this verb in connection with God's Spirit. *Overpower* is used again, once, but it is less evidential for control here because it is used with the preposition *unto* rather than *upon.*

c. Prepositions also connote control by the Holy Spirit. One preposition predominates in respect to God's Spirit: It is *upon ('al),* used twenty-four of the total thirty times a preposition appears. It connotes a more intimate form of contact than the parallel preposition *unto ('el),* and this is in keeping with the idea again of personality control. Also the prepositions *with,* or *in,* both from *be,* are in keeping with the same idea, especially when they are used with the verbs *fill, come,* and *give.* Only once does the preposition *unto* occur, which speaks more of the idea of proximity.

d. Prepositions do not connote control by the evil spirit. In contrast once more, the preposition *unto ('el)* is most often used in regard to the evil spirit. It is used three of the four times a preposition is employed, with *upon ('al)* being the other. This one use of *upon* is with the relatively weak verb *was (hayah),* which reduces its significance.

The above evidence points to the conclusion that Saul was not possessed by a demon working from within his personality, but merely was influenced as the evil spirit worked from without. The fact that different verbs and prepositions are used, when the relation to Saul of God's Spirit and then the evil spirit are in view, cannot be overlooked. An offsetting factor might be thought to exist in that the same verb is used for the departure from Saul of both God's Spirit and the evil spirit. The verb is *sur*, "turn aside," and is used in 1 Samuel 16:14 in reference to God's Spirit leaving Saul and in 1 Samuel 16:23 for the evil spirit leaving him. However, a departure could be either from within a person or from simply being near him, making the use of this verb of little evidential value.

The conclusion most in keeping with the evidence, therefore, is that the evil spirit influenced Saul while merely working from outside his personality. One need not think that the influence was not great, however. Satan and his hosts are extremely clever in their manner of bringing persuasion. It should be remembered, too, that Saul had a natural tendency to be timid, which could well have made for a tension in his personality, not wanting to give into that weakness. While the Holy Spirit had empowered him, he had been able to avoid this tension, but now, with that special help gone, Satan's emissary could have used it to his advantage. The power of Satan and his helpers must never be underestimated, whether actual demon possession is involved or not.

One might ask why Saul alone in the Old Testament is said to have had an evil spirit so influence him — if an outside type of activity was all that was involved — when certainly evil spirits also worked on other people to influence them. In other words, must there not have been something unique about demonic activity with Saul for him to be singled out as the object of a demon's work? The answer is that no doubt there was something special for a specific demon was assigned to him to influence him on a regular basis. Other people were influenced, but normally not as a continuing assignment by a particular satanic emissary. A parallel case appears to have existed later in respect to a demon especially assigned to the king of Persia. His work was to influence this king, who then ruled over territory where Jews lived, to hinder God's program and activity with the Jewish people. A grand heavenly messenger told Daniel that he had been "withstood" by this demon for twenty-one days, as he had come from heaven to bring God's message to Daniel (see Dan. 10:13,20).

In passing, it may be observed that no evidence can be drawn from Saul's relation to the demon for the belief that Christians can be possessed or controlled by demons. Some Bible students have tried to do so, for Saul surely was a child of God, having been chosen by God Himself as Israel's first king. Saul, however, was not demon possessed or controlled. In fact, the Bible does not seem to tell of any cases where a Christian was controlled in this way.

3. The nature of the evil spirit's work. The nature of the work done by this evil spirit is best analyzed by looking at the four different occasions when it is mentioned in connection with Saul.

a. The initial coming to Saul. The first mention appears at the initial coming to Saul, which was immediately after the departure of God's Spirit. Three references to the spirit are made in this context: one concerning the coming proper, in 1 Samuel 16:14, and then Saul's servants refer to it twice in verses 15 and 16. They counsel the king to procure a musician to play music and help alleviate Saul's troubled state when the spirit brought its influence on him.

One word from the context is particularly important for determining the type of work done. It is the word *ba'ath*, translated in KJV as "troubled," but much better rendered "frightened" or even "terrified." The word appears sixteen times in the Old Testament, and in every instance but here the KJV translates it with some word meaning "fear." For instance, in Job 7:14 it is used in the verse, "Then thou scarest me with dreams, and terrifiest me through visions." The word for "terrifiest" is this word. Or again, Isaiah 21:4 uses it, saying, "My heart panted, fearfulness affrighted me: the night of my pleasure hath he turned into fear unto me." Here the closing word *fear* is the translation used. See also 2 Samuel 22:5; Job 3:5; 18:11; Psalm 18:4; et al. There is no reason for changing from this basic idea in the passage concerning Saul.

One aspect of the evil spirit's work with Saul, therefore, was in making him afraid. He was made fearful concerning matters that involved him. A fear complex often couples itself with suspicion, especially in people of position. Saul's actions from this time on show that this truly became the case with him. He became suspicious of others, as both his fear and suspicion became linked in turn to a sense of insecurity. All three elements emerged strongly in his antagonism to David. David was valuable to Saul, being his only military leader capable of defeating the Philistines. But for all this value, Saul's fear, suspicion, and sense of insecurity overrode his better judgment, and he pursued the young man in a persistent attempt to kill him.

It may be noted in passing that Saul's sense of insecurity was probably heightened by the fact of a rather poor performance by himself as king, even while God's Spirit remained on him. When he had assumed the rule, a major task before him had been to unify the tribes into a working whole, but he had not been successful. There is little evidence that this had been accomplished to any significant degree. Criticisms of him in this regard may have been circulating, and this could have been used by the evil spirit to make the sense of insecurity, suspicion, and fear all the greater.

b. Left Saul when David played. The second reference concerns the departure of the evil spirit from Saul whenever David played his stringed instrument. An indication that he did is given in 1 Samuel 16:23: "And it came to pass, when the evil spirit from God was upon Saul, that David took an harp, and played with his hand: so Saul was refreshed, and was well, and the evil spirit departed from him."

The main point of significance concerns a limitation of control on the part of the evil spirit. He would "withdraw" (*sur*, "turn aside, depart") from Saul when David would play. David's instrument was the *kinnor*, a stringed instrument, which produced soothing music. Quite clearly, this type of music was not found compatible by the evil spirit. The tune may also have been something from the ceremonial singing of the Levites, and this too would have been out of keeping with his nature. The demon did not like it and left Saul when he heard it.

In passing, the observation may be made that music regularly carries psychological influence on people, some music for good and some for bad. The type of music one listens to is important. He can either be calmed and refreshed by it, or excited and disturbed. This passage suggests that it may carry even a wider power, one that influences the spirit world. David's sweet music created an atmosphere the evil spirit could not stand. It is only logical to believe that a contrasting type would encourage his presence and activity. Christians of any day need to be careful what kind of music they permit to enter their mind.

A second point to notice is that this passage may provide further indication that the demon did not possess Saul, but only influenced him from without. It would depart from him just as a result of David playing. In the New Testament, people who were demon possessed were not relieved that easily.[8] It took a special act on the part of Christ or one of the apostles to cast demons out of people. The word *sur,* as used here, is not fairly treated, either, by the possible explanation that the demon, while possessing Saul, merely was made inactive for a time. The word regularly speaks of turning aside from, leaving, departing, and is so used approximately three hundred times in the Old Testament.

c. Attempts on David's life. The third and fourth references concern Saul's two attempts to kill David with a spear. The third, 1 Samuel 18:10,11, states that the evil spirit came on Saul and that he then seized a nearby spear and cast it at David, saying, "I will smite David even to the wall with it." The fourth, 1 Samuel 19:9,10, again speaks of the evil spirit coming on Saul "as he sat in his house with his javelin in his hand" and adds that as "David played with his hand . . . Saul sought to smite David even to the wall with the javelin." Both times, however, David escaped without harm. It may be that in the third instance Saul only thrust at David while still holding the spear, for David is said to have "avoided out of his presence twice." In the fourth, however, Saul clearly threw the weapon, for the indication is given that he "smote the javelin into the wall."

It should be realized that many months had passed between the occasions of the second and third references to the evil spirit coming on Saul. The second is made at the time of David's first coming to the palace to play, while the third appears only after he had been there for some time, with both the Goliath struggle and many succeeding battles with the Philistines, having intervened. During this time, he had served as Saul's chief military commander (1 Sam. 18:5) and, because of his several victories over the Philistines, the people had come to speak of him as having killed his "ten thousands" and Saul only his "thousands" (18:7,8). This had given both time and reason for Saul to become jealous of the young military strategist, and this jealousy provides the background for the new situation existent at these third and fourth times.

[8]It is true that the New Testament speaks of demons leaving and returning to people (see Matt. 12:43-45; Luke 11:24-26), but this seems to have been voluntary on their part. Saul's demon, however, did not want to leave, but found the music too incompatible to remain.

In looking at these times, two matters are noteworthy. The first is that in neither case was the evil spirit dissuaded from his work with Saul by David's playing. Before he had been, but not now. These times, rather than departing, he reacted by influencing Saul to try for David's life. It should be noticed, then, that he did react. He did not simply remain with Saul without doing something. The reason for the different form of reaction was no doubt the different situation that now existed. Saul had sinned in becoming jealous of David and this provided the demon with just the advantage he needed to react in the new way. He would not escape the music by running away but by having the player killed. One may believe that even this jealousy had been significantly fostered by the demon; for just because the demon is not mentioned during this extensive intervening time is no reason to think he had not been active. Very likely he had been, and now he was able to build on what he had seen accomplished in Saul's sinful attitude. Because of the jealousy, the demon was able to withstand the opposing atmosphere of the music[9] so that he might influence Saul to make the attempt on David's life.

The thought follows that people, by attitudes and states of mind they permit for themselves, can make the work of Satan's hosts either easier or harder. The apostle Paul warned the Ephesians, "Neither give place to the devil" (Eph. 4:27). Saul clearly had done this. Where earlier David's music had been enough to put the demon to flight, now, because of the permitted jealousy, Saul could be influenced to try for the young man's life. How careful the Christian needs to be in not making Satan's opposing work easier.

The second matter is that these two attempts on David's life give further evidence that Saul's suspicions and fears did concern especially a sense of insecurity on his throne. He could become quickly jealous of David simply because of David's success in defeating the Philistines, seeing him as a rival (see 1 Sam. 18:8). If he had felt secure, he would have been glad for such results, for the Philistines were Israel's chief enemy. Because he did not, Satan's emissary could use the fact to foster jealousy and this in turn to bring the two attempts to take the young man's life.

[9]This idea of withstanding the music may account for the one use of the stronger verb *overcome tsalah*, to describe the demon's work. It occurs in the first of these two instances (1 Sam. 18:10), The evil spirit was able to "overcome" the influence of the fine music on Saul and so influence him to try for David's life.

137

THE HOLY SPIRIT IN THE OLD TESTAMENT

d. Summary. In summary, the nature of the evil spirit's work with Saul was to exploit a weakness Saul already had. The demon worked on Saul's sense of insecurity as a king to make him fearful of losing his throne. Then he employed Saul's recognition of David's success as a reason to influence him to become jealous of the young man. And then he built on this to withstand David's music to influence Saul to kill his talented musician. At first he had found it necessary to flee when David played, but Saul's weakness and sin in jealousy gave him the advantage he needed.

One may safely believe that it was this same continued influence on Saul which brought the distraught king to kill eighty-five priests of Nob and their families somewhat later (1 Sam. 22:18,19). The evil spirit is not mentioned in connection with this tragic occasion, but it logically follows that his influence was at work just as in the earlier instances. One cannot believe that he had desisted in his work with Saul, just because Saul had failed to kill David. This is not the way of Satan and his hosts. It is more likely that he continued to work to Saul's detriment for the rest of Saul's life, though he is not said specifically to have done so.

B. Saul and the Woman of Endor

Our attention now turns to the other type of occasion when Saul had contact with the spirit world. This was the time when he made request of the woman of Endor[10] that she bring Samuel back from the dead so Saul might consult with him (1 Sam. 28:7-25). The occasion has significance in itself, due to its relation to the general idea of contact with the departed dead, and it has significance for the more basic question herein discussed concerning possible involvement of evil spirits and God's Holy Spirit.

1. The incident described. The incident transpired at the close of Saul's life, after approximately fifteen years of influence by the evil spirit. The Philistines had been growing stronger, due for one reason to the fact that David had not been Saul's army commander since having fled as a refugee (1 Sam. 21:10). The Philistines had been able to move north from their own territory (thus against Canaanites who

[10]The name "Witch of Endor" is often used for this woman, but it is improper because she was not a witch. A witch is one who purports to work magic, while the woman of Endor corresponds to one called a medium today.

held the coastal region at this time yet) and then eastward through the Esdraelon Plain. They had moved as far as Shunem (28:4), just west of Mt. Moreh, when Saul arrived with his army at Mt. Gilboa.[11] Apparently Saul's army was much smaller than that of the enemy — due no doubt to lack of confidence in him by Israelites because of his poor leadership in recent years — and Saul was taken with fear. He tried to obtain information from God regarding the impending struggle, but God would not answer him either by "dreams, nor by Urim, nor by prophets" (28:6) — as a result certainly of his wicked ways — and therefore he sought out this woman of Endor. The community of Endor was located on the east of Mt. Moreh, almost straight north of Saul on Mt. Gilboa, thus making it possible for him to visit the woman without coming in contact with the Philistines to the northwest.

In going to this woman, Saul disguised himself and went by night, for he had previously and properly made her kind illegal in the land (28:9). The woman spoke of her illegal status when Saul first arrived, but Saul reassured her and then asked that she bring "up Samuel" from the dead. The woman proceeded with her practiced techniques for attempting to do this.

2. Samuel really appeared. The question has often been asked whether Samuel actually appeared or not. The answer is quite clear, however, that he did appear. It is directly stated in 1 Samuel 28:12 that "the woman saw Samuel," that as a result "she cried with a loud voice," and that she was thus made to realize that her client was none other than Israel's king, Saul. Further, 1 Samuel 28:15-19 records an actual conversation between Saul and Samuel, and Saul could not have conversed with someone who was not there.

The form in which Samuel appeared, however, is not clear; it may have been corporeal or it may have been only as a type of apparition. The woman was able to see the form, but apparently Saul was not, for the woman had to describe Samuel to him (28:14). It may be that the woman, as she saw Samuel, was in a different room from Saul, or it may be that God gave only the woman the ability to see Samuel in the type of apparition God had given His departed saint. The presence of Samuel was real, however, whether in corporeal or apparition form; Saul was able to converse with his departed adviser. If Samuel was in

[11]This would have placed Saul roughly four miles southeast of the Philistines; see Yohanan Aharoni and Michael Avi-yonah, eds., *Macmillan Bible Atlas* (New York: Macmillan, 1968), map 96.

another room, the conversation must have been by means of a door or passageway.

3. No approval of spiritism, however. Because Samuel really appeared and Saul was able to talk with him, the argument is sometimes used that the practice of spiritism is thereby authenticated; the dead really can be contacted. This conclusion does not follow, however, as at least three reasons show.

a. The Bible condemns spiritism. One reason is that the Bible elsewhere clearly condemns all practice of spiritism, and the Bible never contradicts itself. Even before the Israelites entered their land, God made this clear. In fact, he then condemned any manner of divination, speaking of "any one that maketh his son or his daughter to pass through the fire, or that useth divination, or an observer of times, or an enchanter, or a witch, or a charmer . . . or a wizard, or a necromancer," and He included "a consulter with familiar spirits" (literally, "one who asks an *'ob*," the same term as used regarding this woman). He further gave the reason for this condemnation: "For all that do these things are an abomination unto the LORD" (Deut. 18:10-12). God had not changed His mind since the people had come into the land, and even Saul realized this in that he had declared practitioners of these nefarious arts illegal (1 Sam. 28:9). Numerous other passages speak similarly, e.g., Exodus 22:18; Leviticus 19:31; 20:6; 2 Kings 23:24; Isaiah 8:19; Acts 19:18,19.

b. Samuel's appearance was by a special act of God. Another reason is that the appearance of Samuel was not the result of this woman's art but the direct supernatural intervention of God. Several factors indicate this. First, the woman herself was definitely surprised at Samuel's appearance and as a result was made to fear. Saul even counseled her, "Be not afraid" (1 Sam. 28:13). She did not expect to see Samuel, then. She evidently was not accustomed to having such concrete results come from her arts.

Second, this appearance of Samuel brought the woman to a recognition that her client was none other than Saul. Because of Saul's disguise and manner, she had not recognized him before, even having spoken of him in the third person as having cut off such people as herself from the land. That she did recognize him now, then, shows that Samuel's appearance was so unexpected that it made her realize the one inquiring must be unusually important, and she would have known Saul was in the area due to the impending battle with the Philistines. This means also that she must have realized God Himself had made Samuel thus appear, in order to give information to this important person.

Third, the message Samuel gave to Saul, having thus appeared, was clearly from God. It was in no way a message that Saul wanted to hear but only one that he needed to hear, having acted in disobedience to God as he had. In other words, what Samuel did say was what God wanted to be said, and therefore it follows that God was the One who had sent him to say it. Samuel told the king in clear terms the worst possible news: Because Saul had been disobedient to God, God would deliver Israel into the hands of the Philistines and both Saul and his sons would be killed even on the "morrow," with the kingdom then being given to David (1 Sam. 28:17-19). No doubt Saul had come to the woman hoping for some encouragement; what he received, however, was the very opposite. It constituted, really, a further rebuke for Saul, because he had also now disobeyed God in coming to this woman.

It follows that, if God was the One who made Samuel appear, and not the woman, this was not a case of spiritism at all. And if it was not an act of successful spiritism, then obviously no approval for spiritism can be taken from the occasion. It was *in spite of* the woman's techniques that God made Samuel to appear, not *because of* them.

c. Unusual actions of the woman. Still a further reason is found in the unusual actions of the woman, after Samuel had again disappeared; she did not act as a professional of her art would be expected to act. Her conduct showed that she knew something had happened which was beyond her normal powers. She first showed sympathy for Saul, having heard the dire information that Samuel had just spoken to him. Then she offered him food, that he might regain the strength he evidently needed, having fallen prostrate at the news spoken. When he refused this at first, his own servants joined with the woman in urging him to accept her hospitality, which he then did. Her provision amounted to nothing less than an entire "fat calf" besides "unleavened bread" (1 Sam. 28:22-25). If what the woman had experienced in Samuel's appearance had been normal, she would not have acted in this generous fashion toward one who had just tricked her, even if he was the king. She could be expected rather to have set a high fee to such an one for services rendered; this would be in keeping with normal professional conduct, and she really had nothing to fear from Saul as king, for he had come to her and was in her debt, and, moreover, he would die the following day, in view of Samuel's words.

4. Meaning of the term "gods." A question may be asked regarding the woman's meaning when she said, "I saw gods ascending out of the earth" (1 Sam. 28:13). She said this just before describing the form of Samuel to the inquiring Saul. What is the relation between her reference to "gods" and the appearance of Samuel? One part of the answer is that, though the Hebrew word for "gods" (*'elohim*) is plural, it need not be so translated. The term is used hundreds of times in the Old Testament and normally refers only to one deity, usually the true God of heaven. And that it should be translated in the singular here follows from Saul's resulting question, "What form is he of?" in which he used the singular *he*, and also by the woman's answer in describing what she had seen as "an old man," again using the singular. The fact that deity was not intended by her in using the term is indicated also by the manner of the woman's reply. She did not describe a god but only "an old man." Her use of the term was no doubt a way by which she thought to indicate a nonterrestial, nonearthborn being, supernatural in kind.

5. Possible involvement of an evil spirit. The question of whether or not an evil spirit was involved in this occasion is pertinent to our discussion. The term *evil spirit (ruah ra'ah),* used regarding Saul, is not employed here, but another term is, which may refer to a specific class of evil spirits. The term is *'ob.* It is used sixteen times in the Old Testament and frequently in reference to the person himself who practiced as a medium (e.g., Lev. 19:31; 20:6; 1 Sam. 28:3,9; 2 Kings 21:6; et al). A few times, however, it is used for the being such people would contact in this practice. For instance, Deuteronomy 18:11 calls such a person "one who asks an *'ob.*" Leviticus 20:27 refers to such a person as one who "has in them an *'ob.*" Isaiah 29:4 speaks of the *'ob* as being "from the ground." And in our story, the woman is called the "possessor of an *'ob*" twice in verse 7, and in verse 8 Saul asks her to divine for him "by the *'ob.*" All of this suggests rather strongly that an *'ob* was thought of as a spirit by which mediums could bring up departed dead from the ground. The fact that the mediums could themselves also be called by the term may indicate that these people were so closely associated with the 'ob in their work that they came to be practically identified with it.

A further question concerns whether or not such a spirit existed, or if its existence was merely in the minds of people. In other words, Is there a specific spirit or group of spirits that Satan has assigned to work in connection with mediums? The answer these verses suggest is that this may be the case. It is generally accepted that people who claim to be mediums today do have contact with — if not being empowered by — evil spirits. It is only logical, then, to believe that similar people long ago had the same true of them. Since this woman who was consulted by Saul, is called a "possessor of an 'ob," she certainly was believed to have such a spirit. It may well be that she did; and, if so, in this respect at least, an evil spirit was involved in this instance. As has been seen, however, it was not the woman or this evil spirit that was responsible for the appearance of Samuel. He appeared by the supernatural act of God Himself.

By implication, one may safely say that another evil spirit was involved in this occasion also. This spirit was the evil spirit that regularly worked on Saul at Satan's command to influence him wrongly, and here did so in persuading him to make this God-displeasing visit. It must have been this spirit that was largely responsible, for the visit was directly contrary to the revealed law of God, it was something Saul himself had made illegal sometime earlier, and it was just the type of action that Satan would have wanted Saul to do. God had refused to give Saul an answer from any source of information related to Him — dreams, Urim, prophets (1 Sam. 28:6) — and, therefore, Satan would answer him from his false source. Satan's emissary, then, would have been the one to influence Saul to make the visit. Interestingly, though Satan would have been the one to influence Saul, it was God who thwarted Satan in employing the occasion to have Samuel give Saul the message He desired. No doubt Satan had an entirely different type of message to impart through the woman by the more normal procedure.

6. Possible involvement of God's Spirit. Since this appearance of Samuel to Saul was effected by a supernatural act of God, the question is appropriate whether or not the Holy Spirit may have been the specific person of the Godhead who did it. An affirmative answer is likely. Though no mention is made concerning the Spirit, the type of work done in making Samuel appear must be categorized as normal for the Spirit. Samuel was made to appear as a way of bringing rebuke to Saul for his sin in general and now for this added disobedience in consulting the woman. Such rebuke falls under the heading of discipline, and this is an area of work assigned to the Spirit.

This means that the same Spirit, who had left Saul some fifteen years earlier for empowerment in his reign, was still interested in him as to Saul's own life conduct. As seen in an earlier chapter, He would still have indwelt Saul, so far as maintaining Saul as a child of God, and in this capacity He of course was interested in Saul's spiritual relationship with God. Severely grieved at Saul's continued misconduct, He now brought reprimand by bringing Samuel back from the dead to communicate the message of rebuke.

13

SUMMARY STATEMENTS

The following are summary statements of conclusions reached in the preceding discussion relative to the work of the Holy Spirit in the Old Testament.

A. Creation

1. The Holy Spirit as the Third Person of the Trinity had a definite part in creation, along with the Father and the Son.

2. His part was to bring about ("flutter over") the creative work of the six days, thus bringing the universe to its final state of order and design. This work did not involve the formation of substance *ex nihilo,* but to take of both substance and the principle of life (previously brought to existence *ex nihilo* by the Son) and fashion these into all the forms designed from the first by the Father. The crowning aspect in this work was the fashioning of man and woman, making them in the image of God.

B. Empowerment of Old Testament Saints

1. The Old Testament speaks frequently of the Spirit's empowering important people for divinely assigned tasks. These people fall into four groups: judges, craftsmen, prophets (temporary and regular), and civil leaders. The tasks involved were of major significance and each required special abilities above what was normal for the people concerned.

2. Every time the Spirit is mentioned in the Old Testament as coming on or leaving a person, it is this manner of empowerment that

is involved. At no time does a reference of this kind concern the spiritual salvation of an individual.

C. Regeneration, Indwelling, Sealing, and Filling in the Old Testament

1. Since every instance of such a mention of the Spirit concerns empowerment, the question of whether or not the Spirit also regenerated, indwelt, sealed, and filled Old Testament saints must be settled on the basis of other evidence.

2. Evidence that Old Testament people did experience spiritual renewal exists in two directions. One is the exemplary lives of Old Testament saints, explainable only as the result of spiritual renewal. The other is logical deduction on the basis of New Testament truth, which runs as follows: Every man is born lost and the only way of salvation is by faith in Christ. Old Testament people must be included under this truth (since they lived after man's fall in Adam), and therefore they too had to be saved by faith, just as New Testament people. Though their faith in Christ could not be expressed in quite the same way, because they lived before Christ died, they could exercise faith in all that God had revealed, as did Abraham, and have this counted to them for righteousness (Rom. 4:3). Still a third type of evidence exists in the considerable effort Christ put forth to lead people of his day — which was still before His death and the founding of the church — to a saving knowledge of Himself.

3. Evidence that this spiritual renewal included regeneration, indwelling, sealing, and filling exists again in the lives of Old Testament saints. They did experience regeneration, for this is what spiritual renewal means. They must have been indwelt by the Spirit, because they remained children of God all their life (Noah, Abraham, Moses, Samuel, David, and the rest), and the New Testament is clear that this is made possible only by the continued indwelling of God's Holy Spirit. Then they surely experienced sealing, since sealing has reference to this preservation. And they must have understood the idea of filling, for the Old Testament is replete with admonitions to follow close to God and be occupied with doing His will.

4. The reason why the Old Testament does not speak of these truths as such is that they were to be elaborated and explained in the New Testament. This should not be thought strange, for many truths are treated similarly in the Bible. The fact of the truths being in

operation, however, is unmistakably illustrated in the lives depicted.

5. The one work which began for the first time at Pentecost was the baptism of the Spirit. With the gospel provision then made available, there was need for an organism to carry its message to the lost world. This organism was the church, but to become such an organism, a definite act of joining its members into a unity was necessary; this was accomplished by the act of baptism when the Spirit came in power on Pentecost. Since that time, individual believers are baptized into that body then begun. This baptism carries with it an aspect of empowerment: an ability, given to all believers in variant degrees, for evangelizing the world with the gospel message. This baptism along with its resulting empowerment, is the subject of biblical passages that speak of a new coming of the Holy Spirit in New Testament time.

D. Israel's Prophets Were Not Ecstatics

1. Three main passages (Num. 11:25-29; 1 Sam. 10:1-13; 19:18-24) and six supporting passages are cited by many liberal scholars as biblical evidence that Israel's early prophets were ecstatics, like people in Canaan and elsewhere.

2. One evidence taken from the three main passages is that in each case the persons involved are said to have had the Spirit come on them, and this is taken to mean an ecstatic state. Other evidence is taken from a comparison of Israel with other peoples of the day: from the fact that a Canaanite-type high place was involved in one instance, from the playing of musical instruments on the same occasion (music was often used in the rites of ecstaticism), and from the fact that Saul lay in a trancelike stupor for many hours after another instance.

3. An answer was noted for all these arguments, however, as follows: (a) that the Spirit's coming on people had nothing to do with ecstatic frenzy but with a supernatural empowerment for a task; (b) that Israel cannot be compared with contemporary peoples on such a matter, for her basic Law had been supernaturally revealed at Mt. Sinai even before Israel's entrance into Canaan; (c) that the Canaanite-type high place during the time of Samuel, Saul, and David, (when the ark was away from the tabernacle and the temple was not yet built) was approved by God, since even Samuel sacrificed at one; (d) that the musical instruments were not played in a manner suggesting the prolonged, rhythmic tunes necessary to bring on

ecstasy; and (e) that Saul's unusual stupor is better explained as a fit of despair on seeing David in the approving company of the honored Samuel.

4. Three positive arguments against ecstaticism also were noted. First, the basic meaning of *prophecy* taken by ecstatic adherents to mean "to become ecstatic," was found to be "to speak for God"; and the few times of use in an emotional sense were found to add only the idea of "ferventness" to this basic idea. Second, Israel's remarkable resistance to Canaanite influence, in comparison to what is normal in history for comparable situations, can only be accounted for on the basis of strong resistance factors among the people, and prophetism must have been one. If so, it could hardly have been Canaanite in origin itself. And third, the meaning of *prophesy* in the main passages used by ecstatic adherents was found to be a "praising" activity. Evidence that this was a possible meaning for the word was taken from 1 Chronicles 25:1-3, and the idea was seen to fit well in the three key passages involved.

E. The Holy Spirit and the Prophetic Experience

1. The work of the Holy Spirit in the three so-called ecstatic passages was identified. Regarding the seventy in the wilderness, it was empowerment of the seventy to serve as Moses' assistants, with their prophecy of praise as a natural accompanying outburst of thanksgiving. Regarding Saul, on meeting the company of prophets, it was an empowerment for a changed personality, from being timid to having a sense of confidence, with again the prophecy of praise being a natural accompaniment. Regarding Saul, on coming to his three messenger groups all praising along with Samuel's prophets, it was empowerment to praise, so that Saul's attitude was changed from wanting to arrest and kill David, to becoming filled with despair that David clearly was the choice of both Samuel and God.

2. An examination of the prophetic experience in revelation showed that no ecstatic-type factors were existent in any instance. It was observed, however, that the revelation occasion was more than a natural use of a prophet's mind. It involved a proper attitude on his part, a heightened mental ability, and especially a supernatural impartation of knowledge by the Holy Spirit, so that the prophet suddenly knew information that he had not known before. This was found to be an *ab extra* factor, but of a totally different kind from ecstasy.

148

3. An examination of the prophetic experience in declaration was found to involve empowerment further by the Holy Spirit, as He gave special ability for proclaiming God's message to the people.

F. Saul and Evil Spirits

1. The evil spirit that came on Saul, following the departure of the Holy Spirit's empowerment for kingship, was an emissary sent by Satan to influence Saul to wrong actions. A comparison of verbs and prepositions used regarding this demon's work with those used regarding the Holy Spirit's work, revealed that the demon did not possess Saul by working from within and through his personality, but from without.

2. The nature of the demon's work was to keep Saul in a state of fear, due especially to a sense of insecurity on his throne. This made Saul suspicious of others, and this came to the fore most strongly in his opposition to David, whom he saw as a rival. Before this attitude toward David developed, the music of the young man could cause the demon to leave Saul; but, when it had developed, the demon could use this extra advantage to influence Saul to try and kill the young player and so rid itself of the detested music in this way.

3. A climaxing feature of the demon's work was his influence on Saul to visit the woman of Endor, who was probably possessed of another demon called an 'ob. Saul wanted to speak with Samuel, who had died sometime earlier, but, when Samuel appeared, it was not the woman or her 'ob that brought this about, but God — specifically the Holy Spirit — working supernaturally. No biblical support for spiritism, therefore, can be taken from this occasion. Satan had wanted Saul to consult this woman, as his own satanic source of information — since God had refused to answer Saul by any divine source, dreams, Urim, or prophets — but God thwarted Satan's strategy by taking over that source and bringing His own dire message of doom to Saul through the raised Samuel.

G. General Statement

1. All this means that the Holy Spirit's work in the Old Testament was not greatly different from that in the New Testament, except on one important count. That is His work of baptizing believers into the church. There is no reason for denying His work of regenerating, indwelling, sealing, and filling Old Testament saints. All these man-

ifestations of grace were needed by them just as much as by New Testament saints, and there is nothing characteristically New Testament about them. However, there is something that is definitely New Testament in kind about baptism, for this has to do with the church, God's instrument to propagate the gospel. The church could not exist until there was a gospel message made complete and ready for proclamation; therefore, baptism into that church was impossible and its accompanying empowerment for preaching was unnecessary until that time.

Even in respect to empowerment for service generally, there is really no change. Such empowerment existed in the Old Testament and it still continues today. Every servant of God knows the reality of the special power of the Holy Spirit in his life, especially in crucial times. This is empowerment for service, like that enjoyed by a Bezaleel, a Gideon, a David, or an Elijah, so long ago.

2. There is no change either in respect to the Holy Spirit and ecstaticism. He has always been a Person and not a mere manifestation of ecstatic fervor (as ecstatic adherents believe); and He was a God of order and reason in His work with prophets and others in the Old Testament, as He continues to be in New Testament time (see 1 Cor. 14:32).

3. And there is no change in respect to the Holy Spirit and evil spirits. In Old Testament time, evil spirits were Satan's emissaries to hinder the work of the Holy Spirit with God's people, and the same continues true today. The specialized efforts of demons with spiritists, which are opposed to all that the Holy Spirit desires, remain basically the same in this age as then.

BIBLIOGRAPHY

Albright, William F. *From the Stone Age to Christianity.* 2nd ed. Garden City: Doubleday & Co., Anchor Books, 1957.

_____. "Recent Progress in North Canaanite Research." *Bulletin of the American Schools of Oriental Research,* 70 (1938).

Berkhof, Louis. *Reformed Dogmatics.* 2 vols. Grand Rapids: Wm. B. Eerdmans Pub. Co., 1932.

Biederwolf, William E. *Help to the Study of the Holy Spirit.* 4th ed. New York: Fleming H. Revell Co., 1903.

Broomall, Wick, *The Holy Spirit.* New York: American Tract Society, 1940.

Buswell, James O. *A Systematic Theology of the Christian Religion.* Grand Rapids: Zondervan Pub. House, 1962.

Cairns, Earle E. *Christianity Through the Centuries.* Rev. ed. Grand Rapids: Zondervan Pub. House, 1967.

Cambron, Mark G. *Bible Doctrines.* Grand Rapids: Zondervan Pub. House, 1954.

Candlish, J. S. *Work of the Holy Spirit.* Edinburgh: T. & T. Clark, 1883.

Chafer, Lewis S. *He That Is Spiritual.* Grand Rapids: Zondervan Pub. House, 1918.

_____. *Systematic Theology.* 8 vols. Dallas: Dallas Seminary Press, 1948.

Criswell, W. A. *The Baptism, Filling and Gifts of the Holy Spirit.* Grand Rapids: Zondervan Pub. House, 1966.

Davidson, W. T. *The Indwelling Spirit.* London: Hodder and Stoughton, 1911.

Dolman, D. H. *Simple Talks on the Holy Spirit.* New York: Fleming H. Revell Co., 1927.

Dorner, I. A. *A System of Christian Doctrine.* 4 vols. Trans. by A. Cave and J. Banks. Edinburgh: T. & T. Clark, 1888.

Douty, N. F. *Filled with the Spirit.* Findlay, Ohio: Fundamental Truth Publishers, n.d.

Downer, A. C. *Mission and Ministration of the Holy Spirit.* Edinburgh: T. & T. Clark, 1909.

Eichrodt, Walther. *Theology of the Old Testament*. Trans. by J. Baker. Philadelphia: Westminster Press, 1961.

Fisher, G. P. *History of Christian Doctrine*. New York: Charles Scribner's Sons, 1896.

Fitzwater, P. B. *Christian Theology*. Grand Rapids: Wm. B. Eerdmans Pub. Co., 1938.

Frost, H. W. *Who is the Holy Spirit?* New York: Fleming H. Revell Co., 1938.

Goodman, M. *The Comforter*. London: The Paternoster Press, 1938.

Gordon, A. J. *Ministry of the Spirit*. New York: Fleming H. Revell Co., 1894.

Graham, W. C. "The Religion of the Hebrews." *Journal of Religion*, 11 (1931).

Gromacki, Robert G. *The Modern Tongues Movement*. Nutley, NJ: Presbyterian and Reformed Pub. Co., 1967.

Hodge, Charles. *Systematic Theology*. 3 vols. New York: Scribner, Armstrong and Co., 1877.

Johnson, A. R. *The Cultic Prophet in Ancient Israel*. Cardiff: Univ. of Wales Press Board, 1944.

Johnson, E. H. and Weston, H. G. *An Outline of Systematic Theology and Ecclesiology*. Philadelphia: American Baptist Pub. Society, 1895.

Kenyon, John B. *The Bible Revelation of the Holy Spirit*. Grand Rapids: Zondervan Pub. House, 1939.

Kuyper, Abraham. *The Work of the Holy Spirit*. Trans. by Henri de Vries. New York: Funk and Wagnalls Co., 1900; Wm. B. Eerdmans Pub. Co., 1941.

Lange, J. P. *A Commentary on the Holy Scriptures*. Grand Rapids: Zondervan Publishing House, n.d.

Lee, William. *The Inspiration of Holy Scripture*. New York: Robert Carter & Bros., 1854:

Lockyer, Herbert. *All the Doctrines of the Bible*. Grand Rapids: Zondervan Pub. House, 1964.

Manning, H. E. *Temporal Mission of the Holy Ghost*. 4th ed. London: Burns and Oates, Ltd., 1892.

BIBLIOGRAPHY

Marsh, F. E. *Emblems of the Holy Spirit*. New York: Alliance Press Co., 1911.

Moberly, G. *The Administration of the Holy Spirit in the Body of Christ*. 2nd ed. New York: Pott and Amery, 1970.

Morgan, G. Campbell. *Spirit of God*. London: Hodder & Stoughton, 1900.

Murray, Andrew. *Spirit of Christ*. London: James Nisbet & Co., 1888.

Nuttall, G. F. *The Holy Spirit in Puritan Faith and Experience*. Oxford: Basil Blackwell, 1946.

Parker, Joseph. *The Paraclete*. London: Henry S. King & Co., 1874.

Payne, J. Barton. *The Theology of the Older Testament*. Grand Rapids: Zondervan Pub. House, 1962.

Pentecost, J. D. *Things to Come*. Grand Rapids: Zondervan Pub. Co., 1958.

Pope, W. B. *A Compendium of Christian Theology*. 3 vols. London: Wesleyan-Methodist Book Room, 1880.

Pritchard, James B. (ed.). *Ancient Near Eastern Texts*. Rev. ed. Princeton: Princeton Univ. Press, 1955.

Rees, Thomas. *Holy Spirit in Thought and Experience*. New York: Charles Scribner's Sons, 1915.

Ridout, Samuel. *Person and Work of the Holy Spirit*. New York: Loizeaux Bros., n.d.

Robinson, H. W., ed. *Record and Revelation*. Oxford: Clarendon Press, 1938.

Sanders, J. Oswald. *The Holy Spirit and His Gifts*. Rev. ed. Grand Rapids: Zondervan Pub. Co. 1970.

Shedd, W. G. T. *Dogmatic Theology*. 2 vols. 3rd ed. New York: Charles Scribner's Sons, 1891.

Simpson, A. B. *The Holy Spirit or Power From on High*. 2 vols. New York: The Christian Alliance Pub. Co., 1895.

Slattery, C. L. *The Light Within*. New York: Longmans, Green, & Co., 1915.

Smeaton, George. *The Doctrine of the Holy Spirit*. Edinburgh: T. & T. Clark, 1889.

Soltau, George. *Person and Mission of the Holy Spirit*. Philadelphia: Philadelphia School of the Bible, n.d.

Stowell, W. H. *On the Work of the Spirit*. London: Jackson and Walford, 1849.

Strong, Augustus H. *Systematic Theology*. 3 vols. Philadelphia: Judson Press, 1907.

Swete, H. B. *Holy Spirit in the Ancient Church*. London: Macmillan and Co., 1912.

Thiele, Edwin R. *The Mysterious Numbers of the Hebrew Kings*. Rev. ed. Grand Rapids: Wm. B. Eerdmans Pub. Co., 1965.

Thomson, J. G. S. S. "Holy Spirit," in *Baker's Dictionary of Theology*. Ed. by E. F. Harrison. Grand Rapids: Baker Book House, 1960.

Torrey, R. A. *Baptism of the Holy Spirit*. New York: Fleming H. Revell Co., 1897.

Unger, Merrill F. *Demons in the World Today*. Wheaton: Tyndale House, 1971.

Vos, Geerhardus. *Biblical Theology*. Grand Rapids: Wm. B. Eerdmans Pub. Co., 1948.

Walvoord, John F. *The Church in Prophecy*. Grand Rapids: Zondervan Pub. House, 1964.

————. *The Holy Spirit*. Wheaton: VanKampen Press, 1954; Grand Rapids: Zondervan Pub. House, 1965.

Warfield, Benjamin B. *Biblical Doctrines*. New York: Oxford Univ. Press, 1929.

————. *Biblical and Theological Studies*. Philadelphia: Presbyterian and Reformed Pub. Co., 1952.

Weldon, J. E. C. *The Revelation of the Holy Spirit*. London: Macmillan and Co., 1902.

Wolston, W. T. P. *Another Comforter*. London: James Nisbet & Co., 1900.

Wood, I. F. *Spirit of God in Biblical Literature*. London: Hodder and Stoughton, 1904.

Wood, Leon J. "Ecstasy and Israel's Early Prophets." *Bulletin of the Evangelical Theological Society*, 9 (Summer, 1966).

SUBJECT INDEX

Aaron, 108
Abimelech, 115
Abimelech of Gerar, 123
Abraham, 24, 65-66, 68,
123
Adam, 37, 38, 68, 83
Adoption, 21
Agabus, 73
Ahab, 82, 95
Aholiab, 42, 56
Amassai, 26, 44, 58, 130
Amaziah, (Bethel priest),
108
Ammon, Ammonites,
25, 41, 43, 50, 54
Amos, 45, 47, 108
Ananias, 123
Angel of the Lord, 123
Angels, 17, 127
Apollos, 73
Aramaeans of Damascus,
96
Arians, 15
Asa, 43
Asaph, 111
Ashkelon, 41
Asia Minor, 91
Azariah (prophet) 26, 43,
48, 58, 130

Baal, 92, 95
Baal-zebub, 31
Babylonian exile, 28
Balaam, 24, 44, 58, 123,
130
Balak, 44
Baptism of the Spirit, 40,
74-77, 79, 147
Bathsheba, 81, 119
Benjamin, 44, 61
Bethel, 108, 123
Bethesda pool, 67
Bethlehem, 60
Bezaleel, 24, 42-43, 55,
72, 130

Caleb, 54
Canaan, Canaanites, 98,
109-110
Charismatic movement,
11
Creation, 13, 16, 20, 23,
30-38, 145
Cushan-rishathaim, 41,
53

Daniel, 121, 123, 133-
134
David, 25, 26, 32, 42, 44,
51-52, 59-63, 65-66,
68, 83-84, 95, 106,
114-115, 118, 126-
127, 130, 135-138
Demon possession,
129-134
Dreams, 122-123, 139

Ecstatic frency, 13
Ecstaticism, 90-112
Edom, Edomites, 43
Ekron, 31
Eldad, 24, 93, 111
Eli, 119
Elihu, 23, 31, 35
Elijah, 19, 26, 45-46, 48,
82, 95
Elisha, 19, 26, 45-46, 48,
82, 118, 130
Elohim (God), 31
Elymas, 72, 76, 125
Empowerment, 11, 40,
47-52, 53-63, 72-74
76-77, 81-82, 114-
115, 145-146
Ephraim, 61
Esdraelon Valley, 61,
139
Eshtaol, 25, 41
Eternal security, 12, 80
Evil Spirit, 13, 17, 25,
62, 126-144, 149

Execration texts, 44
Ezekiel, 19, 28, 46, 123,
130

Fall of Man, 38
Familiar spirit, 140,
142-143
Feast of Tabernacles, 84
Federal headship, 68
Filling, 13, 40, 71-72,
78-80, 146

Garden of Eden, 37, 38,
68, 83
Gibeon, 104
Gideon, 25, 41, 53, 54,
123, 130
Goliath, 136
Greece, 91

Habakkuk, 47
Hagar, 123
Haggai, 47
Hebron, 127
Heman, 111
Hezekiah, 62
High Place, 98, 103-104,
147
Hiram, 42-43, 55-56
Hosea, 27, 45, 47, 97

Image of God, 36, 37
Incarnation, 35
Indwelling, 11, 13, 39,
40, 41, 69-70, 80, 146
Isaac, 24
Isaiah, 18, 27, 32, 45, 47,
49, 124
Ishbosheth, 61

Jabesh-gilead, 12, 25, 50
Jacob, 17, 24, 123
Jacob's well, 67
Jahaziel, 26, 43, 48,
57-58, 130
Jeduthan, 111

155